BEHIND the MAN

BEHIND the MAN

John Laurie, Ruth Gorman, and the Indian Vote in Canada

By Ruth Gorman

*Edited with an Introduction
by Frits Pannekoek*

UNIVERSITY OF
CALGARY
PRESS

© 2007 Estate of Ruth L. Gorman.
Introduction © 2007 Frits Pannekoek.

Published by the
University of Calgary Press
2500 University Drive NW
Calgary, Alberta, Canada T2N 1N4
www.uofcpress.com

No part of this publication may be reproduced, stored in a retrieval system or transmitted, in any form or by any means, without the prior written consent of the publisher or a licence from The Canadian Copyright Licensing Agency (Access Copyright). For an Access Copyright licence, visit www.accesscopyright.ca or call toll free to 1-800-893-5777.

We acknowledge the financial support of the Government of Canada through the Book Publishing Industry Development Program (BPIDP) and the Alberta Foundation for the Arts for our publishing activities. We acknowledge the support of the Canada Council for the Arts for our publishing program. We thank the Alberta Historical Resources Foundation for its support of this project.

LIBRARY AND ARCHIVES OF
CANADA CATALOGUING IN
PUBLICATION

Gorman, Ruth, 1914–2002.
Behind the man : John Laurie, Ruth Gorman, and the Indian vote in Canada / by Ruth Gorman ; edited and with an introduction by Frits Pannekoek.

(Legacies shared ; no. 21)
Includes bibliographical references and index.
ISBN 978-1-55238-218-9

1. Laurie, John, 1899–1959.
2. Indians of North America – Legal status, laws, etc. – Alberta – History.
3. Indians of North America – Legal status, laws, etc. – Canada – History.
4. Political activists – Alberta – Biography.
5. Educators – Alberta – Biography.
6. Indian Association of Alberta – Biography.
7. Gorman, Ruth, 1914–2002.
8. Social reformers – Canada – Biography.
9. Feminists – Alberta – Biography.
I. Pannekoek, Frits, 1947–
II. Title.
III. Series.

FC3674.1.L39G67 2007
971.23'020922
C2006-906997-2

Printed and bound in Canada by Houghton Boston.

∞ This book is printed on 70 lb. Cougar Opaque.

Cover design, Melina Cusano.
Interior design & typesetting, Jason Dewinetz.

Contents

Acknowledgments ~ vii
Introduction by Frits Pannekoek ~ ix
Notes to Introduction ~ lii
Author's Introduction ~ 5

1. The Mountain ~ 7
2. The Stars Shone Bright ~ 11
3. Strange Omission ~ 15
4. The Winds of Change Blow across the World ~ 19
5. An Angry Young Man ~ 23
6. Laurie Finds the Right Place ~ 27
7. A Horse Did It ~ 33
8. Laurie Finds a Family ~ 39
9. A History Teacher Studies History around the Campfire ~ 57
10. A History Teacher Studies History in Books ~ 63
11. A Red Métis Meets a White Métis ~ 73
12. The Department and Enfranchisement ~ 85
13. The Harsh Reality of Enfranchisement ~ 95
14. Laurie and the Indians Find Me ~ 105
15. The Buckskin Curtain ~ 119
16. Department of Indian Affairs and the IAA ~ 125
17. New Act and the "Man Behind the Throne" ~ 143
18. I Take the Case ~ 151
19. The First Hobbema Hearing 1951 ~ 155
20. After the Hobbema Hearing / I Go Public ~ 167
21. The Appeal ~ 179
22. Senatorship ~ 187
23. Laurie's Death ~ 191
24. Laurie's Funeral ~ 199
25. Laurie's Magnificent Record of Change ~ 211
26. The Brief / I Go North ~ 217
27. I Go to Parliament ~ 225
28. The Vote ~ 239

Epilogue ~ 247
Appendix I: Timeline of events concerning Ruth Gorman and John Laurie's involvement with the Aboriginal people of Canada. ~ 257
Notes ~ 262
Index ~ 269

ACKNOWLEDGMENTS

This manuscript could not have been written without the incredible support of Linda Gorman, Rodney Muir, Neil Watson, Paul Ragona, Gayl Inouye and Judy Bedford. They offered insights into Dr. Gorman that only they could provide, and Linda Gorman permitted unrestricted access to Dr. Gorman's papers after her passing. They read the manuscript several times and were kind in letting me shape the introduction, always questioning but respecting my insights. Dr. Gorman had wished to acknowledge the many people who supported her writing over the years, but she left no detailed notes. She would have wanted to extend her gratitude to the support she received. We had all hoped that Ruth could have seen the completed manuscript and to offer thanks in person, but that was not to be. It must be emphasized that the statements in the manuscript are those of Ruth Gorman, not those of the editors nor the publishers. She took strong views during her life, and every attempt was made to ensure that these were respected.

In addition, the Gorman family would like to acknowledge the following individuals for their special support in the preparation of the book, since they all helped Ruth Gorman at some point, Frieda Abrahamson, Judy Bedford, Dyanne Bigras, Bruce Burns, Alma and Mike Byfield, Ted and Virgina Byfield, Ken and Joan Cope, Catherine Davison, Alex Dawes, Evelyn de Mille, Dr. Gordon (Bud) Dutt, Dorothy Gray, Jacquie Hammond, Flo Harington, Dr. R. (Dick) Harington, Tara Hunt, Gayl Inouye, Shirlee Smith Matheson, Marjorie McIlveen, Dorothy Jean McKay, Will (Billy) Morrow, Carolyn Murray, Marjorie Norris, Judge John Reilly, Dr. Don Smith, Pat Smith, Fred Stenson, Grace Stonewall, Ernestina Velasquez, Ted Washburn, and Shirley Whitehouse.

The University of Calgary Press would like to thank Linda Gorman for allowing photographs and documents from Ruth Gorman's private collection to be printed in this book. Other photographs (as noted) are published with the kind permission of the Glenbow Museum Archives in Calgary.

INTRODUCTION

RUTH GORMAN AND THE JOHN LAURIE MANUSCRIPT

Judy Bedford of Alberta's Historic Sites Service first introduced me to Ruth Gorman in the winter of 1998 at Ruth's home in Roxboro, Calgary. She was hoping I could be persuaded to help Dr. Gorman finish her biography of John Laurie. I had known of Dr. Gorman for the last twenty years, as a heritage preservationist, as one of Alberta's indomitable feminist spirits along with Mary Dover, a friend and sometimes co-conspirator, and as a community activist with strong views on a number of topics.[1] I also knew she had been working on a biography of John Laurie, one of Alberta's key proponents for Aboriginal activism and change and a good friend of hers, for a number of years, years that were going on rather too long.

John Laurie, known to most of his contemporaries and students as Mr. Laurie and to Ruth Gorman as "Laurie," was a man of legend in Alberta of whom too many knew too little, or nothing at all. Dr. Gorman's efforts and admiration had none the less ensured that Laurie's name was attached to a "flat faced" mountain near Canmore.[2] It was known that the mountain had a Stoney name, and it became the first mountain in Canada eventually to have a dual official name: Mount Laurie (*Iyamnathka*). Dr. Gorman had written about Mr. Laurie in *My Golden West*, a regional magazine she founded and edited, but she felt he was owed a lot more.[3] In her mind he was a legend, a hero, a freedom fighter who made a difference to Canada. He freed the Indian people from the tyranny of the Department of Indian Affairs, its bureaucrats, and from the passivity of Canadians by leading them to become full participants in Canada by securing for them the unfettered vote. At least initially that is what Dr. Gorman led me to believe. In fact, the project was infinitely more complex and interesting and touched on many of the new fields in Western Canadian history, including Aboriginal history, women's history, and polyphonic narratives.

I was not really prepared for the scale of Ruth Gorman's project. Over forty large legal boxes of manuscript material were lined up from the front hall, through the living and dining rooms. Initially, I thought I would help her digest the material and edit her manuscript, perhaps checking a few facts. However, as I spent more time with Dr. Gorman, and as I read through the boxes it struck me that this was much more than a biography. It was as much Ruth Gorman's autobiography in the Alberta tradition of feminist activism and service to community as an accounting of Mr. Laurie's achievements. The interconnections between Ruth Gorman and John Laurie, whom she knew so well, and between Ruth Gorman and her book, and between Ruth Gorman and her community, were complex. And the more one investigated the more complex the situation became. Her views and her personality and her gender were ever entwined in the community and Aboriginal politics of the day.

Dr. Gorman had had a number of people transcribing her self-admitted idiosyncratic shorthand and hastily scribbled and sometimes faintly pencilled notes for her book. She was a writer to whom an inspiration could happen at any time. And inspiration must have hit her most often when she was smoking since many notes were on the back of literally hundreds of cigarette packages. Key amongst these volunteers were her grandson, Paul, her good friends, and grant-funded assistants. However, as she realized the real scope of the project and the fragility of her own life, she became anxious to have the project completed.

It needed more than transcription. A number of historians, professor Donald Smith of the department of history at the University of Calgary amongst others, had already contributed to the vision that shaped Ruth Gorman's manuscript. I remember well that fateful moment when Ruth asked if I would take on completing the manuscript and see it through to publication.

After careful reflection and reading into the files and the many boxes, I reluctantly agreed. As I read the material and talked with Ruth Gorman about the numerous stories around Mr. Laurie, so many of which involved her strength of narration, it became clear that the manuscript was in fact already in the boxes. They contained all the variants of Ruth Gorman's writings on every episode that she felt shaped John Laurie's life. While Laurie died in 1959, she believed the victory was not the famous Hobbema Case, but rather the 1961 amendments to the Indian Act, which secured the vote for Aboriginal people without the possibility of enforced enfranchisement. It should be noted that enfranchisement did not necessarily mean the vote, although that was involved. It meant the "liberation" or removal of the Indian from the reserve to "full citizenship." This meant the end to treaty rights and right to live on the reserve. To Ruth it could also mean impoverishment and the end of a way of life.

Like Moses, although she never used the analogy, Laurie never saw this Promised Land. It also became clear in later research, particularly in Senator

James Gladstone's letters in the Glenbow Archives, that Laurie was never persuaded that the vote was desirable. If it cost Aboriginal people the protection of the treaties and reserve, he would have none of it. And in this he did not differ from the majority of Indian leaders of his day. He did argue with Dr. Gorman on the issue. But ever a careful writer and a superb dramatist, Dr. Gorman knew that for a good story she needed a noble cause, a villain, and a hero with a few flaws, and a happy ending. The noble cause was the vote, the villain both the Honourable Jack Pickersgill and the bureaucrats in Indian Affairs, and the hero, Mr. Laurie. He would have to struggle against these flaws with the assistance of his followers – the key one being herself. She was aware of the "gender" implications of how she positioned herself, and the narrative must be read with that in mind. More will be explained about this later in the introduction.

The manuscript was an organic production that could never be finished. As she remembered or found additional materials she added to her files, modifying her chapters and notes. She kept all versions and given the condition of the boxes it was not always possible to determine which variant was the preferred one or the most recent. The bringing together of the manuscript while ensuring the maintenance of Ruth Gorman's voice was not easy. A large number of people, led by Shirley Onn, the former director of the University of Calgary Press, went through each box and typed out Ruth's notes and attachments in their entirety. Lucile Edwards, a dedicated Calgary heritage volunteer, Erin Paynter, a student, Shirley Onn herself, Norma Sieppert, a member of Alberta's Centennial Advisory Committee, and Peter Fortna, one of my research assistants, did Herculean work. I am most appreciative of the considerable work Stéphane Guevremont did in researching obscure points that had eluded me, and in formatting the manuscript for final publication.

Dr. Gorman's chapter structures and chronological orders were largely maintained, although she did start to change the order of the chapters, and added new ideas for ones later in her life. In putting together these chapters the internal structure was kept wherever possible. All repetitions were removed and the most complete variants included. It was realized that the normal editorial process for primary source annotation would have suggested that we take the best version of the manuscript and indicate all variations. While possible, this would have resulted in a several-thousand-page manuscript, and would have detracted significantly from its flow. One of the key issues was that of transition between chapters, particularly chapters five and six, and sixteen and seventeen. Dr. Gorman tended to write in vignettes, or in discrete article form. While she may well have tended to create transition paragraphs there is no sign in her writings and various drafts that she intended smoother transitions. Dr. Gorman was a master storyteller in the Aboriginal tradition, and while many of the stories she told are connected, each is also discrete. It was this spirit and this voice that the Laurie biography captures. When I read the chapters I can in fact hear her telling the stories with passion, conviction, and indeed connection.

Dr. Gorman's life and therefore manuscript was a multifaceted and complex one. In order to ensure that the many strands were connected, an appendix with a timeline was developed to ensure clarity. It should be noted that Linda Gorman, her daughter, Paul Ragona, her grandson, Neil Watson and Rodney Muir, both long-time friends, and Judy Bedford also read the manuscript to ensure that it flowed the way of the many stories she had told them.

As Dr. Gorman came across some of the recent literature on the marginalization of the Aboriginal people of Canada she wanted to include that information as well. She never managed to do so except for Brian E. Titley's *A Narrow Vision: Duncan Campbell Scott and the Administration of Indian Affairs in Canada*, although she was aware of the work of Sarah Carter and clipped media coverage of her early work on Manitoba's Aboriginal farmers.[4] Had Dr. Gorman been familiar with the recent literature on women's narratives by, for example, professor Catherine Cavanaugh of Athabasca University, I am certain she would have significantly revised the biography even further, giving greater agency to her friends in the Calgary Local Council of Women.

Dr. Gorman was persuaded that the box contents were historical documents in their own right. There was only one area where my editorial pen was heavy – and it would have been in any book of this genre. I indicated to her that I would have to establish some balance amongst her notes. She did agree. From time to time in her manuscript she would harangue on the state of the Canadian union or digress with a long section on the benefits or shortcomings of the British Empire. Where these added to an understanding of her interpretation of Mr. Laurie, or revealed something about her own contribution to, for example, the Hobbema Case, or supplied an insight into her own intellectual foundations, the general comments were maintained in the manuscript. However, where they went on for several dozen or more pages they were edited to more moderate length, particularly where they detracted from the main flow of the strong narrative. The complete transcripts of the original notes are presently in the University of Calgary Archives.

Most important, I wanted to ensure that the words in the manuscript were Dr. Gorman's. I believe that her voice has been captured. She never seemed to have developed a writing style that we associate with the legal profession, even in the 1960 brief to the Joint House of Commons and Senate Committee. Rather, and not surprisingly, given her work with *My Golden West*, which she single-handedly managed and more or less wrote, hers was a popular journalistic style. As the manuscript began to emerge, the strength of Ruth's writing and her feminist perspective became increasingly clear. Particularly powerful were the chapters that dealt with her involvement in the Hobbema affair and in the subsequent abolishment of involuntary enfranchisement. It should be emphasized as well that the first twelve chapters were entirely in Ruth Gorman's hands. She had personally finished these before I became involved in the project.

THE CONTEXT

What was the Alberta in which John Laurie and Ruth Gorman found themselves? In 1958, there were 18,525 treaty Indians in Alberta, speaking seven languages and living on ninety reserves totalling 1.5 million acres, the largest, 350,000 acres, being the Blood reserve near Cardston, Alberta. Since the turn of the century and increasingly during the 1930's, Indian Affairs policy was to make as many of the reserves self-sufficient, as independent of Crown financing as possible. The programme was, in short, a failure. Consistent reductions in expenditures and lack of capital for new development made the situation desperate, despite improvements on some of the reserves during the war. Reserves near the larger centres experienced some respite from a life of endless grinding poverty as jobs opened up with the war. In 1949, the Indian Association of Alberta did a survey of the reserves in the province on housing, welfare, employment, and agriculture in support of an eventual submission to the Joint Committee of the Senate and the House of Commons on Indian Affairs in 1960. The situation they found was one of general hopelessness except perhaps on the Hobbema, Saddle Lake, and Gleichen reserves, where agriculture and oil and gas production were beginning to have some success. Altogether there were only 557 farms on all Alberta reserves, 57 government jobs, 2 reserve-based industries and 31 band-paid jobs. The letters in Ruth Gorman's files indicate the plight of an isolated people and their wish for education, inclusion, and validation.

Access to education was minimal. As late as 1958/59, for example, only 34 Indians received provincial vocational training, 19 grade twelve, and 38 grade eleven.[5] In the north of the province there was consistent pressure to maintain and complete the treaty process, to secure reserves and to prevent their sale. In the south, as population densities grew, pressure on land continued. Too often Indian Affairs was too ready to alienate parts of the reserves. As population pressures grew more intense, and the administration of Indian Affairs found itself increasingly less able to deal with the crisis of real need and expectations, it was only a matter of time before political action became the solution. The question would be who, how, and when.

The reserves were located within a province of 800,000 in 1941 and 1.3 million in 1961, forming 1.5 percent of the population.[6] These numbers alone indicate the pressures on the Aboriginal population, which itself was also increasing significantly. Alberta was a province that was emerging from the Depression. Even during that depression the abhorrent condition of the Aboriginal people was recognized by the province's Ewing Commission. The Second World War heralded a new era, one of increasing prosperity, as Edmonton became the centre for the provisioning of the northern war efforts like the Alaska Highway and the CANOL pipeline, while Calgary became the oil city. That wealth also trickled to the reserves, particularly those that had oil, like Hobbema.

Most important, and this becomes clear in Gorman's manuscript, the end of the war brought an interest in a new internationalism with the formation of the United Nations. There was a public belief in human dignity and human equality. Eleanor Roosevelt, a strong internationalist and supporter of human dignity, gave a speech in early March 1949 in Calgary, which Gorman noted was particularly well attended. The call for social justice and reform was one that was impacting politics throughout Canada. The Cooperative Commonwealth Federation (CCF) topped a 1943 Gallup poll, and the following year was elected the government of Saskatchewan. While Alberta was increasingly conservative in its social philosophy, the pressures for human equity were nonetheless pervasive. It was in this environment of economic upswing and concern for economic justice and human rights that Laurie, Gorman, and the Indian Association of Alberta, which had been formed in 1939 at Wabamun, fought for rights including an end to "compulsory enfranchisement."

Before 1960, the Aboriginal people of Canada could only vote in federal elections if they agreed to become or were forcibly enfranchised. Upon "enfranchisement" (i.e., being made "Canadian") they would be removed from the reserve, cease to have treaty rights, and lose their homes, farms, and families. This was accepted until the Indian Association of Alberta, and its Euro-Canadian supporters like Ruth Gorman, secured appropriate amendments to the Indian Act in 1961. It should be noted that to date John Laurie has been given credit for most of the efforts leading to securing the vote, or to ending enfranchisement. Gorman herself has largely given this credit. Out of modesty she felt that it would be inappropriate for a woman to lay the claim – although she would not reject the recognition that would come her way in the future.

It should also be noted that while on reflection the 1961 amendments to the Indian Act were without a doubt a profound milestone, it is not seen as a great milestone in Aboriginal history or in Aboriginal folklore. Olive Dickason, in her definitive *Canada's First Nations: A History of Founding Peoples from Earliest Times*, made no mention of the Hobbema Case, John Laurie, or Ruth Gorman. This is particularly odd given that Dickason is herself a mixed blood, and a woman. Arthur Ray, in his more recent *I Have Lived Here Since the World Began: An Illustrated History of Canada's Native People*, mentions the 1959/1960 Joint Committee in which Dr. Gorman was so dominant, but only in the context of West Coast issues. Again, neither Laurie nor the Hobbema Case is mentioned. Ray gives credit for the reformation of the Indian Act to the 1963 Pearson government, not to the Diefenbaker government who surely started the process. The whole issue of enfranchisement, which was a major impediment to participation by indigenous people in the politics of Canada, is increasingly being ignored. Even the most recent history of Alberta, Aritha van Herk's *Mavericks: An Incorrigible History of Alberta*, chose not to deal with what was truly the odd couple of Alberta Indian politics: Mr. Laurie, the bachelor school teacher and Mrs. John C. Gorman, the Mount Royal matron, women's rights advocate, and lawyer. The memory of the struggle for native rights at Hobbema and all it represented has been lost within thirty years of the events. There are some exceptions but they are few. Howard and Tamara Palmer's *Alberta, A New History*, now out of print but available on the Alberta digitization web site, does mention Laurie, but says nothing about Ruth Gorman.

This reveals an inherent dichotomy in Aboriginal studies, which is evidenced in both Gorman's and Laurie's thinking. They believed that the vote, one aspect of enfranchisement, was the hallmark of democracy, but with the vote also went obligations to pay taxes and to participate in civil society. If this logic was extended it could mean the end of the reserves established by treaty, which both believed were essential to the survival of the Aboriginal people. It is clear that for their part the Aboriginal people did not see the vote as a holy grail. While enfranchisement was an issue, they felt that it had been dealt with as so many other issues had been and would be by appeal to the courts – of which the Hobbema Case was but one.

Enfranchisement was a "strange" European concept, another legal attempt to marginalize and to take away the little that the colonized had left. To the Indians the treaties were their only real protection. So long as they remained intact, their future was protected. In the case of the vote, they knew they were a minority and the vote would do little other than legitimize the hegemony of the Euro-Canadians. One gets the impression from the correspondence that the fight was more a Euro-Canadian fight than an Aboriginal people's fight. But this is not to argue that the fight itself did not have an impact. The fight to secure an equitable place for the Aboriginal people within the Canadian political structure created an organization, the Indian Association of Alberta, an awareness of process, and a generation change of leadership starting with Harold Cardinal that would revolutionize the status and increase the power of Aboriginal people in Canada.

A careful analysis of the events of the 1950's, including the press campaign surrounding the Hobbema trials and the lobbying for an end to involuntary enfranchisement, illustrate that success was largely due to Ruth Gorman's connections through the University of Alberta and the Calgary Local Council of Women and her ability to use the media. This is not to deny that both Mr. Laurie and the Indian Association of Alberta had a significant role. However, without Mrs. Gorman's persistence and ability to mobilize public opinion in Alberta, the Indian Act and the Elections Act would never have been changed.

Officially and in the historical literature, John Laurie is usually given greater credit and Gorman is hardly mentioned at all. But he was hardly as supportive as was Gorman. He, as well as the Indian Association of Alberta, had to be persuaded that this was the ultimate prize. Had he been alive in 1961 it is not certain that he would have supported Gorman in her cause at the Parliamentary Committee. The Indian Association of Alberta trusted Gorman, although they had continuing concerns that she was a woman. Many within the organization felt that the dangers of "enfranchisement" were too serious, and at least once Gorman had to storm out of a meeting after she had suffered more abuse than she cared for. Many felt that once they had the vote, Euro-Canadians would argue that with the vote go responsibilities – this ultimately would lead to a weakening if indeed not the abrogation of the treaties. Gorman never openly advocated that. She publicly believed that the treaties were inviolate, but that only through the vote would Aboriginal people gain control over their destiny and end the crippling trust relationship with the Crown.

JOHN LAURIE

John Laurie remains a man of mystery. Even those closest to him, for example contemporaries like Ruth Gorman, never really got to know him. Born in 1899, he died in 1959 at a relatively young age of heart problems exacerbated by his punishing pace as he in effect did two jobs – one as an English teacher and the other as secretary to the Indian Association of Alberta. He had accomplished enough in this life, however, to have accumulated an honorary doctorate from the University of Alberta, a mountain name near Canmore, and a freeway name in Calgary. He was adopted by the Stoney and was known to them as White Cloud, and to the Sarcee (*Tsuu T'ina*) as Sitting Eagle. Ruth Gorman believed him to be the Dr. Schweitzer of the Canadian Plains. He was a man who touched the many who got to know him.

In a brief puzzling "deathbed" autobiography, which was only added to his papers after his death, John Laurie invented for himself a "Grey Owl" childhood. He had himself immigrated to Canada and then in his youth was transported back to England to live with an aged and strict grandmother. None of this was true, although it was believed by Ruth Gorman in this biography and informed her assessment of Laurie. She therefore purposefully included it in the book.

Even more interesting is the fact that Laurie claimed Aboriginal ancestry. Dr. Donald Smith knew of this claim, although Laurie's sister maintained in a conversation with professor Smith that she had no evidence of it. Ruth Gorman's daughter, Linda Gorman, who knew Laurie as well, did not know of any basis for this claim. In any case, further investigation may well be worthwhile. In a letter to Senator Gladstone, president of the Indian Association of Alberta, Laurie confided that he was in fact eligible for treaty status under the Indian Act:

> My great-grandfather who was probably a mixed blood drank too much rum, fell into a fire and died of burns. My grandfather was taken in by white people, brought up by them, educated a little by the Church in Ontario (Bishop John Strachan had most to do with it). He married the daughter of this family and that is why I have the name I have. My father was properly brought up by this family – really his mother's family – and he married white. I can prove all of this by letters and papers. I never told anyone this but it is not quite unknown to Six Nations people. My great-great-grandfather was simply called William of Canajoharie from the village he and his mother lived in New York State. Properly speaking we are entitled to Indian status under the definition in the present Indian Act. I know where great-grandfather was buried not very far from Brantford. My dad used to show me his grave.[7]

Despite twenty-five years of association, John Laurie rarely dropped the shield of his privacy to Ruth Gorman. She certainly was not aware that he might claim Indian blood, nor did she know of his "English" fantasy. Perhaps Laurie fantasized with everyone but Mrs. Gorman, who might have had some sharp and straight thoughts had she known. John Laurie's letters do illustrate a certain mischievous humour and his "recollections" of these early years may have been that. These multiple identities, none of which were formalized, may also have been an attempt to disassociate himself from his family. Ruth Gorman was appalled that when John Laurie died, his sister expressed little interest in him personally. Her single concern, according to Gorman, was the residue of his estate.[8] Perhaps Laurie's sister simply chose to "deny" her Indian antecedents because it was not "fashionable" in her community and to her friends. In any case, Donald Smith gathered in his discussions with John Laurie's sister that relations may have been somewhat strained.[9] Perhaps it was John Laurie's indirect way of indicating a wish to distance himself from his past.

His revelations to Senator Gladstone, however, are interesting. Was he trying to establish a relationship with Gladstone, who himself was Cree-French mixed-blood, through the creation of a common heritage? Whatever his motivation, this confession has a ring of truth and was written in Laurie's own hand, and is worth exploring further.

Professor Donald Smith does prove that Laurie, whatever his heritage, came to life on 23 October 1899 of Ontarian-born parents on a farm in Blenheim Township, Oxford, Ontario.[10] This does not contradict Laurie's confessions to Gladstone. He was entirely educated in Ontario and graduated from the University of Toronto in 1923, arriving in Calgary on 30 June 1926. There he taught high school English at Crescent Heights for his working life. In his later years, he did some contract work for the Glenbow Museum as well, a kindness by Eric Harvie, who valued his efforts with the Indian Association of Alberta and his knowledge. But his real motivation was to help Laurie's desperate financial situation. When he left the school board due to ill health, his resources were limited. Harvie wanted to ensure that his work with the Indian Association of Alberta could continue.

Laurie had excellent contacts, which he used to further the cause. For a few years at least, William Aberhart, later the premier of Alberta, was his principal. His colleagues there included Douglas Harkness, who was always a key supporter and was a one-time minister of defence in the Diefenbaker government.

Gorman argues that as Laurie became more involved in Calgary, he came to learn of the marginalization of the Aboriginal people who lived in the area around Calgary, particularly the Stoney, the Sarcee, and later the Blackfoot and the Bloods. Passionate about education as a teacher, he boarded in his home, at his own expense, Eddie Hunter, Gerald Tailfeathers, and Gordon Crowchild, all young Aboriginal male adults who would have been denied education in the city otherwise. While unknown to Gorman, it is interesting that this replicated Laurie's version of his own father's experience. All became lifelong friends and gave him entrée into the reality of Aboriginal life in Alberta in the 1940's to 1950's. He was adopted as a son by Eddie Hunter's family – an adoption that meant a great deal to him and which he took, as did his adoptive family, very seriously. It is interesting to note that the Hunter family had also adopted Ruth Gorman's father, Colonel M.B. Peacock, and honoured his daughter with the name "Mountain White Eagle Girl" on 25 July 1937.[11] Although later she valued the honour, Ruth always claimed she wasn't alerted that the ceremony was to take place and was somewhat embarrassed about the circumstances.

While Ruth Gorman sees Laurie's connection with Calgary's Aboriginal community as a gradual awakening, there is little in the Gladstone correspondence that would support this, particularly if Laurie himself believed in his own native ancestry. He may have sought out connection with his heritage. If this is indeed the case, it may explain his motivation throughout his life. In the 1950's, it was not fashionable to claim a native heritage. It would also explain his real understanding of the League of Indians of Canada, founded by Fred Loft, a member of the Six Nations.

In 1944, John Laurie, who at least publicly had become increasingly committed to changing the situation of the Aboriginal people in Alberta was, according to Gorman, persuaded by Malcolm Norris, the great Alberta Métis leader who was instrumental in the revival of the Indian Association of Alberta and the Métis Association, to become secretary of the Indian Association of Alberta.[12] There is contrary evidence in the Minutes that it was Enos Hunter, his adopted father, who persuaded him.[13] Whatever the origins, this was a position he held almost continuously until a few years before he died in 1959 when his health would no longer permit him to provide the service he felt the Association needed.

While Laurie was very much the servant of the executive of the Association, who were always key Aboriginal leaders, it is clear from the correspondence that Laurie was not without influence. He would persuade, he would argue, and he would counsel both privately and in meetings to ensure that his perspectives were heard and adopted. Most often, members of the Association and its executive shared them, but sometimes there were divisions. There was a feeling by some that perhaps he was over-zealous in his views, but there is no doubt he was held in the highest esteem even in argument.

When the Indian Association of Alberta decided to make him an honorary member, he accepted with great humility. However, when they also wanted to give him the vote, he strongly objected. Those present argued that Laurie was an elder and leader of distinction, and whether Indian or non-Indian, it would be wrong not to have your most honoured members vote. Given Laurie's own views on the franchise, one wonders if he saw the irony of the discussion.

On one point he was passionate about and would not compromise. When it appeared that the Blackfoot-speaking members of Treaty Seven were considering separation from the Indian Association of Alberta, John Laurie was blunt. If this happened, he said in a letter to Senator Gladstone, he would resign. So would Ruth Gorman. It is likely that this threat more than anything kept the Association a coordinated body.[14]

Laurie had several core unwavering beliefs that governed his actions. As will be seen, they were for the most part congruent with those of Ruth Gorman. However, there were also significant differences and in some, but not all cases, Laurie kept these to himself. In others it is likely that Gorman chose to blind herself. When she was committed to a cause, she believed all should be of one mind, and often chose to ignore differences. This will explain why in some cases in the manuscript she will position Laurie as arguing a case in her manuscript, when Laurie's own confidential correspondence suggests that he had alternate views.

First and most important, Laurie believed, as did Gorman, in the sanctity of the treaties. When he was reluctant to move forward on an issue, it was usually because he felt that the treaties might be compromised. For example, throughout the later 1950's Laurie was not convinced, and neither were many of the executive of the Indian Association of Alberta, that they should pursue the vote. They doubted that it would end the oppression by the Department of Indian Affairs; most important, they thought it would compromise the treaties. The vote could mean an obligation to pay taxes, and to accept other burdens, which would certainly compromise the promise of the treaties. Laurie and some leaders were also opposed to liquor on the reserves. Although it might be argued that this was driven by Laurie's racial stereotypes of Indians, there is more evidence to suggest that Laurie felt that since some of the treaties forbade liquor, that any change would encourage the Department to see the treaties as vulnerable. In reading the Gorman manuscript it is critical to keep this in mind. His strong views on these topics do not come through, because Gorman believed him converted to her perspectives. This, though, was not the case. In a 1957 letter to Senator Gladstone, he related a conversation he had with Ruth Gorman:

> She [Ruth Gorman] argues that the PC's must have the support of the CCF to pass any amendments and the CCF is likely to insist that a federal vote must be given. My argument is that Indians must choose whether they want to vote at all or not and that I am suspicious that opening one gate into the hayfield leads to opening other gates until there is not even a fence. She replies that Indians accept the old age pensions, the old age assistance payments, blind pensions, school grants at the taxpayer's expense and also that it is a general principle that accepting anything not originally provided for in Treaty also calls for accepting responsibility. Think it over and make up your own mind about it.[15]

Second and perhaps even more important, Laurie loathed the Department of Indian Affairs and its various incarnations. To him even more than his

Indian friends, it was evil incarnate. He felt that the Department was systematically undermining the treaties in an attempt to cut costs, and to force assimilation. He saw the various changes in the Indian Act, and the enforced enfranchisement of treaty Indians in the 1940's and 1950's as examples of this policy – a policy he felt should be stopped at all cost. Ruth Gorman knew these views and they continued to influence her actions. In *My Golden West*, she indicated in an editorial that she was always suspicious when Indian and Northern Affairs made a conciliatory gesture. She always asked herself, "John Laurie would question – what are they up to now?"[16] While Laurie held these views with considerable strength, they were reinforced but also moderated by the presidents of the Indian Association of Alberta, with whom he was in constant communication.

In his correspondence with the presidents, he was completely open in sharing his views. It is difficult to detect any tone of condescension in the letters, but it is clear that something was felt. Laurie had a certain generational, more traditional view of the Indian that may have been accepted by both the older leaders, and perhaps the public, but it chaffed the younger generation. Laurie for example lamented the lack of leaders amongst the younger Aboriginal people of Alberta to Senator Gladstone.[17] Yet, this was the generation that would produce the most dynamic leaders of all, starting with Harold Cardinal. It was this new generation who would work with Indian Affairs, and the federal government, to maximize opportunities that worried Laurie, bound by his own prejudices. Hugh Dempsey, Laurie's successor as secretary to the Indian Association of Alberta, and Senator Gladstone's son-in-law, believed that Laurie had a stereotypical "noble savage" view of the old Indian leaders. At Laurie's funeral Gorman indicated she understood his views, by requesting some of the Indians to wear the traditional dress that Laurie so loved.

Laurie died without knowing whether his work was the foundation for the next generations of activism, or whether he had mired the Association in controversies that would become largely irrelevant. Would the changes he fought for have occurred in any case given the pressure that the international community was placing on human rights issues? It has even been suggested by some academic authorities that the famous Hobbema Case would have had a benign outcome regardless of Laurie's involvement. Professor Douglas Sanders argues that the judiciary generally did not side with the Department of Indian Affairs in enforced enfranchisements.[18] Yet, to argue that individual actions were irrelevant is specious at best. If Gorman had not acted, the Indian Association of Alberta would not have gained the experience needed to shape a future determined by the Aboriginal people themselves.

Laurie and Gorman's activism was based on a belief, shared by the native people, that both the political and legal systems would accommodate justice and human dignity. This legacy may well explain why in Canada the Aboriginal communities still use the law as recourse to injustice, while many indigenous people elsewhere in the world, including the United States, believe that violence remains the only recourse.[19]

There are those who would argue that Gorman and Laurie's suspicions of the bureaucracy were well-placed. Professor Dean Neu of the Haskayne School of Business at the University of Calgary and Richard Therrien, poet, researcher, and writer, in their *Accounting for Genocide: Canada's Bureaucratic Assault on Aboriginal People*, argue that

> Relationships between indigenous people and governments are filtered and managed through a complex field of bureaucratized manipulations, controlled by soft technologies such as strategic planning, law and accounting. By the time individuals sit down to negotiate face to face, the choices available have been severely diminished. Those government processes are firmly entrenched within the broader phenomena of modernity, colonialism and genocide.[20]

Laurie would have understood and accepted this argument. Ruth Gorman believed that if watched and controlled bureaucracies could be functional. She believed that if there was to be a department responsible for Indian affairs, it should be staffed by, controlled by, and accountable to Aboriginal people.

Laurie died just after the Hobbema Case was "won," at the height of the press coverage, and in the throes of victory. The funeral held both in Calgary and at Morley was accompanied by much mourning – that usually accompanying a key much-beloved public figure. He didn't have decades to diminish in the public consciousness as Ruth Gorman, whose funeral was more modest and less acclaimed, did.

RUTH GORMAN

Ruth Gorman's biography of Laurie does not necessarily explain the subtleties of his motivation and interrelationships with the Alberta Aboriginal community. It is, however, an intimate perspective of the mutual intersection of John Laurie's world with hers. Laurie was clear in his own mind as to how Ruth Gorman fit into his passion for reform. She was to be the legal standard bearer, to both preserve the treaties and to fend off the Department that was intent upon Aboriginal genocide. She was to be his legal, community development, and publicity instrument. She accepted this role, not only because she believed in the fundamentals of the cause, but also because she was good at it.

Ruth Gorman had many lives, all passionate, most of which were devoted to correcting a major injustice. She kept these lives separate, but they all had this common thread. She was central in ensuring changes to the status of women, to the status of Aboriginal people, to the status of the handicapped, and to the status of Western Canadians. Her strong belief in justice and equality were built upon an equally strong belief in the common sense of her fellow humans. This tradition of championing the disadvantaged was one accepted, and indeed sought after, by Western Canadian women of strong spirit, according to Catherine Cavanaugh.[21]

As noted earlier, she would accept that bureaucracies and elected officials were necessary but believed they had to be watched by the people and constantly held accountable. This more than anything explained her later role in founding the Western Canada Concept Party, her single-handed successful opposition to the relocation of the CPR rail track in Calgary, and her opposition to the repatriation of the Trudeau constitution, which she felt would seriously impact on property rights. She was particularly upset about the constitution. To her it was a fundamental document that should have been endorsed by all Canadians in a much more consultative and meaningful way. Her magazine *My Golden West* provides the best, sustained documentation of her belief system. Sometimes her too forthright manner in presenting her ideals would offend, but she would put that down to her training as a lawyer. She often stated that the legal profession did not really allow women to be "ladies."

Ruth Gorman was born in 1914 into a privileged Mount Royal environment in turn-of-the-century Calgary. She graduated from the University of Alberta with a bachelor of arts degree in 1937 and with a law degree in 1939, and then articled in her father's law firm. Her father, M.B. Peacock, a key influence in her life, was a close friend of Banff's Norman Luxton, who had married into the famous McDougall missionary family of Morley, Alberta. Her father was easily persuaded to become involved with the Aboriginal communities between Calgary and Banff, particularly those connected to the work of the missionaries. Donating his services, he fought the famous Wesley case (Rex v. Wesley, 26 Alta. L.R. 433, [1932] 2 W.W.R. 337, 58 C.C.C. 269, [1932] 4 D.L.R. 774 (C.A.)), which clarified the hunting rights of the Stoney, and worked through his Sunday school classes at Wesley United Church in Calgary to build bridges.[22] They often went to the reserve to play hockey with their native neighbours, hoping to develop closer connections between the city and the reserve. Because of her father's work and contributions, Ruth Gorman herself was made an Indian "princess" in 1937 when she was twenty-three years old, well before any of her activism, an honour she admitted she did not appreciate until later.[23]

While Dr. Gorman would argue that she only became familiar with and concerned about her Aboriginal neighbours after John Laurie invited her to become involved, it is clear that she would likely have had considerable sympathy and familiarity as a result of her father's involvement. It is also not unlikely that John Laurie would have known of her father's work, particularly in the Wesley case, which did receive newspaper coverage. Calgary after all was a small town and everyone knew everyone.

Because she was one of the few women lawyers in Calgary, and perhaps because her mother had held the position, or more likely because her father was a lawyer, when Ruth Gorman returned from university, she was asked almost immediately to be the convenor of laws for the Local Council of Women. She held the position until 1963, and during much of that time she also served as the honorary convenor of laws for the Canadian National Council of Women.

While her activities with the Local Council of Women might not seem connected to her work with Laurie, it produced for her a natural and continuing power base. These were women of her class, natural allies, who saw themselves at the leading edge, as they indeed were, of social reform. But her tenacity and ability to persuade, to engage, to badger, but always to point out social injustice, ensured significant and continuing support.

One of her first causes put to her by the Local Council of Women, before she became involved with the Indian Association of Alberta, was the need for an amendment to Alberta's Dower Act. Her persuasions ensured further amendments to the effect that a wife's recourse was not only against her husband, but also against anyone who had subsequently acquired an inappropriately alienated family home or farm. To ensure passage of the Act, according to her account published in *A Leaven of Ladies*, she went directly to Aberhart to get the law changed. He must have admired her because, according to a conversation I had with Gorman, he asked her to become his attorney general, an offer she did not accept given her family obligations. This refusal to enter formal public life was always a struggle for Gorman, who felt the tensions between her soul, which demanded social reform, and domestic duty, which demanded time. As the Council's legal convenor she also fought for the marketing of skimmed milk, and for women on the police force. She also worked to help create Calgary's Indian Friendship Centre and founded the Calgary Rehabilitation Society for the Handicapped. To both she was the critical legal counsel who got established the legal foundations that allowed them to flourish. Ruth was also involved in Alberta penal reform and in the United Nations human rights movement.

The League of Women's membership reflected the better off of Calgary, the wives of the professionals and the moneyed. It had been formed in Calgary during the 1895 visit of Lady Aberdeen, the wife of the governor-general of Canada. The women involved, according to Ruth Gorman, while the victims of a more restrictive age in that they could not work, assigned themselves the role of social reformers and keepers of the country's morals. While Gorman herself did not necessarily agree with the assigned role, she not only accepted it, but also made the best of it. Her thoughts on the role of women were clearly expressed in *My Golden West*.

She believed, for example, that women should reflect on the real meaning of marriage, and determine its new meanings:

> Marriage could be entering a new and exciting era based on both sexes' mutual needs and less on legal bonds, but the women of today are going to have to work as a group and study to find brand new rules and standards for this or just give up the marriage institution.[24]

Gorman formed an equally important link with the press. These links are outlined in the following Laurie biography. Connections with the publisher of the *Calgary Herald*, with reporter Richard (Dick) Snell, and others were a result of both her social and university contacts, but also a result of her activities with the Calgary Local Council of Women and with the Canadian Bar Association. Her ability to use and motivate the media became a key feature of her campaigns. It was her canny populist sense of what the public would consider an issue that made her campaigns, particularly in the Hobbema Case, such a success. She repeated her press strategy again in 1963 when she successfully fought Mayor Harry Hays in his attempt to relocate the CPR mainline track to the south bank of the Bow River, which would destroy valuable future park land, now Prince's Island. In 1955, the city had agreed with the Local Council of Women that the area to be impacted would be a city park. They were now going to break their word, something that no one did to Ruth Gorman without consequence.[25]

She attempted to use the press in one other key issue, the repatriation of the Canadian constitution in the 1980's. Her fame as a public figure ensured that she would get coverage, but she was unable to mobilize key power brokers to oppose the repatriation, which she believed abrogated property rights. Her visceral opposition to the constitution made her an easy and willing recruit for the Western Canadian Concept movement. As with most causes she believed in, she became involved with the political party with a passion. She developed its constitution and did much of its legal work. Her love for the Canadian West is obvious in *My Golden West*, but she was not a Western separatist. The Western Canada Concept was the last of her great causes, all of which were to rectify injustice.

The context of the manuscript is critical to its understanding. As indicated earlier, Gorman's biography of Laurie is really at the same time her autobiography. When I first asked Dr. Gorman about this possibility, she confessed that indeed it was. She hoped it was not too apparent! She felt that it was not acceptable in her generation for women, particularly women of her social rank, to take precedence over men. After all she was a Mount Royal matron! Indeed, in the *Calgary Herald* of 5 March 1966, she mused about herself: "law makes you argumentative which is not the natural bent of females. It is extremely difficult for a woman to become a lawyer, and you are not welcome." She certainly felt she had to use flattery as well as brains to succeed in law school, and that she had to play the gender role that society set for her.

Although not a conventional thinker, she was not ignorant of the ties and benefits of convention. For example, she only worked for one year in her father's law firm, before she married and decided to become a full-time mother and Mount Royal "lady." She stepped into a role that, while on the surface might seem unusual, had been set for wealthy educated women of her generation – social activism. In Calgary this was particularly acceptable by the 1940's. The pathways had been set by Annie Gale, the first women elected to council in the City of Calgary, and by Nellie McClung and the others of the Famous Five, to whom Ruth Gorman was a real successor. The Calgary Council of Women had also been active for several decades, and she followed a trail that was well marked.

Her book, then, is the story of her friendship with Laurie, her own work on the Hobbema Case and her work in presenting the Indian Association of Alberta case to the 1959/60 Joint Senate and House of Commons Committee on Indian affairs. What she described as her successes were a result of her worldview and the tenacity with which she held it. Dr. Gorman had a distinct view of right and wrong, the role of women, the role of men, the responsibility of friends, the role of elected officials and the role of bureaucrats. She was an articulate "freedom fighter" but at the same time she was not prepared to be a revolutionary. Everything Dr. Gorman did was within the law and pushed but did not overstep the social conventions of her time. Although himself involved with the CCF, Laurie had trouble with the "social liberals" with whom Gorman surrounded herself, and referred to some of the more rabid as "communists," but he never labelled her as such.[26]

Ruth Gorman was instilled with a strong sense of social justice and a belief that individuals, when acting collectively but particularly individually, could make a difference. She admired Gandhi and believed in non-violence: "The time is now for the non-violent to act together in determined resistance by simply backing up our land and our police."[27] She believed that the greatest contribution of the North American Indians was what she saw as their commitment to "non-violence." She believed that Indian culture was based on "respect for the older, tolerance for the weak and a voluntarily shared tribal life." She believed that they only took to violence as "a means to rectify a wrong or to gain daily bread." She argued, in *My Golden West*, that "we desperately need their secret of non-violence in order to survive."[28]

Her views on Aboriginal people were distinct and may have caused some of her contemporaries offence. She noted with agreement George MacLean's (Walking Buffalo) deathbed advice to his people: "Do not lose your Indian ways, the poor white savage may need them someday."[29]

She passionately believed that Canadian society was not living up to its treaty obligations, and that if Canadians as a whole knew of their shame – there would be change. She at no time believed that she was engaged in "uplifting" the Aboriginal condition. She believed that if there were "a condition," it had been imposed by the Canadian government and particularly its Department of Indian Affairs. To her, its parsimony and its passion for self-preservation impoverished and stifled the rich culture of the people she knew. She was motivated by equal amounts of indignation and shame.

The righteous, of which she was one, had an obligation to combat evil. She also had an overwhelming belief in the sensibility of the common man. If he or she knew what was going on, injustice would be corrected. She frequently related the comments of a cab driver who asked her on one of her trips to Hobbema what she did and where she was going. After telling him, he indicated he felt that the Indians deserved a much better deal than they were getting. She believed in a world in which the common man or woman, if the truth were provided, would make change.

She also believed strongly in parliamentary democracy, but also that the citizen had to hold parliament accountable. She believed that bureaucracies were to be feared and that by nature they would indulge in self-preservation and self-aggrandizement. She also believed that they were essential to the sound functioning of government. To her the Department of Indian and Northern Affairs had run amok. It should be destroyed, and, as soon as possible, the Indians should be given not only the right to self-government, but the fiscal instruments as well. Dr. Gorman also believed that if the Indians got the vote, then and only then, would parliamentarians begin to pay them the attention they deserved. Treaties should be rigorously upheld and not an inch of leeway should be granted by the Indians in their negotiations.

She also firmly believed in group action. A strong supporter of the Indian Association of Alberta, she was fearful that if it became fragmented, the Indians would be victimized by the Department of Indian Affairs. She was ever fearful, as was John Laurie, that if the Indian Association of Alberta became divided between north and south, only the Department would be the winner.

Those she counted as her friends, for example Mr. Laurie, did not necessarily understand her views. It is clear from the minutes of the Indian Association of Alberta that she differed from him on two very key issues. Dr. Gorman believed certainly more adamantly than Laurie, and the executive of the IAA, that the unencumbered franchise would be the solution for any of the problems facing the Aboriginal people of Canada. As a populist, she had to believe that politicians would listen to the voting Aboriginal people and their supporters, the "common man." She believed that if the reserves voted strategically, they could make an incredible difference. But her belief in the vote did not end with the franchise. If she had had her way, the Aboriginal people would have had their own legislature, and both staff and control the Department of Indian and Northern Affairs. She was a generation ahead in her support of self-government.

But John Laurie was reluctant to press for the vote during his lifetime. He was extraordinarily suspicious of the Department of Indian and Northern Affairs and its various iterations. He believed that the key to the well being of the Aboriginal people of Canada was strict adherence to treaty. To him the moment the Aboriginal people accepted something that was not in the treaties – and the treaties were silent on the vote – the entire treaty might be abrogated. He felt that the Department of Indian Affairs might very well forcibly enfranchise Indians if they engaged too openly in political activities. Certainly this is why he was so careful to distance the IAA from the Hobbema Case. In his correspondence with Senator Gladstone he made it quite clear that he had distanced the IAA from Gorman's litigation.[30] It may be that he felt the Department might well forcibly enfranchise those involved.

A second point on which Gorman and Laurie differed was on giving the Aboriginal people the right to consume liquor. John Laurie was adamantly opposed for two reasons. He believed that the Aboriginal people were genetically predisposed to be more severely impacted by alcohol than Euro-Canadians. But most importantly he believed that if treaty Indians acquired the rights to consume and sell liquor, this would be another chipping away at the validity of the treaties. Several of the treaties were explicit in the exclusion of alcohol. This issue was to be one on which Senator Gladstone, an Aboriginal adherent to the Bloods and Canada's first native senator, and Laurie would never agree. John Laurie did feel that Ruth Gorman should support him in his opposition. However, when carefully queried at an IAA meeting, she indicated that the choice to consume liquor should be left to the individual. It is interesting that these disagreements with Laurie are not outlined in her biography of him.

John Laurie did not conceal his concerns about the issue of the vote from Ruth Gorman or from others. In a revealing letter from Laurie to Gladstone, he outlines his concerns in an almost state of panic:

> Have you any idea how much fighting I have to do to keep people like the Friends from openly advocating enfranchisement, and other well-meaning people also who think voting is the great solution. To my mind, education in the reserve is the solution. Give back to our brothers the self-respect and self-reliance that was once theirs. Fifty years from now they can start talking about votes if they feel like it. But now such a step would be the complete damnation of our brothers. This is my idea anyway.[31]

Gorman tended to either "believe" in a person and forgive all faults, or condemn an individual if they failed a key test of her belief structure. John Laurie passed her tests.

When Laurie died, Gorman saw herself as the steward of his incomplete legacy. She believed that it was her duty – indeed her purpose on this planet – to complete that mission. To her, it was the change to the Indian Act in 1961 that would see the removal of Section 112, compulsory enfranchisement. The months she spent touring Alberta's key native communities in 1959/60 were the highlights of her years with the Indian Association of Alberta. She was firm that the communities must support that change, and the trek was in the tradition of a political campaign rather than a fact-finding mission. While removal of enfranchisement provisions were key, the Indian Association of Alberta added concerns about education, welfare, and hunting and fishing rights – for a total of fifty-seven resolutions. While Gorman supported all of them, it is clear from her argument (for it was argument rather than testimony) to the Joint Committee of the Senate and the House of Commons on Indian Affairs in 1960 that her own efforts were in the removal of Section 112.

As in her Hobbema fight, the resolutions were endorsed by the Friends of the Indians Society in Calgary and Edmonton, a group of largely white women and their male supporters who wanted to support political action by the Indians, and by the Canadian Bar Association. The great trek in 1959/60 by the executive members of the IAA throughout the province created incredible expectations. The executive first went to the Sarcee reserve, and then to the Stoney reserve. This was followed by meetings in Cardston with Chief Clarence McHugh, and Chief Shot on Both Sides, then on to Hobbema and then to Lesser Slave Lake and Cold Lake. These five large meetings elected representatives for a consolidated meeting at Hobbema to draft the final resolutions.

The IAA correspondence on the preparation of the brief to the Joint Senate and House of Commons Committee indicate how seriously the communities considered the process. Indeed, the committee's minutes are probably one of the best snapshots of the concerns of the reserves throughout Alberta. There was by no means consensus on all of the issues at the final Hobbema meeting, and, in fact, some of the delegates felt that where issues had not been fully dealt with by their communities they should go back for further consultation. This tendency concerned Gorman who felt that elected delegates should have the latitude to shape the resolutions. It also threatened any sense of unanimity. The degree of public consensus that the IAA managed to achieve is evident in the minutes of proceedings and evidence of the Senate and House of Commons Committee on Indian Affairs, a copy of which was one of Ruth Gorman's most cherished possessions.

Particularly contentious was the discussion on the vote. Gorman put the matter to the Indian representatives in Hobbema very succinctly. Individuals were to be for the vote, against the vote, or could reserve the decision. Peter Many Wounds felt that each band at home should settle the questions. He felt that they represented only a fraction of the people – only all of the people should decide. Gorman strongly argued that the resolution could not be taken home: "You as delegates here today have the vote of your people." Fred Gladstone spoke in favour of the third option in that he didn't "want the IAA to commit itself one way or the other." John Samson was clear that

> By now we are all quite familiar with those resolutions and a lot of us should know by now the general feeling of the people on our reserves. As far as we are concerned at Hobbema we do not want the provincial vote at all.[32]

When queried by Fred Gladstone as to whether he meant the federal vote as well, he replied "none at all – no vote. There is no guarantee we would not lose any of our treaty rights." There was obviously doubt in the room that the vote would bring anything but anguish. Senator Gladstone did indicate that the vote would bring some benefits. He emphasized that their rights – particularly treaty rights – would not be diminished. Joe Jiroux was concerned that the vote might mean additional taxation, but he did concede that Indians would likely have more say in their affairs. In the end the consensus was as Gorman wanted – they would oppose the vote until Section 112 was removed.

Liquor, a continuing issue particularly to Senator Gladstone, who felt that the legal restrictions on alcohol made Indians second-class, was another issue. Gorman believed that liquor privileges should be entirely an Indian matter.³³ She understood Laurie's opposition when he was alive, but was not prepared to press. John Samson and David Crowchild voiced opposition.

At this point the meeting became somewhat heated. It was obvious that the Hobbema meeting was guided by Mrs. Gorman's strong hand and voice. Someone commented, "for two days now it seems as though it is this woman's meeting."³⁴ At that point Mrs. Gorman left the meeting refusing to accept the insults. In camera, the president said:

> We would like Mrs. Gorman back. We do not want a new lawyer. Time is getting short. We have to meet the Joint Committee with someone who knows it and who can make a good job of the brief. I know some of you are confused. She has tried her best in her own way – she's helping us.

Mrs. Gorman, who was not paid for her legal counsel, was persuaded to return but remained resolute and not cowed. She stated that there were still

> long legal questions of your brief which you have not okayed. I would suggest that you form a committee who can authorize the brief. I want you to take a vote whether you want me to stay as your lawyer or not. All the things I have done today, drawing the resolutions from your old minutes, new resolutions I talked on my tour to your various reserves and they were all approved by your own executive. I have never in my life done anything that was not passed by the IAA without the consent of your executive. I do understand what an effort you have made and it is that reason why I am glad to help you. I want to thank Hobbema ladies for their wonderful courtesy to me. I will go home now and I won't even cross a T until I have talked to your committee.³⁵

The emphasis on "your" is not to be missed.

The proceedings in Ottawa also suggested that Gorman again dominated the discussions, although she was accompanied by Howard Beebe, president of the IAA, and Chief John Samson, northern representative. Gerald Tailfeathers was also there representing the Blood Indian reserve Protestant group. Senator Gladstone was the senate chair. The honourable John (Jack) Whitney Pickersgill was on the committee, although he did not speak and there is no record of his attendance.

While there is no doubt that the bulk of the brief was written by Ruth Gorman, officially it was prepared by Howard Beebe, Peter Burnsstick, Albert Lightning, Mrs. Nora Matchatis, John Samson, and Ralph Steinhauer, as well as Hugh Dempsey. The presentation is an extraordinary document. There is no doubt that while Gorman may have written much of it, it did reflect the interests and stories of the Aboriginal people of Alberta. The brief is clear that in the last years of the nineteenth century and in the first years of the twentieth, individual Indians were successfully making the transition to the capitalist economy. Whether this is something that Gorman got out of reading Lucien Mason Hanks and Jane Richardson Hanks's *Tribe Under Trust: A Study of the Blackfoot Reserve of Alberta*, for which she wrote an extensive eye-opening review for the *Calgary Herald*, will not be known.

Gorman's brief documents the Indian economic successes of the 1880's and 1890's. Black Horses, for example, owned a coal mine during the 1890's, employing 128 with several Indians. Chief Moon, a Blood, was in the hay-contracting business, successfully competing for contracts with white ranchers. Big Swan, a Peigan, and Coyote from Hobbema operated stopping houses. The brief suggests that changing attitudes in the Department of Indian Affairs in the early 1900's stifled the initiatives, forcing instead the sale of "unused" lands and the breaking up of reserves. It was during this period as well that "trust funds" that resulted from these sales were used for the education and welfare of the respective reserves. Gorman felt, and strongly stated these feelings at the committee, that this was in breach of the treaties and normal conditions of a legal trust. She saw the Department as engaged in ever-tightening its control of the reserves, with the amendments to the Indian Act in 1919 being particularly evil. The new amendments of that year encouraged enfranchisement by offering those who took it ten years of treaty payments in one lump sum. As she pointed out, in 1919 only 102 Indians had ever chosen enfranchisement, but since 1919, 487 had chosen it.

As a whole, the brief was an extraordinarily powerful one – one that should have induced shame and did from some, although not from all, of the committee's members. Senator Hugh Horner, for one, was hardly sympathetic and there were other members as well who were always careful to compare the rights of native people with those of the rest of Canadians. Gorman repeatedly pulled the committee back to the reality of the treaties and the realities of marginalization. John Samson stated it clearly:

We want our people to progress, but not at the expense of our basic rights as treaty Indians. We feel that it should be possible for us to be able to live on an equal footing with the white man, without having to give up our right to live on our reserves if we so wish or to lose our legal status as treaty Indians."[36]

The word "enfranchised" caused the committee some confusion. It meant "liberation," although to some Canadians it meant getting the vote. In some provinces Indians already had the vote, and in the Dominion Elections Act Indians were allowed the vote provided they subject themselves to the payment of taxes.[37] It became abundantly clear, however, to the committee that Indians would refuse the vote until Section 112 was removed.

While the whole enfranchisement issue was one that dominated the discussions, another issue that preoccupied Ruth Gorman was the status of Aboriginal women, who were marginalized by the Indian Act. Married women were the responsibility of their husband's reserve, as were their children. However, unmarried women and their children were the responsibility of the mother's reserve. Decisions as to whether or not to marry became economic. In the case of Hobbema, for example, the illegitimacy rate was high simply because it would be to the economic benefit of any Hobbema woman's children and husband to be able to continue to secure her monthly trust income. Amendments were suggested to ensure that the husband would continue to be responsible for the children upon abandonment. Gorman was also concerned that Aboriginal women who married white men should be able to return to the reserve should the marriage fail. There was also a considerable discussion about the interest of white men in marrying Aboriginal women for their share of the trust funds.

What these discussions did for the committee was to bring into focus the pain of governing every aspect of a people's life through contradictory and poorly thought out legislation and bureaucratic processes. Discussion of education, business financing, and fish and game policies offered similar imponderables. The Department had its bureaucrats out in full force at the committee meetings and they protected their interests well. Reading between the lines, some found joy in catching Gorman out in small details – but for the most part the sense is that they preferred to avoid jousting with the legal advisor to the Indian Association of Alberta.

There is much of Gorman the lawyer throughout the document, particularly in the language. The issue of "trust" is one that she held dearly and referred to often. She believed firmly that any sale of reserve assets, including land, should not be used for the social and/or welfare issues facing so many reserves. She felt that these were responsibilities that should be fully funded by the federal government out of general revenues. Capital expenditures to generate new income might be eligible – but even here she felt that there was a considerable obligation in the treaties to provide this kind of support. What was clear is that the federal government's responsibilities should not be foisted off on band trust funds. Education was a primary concern that was well articulated by John Samson, who said, "we do not want education that will turn us into second class white people; rather we want to become first class Indians."[38] But they wanted education that was community-based, not residential-school-based, and that could be had at neighbouring Canadian schools if desired. They asked for equitable treatment to Canadians, but Gorman more than once interjected that she felt they should have more than equitable treatment. They also wanted change to the general school curriculum to ensure respectful treatment of Aboriginal people – further, they wanted the skills not only to be healthy in their own community and culture but also in the wider Canadian culture should they chose their future there.

In the end, this committee report caused amendments to the Indian Act removing Section 112. To Gorman, this was the revolution. Once democratic rights were available, she believed they would be exercised and in time the Indian people of Canada would assume control of their own destiny. If in the end she had any regrets, it was that reform had not moved quickly enough.

INTERPRETATIONS OF JOHN LAURIE

Both John Laurie and Ruth Gorman have been subject to historical analysis, although not with the same fervour and rigour as other Western Canadian or Canadian figures. In writing her book, Ruth Gorman was aware of other interpretations of John Laurie, her superhero. She most appreciated Donald B. Smith's "A Good Samaritan: John Laurie," in Max Foran and Sheilagh Jameson's *Citymakers*. Smith offers an even-handed account of Laurie, appreciates his activities, but makes no interpretation. Smith's neutrality should not go unnoticed. Given the occasional conflict between Ruth Gorman and some of her contemporaries, he probably avoided anything that might upset her.

Smith's major contribution is the clarification of John Laurie's childhood, although as indicated he knew of, but decided not to include, Laurie's claim to Indian ancestry. Laurie rarely spoke to Ruth Gorman about his past, and she says so in her manuscript. When his dictated notes on his early upbringing were released by Eric Harvie's office upon his death, they certainly shocked Gorman. In these notes he claimed that he had been brought up in Oxford, England, by an aged and somewhat imposing grandmother. In fact, he grew up in Ontario and his grandmother came to live with them in Canada. It is interesting to note the similarities with Grey Owl's upbringing and, while there is no evidence, it would not be surprising if Laurie were not familiar with the Grey Owl story. Grey Owl, the greatest of the Indian impostors, had been brought up in England by aged aunts who very much shaped his younger years.

But most shocking to Gorman would have been Laurie's probable Indian ancestry. He indicated in his correspondence with Senator Gladstone on more than one occasion that he was "part" Indian. If Laurie had not lied about his upbringing in the dictated story of his childhood, this might be easier to believe. Did Laurie mean he was spiritually Indian? Was he referring to his Six Nations great-grandfather? What is interesting is that Gorman chose to believe Laurie's revelation about his English upbringing to Marjorie Bond, the secretary who typed his deathbed confession, and attributed to Laurie's youth variations of his lifelong habits. What she would have thought had she known he was a confessed mixed-blood can only be speculated.

Hugh Dempsey's interpretation of John Laurie, which is to be found in his *The Gentle Persuader: A Biography of James Gladstone, Indian Senator*, flies directly in the face of that offered by Ruth Gorman. There are several key points of difference that must be noted. Again, context is critical. Dempsey, as Senator Gladstone's son-in-law and as future secretary of the Indian Association of Alberta, knew Laurie and worked with him, as did Senator Gladstone. So, that biography is as much a reflection of a family life as it is deliberated "academic" history.

Dempsey saw Mr. Laurie, as he wished to be called, as an old-fashioned man who was intent upon keeping Aboriginal people "in their place." On the issue of enfranchisement, Dempsey states that

> Laurie believed that the suggestion of Indians obtaining the federal vote was simply a way to introduce taxation, which would ultimately lead to the dissolution of reserves and the end of any special status for native people.[39]

This statement would have appalled Gorman, since she believed Laurie was supportive of the franchise. She knew that Laurie was initially cautious for more complex reasons. First, Laurie believed that if the Indians obtained the vote they might well be forcibly enfranchised (i.e., removed from the reserve). Second, since the vote was not part of the treaty negotiation in the first place, it might well mean that sections of the treaties could be abrogated. Third, he didn't trust the Department of Indian Affairs and believed they would act out of malice, even if the Act was changed. It is also clear in the IAA minutes that those Indians on reserves were not keen at all on fighting for the vote. Ruth Gorman had so frightened them with the Hobbema enfranchisement fight that they saw no value in the vote. If they no longer feared enfranchisement, they feared taxation, and most emphatically they did fear the erosion of treaty. There were also other issues that mattered more on a day-to-day basis such as education, housing, and hunting rights.

Dempsey makes much of the differences amongst Laurie and Gladstone over the liquor issue. Senator Gladstone believed that Indian people should have the right to consume alcohol like any other Canadian. Laurie believed that alcohol would exacerbate social problems, and most important of all, since it was mentioned as prohibited in some of the treaties, the change might well call the entire treaty into question. Again, it was his suspicion of the Department of Indian Affairs. Gorman captures this hatred in several of the chapters in her book. However, Dempsey sees Laurie's caution as one based on racism. He states that while Gladstone saw liquor rights as a step towards equality, which was fraught with potential dangers, Laurie saw it as a means towards destroying the Indian "race." Dempsey unfairly argues that Laurie was a Calvinist bachelor who had some rather uncompromising views of the world that did not involve liquor. Laurie's belief that his great-grandfather was an alcoholic might have played a role, or it may have been invented to make a point. He also argues that Laurie romanticized the Aboriginal culture and had difficulty working with those who did not fit his stereotype. Also, Dempsey did not believe Laurie's claim that his great-grandfather was Aboriginal.

There were tensions amongst Laurie, Gladstone, Dempsey, and Gorman, the roots of which are not clear. Perhaps they can be traced to the issue of the senatorship. According to Ruth Gorman, she was offered a senate seat by Diefenbaker but turned it down hoping that John Laurie, who had the greatest difficulty in financing his work with the Indian Association of Alberta, would finally have a reasonable income. This claim may well be true. It has been claimed that the publicity she generated around the Hobbema Case was a key factor in the electoral success of the Diefenbaker government. She had a close relationship with Diefenbaker, and there is evidence that she had frequent discussions with him over a variety of issues.

She was horrified when Laurie offered the seat instead to the president of the Indian Association of Alberta, who at that time happened to be James Gladstone, a Cree mixed-blood adopted by the Blood people and married into one of its prominent families. In her mind the senatorship would likely have been offered to whomever was president, and it was Gladstone by accident. She minimally hoped that Laurie would at least become Gladstone's assistant, but that was not to be. Gladstone's senate office, according to Gorman, was to remain a family affair at his direction.

However, the Laurie-Gladstone correspondence around the senate appointment would suggest that Laurie knew what was going on before Gladstone did.[40] He certainly did not communicate Diefenbaker's offer of a senate seat made to Gladstone to Gorman. But Laurie was a very private and circumspect person, and it would have been unusual for him to tell Gorman. It would also not be a surprise if Laurie had been offered the senatorship, although there is no evidence that this happened. It would have happened verbally and no one would have known. However, Laurie did know that Gladstone was to be offered the senatorship, so it is likely that he was one of the key advocates for the appointment. He may also have suggested Ruth Gorman, although there is no evidence of this. But Laurie did have influence. Doug Harkness, a minister in the new Diefenbaker government and a former colleague, was in careful communication with Laurie over the appointment. The Gladstone-Laurie correspondence also suggests a strong friendship between Gladstone and Laurie that ran for several years before the senatorship. Whatever the sequence of events, it is clear in the manuscript that Gorman felt that Gladstone did not fulfill the job to her satisfaction. He should have been a much stronger advocate, according to Gorman, for changes to the Indian Act.

The best work to date on the Indian Association of Alberta and John Laurie's and Ruth Gorman's roles is *The Indian Association of Alberta: A History of Political Action*, by Laurie Meijer Drees. She accepts Dempsey's interpretation of Laurie as a conservative who was a brake on the Indian Association of Alberta. She may well have been right, at least on this point. The minutes of the Association indicate that the executive was very much in charge; they also demonstrate the subtle influence that Laurie held and, as time went on, that Gorman had, particularly on matters that involved legal issues. Drees does not admit, however, that at the same time the Indian Association of Alberta developed future strategies and tactics to which can be directly linked the activist environments created by Gorman and Laurie.

Drees also tends to anthropomorphize the Indian Association of Alberta. She sees it as a body which Laurie and Gorman acted upon or manipulated, rather than a dynamic group of characters of which they were a part. It can be argued that Laurie was as much a part of the anthropomorphized body as was Gladstone or any of the key Indian players. In another matter, Drees might be technically correct that Laurie, through Enos Hunter, recommended Gorman as the lawyer to act as their volunteer counsel in the Hobbema Case, but his influence was such that it was a suggestion that was hardly going to be declined. Furthermore, she ignores the fact that Ruth

Gorman's name was hardly unknown to Enos Hunter, who had worked with her father, who had also volunteered his service. Laurie cleverly picked a lawyer with family "tradition" amongst the Aboriginal people.

Drees's interpretation of Laurie's motives in keeping the Indian Association of Alberta out of the enfranchisement issue is unclear. She makes it appear that Laurie had to be pushed into opposing the expulsions at Hobbema. This certainly is a different version of events from that presented by Gorman. At Gorman's meeting with Laurie, it was clear that he was extraordinarily upset and that he wanted her to act – and act immediately. Drees also doesn't mention the fact that Laurie was very worried that any protest or political involvement by the Indian Association of Alberta as an organization might expose the leadership to enfranchisement. While this is not likely to have happened, Laurie did not want to put his friends at risk of losing their homes and community. At one time Gladstone was afraid that he might be targeted. Laurie, for whatever reason, did not want to become involved in the Hobbema challenge himself except as an observer. The strength of his conviction must not have been clear to Gorman, and is rather puzzling.

On 28 March 1954, Laurie wrote Gladstone that he had turned the Hobbema Case over to Mrs. Gorman. "Apart from helping her to gather evidence, I have no part in it." Laurie was however there as a reporter for the *Calgary Herald* to ensure that he could not be excluded: "Mrs. Gorman will assist the Indians to carry their appeal.… I do not mean to involve the IAA as part of the defence."[41]

Drees also fails to acknowledge that much of the strategy behind the public protests and the political machinations was Gorman's. The approvals, however, were entirely that of the executive. Initially, for example, she did not support a petition to the Queen for redress at Hobbema. She thought it of little use. But she soon changed her mind and saw the political possibilities when the government refused to forward the petition to the Queen. She made sure it unleashed Diefenbaker's thunder. Drees also minimizes the Hobbema fight when she supports Professor Douglas Sanders at the University of Calgary in his contention that Gorman and the Indian Association of Alberta had little reason to fear since "in hindsight band membership cases such as the one at Hobbema, when taken to court elsewhere in the country, were generally won by the complainants on humanitarian grounds."[42]

Certainly Laurie and Gorman did not believe this to be the case. It is peculiar indeed that she would state this when so many in other reserves were in fact "enfranchised" against their wills. As Gorman clearly points out, many of the cases of voluntary enfranchisement were in fact ones involving subtle coercion, such as status Indian women marrying non-Indians. If you opposed enfranchisement and were forcibly enfranchised, you would not be eligible for your modest share of community property. If you voluntarily enfranchised, you would be eligible for a portion of the reserve's trust. There were few protests simply because the Department engineered this intimidating alternative. Drees also minimizes the amendment to the Indian Act that ended compulsory enfranchisement. Yet, to Gorman, that was the reward for a lifetime of struggle. It was the greatest achievement.

Drees sees the real struggle of the Indian Association of Alberta to be "self-government," that is, moving ahead without the Euro-Canadian influences of the secretary and his lawyer. The Department of Indian and Northern Affairs and its various iterations are hardly evil to Drees. But both Gorman and Laurie believed that the Indian Act was so carefully constructed that the Indian people did not have the same legal instruments as other Canadians had to redress the evils visited upon them by government. Drees's manuscript on the Indian Association of Alberta was written in the 1990's, when the country's sentiments on the place of native people in Canada had changed. Contemporary correspondence, however, supports Gorman and Laurie in their position. Many believed that the Department of Indian Affairs mismanaged both reserves and trust funds and that they were more interested in their own preservation than in meeting the moral and legal obligations of the treaties.

Drees's interpretation of Laurie is expanded in her fourth chapter, "Outside Help: John Laurie and Non-Indian Supporters of the Indian Association of Alberta." The title reveals all, and there is no doubt that she sides with Harold Cardinal's assessment in his *Unjust Society*:

> Unfortunately, these do-gooders get involved in spheres of activity ranging from simple, charitable church projects to the political arena, where self-appointed spokesmen for the Indians do incalculable harm. Their view of the Indian almost always, even if subconsciously, is that native people are incapable of handling their own affairs.[43]

While Drees believes Cardinal's assessment and it is not without merit, it is difficult to apply to Gorman and Laurie. Drees acknowledges, for example, that the IAA purposely decided to get outside help. Malcolm Norris and Hunter specifically identified John Laurie as someone who could help. It is clear that the Indian Association of Alberta retained both Gorman and Laurie because the Association wanted their expertise but could not provide a salary to Ruth Gorman. Drees argues, as does Dempsey, who was interviewed for her study, that Laurie was a conservative brake on the aspirations of the IAA, although he was influenced by "the intellectual climate of the time," whatever that might mean.

Gorman argues, as does Drees, that the "winds of change" did impact Alberta. Both accept that there was a real interest in regenerating Canadian society after the war. While Drees suggests that their motive was to "bring" the Aboriginal people up to where they could be part of the social, economic, and political fabric of society, a careful reading of Gorman's manuscript would not support this observation. In fact, this is the exact opposite to what Gorman argues. She actually believes that the Canadian Indian should be able to make his or her own choices, and she did not expect that the choice of many would be assimilation.

Professor Douglas Sanders in his article "The Queen's Promises" offers probably the most sophisticated view of the Hobbema Case as well as of Ruth Gorman and, to a lesser degree, of John Laurie. He argues that it was three non-Aboriginals, John Laurie, Ruth Gorman, and Hugh Dempsey, who acted as the lawyers or political intermediaries to ensure that Aboriginal issues were discussed and that redress was obtained both through the courts and through parliament. He argues further that these "brokers" are worth studying because they were the critical links to Canada and its court system. Sanders' observations are worthy of further consideration. It can be argued that the IAA and its foundation was built by a "broker" people, the Métis. Gladstone himself was Métis. It could be argued that the IAA was a construct that allowed Métis leaders to bring together their Indian and European heritage to achieve enlightened justice for both.

Murray Dobbin, in *The One-and-a-Half Men*, would probably have supported that argument. He believes that it was Malcolm Norris, John Calihoo, and John B. Tootoosis who in varying ways brought the Indian Association of Alberta together. He accepts that John Laurie ran the "bureaucracy," such as it was, and maintained contacts with the Calgary activist community, but its policies and actions were the responsibility of its council and presidents. Dobbin spends little other time on Laurie's work and none on enfranchisement. But then, his interest was in discovering a new Riel, not in an analysis of a "white" civil servant. Had he known that, privately, Laurie was a self-declared mixed blood, his interpretation might well have changed.

INTERPRETATIONS OF RUTH GORMAN

As mentioned earlier, the Laurie biography is as much an autobiography of Ruth Gorman. In her best-selling *Writing a Woman's Life*, Carolyn Heilbrun, the Avalon Foundation Professor in the Humanities at Columbia University, suggested that:

There are four ways to write a woman's life: the woman herself may tell it, in what she chooses to call an autobiography; she may tell it in what she chooses to call fiction; a biographer, a woman or man, may write the woman's life in what is called a biography; or the woman may write her own life in advance of living it, unconsciously, and without recognizing or naming the process.[44]

Gorman chooses none of these. Instead, she writes about herself through her experiences with John Laurie. The narrative is very much Ruth Gorman's and, after the first few chapters, is largely about her. The recent writings on women's narratives are particularly instructive in providing a meaningful guide through the Laurie biography. They explain much about Gorman's perspective and give insight into her construction of the Laurie biography. The few critical writings about Gorman can also be better understood as a product of the domination of the Western narrative by men.

There are several characteristics that emerge in Gorman's writing and in her life. First, she was what may be called a "strong-minded woman."[45] Strong-minded women are single-minded in their purpose, and intend to want to make the world a better place. While many "strong-minded" women were forgiving of their persecutors, it is fair to say that Gorman was less forgiving. Jack Pickersgill or the Indian Affairs bureaucrats are offered no forgiveness. Equally, most strong-minded women, according to Margaret Thorp, who has reflected on the archetype in *Female Persuasion: Six Strong-Minded Women*, do not reject the domestic sphere, but they do smooth it out and arrange it so as to ensure that there is time for "the fight." This was certainly the case with Ruth Gorman. She was always aware of the need to balance family responsibilities and the needs of her child and husband with her cause. In the Laurie manuscript there is frequent mention of her inability to attend a meeting, or of the need to return to Calgary to care for a family issue. In the Gladstone correspondence, John Laurie himself frequently mentions that Gorman is on the threshold of resigning from her position as "unpaid solicitor" to preserve her marriage and family. However, as with many strong-minded women, she was successful in part because of the support of her husband. Certainly in the case of her work with the Indian Association of Alberta, Gorman was assisted by her husband, who was frequently the lawyer of record when she could not be.

Gorman was in part an American and Commonwealth phenomenon, or so Jill Ker Conway would have argued in *In Her Own Words: Women's Memoirs from Australia, New Zealand, Canada, and the United States*. She observes that "for rebellious and ambitious Commonwealth women, almost the only escape from family and the requirements of respectable society was into political commitment to left politics."⁴⁶

Gorman would likely have disagreed with this observation. She was proud of her status within Mount Royal society and did not reject it. Rather, she consciously used the status to mobilize her forces and to press whatever cause she was pressing at the time. The suggestion that Gorman had a commitment to "left politics" would either have amused or annoyed her. While John Laurie certainly had CCF connections, Gorman (if she was anything) was a Conservative and populist. She certainly saw herself as a human rights activist, but would not see that at all in opposition to her support of the Diefenbaker government, or contrary to her fight against the Trudeau constitution. Gorman may also have been unusual amongst women activists of her time in that she was not only born in Calgary, but she had strong Canadian, indeed United Empire Loyalist, roots.

But what Gorman does share with the female radicals of her time is her incredible devotion to human rights, and to fairness and justice. What she has in common with so many strong-minded women of her generation is her strong drive to document – to write about – to share her experiences. One senses too in Gorman's writings in *My Golden West* a continuous struggle to break out of the restrictions of class and convention. Her writings on marriage and on convention themselves give a sense of "suffocating confinement."⁴⁷ But in the end the conventions were so strong that she confided, in one of her interviews, that the reason she did not write her own autobiography and chose John Laurie as her vehicle was that "it would seem to be boasting" and would seem to take away from John Laurie, i.e., a man's contribution.

Gorman is fully involved in a man's world; indeed she stands continuously on the "threshold of a man's world," always looking over her shoulder at what she doesn't want to leave behind. While Gorman certainly acknowledges the Calgary Local Council of Women, in the Laurie narrative they are infrequent actors. They are cast in a supportive role. It can be argued that Gorman has cast herself as the ultimate "supporter." John Laurie is front and centre; she is the supporting lawyer. Yet, there is considerable frustration in her own type-casting. She knows that it is her expertise, vigour, and sense of injustice that wins the day. He has the need; she has the professional skills. But Gorman also knew the limits of her own professional abilities by frequently bringing in her male university classmates or her husband to fill in where she felt that their expertise would be beneficial. There is no doubt, however, that she is the key strategist, and that she was frustrated at a number of points by the unwillingness of some men to recognize her mind and abilities. She handles the Aboriginal anti-feminist outburst at a key Hobbema strategy session as culturally based. She puts her own outspokenness to her training as a "lawyer." She is aware from her law school days that she was often a "token woman" amongst men but that she could succeed because she believed that, in the end, she was in fact more able than some of her classmates.

Gorman is also interesting in that she always saw herself as very much her father's daughter. While she certainly acknowledges his influence, she argues that she fought against it. She did not want to go to law school, after successfully completing her B.A. degree. But the alternative was caring for her mother and the endless propriety of being a Mount Royal debutante. One senses in her letters and papers that there was a continuous struggle between her mother's expectations for respectability and her father's for achievement. She felt that her service to Indians, to those struggling to preserve Prince's Island, or to those trying to get changes to the Dower Act were "radical" steps of achievement within convention. They were all achieved within the "expectations" and traditions of her time. Her father had donated his services to Aboriginal people and to community, as had her mother as legal convenor for the Calgary Local Council of Women.

However, she was, as were a number of female leaders of her generation, a professional in her own right. For the first time women did not have to rely on professional men as their advocates. Perhaps this tension contributed to her marriage difficulties. Gorman did eventually break out of the mould set for her by the professional male patriarchs. After Laurie's death, she became her own advocate and self. She was the key spokesperson at the 1960 parliamentary hearings for a group of men. When she retired as legal counsel to the Indian Association of Alberta, she also became the single voice, through *My Golden West*, for her favourite causes, including Indian, Western, and status of women issues. It is probably in that magazine that Gorman found her own distinct voice, again pushing what she thought were the boundaries of her community and culture. She also wrote a private work of fiction in which she reflected a more radical perspective on the relationship of the genders. It is not the purpose of this introduction to go into depth into these boundaries. Her personal papers are rich and give incredible depth of the life of a Calgary professional woman living on the threshold of what was acceptable to her gender in her day, and the radical alternative.

It is not surprising that Gorman came out of a Calgary environment. Cathy Cavanaugh and Randi Warne have summarized it best. Although talking about single upper-class British women immigrants – their statement certainly applies to Gorman:

> Women ... were able to expand their spheres of influence and to
> exercise great personal autonomy. In some cases close contact with

indigenous people altered women's perceptions of natives as the "exotic" Other and/or raised for them personal questions about an assumed racial order.⁴⁸

While she saw herself as pushing the boundaries, and the nation certainly recognized that through her many awards, these same awards were provided by the nation's establishment.⁴⁹ She was a radical within the boundaries of gender convention.

What the Gorman narrative reinforces is the defining role that women played in the Western narrative. Gorman's narrative is one of the more unusual in that it attempts to intertwine the role of the supporting woman to the male hero. But the subtext is clear – the hero is really in the supporting role – the centre of the story is really Gorman herself. This is one of the few manuscript biographies of a man, written as an autobiography of a woman. It remains rich in symbolism, and rich in suggestions for further reflection and study. Gorman has carefully positioned herself at the centre of the narrative, first by writing it, secondly by positioning Laurie as a faltering hero who dies before the end is achieved, and thirdly by positioning herself as a non-radical champion. By so doing she defines what she believes were the boundaries of acceptable activity for women of her day. But she was always ready to ruminate about those boundaries in *My Golden West*.

Various other interpretations of Ruth Gorman are scattered throughout the literature on Calgary, on the Calgary Local Council of Women, and in specific native histories. Most, except for *A Leaven of Ladies*, in which Gorman had a strong hand, are by men who for the most part marginalize Gorman. Hugh Dempsey, for example, gives little agency or credit to Ruth Gorman in *The Gentle Persuader*. She is ignored for her work as a volunteer lawyer, a status of which Ruth Gorman was extremely proud. He rather gives her credit, which she deserved, for the ingenuity she showed in managing the publicity around the Hobbema Case. By cleverly delaying the filing of the case as long as possible, she encouraged a swell of anti-government opinion. If she had filed earlier, the press could not have commented, and the government's sole comment would have been "it is before the courts." Dempsey also makes it clear that her connections with the Local Council of Women and her ability to mobilize them were key to the success of the case. *The Gentle Persuader*, however, minimizes her role in amendments to the 1961 Indian Act, which to Gorman were the culmination of several decades of work. By doing so, Dempsey, who sees himself as a key actor, has effectively, but perhaps not intentionally, diminished her work.

There may well be an explanation for this inadvertent marginalization. In 1965, there was to be a rift between Senator Gladstone and Hugh Dempsey, and Ruth Gorman, that was not to be repaired. She honestly felt, as did Laurie before his death in 1959, that Gladstone was not representing the interests of Canada's Aboriginal people in the senate. Laurie was appalled at the senator's support of liquor, and Gorman felt he did not do enough to support the end of compulsory enfranchisement.

Despite this, Ruth Gorman has considerable respect for Pauline Gladstone, Hugh Dempsey's wife, and recommended her to succeed Laurie when he was too ill to continue as secretary of the Indian Association of Alberta. In 1965, however, a gulf between Gorman and Dempsey so deepened that it could never again be bridged.

Ruth Gorman was one of the key movers behind the creation of the Calgary Indian Friendship Centre along with Mrs. Grace Johnson, vice-president at the time of the Calgary Local Council of Women. It would be a mistake to suggest that the Local Council of Women were not sensitive to the issue of minority representation. Daisy Crowchild, for example, was an executive member of the council. It was the intention of both Ruth Gorman and Grace Johnson that all of the staff of the centre be Aboriginal, and its first executive director was Lawrence Whitney, from the Sarcee nation. For whatever reason, Pauline Gladstone-Dempsey did not support Whitney. Indeed, she thought he was weak and under Gorman's and Johnson's influence. When Gorman and her supporters (Lawrence Whitney and Ed Many Bears) were off on a visit to Gleichen, Pauline Dempsey circulated a petition for an investigation into the affairs of the centre. Senator Gladstone happened to be in the centre at the time and signed the petition. Gorman, who was never one to avoid speaking her mind when she thought that any behaviour was less that totally open, was so angry that she wrote the senator with what can only be described as a "piece of her mind." The senator uncharacteristically exploded and put his feelings to pen. He said:

> I gather from your letter that you imagine that Pauline is accusing Mrs. Johnson of doing something to hurt her.... I think you are being really cruel to Pauline, and for God sakes why don't you all get together and make rules that could be followed to make the centre what it should be.... What distresses me most is the way you have been persecuting her. For goodness sake stop calling the Indians "as your Indian children" and treat them as your friends.[50]

Admittedly, Ruth Gorman's use of the possessive in describing Indians would have more than rankled. The following chapters are riddled with vocabulary that would offend today, and that obviously offended people of her generation, although she never intended to do so.

It is easy to understand why Gladstone might have been offended by her continuing reference to Indians as her "children," but Gorman took her honour of being made the "mother" of all the Cree at the conclusion of the Hobbema Case seriously. So did the Hobbema Cree. John Samson certainly referred to her as that and sent her cards emphasizing that honour on Mother's Day for many years.[51] She may have taken that too literally in front of non-Cree, although she was not ignorant of the divisions between the Cree and Blackfoot, and amongst the Blackfoot themselves. But whatever the roots of the feelings, they were now out in the open.

Hugh Dempsey himself had also entered the fray. In an earlier 28 February 1965 letter to Mr. Deane Gundlock, M.P., he alleges that Ruth Gorman dominated the centre with complete disregard of the wishes or suggestions of the Indians. Worse than that, Gorman and Johnson displayed an inability to "really understand the Indians."[52] While the details of what happened at the centre were important at the time, they best indicate a growing rift between the Gladstone clan and the old guard and their Euro-Canadian supporters who had worked with the Indian community to create what was in effect a revolution. It also reflected the fact that Ruth Gorman did not behave as an Aboriginal woman would have in similar circumstances. Whatever the real issues, by 1969 both Grace Johnson and Ruth Gorman had turned the entire management and operation over to the Aboriginal community and were no longer involved.[53]

This conflict must have been particularly painful to Ruth Gorman, who believed herself to be aware of prejudice and its consequence. She recounts an event in the late 1950's in Banff. She was to attend a gathering of lawyers and arrived early. In an effort to promote Aboriginal arts, she wore (something she did infrequently) her full native costume that had been given to her by the Stoney in 1937. She must have looked the part because when she sat down to wait for her party, she experienced what every one of her Indian friends had many times over:

> I said to the waiter – may I have a cup of coffee and he said "get it yourself in the kitchen." So, there I sat and suddenly I felt the strangest thing. I can only describe it as a subtle drawing away from me. I was left in a small circle of aloneness. My attempts at conversation received only short and quick replies. The backs were there and all against me. Suddenly I knew how the Indians felt. It is something you can't put your finger on. This aloneness, this subtle you're here but not really included was what my Indians had often tried to tell me in halting words – we miss friends talk.[54]

Her feelings as usual were open and honest. She realized that tolerance would always be a struggle for all human beings, but that tolerance could be learned:

> I was fortunate. I acquired the gift of tolerance. I don't believe any of us are naturally tolerant. We appreciate ourselves and anything that differs from us creates curiosity and even fear, and unconsciously intolerance enters our life ... we can do little to prevent the original flashes of warning "they are different" that is the basis of all intolerance. It's the smell, the touch of a dark hand, the ... hair, the laugh, a joke we can't understand that create a constant state of insecurity.... Fortunately, I had a mother and father who practiced tolerance. My father's Chinese clients bought gifts they gave me, my father's Indian clients sat in his waiting room smoking their interminable brown stained cigarettes down to the last puff. I walked to school with a Jewish girl I loved dearly.[55]

She counted Walking Buffalo as one of her real friends – a teacher and a humanist. She was once at an event in Banff and heard some intolerant comments from Canadians at the CPR hotel about the smell of Indians. She was furious and left the hotel to join her friend Walking Buffalo. Just as she was to relate what had happened to her, Walking Buffalo said, "white savages smell so bad." Gorman was somewhat taken aback but asked him why. He said he found the use of cosmetics offensive and that Canadians smelled of gasoline – of cars. But despite this smell, it would not change their humanity. It was from frank encounters like this that Gorman learned her approach to tolerance. Any group can be intolerant if it focuses on differences.[56]

She remained firm in the belief, as did Walking Buffalo, that when people are working together intolerance can be overcome. She also believed that intolerance could breed exploitation and marginalization. She felt very strongly about the faith and the bond that developed between her and the Indian people – "neither of us used one another, we righted injustices only." But Gorman had a strong personality, and the strength of that personality was the root both of the celebrations of her successes by some and her demonization by others.

If Dempsey then politely ignores Gorman, Marjorie Norris's *A Leaven of Ladies* devotes at least two chapters to Gorman. In this book Gorman emerges as a key mover behind several major issues, one of which is the Hobbema Case. While the Local Council of Women in Calgary was heavily involved in supporting the Hobbema Case protests and in the 1961 amendments to the Indian Act, Majorie Norris claims that Ruth Gorman told her

Introduction *xlvii*

that the "most lasting and effective move for Calgary in the legal field of LCW's efforts"⁵⁷ was her (Gorman's) fight to prevent the move of the railway to current Prince's Island, now a park preserve. It was definitely seen as a Council of Women's initiative, with Gorman as the leader. The Hobbema and Indian Act issues are seen more as her personal issues, which for this reason had the Local Council of Women's support.

In *A Leaven of Ladies*, Ruth Gorman was asked to contribute her own biography. She noted that the Local Council of Women had supported John Laurie before she "came on the scene." She confirms the importance of the Local Council of Women and particularly its national organization in the Hobbema and Indian Act fights, but if space is an indicator of importance, she devoted only half a page out of five to these two issues. If there was one theme she felt ran through all her causes, it was "tolerance" and fairness.

Laurie and to a much larger extent Gorman were both subject of extensive newspaper coverage. Laurie is uniformly seen as a positive force working to support the Indian people, particularly of the Calgary area. For the most part, Gorman received similar accolades. The *Calgary Herald* or the *Mountie* in particular offered positive interpretations of her activities with the IAA. The *Mountie*, for example, titled the article on Gorman in November/December 1963 "Guardian of Indian Rights" and focused entirely on the Hobbema Case and the Indian Act amendments. The story is replete with the tidbits that would reinforce the need for a reinterpretation of Gorman's involvement with Alberta's Aboriginal people. It has Ruth becoming Princess Mountain White Eagle Girl when she was twelve, when we now suspect it happened in 1937, when she had just graduated from university. The same article indicates that she was a frequent visitor to Morley and a "popular leader in the tribe's youth and church organizations." The article states that in 1946

> ... her father died, and Mrs. Gorman was asked by a delegation of Stoney who visited her home, to succeed him as a solicitor of the Indian Association of Alberta.... Mrs. Gorman tactfully declined.... But the delegation after a brief pow-wow, pointed out that their hostess was an Indian princess, a position that carried certain responsibilities. Mrs. Gorman grudgingly gave in....⁵⁸

It can be assumed that this plea probably happened just before or after the meeting that Laurie arranged in the basement of the Anglican church. Gorman's probable involvement in church youth leadership would, however, suggest that she was not entirely unknown to the Stoney community. The same article also offers an expanded version of how Mrs. Gorman became involved in the Hobbema Case. It sheds additional light on her account in the Laurie biography. While the visit to Laurie's house is thoroughly plausible, she was aware that there was some resistance to her taking on the rather more important Hobbema Case by Indian males. She observed to the reporter that

> ... Indian males class women with curs and cuyuses ... and the idea of a mere woman handling a crisis of this sort set off a terrific howl. Fully 90 percent of the men were violently opposed.[59]

Apparently, an old respected chief argued the case for her involvement. He pointed out that first they didn't have the money. Second, "I have been told that Mrs. Gorman is smart for a woman, but not so smart that she can't be talked into working for nothing." The article continues with a reasonably accurate account of the Hobbema Case, fails to deal with changes to the Indian Act and the vote, but does spend more time than any other article on Gorman's staunch advocacy for Aboriginal education. She believed that education should occur on the reserves, not at residential schools, and that education should continue to high school and vocational schools. When asked what Canadians could do to support Aboriginal people, she bluntly replied, "employ them," allow them to contribute to Canada.

The *Calgary Herald* saw her as a heroine for both her work in the Hobbema Case and in the railway controversy in that order. There is no doubt that it was the twenty-five years of voluntary work as the solicitor for the IAA that was considered her most important contribution. The *Albertan*, never a staunch supporter, did an article on her on 29 June 1967 when the Canadian Council of Christians and Jews chose her as Alberta's woman of the century. It barely mentioned her work with the IAA.

James Henry Gray's "Queen Mother Morningstar: The Non-Practicing Lawyer Who Scalped Indian Affairs," in *Talk to My Lawyer: Great Stories of Southern Alberta's Bar and Bench*, offers a folkloric interpretation that takes full advantage of Gray's narrative style. He focuses mostly on the Hobbema Case and captures the power and excitement that it generated. He helps more than anyone to create Ruth Gorman as a larger than life, almost mythical, female figure.

Professor Douglas Sanders offers one of the few academic interpretations of Gorman's work in "The Queen's Promises." As noted earlier, he deals with both the Wesley and the Hobbema (more properly the Samson case) cases and interprets them as connected by more than father and daughter. To him, both contributed significantly to the politicization of Indian judicial cases. He isolated several interesting elements in the case. First of all,

Peacock (called Chief Walking Bear by the Stoney)[60] absorbed the cost of the litigation. This was in the Western Canadian tradition. Other lawyers like William Morrow, who helped Ruth Gorman, or John Diefenbaker also never charged their Indian clients. Ruth Gorman's refusal to charge for her work was in the Western Canadian and in her family's tradition.

Of greater interest is Sanders' analysis of the Hobbema Case. He notes that the Hobbema Case was possibly the most serious in a long line of forced enfranchisements. There were several ways in which individuals could be removed from the reserve. The most serious cause was for someone or their ancestors to have taken Métis scrip, and then return to the reserve. For example, in the first half of the 1940's, seven hundred were removed from the Slave Lake area reserves. The action was challenged and probably half were reinstated. But the challenges to Indian status continued. It was the Lesser Slave removals that caused the Indian Association of Alberta to reorganize itself so it could protest more effectively. The federal government retaliated by reinforcing the authority of the Department and the minister to unilaterally remove people. But the real crisis happened in 1951 when the Indian Act was revised so as to allow any ten individuals on a reserve to protest the inclusion of any other based on certain criteria, including whether someone's ancestors had taken scrip, or whether their birth or that of their ancestor had been "legitimate"! Sanders has the most cautious and accurate account of the Hobbema trials. On 15 January 1952, ten members of the Samson band on the Hobbema reserve protested the membership of twenty-seven individuals who, with their children, numbered 103, or one third of the band. The situation was a serious one and not necessarily understood by everyone. Some who protested individuals themselves ended up on the list because of their relationship to the person protested. The initial hearings began on March 29th in Hobbema. Sanders argues that this was the first of the seriously politicized Indian cases and accurately describes the careful politicization of the case through the press. To him the Samson and subsequent cases were unusual, but they should not have frightened Gorman. He suspects that the reason for the enfranchisement drive was simply overzealous bureaucrats and believes that the 1951 legislation would have never been enforced by the courts. Sanders states that

> ... the group of cases makes it clear that judges, particularly when they were not subject to appeal, responded on humanitarian grounds and justified their decisions on dubious technicalities. The extent of this pattern was not known to Ruth Gorman, who was aware of only three other membership cases. She had concluded that the case had to be fought politically.[61]

Sanders argues then that Gorman's fight at Hobbema was unnecessary. His interpretation takes the legal wind out of Gorman's sails. But he does concede that the case marked the beginning of the "political re-emergence of the Indian questions in post-war Canadian political life."[62] Sanders further says that "the Diefenbaker period was marked by some reconciliation and recognition and moved Indian questions much more clearly onto a national political agenda." If anything, then, in his eyes, this was Ruth Gorman's contribution. But while Diefenbaker was sympathetic to Gorman's political storms – she used tactics he much admired. Gorman still had to fight Ellen Louks Fairclough, the first woman appointed federal cabinet minister in 1957 (Secretary of State and later Minister of Citizenship and Immigration), who was not always sympathetic to the Indian cause, and with the bureaucracy who were even less so to achieve change. The extent of the argument is evident in the 1959/60 Joint House of Commons and Senate hearings. It may well be that Gorman saw life in adversarial terms, but the correspondence in the national archives indicates that her perspectives were not without justification.

Today, the Hobbema Case and Ruth Gorman's efforts have withered in public mythology. While over a dozen of her Indian friends came to celebrate her honorary doctorate, none came to her funeral. Probably none knew of her death and today's generation has forgotten her. But some of the new communication web sites celebrating Alberta's heritage are attempting to rectify this.[63] The Alberta community heritage site has dramatized the Hobbema Case and entitled it "The Righteous Anger of Queen Mother Morning Star." The site is divided into "Setting, The Trial, People and Significance." Gorman is interviewed by a Mr. Grant while in Ottawa during the 1950's. The sound bites are excellent, and true in tone to Dr. Gorman's beliefs. The script deals with her first meeting with the Indians in Paget Hall, and then with the issues surrounding the Hobbema enfranchisement. While the characterization of Gorman may be fair, it is disparaging in its imitation of Cree accents. However, the power of the "radio" play is great and personalizes the issue – as only radio can do. While the internet has become the vehicle of modern historical discourse, there is room for Gorman's own view of the past and its dynamics. Her "biography" of John Lee Laurie offers the beginning of an understanding of the interaction of strong-minded women, the reformation of Indian affairs, and their contribution to the liberation of the Aboriginal people of Canada.

Frits Pannekoek
Calgary, 24 March 2006

NOTES TO INTRODUCTION

1. For a biography of Mary Cross Dover, see Sherrill MacLaren, *Braehead: Three Founding Families in Nineteenth Century Canada* (Toronto: McClelland and Stewart, 1986), pp. 383–90.
2. Aphrodite Karamitsanis, ed., *Place Names of Alberta*, vol. I: *Mountains, Mountain Parks and Foothills* (Calgary: University of Calgary Press, 1991), p. 136.
3. *My Golden West*, 14 vols. (Calgary: Golden West Publishing, Christmas, 1965 to Spring/Summer, 1970) and was later known as *Canadian Golden West* (Fall, 1970 to Winter, 1979).
4. Sarah Carter, *Lost Harvests: Prairie Indian Reserve Farmers and Government Policy* (Montreal and Kingston: McGill-Queen's University Press, 1990).
5. Canada, Parliament, Joint Committee of the Senate and the House of Commons on Indian Affairs, *Minutes of Proceedings and Evidence*, no. 3 (Ottawa: Queen's Printer, 1960), p. 168.
6. Robert Stamp, "Alberta," *The Canadian Encyclopaedia* (Edmonton: Hurtig, 1988), p. 51.
7. Glenbow Archives (hereafter G.A.), Gladstone Papers (hereafter G.P.), M7655, file 330, "John Laurie to Senator Gladstone," 28 September 1956.
8. Conversation with Ruth Gorman.
9. Conversation with Donald Smith.
10. Donald Smith, "John Laurie," in Max Foran and Sheilagh Jameson, eds., *Citymakers: Calgarians after the Frontier* (Calgary: The Historical Society of Alberta, Chinook Country Chapter, 1987), pp. 263–74.
11. *Crag and Canyon*, 30 July 1937. "On Sunday afternoon Miss Ruth Peacock, daughter of Mr. M.B. Peacock of Calgary, was taken into the tribe as a blood sister. This was a very colourful and solemn ceremony."
12. Murray Dobbin, *The One-and-a-Half Men: The Story of Jim Brady and Malcolm Norris, Métis Patriots of the Twentieth Century* (Vancouver: New Star Books, 1981).
13. G.A., IAA Papers, M7155/2, 25–26 May 1944, Fifth General Meeting, Indian Association of Alberta, Hobbema. It indicates "John Laurie nominated by Enos Hunter and Same Minde (Hobbema)."
14. G.A., G.P., M7655, file 330, "Laurie to Gladstone," 3 July 1957.
15. G.A., G.P., M7655, file 330, "John Laurie to Senator Gladstone," 11 November 1957.
16. Discussion with Ruth Gorman.
17. G.A., G.P., M7655, file 330, "Laurie to Gladstone," 25 February 1959.
18. Douglas Sanders, "The Queen's Promises," in Louis A. Knafla, ed., *Law & Justice in a New Land: Essays in Western Canadian Legal History* (Toronto: Carswell, 1986), p. 127.
19. Frits Pannekoek, "Cyberimpérialisme et marginalisation des Autochtones au Canada," in Jean-Paul Baillargeon, ed., *Transmission de la culture, petites sociétés, mondialisation* (Ste-Foy, Quebec: Les Presses de l'Université Laval, 2002), pp. 85–104.
20. Dean Neu and Richard Therrien, *Accounting for Genocide: Canada's Bureaucratic Assault on Aboriginal People* (Winnipeg: Fernwood Books and Zed Books, 2003), p. 5.
21. Catherine Anne Cavanaugh and Randi Ruth Warne, eds., *Telling Tales: Essays in Western Women's History* (Vancouver: UBC Press, 2000), p. 21.
22. Sanders, "The Queen's Promises," p. 104.
23. Gorman Papers (Private), 1937, newspaper clipping from the *Calgary Albertan*. For a narrative autobiography, see Marjorie Norris, *A Leaven of Ladies: A History of the Calgary Local Council of Women* (Calgary: Detselig, 1995), pp. 231–62.
24. *My Golden West*, vol. 4 (Spring 1969), p. 31.
25. Norris, *A Leaven of Ladies*, pp. 197–212.
26. G.A., G.P., M7655, file 329, "Laurie to Gladstone," 29 May 1955. "I suspect Mrs. Rowan of collaboration since she is a Labour Progressive, another name for Communist." Reta Rowan, wife of famed zoologist William Rowan, was an influential Edmonton lady who chaired the Council for Canadian Unity from 1942 to 1950 and was corresponding secretary of the Friends of the Indians Society until 1960. She was an observer at the Indian Association of Alberta until 1957 when she was appointed to its advisory board. She left Alberta in 1977 and died in Toronto six years later. See the Reta Rowan Fonds at the University of Alberta Archives at *http://archive1.lse.ualberta.ca/FindingAids/RetaRowan/RetaRowan.html#biography*

27 Rodney Muir has identified Gorman's admiration of Gandhi as critical in the formation of her advocacy of non-violence.
28 *My Golden West*, vol. 4 (Spring 1969): 3.
29 *Canadian Golden West*, vol. 9 (Fall 1972): 7.
30 G. A, G.P., M7655, file 329, "Laurie to Gladstone," 28 March 1954.
31 G.A., G.P., M7655, file 328, "Laurie to Gladstone," n.d.
32 G.A., G.P., M7811, file 2, "Verbatim Copy of Minutes," 20–21 November 1959.
33 Ibid., M7655, file 308, "Advisory Board Report," 21–22 June 1958.
34 G.A., G.P., M7811, file 2, "Verbatim Copy of Minutes," 20–21 November 1959.
35 Ibid.
36 Canada, *Minutes of Proceedings and Evidence*, p. 131.
37 Ibid., p. 132.
38 Ibid.
39 Hugh Aylmer Dempsey, *The Gentle Persuader: A Biography of James Gladstone, Indian Senator* (Saskatoon: Western Producer Prairie Books, 1986), p. 119.
40 See, for example. G.A., G.P., M7655, "Laurie to Gladstone," 25 February 1959.
41 G.A., G.P., M7655, file 329, "Laurie to Gladstone," 28 March 1954.
42 Laurie Meijer Drees, *The Indian Association of Alberta: A History of Political Action* (Vancouver: UBC Press, 2002), p. 151.
43 Ibid., p. 42 as quoted by Drees.
44 Carolyn G. Heilbrun, *Writing A Woman's Life* (New York: Norton, 1988), p. 11.
45 Margaret Farrand Thorp, *Female Persuasion: Six Strong-Minded Women* (Hamden, CT: Archon Books [1949], 1971), p. 1.
46 Jill Ker Conway, *In Her Own Words: Women's Memoirs from Australia, New Zealand, Canada, and the United States* (New York: Vintage Books, 1999), p. *ix*.
47 Ibid., p. *xi*.
48 Cavanaugh and Warne, eds., *Telling Tales*, p. 14.
49 Some of the awards that Ruth Gorman received in her lifetime include: Calgary's *Woman of the Year* (awarded by the Local Council of Women, 1960); *Citizen of the Year* (awarded by the Calgary Junior Chamber of Commerce, 1961); *Alberta Woman of the Century Medal* (awarded by the National Council of Jewish Women, 1968); Officer, *Order of Canada*, 1968; Legal Humanities Award, 1988; Lifetime Achievement Award (Calgary Access Awareness, 1991); *Confederation Medal*, 1993. She was also the convenor of laws to Canada's National Council of Women; a member and on the founding board of Tweedsmuir School, Calgary; a past chairman of the civil liberties section of the Canadian Bar on Indian Law. From Elizabeth Lumley, ed., *Canada's Who's Who*, vol. 38 (Toronto: University of Toronto Press, 2003), p. 523.
50 G.A., G.P., M7655, folder 79, "Gladstone to Gorman," 10 April 1965.
51 Gorman, Private Papers, "Mother's Day Cards from Johnnie Samson."
52 G.A., G.P., M7655, folder 79, "Dempsey to Gundlock," 28 February 1965.
53 Gorman Papers, Private Papers, "Grace Johnson to Gorman," n.d. It was a brief manuscript on the history of the Calgary Native Friendship Centre.
54 Gorman Papers, Private Papers, File Autobiography, "Tolerance."
55 Ibid.
56 Gorman, Private Papers, "Tolerance" file, n.d.
57 Norris, *A Leaven of Ladies*, p. 197.
58 Gray Clarke, "Profile Guardian of Indian Rights," *The Mountie* (November/December 1963).
59 Ibid.
60 The family tradition has him called Chief Walking Bear, although Sanders uses Walking Bear. *Crag and Canyon*, 26 July 1935, indicates that he was formally Chief Walking Bear.
61 Sanders, "The Queen's Promises," p. 126.
62 Ibid., p. 127.
63 www.albertasource.ca/lawcases/constitutional/morningstar/morningstar.htm

BIBLIOGRAPHY

Interviews
Ruth Gorman (Frits Pannekoek)
Ruth Gorman (Susie Sparks, deposited in the Glenbow Archives)

Archival Sources

GLENBOW ARCHIVES, CALGARY
James Gladstone Papers
John Laurie Papers
Indian Association of Alberta Papers
Hobbema Agency Papers

NATIONAL ARCHIVES OF CANADA
Record Group 10, Indian Affairs

PRIVATE
Ruth Gorman Papers, Private Family Collection (60 metres)

Newspapers
  Calgary Albertan
  Calgary Herald
  Canadian Cattlemen
  Crag and Canyon
  The Mountie

Magazines
These magazines, published sequentially, were owned and edited by Ruth Gorman and contain the best examples of her views. It should be noted that she also wrote in the magazine under her own name as well as M.W. Eagle and M. Starr.
  Golden West
  My Golden West
  Canadian Golden West

Parliament
Canada. Parliament. House of Commons. *Debates*, 1949–1966.
Canada. Parliament. Third Session – Twenty-fourth Parliament, 1960. Joint Committee of the Senate and the House of Commons on Indian Affairs. *Minutes of Proceedings and Evidence*. Ottawa: Queen's Printer, 1960.

SECONDARY SOURCES

Baillargeon, Jean-Paul, ed. *Transmission de la culture, petites sociétés, mondialisation.* Ste-Foy, Quebec: Les Presses de l'Université Laval, 2002.

Cardinal, Harold. *The Unjust Society.* 2nd ed. Edmonton: Hurtig (1969); Vancouver: Douglas and McIntyre, 1999.

Carter, Sarah. *Lost Harvests: Prairie Indian Reserve Farmers and Government Policy.* Montreal and Kingston: McGill-Queen's University Press, 1990.

Cavanaugh, Catherine Anne, and Randi Ruth Warne, eds. *Telling Tales: Essays in Western Women's History.* Vancouver: UBC Press, 2000.

Conway, Jill Ker. *In Her Own Words: Women's Memoirs from Australia, New Zealand, Canada, and the United States.* New York: Vintage Books, 1999.

Dempsey, Hugh Aylmer. *The Gentle Persuader: A Biography of James Gladstone, Indian Senator.* Saskatoon: Western Producer Prairie Books, 1986.

Dickason, Olive Patricia. *Canada's First Nations: A History of Founding Peoples from Earliest Times.* 3rd ed. Toronto: McClelland and Stewart (1992), 2002.

Dobbin, Murray. *The One-and-a-Half Men: The Story of Jim Brady and Malcolm Norris, Métis Patriots of the Twentieth Century.* Vancouver: New Star Books, 1981.

Drees, Laurie Meijer. *The Indian Association of Alberta: A History of Political Action.* Vancouver: UBC Press, 2002.

Foran, Max, and Shellagh James, eds. *City Makers: Calgarians after the Frontier.* Calgary: The Historical Society of Alberta, Chinook Country Chapter, 1987.

Friesen, Gerald. *The Canadian Prairies: A History.* Toronto: University of Toronto Press, 1987.

Gray, James Henry. *Talk to My Lawyer: Great Stories of Southern Alberta's Bar and Bench.* Edmonton: Hurtig, 1987.

Hanks, Lucien Mason, and Jane Richardson Hanks. *Tribe Under Trust: A Study of the Blackfoot Reserve of Alberta.* Toronto: University of Toronto Press, 1950.

Heilbrun, Carolyn G. *Women's Lives: The View from the Threshold.* Toronto: University of Toronto Press, 1999.

———. *Writing A Woman's Life.* New York: Norton, 1988.

Isaac, Thomas Francis. *Aboriginal Law: Commentary, Cases and Materials.* 3rd ed. Saskatoon: Purich (1995), 2004.

Karamitsanis, Aphrodite, ed. *Place Names of Alberta.* Vol. I: *Mountains, Mountain Parks and Foothills.* Calgary: University of Calgary Press, 1991.

Knafla, Louis A., ed. *Law & Justice in a New Land: Essays in Western Canadian Legal History.* Toronto: Carswell, 1986.

Kulchyski, Peter. "Considerable Unrest: F.O. Loft and the League of Indians." *Native Studies Review* 4, nos. 1–2 (1988):. 95–117.

Lumley, Elizabeth, ed. *Canada's Who's Who.* Vol. 38. Toronto: University of Toronto Press, 2003.

MacLaren, Sherrill. *Braehead: Three Founding Families in Nineteenth Century Canada.* Toronto: McClelland and Stewart, 1986.

Miller, James Rodger. *Skyscrapers Hide the Heavens: A History of Indian-White Relations in Canada.* 3rd ed. Toronto: University of Toronto Press (1991), 2000.

Neu, Dean, and Richard Therrien. *Accounting for Genocide: Canada's Bureaucratic Assault on Aboriginal People.* Winnipeg: Fernwood Books and Zed Books, 2003.

Norris, Marjorie. *A Leaven of Ladies: A History of the Calgary Local Council of Women.* Calgary: Detselig, 1995.

Palmer, Howard and Tamara. *Alberta, A New History*. Edmonton: Hurtig, 1990.
Ray, Arthur J. *I Have Lived Here Since the World Began: An Illustrated History of Canada's Native People*. Revised edition. Toronto: Lester (1996); Key Porter, 2005.
Stamp, Robert. *The Canadian Encyclopaedia*. Edmonton: Hurtig, 1988.
Thorp, Margaret Farrand. *Female Persuasion: Six Strong-Minded Women*. Hamden, CT: Archon Books (1949), 1971.
Titley, Brian E. *A Narrow Vision: Duncan Campbell Scott and the Administration of Indian Affairs in Canada*. Vancouver: University of British Columbia Press, 1986.
Van Herk, Aritha. *Mavericks: An Incorrigible History of Alberta*. Toronto: Viking, 2001.

BEHIND the MAN

Ruth Gorman

Dedicated to my father,
Colonel Mark Bennett Peacock, K.C.,
who inspired this journey.

AUTHOR'S INTRODUCTION

I wrote this biography of an unusual person, because I know so many untold parts of his story.* He was an unforgettable man to any who knew him; now, I'm probably the last person alive who intimately knew the extent of his efforts on behalf of the Indian people of southern Alberta. I had the great good fortune to share many parts of his life with him. I want to supply the missing historic link in his story and to recognize the significant changes he made in Canada's history.

The man's name was John Lee Laurie. We call the unknown people he helped the Indians, and what he did came after a hundred years of denial. I call the Indians the unknown people – unknown because so rarely have we met them as persons or friends, or on a face-to-face basis. I had the good luck to deal with them for almost twenty years of my life and to be directed during that time by John Laurie who had such a deep understanding of them. They add greatly to the Canadian mosaic. Their tolerance towards the whites has continually amazed me, when one considers that they cannot help but realize that the treaties were an unequal payment to them and have been to some degree misrepresented to them, and that following the treaties, they were put under the dictatorial control of the Ottawa bureaucrats. Yet, the Indian has never shown me hatred towards the non-Indians.

John Lee Laurie's life story has all the elements necessary to create a legend of Western Canada. We never quite let our legends die. Legends are the longest, best sellers of all literature. Their popularity never goes away. We have to keep them alive because they are what gives importance to our own individual lives and justifies our existence. They are always the same story of how one man alone is able to overcome vast forces of evil.

---

* During the writing of the manuscript, according to Gayle Inouye and Judy Bedford, Dr. Gorman considered using the title *Triumphant Tolerance, The Story of John Laurie*. However, no written evidence of that proposal was ever found, and as that title did not include any references to either the aboriginal vote or Dr. Gorman's role in assisting John Laurie, it was not used as the title of this book.

We retell these legends down through the generations, sometimes in a different form, but we never let a legend die, we can't let it die. It is the consolation we need in our own private mind, to reassure us that each person's life can be important, that there is a just peace for each one of us to find, and there is a hope that our life too would have made a change in the world around us.

The times were right for Laurie, but what was in his character to raise an ordinary man to become a legend? A few lucky people have come into this world with talent. They are people who will paint a picture, or they are great wordsmiths whose written phrases come down through the centuries, or they write music which we find ourselves humming. Laurie did not have these gifts or talents. Nor would he have the ability to create wealth. He was so poor when he died, there was hardly enough money to bury him. Nor would he have the ability to inspire a great group of followers and so become a leader for change. The only special talent he had, was one we all have – that is concern for our fellow beings, but in Laurie's case he developed that into an unusual greatness. This concern for the life in all living things would become the theme of his life. How he acquired that and how he used it is the story of a legend. It is the story of how one man, one small single man, a school teacher who was able in his lifetime to win, against forces which seemed impossibly large, the political freedom of the Canadian Indian. It is a true story that I know, because fortunately, I had a small part in it.

How did he do it? He had to have been just the right man, at the right time, at the right place. I had not met that man until 1942, I was almost 28 years old and he was 35 or seven years older than me.[1] We called one another friend, but we were more than friends and yet in many ways less than friends. As I look back on those 20 years together, I realize our relationship was more of two soldiers fighting side by side rather than friends. Unlike friends, soldiers who find they are fighting together get to know their fellow warrior in a strange way. They may know that secret place, the very bottom of each others' fear, the foolishness of our hopes and what help we can find when there is a need. Yet, on the other hand, you may not even know what kind of a house your fellow warrior lives in, his job, his bank account, even his friends and what he does each day. Fortunately, Laurie and I lived in the same place, and that was in the City of Calgary, Province of Alberta, Canada, that lay on the great sweep of Canadian land that flowed from the high western Rocky Mountains ever eastward into the Atlantic Ocean.

Ruth Gorman
Calgary, January 2002

1: THE MOUNTAIN

Mount Laurie in 1972 (Photo: Patrick Morrow).

John Laurie was a man seeking not just knowledge, but also understanding of the lives of other humans. He was able to turn that into benefiting thousands and to find a life of achievements and success through his efforts to permanently change forever, the history of his own beloved country – Canada.

Canada is a blessed country. Nature has provided her with the most beautiful monuments in the world. Today, we call them the Rocky Mountains. As you speed sixty miles west of Calgary on the Trans-Canada Highway, you come to the first of these monuments. They soar sky high, straight up from the 2,000 miles of the flat plains to the east of them. Ever since the first pale-faced Canadian land explorers, and later dilettante English travellers, like Lord Milton, Dr. Cheadle and the Earl of Southesk, first gazed on those mountains, they have been arrogantly sprinkling their own white names onto every mountain they saw. Today, we know by scientific measurement that other humans were here six thousand years before the arrival of these white men. They too had given each mountain a name.

The guide book tells you that the first mountain you encounter on the highway west of Calgary is called *Iyamnathka*, but in 1961, that name was changed to honour a white man, John Laurie. Guidebooks are of necessity small and can barely list the facts. They cannot tell the stories that lurk behind a name. This mountain has been unique in that it was one of the few mountains to keep its ancient Indian name. The Indians themselves chose to surrender their Indian name in order to honour that white man, John Laurie. The story of why they did so has never been told.

On 5 April 1961, the mountain, which is today popularly called *Yamnuska* was officially designated Mount Laurie (*Iyamnathka*). The Indian portion of the name means 'flat-faced mountain.'[1] Present at the ceremony were top representatives of the Canadian and Alberta governments. More important were the native people present, from nearly every tribe in Alberta, some of whom had travelled over 500 miles to be there. I came at the request of those native people. I came as a friend of the Indians, John Laurie, and as a past-honorary Princess of the Indian tribe who lived beside that mountain for thousands of years. The Indians then asked that I serve as the master of the naming ceremonies.

I met John Laurie when I was twenty-six years old, and he was forty-two.[2] We worked together as friends and associates of the Indians for twenty years of his life. The culmination of our efforts was attaining the vote for all Canadian natives. This had been denied to them for 300 years in this country where they had forever lived.

The story of how the Canadian native achieved full voting status, and the story of John Laurie's role in that achievement, has been almost lost. It is a story of one of the most vital changes made in Canadian history and, just as in the story of Julius Caesar that Shakespeare told, political chicanery more than anything else buried it.

Laurie used to climb and hunt on the mountain that was later named after him, Mount *Yamnuska*. Enos Hunter[3] used to tell many stories about this mountain, legends of the angry spirits that lived in it causing snow slides to fall on the unwary. On one occasion Laurie was taken by his family to a secret very small cave. On its bottom was a tiny pool of steaming water. There were great white stalactites formed by the drippings of centuries hanging on its roof.

On that day in 1961 when Mount *Yamnuska* became Mount Laurie, the sun shone bright, but John Laurie was not there. He had died two years before. On the drive home after the ceremony I was thinking about how very generous those native people had been to donate to a white man one of the few remnants of their own past that we hadn't already taken from them. I wished I could have told them of what I hoped would be John Laurie's final and greatest gift to all of them. However, all I had was a politician's promise, and I know those promises are just a politician's stock in trade. Until it was a reality, it would be unkind to, once more, only raise their hopes.

As I drove home, it became clear to me how that lone, seemingly ordinary man, John Laurie, was going to maybe do the impossible: change the past and the future history of his own country, Canada. How had he accomplished it?

He must have been just the right man in the right place at the right time! We are all given control to change ourselves into the right person, and we can find the right place. But your allotted space in time's inevitable march is beyond human control. We are just thrust, resisting and squirming, into our good spot in time's eternal stream. We even need a slap on our back by another to get our first breath of air.[4] Also, time is beyond any human's control: it comes pushing out of our past. Yet, despite that, John Laurie had found the right time, and the right place, to personally change the history of his own country – Canada.

As to the right person, John Laurie was a person concerned with human inner spirituality. He always had that concern for others. He was a student of history all his life so intellectually he knew how history could be changed. Most importantly was his empathy with all other persons.

Most of his friends described John Laurie as a very "private sort of person." It was more than his Scottish nature – it was modesty, I used to think. Despite the fact that he taught English, he never realized 'I' was a pronoun as well as a letter in the alphabet and it was one I rarely heard him ever say. It was he who would teach history to me.

2: THE STARS SHONE BRIGHT

The stars shone bright on the night John Laurie was born, or so his mother had told him and he in turn had told me. To them the stars were all that seemed familiar, steady or even beautiful. She told him that she and his father had seen those stars from the top deck of a ship that was bringing them from their native land, Scotland, to a new land, Canada.

On that night his young parents could no longer endure their sleeplessness, nor the stuffy air of the ship's cabin. They climbed the narrow ship's stairs to the top deck hoping to see a glimmer of shore lights. They knew that soon their first-born would arrive so they were hoping to reach land before that happened. However, it would not be so; he had been born that night while the ship was still at sea. To the young parents the small boy seemed a miracle of their own creation. The proud crew, the only assistants, of whom one unidentified member had taken the St. John's Ambulance bandaging course – hardly suitable for the occasion – noted with relief that the boy had come with all "the appropriate appendages."[1]

On landing, the crew allowed the new parents to be the last to leave the ship. The mother's long elegant skirts trailed on the already filthy gangplank and dock as she descended, clutching tight the tiny baby while the father wrestled with leather portmanteaus and tin chests that contained all their worldly possessions.

Possibly symbolic of his future, John Laurie had been born without a home, because never in his life would he own a permanent one of his own. Also, he had been born between the opposing elements of earth, sea and sky and located between the old known continent of Europe and the new yet unknown land of Canada. The time too seemed significant. It was just at the beginning of a new century. They were stirring times that he would live in and even play an important part in. If John Laurie had been born in either a later or an earlier time, he might have just been known as 'the nicest man who lived on our block.' Instead, this baby was a man totally in time with the age he was born in. He was privileged to be born in an age that history accepted as the age of freedom fighters,[2] and he would become one of Canada's greatest.

When the ship docked at the port of Quebec City, the new father hurried ashore to purchase a farm. It had to be in Protestant Ontario because his wife was determined to have her son, whom they named John Lee Laurie, baptized in a Scottish Presbyterian Church. Ashore, sight unseen, his father Andrew had purchased a farm with cash. The real estate agent advised him against acquiring the still available free homestead land, because, as he said, you must first clear the heavily wooded land, fence it and build a house before you can acquire the title.

John Laurie's father may have chosen that land knowing it had a Scottish name. After all, his favourite Scottish poet Robert Burns in his poem 'Tam O'Shanter' saw the drunken Tam escaping his pursuing witches by riding his horse Mag over the flowing water, crossing the river called Aimes. He was saved, because there was a superstition at that time that no witches could ride their brooms over running water.

However, the farm turned out not quite as represented by the real estate agent. It had a house, but the four rooms were small, and as for clear pasture land, the original homesteader had just cut off the tops of the big trees leaving the giant stumps still in the ground, and used the tree tops to make the necessary zigzag fence so common to early Ontario farms. This left an unsuitable pasture. The only water came from a small stream on the edge of the property, which his father always called "the spring stream." That was the stream that found a solution to his problem of getting help.

One day, there appeared at the farm door a tiny wizened Indian woman named Betsy Dickson. Beside her stood her two very tall, strong and stalwart sons and peeping out from behind her skirt were her two grandsons. In perfect English she explained that her people lived on the Six Nations reserve next to their land on the other side of the stream, and had for centuries used the willows that grew along the banks of the stream to make their baskets from. She was now asking for permission to cut down some of these branches on their land to make baskets with and she wished permission to camp.

Laurie's father, seeing the solution for getting help in clearing the backbreaking giant stumps, and also possibly someone to help care for his still ill wife and small baby, quickly gave his consent. Betsy and the Indians moved beside the stream next to the Laurie farm. So, John Laurie had a nanny, not the usual British ones that his parents had, but it would be help for his delicate mother. His nanny was an Indian woman, and his first playmates were the Indian children. For fun they taught him to set traps, shoot, and play bow and arrow. He also accompanied Betsy and her children when she sold her baskets, sometimes full of berries, to the white settlers.

I almost envied what John Laurie had told me of this idyllic childhood spending his days playing with the young Indians and often eating his meals around an Indian campfire.[3] My long association with John Laurie was unusual in many ways. I was the only white woman volunteer lawyer and John was the white volunteer secretary for the Indian Association of Alberta. I was a woman happily married to a Calgary lawyer and a mother of a small daughter (Linda) whom I love very much, and Laurie was a bachelor schoolteacher. I was content with my life, and Laurie had involved me reluctantly at first, to aid him in his determination to help Canada's forgotten native people, who then were reduced to living in hunger and poverty and separated by invisible barriers on their far apart isolated Alberta reserves.

During those almost twenty years, I helped this man whose life work so materially changed the life of all Canadian Indians and indeed the history of Canada in his lifelong battle to bring justice to a whole race of people: our first people of Canada, our native people, the Indians.[4]

Conversations between Laurie and I were only about our Indian pursuits together. Both of us had busy lives and much to accomplish so we had no time for casual conversation. Laurie at this time did not have a car. His old car had broken down under the strain of the long journeys to the reserves, and he was too poor to buy a replacement. Sometimes, he was able to get a ride from the Indians to their reserves, but it too was uncomfortable to squish into the small crowded cars. Once I began working with Laurie, I naturally offered to drive my car to the reserves, often over 400 miles round trip. I would have been safer to spend the night, but my family duties required me to return home after each long meeting.

Tired of talking Indian business, I suspect, Laurie spoke to me of the tales of his own past on our long night trips from the remote reserves to keep me, the driver, awake. Sometimes, he would even sing in his fine voice the Scottish songs his father had sung in Gaelic. I liked best 'Annie Laurie,' which he always claimed was his 'family's national anthem.' In these long night drives I learned more than most, the tales of Laurie's past, and they are wonderful! I learned that Laurie was always honest except for the stories of his childhood.

3: STRANGE OMISSION

I didn't know Laurie's earlier life, only what he told me during the twenty years that I had worked with him, and only what he chose to tell me. Fortunately, that was a lot, but later I would learn that there was a strange omission.

In the cynicism of today's age, the deliberate exposure of publicly admired characters has been a source of many best-selling books. We feel almost relief in finding a human flaw in our past heroes. Only when I began to write this book did I realize that the great Laurie, in having his secrets, was no exception to this rule.

I envied John's early years on the Ontario farm that he had described to me on our long late night drives from the reserves. It was a shock to me when over 60 years after John Laurie's birth and 15 years after his death I learned that his childhood story was a lie, by omission. Only when I began to write this book did I discover what had truly happened. I read of it in John Laurie's own files which I advised the executor of his estate, John Gorman, to give to John Laurie's benefactor, Eric Harvie's Glenbow Museum. This is Calgary's only museum which Mr. Eric Harvie had built, filled and given to the City of Calgary, and which had been modestly named after his own Alberta ranch.

In these files I came across an eight-page document titled "John Laurie's Autobiography." It was out of character for John to speak about himself, so I was surprised to find this treasure. I read it with amazement! John Laurie's youth had not been entirely happy with his loving father and his Indian playmates. Instead, he had at the tender age of five years been given away by his family to his English grandmother who had kept him at her mansion in Oxford, England, until he was almost 14 years old.[1]

He told me nothing between his time on a Canadian farm, and the time when he attended a white man's school. It was such a secret and an unexpected virtue that it went untold. Laurie was not one who could ever gain any comfort or stature for himself by condemning others. At Oxford, John's grandmother was a fortunate woman of her time when upon the death of her husband, a trader, she had inherited a great deal of money.

Laurie in his own unfinished biography had made a special note to say that she had her way because "she had the money." In Oxford she did not send him to any of the nearby private schools, but instead hired private tutors from Oxford with the instructions that he be well versed in the importance of England as a world ruler. It was as though a shell had surrounded him. Laurie stated his dislike of his grandmother. She was one who would break a boy's handmade fishing rod if provoked and would boss everyone because she had the money.

Under the Oxford student's intensified study of England's greatness, he noticed their tendency to not destroy, but rather absorb the races inhabiting the country they were invading. It was this ability that helped to build an empire.

In England, each night, the small boy in his high-canopied bed with the covers pulled high watched the shadows crawl like dark monsters from the corners of his room, lying on his back so that the ghosts they said haunted the house could not sneak up on him. He squeezed his eyes tight to stop the tears and try to remember home. But when he excitedly reached home, all was different. His family had moved from the farm into town.[2] Gone were his Indian friends and the nature walks with his father. Why Laurie's grandmother decided to leave England and return to live closer to her only daughter is never explained.[3]

From his tragic "Oxford banishment" Laurie had gained a fine basic education. His Oxford tutors had done a fine job that made an easy entry into Canadian schools and eventually led to his acceptance at Trinity College in Toronto. But his "assimilation" into the school system was not a smooth one. He felt a misfit because of his aristocratic English clothes, he could not skate or play hockey, and he had an accent and could not even relate to girls at 14 years of age.[4] When he returned home he felt displaced by a new baby sister who captured the family's attention. This sister later denied Laurie's abandonment by his parents in a "conversation" with professor Donald Smith, and claimed that Laurie always remained in Canada. Back in Canada, he had to ride a train to school and so was further isolated from his family each day.

Why had he chosen at last to speak of it? It was in his first year of retirement, always a crisis point in one's life, that he decided to confess secrets about his past life. Marjorie Bond, his stenographer and former adoring pupil at Crescent Heights, had been shocked on a visit to find Laurie frail, ill and homebound. Laurie said that it was suggested to him that he write his autobiography. Because he was ill and always disliked typing he asked

Marjorie if she would consider writing it with him. She was terrified because she had never written anything in her life, so he said not to worry, he could dictate it to her.

The result was eight typed pages corrected by Laurie himself, the schoolteacher, with a red pen. Too ill to continue, he never finished the autobiography, but nonetheless, it provided important clues to understanding him and his life's work. I sometimes feel that it was a dying confession. Laurie, like the great Mahatma Gandhi whom he so admired, had as his first precept, honesty. Like Gandhi, Laurie gave the most importance to how you transfer honesty into action.

His other friends when speaking of him almost invariably called him 'a very private person.' It was not due to his Scottish natural reticence, but more to an inordinate modesty. He never spoke of any personal hardships or triumphs as a rule. However, it is inevitable that in over 20 years of friendship, you learn a great deal about your friend's past dreams, disappointments and even past activities.

Laurie, I guess, felt it wasn't vital and so he did not mention this sad time in his life to either his friends or early biographers. The only other piece of real evidence of his life overseas, other than his autobiography, was a painting of a fine rather elegant stone Norman Lord type manor that he was careful to take with him on each move and pin on the wall of whatever temporary lodging he lived in.

4: THE WINDS OF CHANGE BLOW ACROSS THE WORLD

The winds of change on the Western Canadian plains flew through the air travelling faster than a flash of lightning. In Canada, where Marconi sent out the first sound across the airwaves, the radio changed our history. Before the radio, all you could hear about was your neighbour. We would have to wait until the radio brought the world into our prairie homes.

Across the great lonely land where even neighbours were miles apart, the Canadian Mr. Bell's invention, the telephone, first helped! Each area was gathered in what was called a "party line," and each person's telephone had a series of long and short rings, so every neighbour knew who was communicating with whom. They were inclined to lift the receiver and listen in – they called it 'rubbering.' It was a means to lift the loneliness of the plains and also to keep in touch with what was happening with others – after all gossip has always been fun. There were no phones on the Indian reserves; they were still isolated on the great silent plains, just as they were confined and locked in on their reserve land. One advantage was the telephone was cheap, and these were hard up times, so it was one recreation most non-Indians could afford.

The winds of change were blowing politically too. The Depression had given rise to new political solutions and new political parties. Alberta elected the first 'farmer's government' in the world, officially called the 'United Farmers of Alberta' (UFA).[1] It was a secure organization which only a scandal – and one came – could corrupt.

Alberta's married Premier Brownlee supposedly had an affair with a babysitter. Today grave doubt exists about the charge's validity.[2] Rumour had it, the lawyer who took it had a grudge regarding his own charge of drunkenness that Brownlee would not set aside as he requested. Certainly nothing but a sex scandal could unseat the government, and it did. My sex education was largely obtained from reading the daily papers' long accounts of the trial's evidence in the now defunct *Edmonton Bulletin*. However, Alberta did obtain other years of good government from that party.

The farmer's government was replaced by an even stranger form of government, again unique to the world, called Social Credit. This was led by John Laurie's ex-principal at Crescent Heights High School, William Aberhart. He was one of the first to take advantage of radio and became one of the first religiously evangelistic broadcasters that today are so numerous. He believed in the prophecies of the Old Testament that we would come to doom unless we reformed our morals, and for this he made his own religion in a Calgary church, which he called the Prophetic Bible Institute. He gained this by asking listeners to send a dollar for a brick. As a result, he built on one of Calgary's main streets, 8th Avenue near 4th Street S.W., a fine brick building under his own control.

Aberhart had also read the writings of an Australian named Major Douglas who had a new monetary theory, that wealth should be based not on the gold held in banks, but by the value of a province's resources, both agricultural and mineral.[3] On that basis, the provincial government should be able to issue a useable currency. The holders of this currency would buy goods in the area, and the government would issue $25.00 of this currency to each person per month. Whether it would have succeeded or not, we will never know. The Canadian banks promptly took Aberhart to court, and the Supreme Court declared this practice illegal. Hence, Alberta came to be known as the province with 'the funny money' theory.

Fortunately for Alberta, Aberhart's radio broadcast had reached the arid plains of Saskatchewan where there was a young man named Ernest Manning. His family gave him an old car and he asked if he could attend Aberhart's College in return for janitorial aide and other services.

Dissatisfied with the rumour of scandals of the past government and suffering from poverty, Aberhart gained a surprising victory in the polls in 1935. Everyone wanted a change and whether they admitted it or not, a bonus of $25 per month. Today, every child in Canada receives a government 'baby bonus' which is issued through banks and is not considered illegal. Fortunately for Alberta, but not for Premier Aberhart, Aberhart had a fatal illness and was forced to name young Ernest Manning as his successor. Manning swept into power and gave Alberta many years of excellent government. There were no scandals. He quickly nipped them in the bud. He personally went to New York and spoke to the big petroleum companies about the value of Alberta's petroleum products, which brought investment and the first wave of prosperity to this province. Fortunately, he proved in the future to be a loyal admirer of John Laurie as a person.

Another new Canadian political party was arising from the public's discontent of the old government. It too was founded by a minister, Reverend J.S. Woodsworth. He preached in British Columbia that reform was needed in government. He called his party the Cooperative Commonwealth Federation (CCF and today's New Democratic Party or NDP). His proposals had appealed to two of John Laurie's friends, Alexander Calhoun, Calgary's head librarian, and his fellow teachers, the Liesemer brothers.[4] When it was proposed that Woodsworth would come to Calgary to present his views, a secret meeting was carefully planned. The meetings were secret because the old party propaganda had labelled this new party as communist, as the Soviet government at that time proclaimed its intention to conquer the world with its new political party. What is more secret than an empty locked up library at night? The meeting was consequently held there. Woodsworth brought to the meeting a young RCMP officer named Ramsey Norris who, Woodsworth explained, had a group in Northern Alberta which was also interested in hearing the plans for a proposed new government. He was an attractive young man and, like Laurie, was quiet, thin and wore glasses. Laurie, thinking of his own past occupation in army barracks, offered to drive him home and, on the way, suggested a stopover in his small rooms for a nightcap to discuss the new party they had called the Cooperative Commonwealth Federation (CCF). Fortunately, he proved to be a loyal admirer of John Laurie as a person too.

As a writer concerned about the troubles of his native people, Laurie wrote an article and even started a small newspaper he handed out to the native people to help them in their struggles. At that same time Gandhi was making his move to free his people in India. Also, it was a time when Einstein, the scientist, was studying how to dissolve all matter.

5: AN ANGRY YOUNG MAN

The attention-getting date of 1890 brought thoughts of the emergence of a new century and introduced to humanity world changes and tragic results. In America the cult of admiration for the "self-made millionaire" thrived. They printed 'in God we trust' on their coinage, but in reality they paid homage to their interest-growing bank balances based on paper credit.

The 'self-made millionaire' families of the Fords, Duponts and the Rockefellers became national heroes. In the newspaper field, the financial giant was William Randolph Hearst. At the emergence of the 20th century, Hearst personally wrote the editorial on his masthead newspaper *The New York Journal* in which he wondered about 'The Christmas Peace on Earth' celebration. He noted that Europe had never before had such a proportion of its population under arms, and in financial circles the richest man in the world was rumoured to be a man of mystery and a European arms dealer.

In Europe, countries were out seeking alliances. Treaties of alliance once achieved by royal marriages were now being assured by paper between countries to maintain peace. The absolute monarchies of Europe – Germany with a Kaiser, Russia with a Tsar, and Austria and the Balkans with their Kings – tried to take a vise-like hold over central Europe. That was soon to go with the shooting assassination of the Archduke Ferdinand of Austria by a Serbian. The popular thinking billed in the press as the catch-phrase "the shot heard around the world" contributed to the outbreak of the First World War. In reality that shot was only the start of a long-planned conquest of Europe.

The world blundered on in confusion, but it was the crossing and conquest of the tiny country of Belgium that dragged its allies, France and England, into the war. In retrospect, the blundering and false pride seem pathetic, but the resulting four-year war was the most destructive the world had seen to that time. It affected everyone's lives. At least two million young men in their prime were killed. Probably another four million were permanently wounded and destined to be impoverished and unproductive. Nearly every home in the whole world underwent tragic changes by the time peace was signed on 11 November 1918.

The United States' isolationist foreign policy kept it out of the war at first and allowed the making of private fortunes by supplying goods to the beleaguered allies. Only with the threat of defeat of the more democratic allies did the U.S.A. enter the war with vigour and enthusiasm.

Canada, with few defences itself, joined Britain in the fight, although Quebec rebelled at being conscripted to aid the English or protect themselves. Canada suffered huge casualties as it fought the long war from disease-ridden trenches. Canada had some glorious victories to their credit at Mons and Vimy Ridge where neither the French nor British had succeeded in taking the hill, but the Canadians did with severe losses. Their publicized victories were of the lone fighter pilots of the Royal Flying Corps. Names such as Billy Bishop of Winnipeg and Freddy McCall of Calgary became legendary heroes. All alone they had ventured forth in canvas and wooden airborne crafts against the older and better prepared Imperial German Air Service pilots led by the German 'Red' Baron (Manfred von Richthofen).

With Canada's involvement in the First World War, Laurie was on fire to join the Canadian "knights of the air." Lying about his age he enlisted with the newly formed Royal Air Force in 1917.[1] He spent most of his time in stuffy, over-crowded barracks, running around training fields and being ordered about by aged infantry veterans. When peace came in 1918, disillusioned "angry young men" like John Laurie were trying to keep alive the promises made to the dead, of creating a world without war.

Out of the war, John Laurie emerged with the seeds of a freedom fighter planted within him. The war ended with a victory for the democratic allies on 11 November 1918. Because of his age John Laurie had not seen overseas active service, but he would not be discharged for another year. During this period he identified with other young, enlisted men who were either expecting to fight, or were already in the midst of war, or by now, dead or wounded. He was aware of how many had actually profited by the war in comparative safety on the North American continent. Employment and wages were increasing and suppliers of war materials were becoming wealthy. This was especially true in Quebec where many had opposed aiding the English, and in the United States, delaying the entry into the war until victory was near.

The First World War was a "young man's war." They died in vast numbers, were wounded and had given their finest years to the cause. Canadian casualties had been proportionally very high. On their return home many young men faced unemployment. Labour unions had formed strong rules to prevent the discharge of employees hired in the absence of the soldier. The young men had gone to war suffering from lack of decent employment and prepared to make a sacrifice because they had been promised it was "A War to End All Wars."

The plans to achieve a permanent peace by a League of Nations had been blown away with the collapse of that League. This occurred when the League's most powerful supporter, the United States, withdrew. The American people had defeated their President and League sponsor, Woodrow Wilson, leaving the new-borne League a very lame duck indeed insofar as its ability to support decisions of the peace seekers.

The defeated nations discarded the absolute monarchs who had led them to war: the German Kaiser was banished, the Russian Tsar was assassinated, and Germany acquired a magnificent written constitution. In the extreme poverty following the war, Russians turned hopefully to newly-conceived political solutions being expounded by Karl Marx in his communist manifesto, and Germans read Adolf Hitler's *Mein Kampf* and created the new National-Socialist Party. Young men lined up under the banners of militarism in both the Soviet Union and Germany.

In the democratic post-war atmosphere in the allied countries, the disillusioned young men were adopting a new philosophy led by poets and writers. They had no political party organizers or leaders, but were united only by a turnabout in their way of thinking: they desired to find a better world with a way of thinking different from that which led to the disastrous world war that had benefited so few. They were labelled "angry young men."

Back at college following the war, John Laurie admittedly became one of the angry young men – dedicated to helping individuals find a better life. In the society he lived in, Laurie would see he had to be a rebel. The majority in Canada were not on the Indians' side. Could he be a rebel and was he a rebel with a cause? A rebel without a cause is but an idiot, shaking his fist at the sky above only from personal anger and hurt.

The cause would be clear. Here would be a good people, a fine people, being abused and even in subtle ways imprisoned and unable to even speak out against their injustices without severe punishment. Laurie's cause would be right, but what form his rebellion should take was not. He would not be the one who needed to rebel; his life would be a good one. He would have a job he liked, a horse he liked, good friends and good health. It would be a life of his choosing. The question would be, why did fine people suffer and he endorsed it by being part of the group that caused their suffering. His newly found knowledge of the Indian people's suffering would make his own life not truly satisfactory. He could go on just being lord bountiful offering them his food, assisting them with his knowledge and his goodness, but that was like putting a bandage on a great festering sore and saying 'that doesn't hurt now.'

At the same time, the war had stimulated major changes in the thinking of Canada's native people. The Indians, whose background had always provided for and honoured warriors in their tribes, understood war. They were, as they had always been, excellent warriors. In the First World War they volunteered to enlist in large numbers.[2] In fact, one reserve was almost depleted of the male population. Their young men had flocked to the enlistment office thinking that anything, even possible death, was better than half-starvation, frustration and the idle life of the reserve. They made magnificent fighters in the Canadian forces. For most of the Indian soldiers overseas it was the first time in their lives that they found themselves treated as equals with non-Indians. They were exposed to a whole new life where they were totally accepted by their fellow non-native warriors. It was an exhilarating and enlightening experience. Indian veterans came back to an even bleaker future than the Canadian non-Indian veterans. The disillusionment they met on their victorious return turned them into angry young Indian men too.

They attempted to initiate reforms and improvements in their own lives on the reserves and as a result, small Indian associations began springing up all over Canada. Ever since the first trade guilds were formed the white man knew he was defenceless against those who governed him unless he united. Later, at the end of the Second World War, veteran Indians began to fight for the rights they knew they were denied.

6: LAURIE FINDS THE RIGHT PLACE

Laurie (right), Norman Holt (centre) and a friend in 1925.

John Laurie with his polite intelligent ways and his obvious humour was an attractive personality. He was highly regarded by students, and by adult women and men. He made an admirable ambassador to introduce Canadians to their own unknown Indian people who they had isolated on the reserves. Aid for the Indians on the reserve and acceptance and honour off the reserve became the lifelong role Laurie assumed. First he sought out individuals to influence and then he sought out groups.

The first individuals he chose were ones who already had knowledge of the Indians. The great missionary John McDougall had three sons-in-law: Banff's Norman Luxton, sheriff Fred Graham and the lawyer politician, Calgary member of Parliament George Ross. They became Laurie's contacts. Next he sought out church leaders in Indian work, then authors and journalists.

Fortunately, one of his early journalist contacts was Fred Kennedy of the *Calgary Herald* (1927–1957) and the *Albertan* (1965–1979). Later there were journalists Blair Fraser, Basil Deane and Richard (Dick) Snell. Fred Kennedy was a long-time Calgary columnist and became an early convert and friend. He was therefore able to leave us a portrait of Laurie's earliest Calgary days. He probably first met Laurie around the racetracks, or on the hunting trips. They were both addicts to the love of the horse.

While attending university in Ontario, Laurie visited a friend's ranch in Saskatchewan and learned to ride and love horses. After graduation, Laurie decided to come west and got off the train at Calgary in 1919.[1] He never told me why, possibly because he was running out of money. When Laurie looked down on Calgary's sparkling Bow River for the first time, he was reminded that this land had once been called Rupert's Land, long before its name was changed to Alberta, when it had become a province in 1905.

Laurie was amazed to discover that Calgary had fifteen hotels. The Canadian Pacific Railway's Palliser Hotel next to the train station was about ten years old and the tallest building in Western Canada.[2] Laurie was impressed with the Palliser's interior design, its huge lobby and big crystal chandelier. Obviously this was too expensive for him. As Laurie sat in one of the soft leather chairs, an old man next to him handed him a section of his newspaper to read. When the man discovered that Laurie was a newcomer from down East, he suggested that Laurie take a ride on the hotel's elevator to the top floor to the sunroom and look out the windows. There he was able to see the glorious Rocky Mountains.

It was a beautiful morning: the sky was solid blue, the mountains were covered with glistening white snow. They seemed so magnificent and close that Laurie thought he must take a walk there. Fortunately, before he undertook the walk someone told him that they were about eighty miles away. Luckily, he did not fall into the trap of other newcomers to the city who, without any extra food, were sometimes foolish enough to try to attempt what they expected to be a small walk and had to be rescued as the always retreating mountains reduced them to fatigue.

After breakfast at the Palliser Hotel, Laurie found a hotel he could afford, the St. Regis, which had no bar. However, when Laurie found out its owner Albert Johnson had made his grub steak in the Klondike gold rush, it gave him the feeling of being in a new exciting land.

Behind the hotel clerk, pinned to the wall, was the most majestic drawing Laurie had ever seen of a man riding a fiercely bucking horse that seemed to be advertising some coming event. The cowboy artist was Edward Borein, believed by Laurie to be a friend of Guy Weadick, who once worked for Buffalo Bill's "Wild West Show." Weadick had arrived in Calgary in 1912 and convinced four wealthy ranchers – A. E. Cross, Pat Burns, George Lane and Archie Maclean – to finance an outdoor wild west show at the same time as they held their more sedate yearly agricultural fair. The clerk launched into an exciting explanation about the coming Calgary Stampede and told Laurie it was something one couldn't afford to miss. He convinced Laurie that he should stay with them until he saw the Stampede and suggested that he take the streetcar sightseeing tour of the city.

The next day, the hotel clerk awakened Laurie so he wouldn't miss his city tour on the sightseeing streetcar. The streetcar itself was a sight to behold. It was roofless, with the seats raised in tiers like those of a theatre, so each passenger got an unobstructed view. The most amazing thing about it was its mirror-covered outside. This faced the streets and invariably small children paused to make faces or wave to themselves, and adult passers-by sneaked quick, surreptitious glances at their own reflections. In movement it was a constantly changing kaleidoscope of moving, coloured reflections.

At its passenger entrance steps stood a fat man in a red blazer, wearing a straw hat set at a rakish angle. It was a narrow-brimmed flat crowned one, of the type Laurie had learned to call a 'boater' in England, and the band had a wide, bright red ribbon. He shook each of the passenger's hands as he extracted their twenty-five cent fare. When the car at last moved off with a clatter, in a hoarse voice he bellowed continuously at the passengers through a large megaphone. He held it in one hand and only occasionally paused to vaguely wave it at some passing building.

Laurie decided that the man knew only two adjectives, 'magnificent' and 'new,' which he used to describe everything. He reminded Laurie of the barkers he had seen at British fairs enticing passers-by into the freak show tents. The guide seemed very proud of city hall, which to Laurie was an architectural horror of mixed styles. The guide thought the architectural style magnificent, and explained that they had been careful to make it representative of all Calgary's citizens. It had a clock tower like London's Westminster, a dome like St. Peters in Rome to keep the European Catholics happy, and narrow windows like those in a French chateau. He proudly added that it was built of stones found only in Southern Alberta along its rivers, and called after their colour – sandstone.

Laurie had noted several office buildings and even a couple of big houses built of that stone. It had given the city a sort of elegance in contrast to the wood and brick buildings of other Western Canadian cities.

The most exciting thing he saw on the tour was the Carnegie library. This building was classically elegant and it reminded him of the Oxford Museum into which he and his tutor had often escaped the stuffy atmosphere of his grandmother's mansion and the old people who occupied it.

Laurie spent his lifetime in the narrow confines of one city. Although his roots were locked in one place, that place would be swept with such a variety of events during his lifetime that almost daily he was exposed to constant change. This was as exciting for him as for those who rush from place to place in the hopes of finding variety to titillate their thoughts.

Laurie's life with the Indians was like watching a drama where the plot is the changing of man's problems, not across a day, but across centuries. It presented him with a pageant of time. When Laurie first met the Indians, he encountered the drama and excitement of men who had lived close to a beautiful, untouched land for centuries. He was able to trace the changes in the human condition across centuries. The native in his very person, with his carefully guarded memories of a past barely interrupted by civilization could reveal what had been lost and what had been gained in our march to so-called civilization. This civilization had all too often merely sought the glitter of gadgets in substitution for true progress in the human condition.

In the city where Laurie now lived, he watched the rapid changes that come to a country only a hundred years old. The local scene changed as violently and rapidly as a storm that swiftly disappears, only to be replaced by a rainbow. To live in Calgary was to watch a constant panorama of change.

All his life John Laurie would have just one profession – a high school teacher – and all his life he would live in one place – Calgary, Alberta.

Calgary is a place of contrast – you can lift your eyes high to the great splendour of the sky-piercing mountains or slide them over miles of flat, flat prairie fields. It was a place with a change of view, where you can accept a change of viewpoint.

Laurie's life was expanding. No longer was he just a young man testing life's ways in college, and city. His time visiting his university friend's Saskatchewan ranch and racing his horse across open fields under a vast sky had opened for him new knowledge of nature's vast beauty and peace. This made it possible for him in the future to grasp and understand the Indian people's preoccupation and reverence for nature. However, being young, he still had an 'itch' for the excitement and variety of city life.

While drinking hot coffee in a farmer's kitchen, Laurie watched the frustrated farm wife try to explain a math problem to her little children. This was the time when, unable to cope with the difficulty of riding miles to the few existing country schoolhouses, many farmers' children had to rely on correspondence courses. Watching the housewife fumble with the math problem, Laurie couldn't resist leaning over and saying "This is how you do it." The delighted housewife said, "From now on that is a part of your chores," and by the end of the winter he was teaching four other children from nearby ranches on a daily basis.

What John Laurie really would be all his life was a teacher. His teaching career had begun teaching very small children around a kitchen table, had grown from a one-room school house to a private boarding school, and eventually to a high school in Calgary. Teaching was his life-long profession and the techniques he learned in that profession enabled him eventually to encourage the Indians to go back to the dignified life they once had and the white people to learn to accept and live with the Indians and for all of those people to work in unity for achievement. He lived and died a teacher.

An opportunity came for Laurie when he heard of a teaching vacancy at Western Canada College in Calgary, on the site of Calgary's Western Canada High School. The college was the brainchild of the last of the maverick characters who had seen the Canadian Pacific Railway's European posters advertising steamship and railway tickets. Reverend Dr. Archibald Oswald MacRae personally raised the building funds and paid students, it is rumoured, with a Bible in one pocket and a flask in the other. By reaching into the right pocket for the right approach, he had opened Western Canada's first college. To find students, he kept the teacher's fees comparatively low, but their duties as understaffed boarding school teachers were strenuous.[3]

For John Laurie it had a double appeal: it would enable him in his spare time to obtain an Alberta teacher's certificate, and just down the street there was a livery stable where his horse could live. The still living pupils speak fondly of him. To this day in the Calgary high school where he taught only one remembers getting the cane from Laurie. On his birthday, pupils who now only hear of him list it in their school newspaper. The picture that ran in the newspaper when the young Calgary businessmen in the chamber of commerce chose him as 'Citizen of the Year' shows Laurie surrounded by young happy faces. The reporter noted that, interestingly enough, a great many in that room were taught by John Laurie. They were now young successful businessmen in Calgary, but not one of them had forgotten their old teacher.

Calgary author Shirley Matheson discovered that John Laurie had been a teacher in the small one-room schoolhouse she had first attended when she went to a school reunion there. She was amazed to find on its wall a picture of John Laurie. She had grown up in an era when Calgary's only vague memory of him was contained in the name of the city boulevard they drove down daily. There is nothing like a school reunion to bring alive lost memories. The sense of *déjà vu* as you look out those windows on the scene that was engraved upon your mind so long ago, and the smell of chalk, gives us all a new perspective on our lives since then.

At the reunion were elderly persons who travelled quite a distance and among them were several who remembered John Laurie. There were several, now very old persons, who remembered their teacher well. They all remembered his horse and the way their teacher came flying across the fields on this fast horse and sometimes even cleared the fence instead of going around to open the gate. One student, now in her eighties, had travelled from Vancouver to her reunion. When I asked her if she remembered Laurie as her teacher, her eyes filled with tears and she said, "Oh, I never forgot him, he was so kind. My mother, because of early illness, would not let me travel the long distance to the only school in the district and so I was behind all the other students of my age. We were all of course in different grades in the one classroom, but I was embarrassed by my lack of knowledge. It was as though Laurie instinctively understood this. He always made sure that my desk was near the old Franklin heater in the cold school room and when I was having difficulty, he would just stop by my desk and take a little extra time to help me catch up with the other students. I will never forget him."

The first pupil I was able to contact whom Laurie had taught in the years he was at the private boarding school, Western Canada College, was quite brief with me on the phone. He said, "Yes, I remember him well. He gave me the strap." When I asked, "Well, what for?" he remembered that well too. He said, "I guess you would call it impetuous." So there was another side to the schoolteacher, a stern disciplinarian. The memories of another well-known and respected old-timer in Calgary were quite different. His family had a large ranch close to Calgary and he had been sent to what was literally Calgary's first urban high school, Western Canada College. He wrote of wonderful memories about how Laurie had him and his best friend over on the occasional evening to enjoy a cup of tea in his rooms. Like all who leave the home environment and go to a residential school, they were suffering slight pains of homesickness and confusion. Laurie not only helped them with their homework, but let them discuss the problems of life.

The conscientious Laurie was concerned about the exams and the textbooks he would teach from so he wrote to the Department of Education in Edmonton. They were shocked to discover an unregistered teacher. They directed a school inspector at High River to check the matter out. Now it seems to me an impossible coincidence, but the inspector from High River sent to question Laurie was my future father-in-law, George Gorman, who later became a deputy minister of education for Alberta, and was known for creating the system of bus transportation for rural schools. George, a university graduate of McMaster University himself, recognized John's abilities as a graduate from the University of Toronto and signed Laurie in as an official Alberta schoolteacher. Much later, Laurie acquired the authentic credentials from the University of Alberta necessary for the job.

7: A HORSE DID IT

Laurie loved horses. He kept his beloved horse Paddy a block and a half east of where Western Canada High School is now located, in Ruttle's livery stable. The boys were convinced that Laurie had chosen to teach at the boarding school because of the closeness of the school to the stables. Often in the evening they would hear Laurie exercising Paddy round and round at a full gallop in the playing field that is still behind Western Canada High School in Calgary.

The Ruttle stables were much a part of Calgary's history and I would say even helped form the character of Calgary. When the stables opened they were a very important part of the community. They were the equivalent of Calgary's first car rental system but for poor people who couldn't afford their own carriage and horse. Here is where you rented one for the big occasions like a wedding or even a funeral where horses would draw the hearse. It was also a place where hundreds of Calgary's children who never could afford a horse of their own learned to ride.

I rode a horse out of the Ruttle stables, which was close to my own home in Mount Royal. I was, of course, younger than John Laurie and never saw him there. Many Calgarian children grew up living in the city yet rode horses for most of their lives. It seems almost unbelievable to me now, but in my youth you could ride your horse out of the Ruttle stable precariously across the cement and the streetcar tracks that ran down 17th Avenue S.W. and after that, by using back lanes and open fields, you could reach near where Earl Grey School is built on a hill, across the hills that were then green grass, descend and ford the river and ride all the way to De Winton with your horse.

With the growth of the city, the stable property was desired by developers. Nearly every year a developer would appear and try to get city council to declare the livery stable dangerous to public health and pull it down so they could acquire the property. For every developer there were Calgary mothers who remembered the joy that the livery stable had brought their children. Some of those boys had grown up to be quite prominent citizens so an equally angry group of citizens appeared to demand that the stable be allowed to stay. It did stay until George Ruttle, himself a very old man, decided to retire. It was probably the presence, however, of that horse stable sitting in an almost central Calgary area that caused eastern reporters to label Calgary a 'Cowtown.' On the other hand it was Calgary's deep respect for the courage and the hardships that had gone into creating the early roots of the West that made it possible for John Laurie to later win their support with his plea for understanding the native people, the first people here. It was this citywide backing that eventually allowed John Laurie to bring the Canadian Indian the vote.

I was six years old when John Laurie first came to Calgary. I have happy memories about my life in Mount Royal and my family's Sunbeam car. We kept the car in a barn with a wonderful horse and hayloft. On Christmas day my father would take us all in a cutter and drive the horse around town and wave to our neighbours. Patricia Kathleen Page, a well-known Canadian poet,[1] remembers that time as a child when her father was Colonel of the Lord Strathcona's Horse Regiment in Calgary, and the important part the horse played in transportation in Calgary's early days. Ladies came to her mother's teas often dressed in their elegant riding costumes and left their horses tied to the fence outside. Mrs. Gladys Alma Egbert, who became one of Canada's finest music teachers,[2] remembers how she used to ride her pony clear across the city to take lessons.

On the surrounding ranches were many persons of similar background to Laurie. They were second and third sons of nobility who found that a life of poor gentility was much better in Canada than in England. On their ranches they played polo and even on occasion put on red jackets and loudly blowing horns chased a rather confused coyote across the country. The versatile horse Paddy turned out to be as good a polo horse as he was a racer.

In Calgary, they held not only races and horse shows, but also an outdoor Buffalo Bill Wild West style show that was combined with the usual staid indoor agriculture fair, today's Calgary Stampede. Now, over a million people go to the Stampede each year to watch 10 days of contests between man and horse and to watch the marvellous chuckwagon races where 32 horses wheel gracefully around barrels and come thundering down a narrow track often almost touching each other. Each year of his life, one of Laurie's indulgences was to attend the Calgary Stampede.

Laurie loved Stampede time, but he never wore a cowboy hat. Calgarians, even those who had the meekest jobs, wore tall wide-brimmed cowboy hats, not black ones, during Stampede week. They pretended to be 'the good guys' and wore white hats.

Laurie loved the chuckwagon races and so did the Indians who were usually unable to race, because they did not have the money to get a wagon together. Laurie understood that as horsemen they wanted to be in the race and he also understood that those without hope must have some fun. In those days the racehorses were largely quarter horse types more ideally suited to pulling the ton-heavy wagons. One of the unknown secrets of Laurie's life, which I discovered only when I looked into his cash box after his death, was that at his death Laurie owned horses that ran in the Stampede chuckwagon races. He had been so anxious that Indians would not be just spectators, but would be allowed to compete at the Stampede that he and David Crowchild put their heads together and out of his limited funds the teacher purchased the horses. He helped finance his friend Dave in setting up a chuck outfit and for many years the Sarcee had a wagon in the races. I think all they ever won was day money once; the horses were never quite fast enough. However, each year Dave drove in the race and he drove well to the delight of the crowd and no doubt to the great inner satisfaction of John Laurie.

The fact that Calgary's mild-seeming, very proper school teacher was a participant in the tough wild chuckwagon races would have shocked most people who knew him, his pupils most of all. But hanging over the rail and watching the horse come charging into the finish line was concealed in the heart of the young adventurer who had first come west and fallen in love and raced his first horse, the glorious Paddy.

Horses would not let Laurie down either. While in search of a stud for a chuckwagon mare he found the Parkers of Cochrane. Geoff was an excellent polo player. Laurie had replied to an ad for 'at stud' over the phone and the Parkers were a little shaken when David Crowchild appeared at the door with a mare to be bred that was now too old and slow for the race track. It had an unlikely name for a racehorse, 'Mama Poke.' I suspect it was a joke of Laurie's. When she threw a fine colt, Laurie came to see it and named it 'Baby Poke.' Out of these encounters came a permanent friendship with the Parkers and he convalesced in their ranch home after his heart attack at the first Hobbema trial. They became lifelong friends. Geoff was one of the four white pallbearers who carried Laurie with his four Indian friends to his final grave on the nearby Morley Reserve.

The Indians who moved into Calgary for the Stampede, often over 200 of them, actually lived down on the Stampede grounds in their magnificent tepees. Laurie spent time with his Indian friends behind the show tepees on the grounds. He did not want them to be turned into another mid-way sideshow.

Laurie and I decided to make sure of this. The Stampede board, despite all the financial dress up, was just another moneymaking company with a closed list of shareholders and had come to look upon the Indians as a 'piece of property.' They laid down the bucks and they expected a performance. The board paid them a dollar a day to come in their own beautiful expensive native costumes, bring their own tents, and ride their own horses on hot paved streets in a two-hour parade. What really upset Laurie and me was that in the early Stampede years, they had no water or toilet facilities. There was one iron pipe with a lawn faucet of cold water for the whole camp. Toilets were blocks away in the basement. But worst of all there were no patrols and all night long some drunk with a flask of booze tried to bait young Indian women. The camp needed night security guards. I made the request to the board and was shocked at their quick blunt NO! Then, I let my temper go and as we rose to leave, I said, "You are so proud that the sun always shines Stampede week for you. What if the Indians won't do their sun dance?" My remark, of course, was based on the whites' ignorance. They always thought of the sun dance as some kind of dance that drove away the rain.

I was heartily ashamed of my waste of temper, as we left with no concessions, but the funniest thing happened. When the guest of honour for the Stampede that coming year stood on the open-air platform to read out his speech, there was a great crack of thunder and one of the heaviest rainstorms ever drenched performers on the open stage and audiences in the grandstand. For the first time in years the Stampede was nearly rained out. The next year the Indians needful requests were met. Such is the superstition of non-Indians.

The Indians loved the Stampede. Photographs of Calgary's first exhibition were almost entirely of Indians trailing travois with small children in them. They also were performers in the Stampede. The bucking horse champion was Blood Indian Tom Three Persons riding notorious outlaw horse Cyclone. Unfortunately, Tom Three Persons, the best rider, was jailed because he had had a celebration drink, which was not allowed for an Indian. The more experienced riders from the South (Americans) were about to take home the high prize money being offered when, luckily, Tom Three Persons' bail appeared and he won and kept the championship in Canada.[3]

Calgarians' love of horses operates on strange levels in strange ways. One morning, a man on his way to work saw the many old toothless horses waiting to make their final contribution as dog food in the corral of the dog food plant. There, an old mare had just given birth to a colt. He phoned Bill Knights' radio program to ask if he would mention this. As soon as the news reached out over the airwaves another unnamed resident drove his car over and paid the money to save the mare and colt from extermination. A farmer just outside the city telephoned in and offered free pasture "for life" for the mother and colt. Another citizen got in his truck and drove them there. By noon, without any protests, or any official arguments the mare and colt were resting peacefully, lying down together in the sun in a lush green pasture.

Laurie's high degree of education, but lack of experience in any specific field, made job hunting difficult. He finally found work with a horse trader who plied his trade travelling all summer from one small town fair to another. The ranchers loved horse races and nearly every town held a yearly one. Even today in a small area south of Calgary, now called Millarville, they still hold an annual race. In fact, it is the oldest annual race meet in Canadian history.

At a sale at one of these race meets, Laurie couldn't resist the appeal of a horse no one bid on because she was past her prime as a racehorse. Now, he had doubled his responsibilities. The trouble came in winter when his employer closed down operations. Laurie was now running out of his money saved from his army pay and had to find a place for both to live. He hit on the happy idea of applying for a job on a ranch that would give them both cover for the long winter.

In the Royal Canadian Mounted Police stables where the musical ride horses were housed, you will find the battered motto: 'The Best Thing for the Inside of a Man is the Outside of a Horse.' This proved true for John Laurie and was part of the healing process of the trauma of his unloved youth.

While moving some horses from Millarville to Rocky Mountain House where he lived at the time, Laurie spent his first night at Morley. While out riding west of Calgary between the Jumping Pound Creek and the Morley station his saddle horse had cast a shoe. Urgently he needed a blacksmith, and after inquiries he was directed to Dan Wildman, official interpreter, stockman, and blacksmith on the Stoney reserve. The blacksmith shoed the horse, and invited him to stay overnight. He did and in the years to follow he returned to Morley many times.

8: LAURIE FINDS A FAMILY

Laurie was now in his mid-years and he felt good, strong and content in the life he had carved out for himself. It had been luck that by birth he had found Canada. Every year of his life convinced him of that. He loved saying its name. One of his favourite writers was the Westerner Bruce Hutchison. He said, "Canada, its name sounds more like the call of a song bird, than the name of a country." For Laurie it was an inner song he always heard. Possibly it was those long eight years of isolation in grandmother's big Oxfordshire English manor when each day he longed to be back in Canada in the woods – long walks in the woods with his beloved gentle father; wild games he played first with his small Iroquois playmates. He was content with the Alberta he had found with its great blue dome of sky. He managed to enjoy the stretch of plains almost into infinity and the ancient force of the mountains. The teaching he had to do each day absorbed him. He rose each day to gladly meet it. He was a content man. His friends, his students filled that sense of aloneness he had blocked out and the fear of those years of rejection.

It was a good life he led, and he filled every moment of it enjoying what he did. There was not much money, but he had watched the miserly concern for money and its power in grandmother's house. He could do without the cowing dependent relatives and his grandmother's frugal attitude. He had no memory of a family. He would stay away from that as a source of great joy. He hadn't the money to acquire a family, a wife and home of his own anyway, so why chase what to him had proven to be a source of unhappiness. He was a young man in a young country and each day's problems were the only easy challenges he enjoyed solving.

It was in just such a contented mood, enjoying the sunny day, that he undertook the job of helping his Cochrane ranch friend repair the old original McDougall Church at Morley in the 1920's. It was one of Southern Alberta's first churches sitting alone on fields of prairie grass at the foot of where the Rockies suddenly emerge to rear themselves up from the bowels of the earth and to dominate both land and sky. It was probably the first church built in

Southern Alberta. Reverend George McDougall had carefully constructed it with Indian labour, adding to it section by section until his three small log cabins grew into one church. He had even hopefully added a steeple with a tower bell window, hoping someday to acquire a bell so he could ring it out across their prairies and call his Indians to service. Even the memorial monument in front of it was disintegrating. It was a cairn made of the round, smooth stones so often found on the prairies that had been scraped smooth by glaciers thousands of years ago. However, the cement holding it together was cracked and some stones had even fallen out. The church was no longer in active use. It had been vandalized.

It was a lovely summer day when Laurie arrived to help in the repair job and he was the first there. While he was beginning to work at it, a car drove up and a tall vigorous man with scholarly glasses and a thick shock of black hair stepped out. He introduced himself as the Reverend Staley, both missionary and the superintendent of the nearby Indians' residential school on the Stoney reserve. The two teachers fell easily into shop talk and Staley, who had long ago given up too much hope of getting assistance from the Department of Indian Affairs, was always seeking to interest and find concerned non-Indians to help. He offered Laurie a teacher's job but, when Laurie heard the low wage, he was quite shaken and realized the Reverend Staley's difficulty in obtaining able teachers.

However, Staley, like many another missionaries, was a determined and dedicated man. He had turned his back on the ease offered by civilization in their cities and the better wages. He didn't give up easily. He did persuade John Laurie to agree to come and serve as an impartial judge at the Indian school's next concert. Laurie, in turn, remembering the kindness and pleasure he had had in his overnight stay with the Indian blacksmith consented to come.

Laurie's life that sunny morning, without him realizing it, was set upon a whole new future. He had taken his first step down a path few other white men would ever walk. At the school concert a few weeks later a thin, dark-haired young Indian, Eddie Hunter, played the violin, an unlikely instrument for an Indian. Laurie learned that a past teacher had taught Eddie to play the violin and when she left, she gave him her old one. He had no further lessons. Laurie knew a violin teacher in Calgary and suggested that Eddie come and take lessons from her. After his first lesson, Eddie missed the bus back to Morley and he stayed overnight at Laurie's, who drove him home the next day. After that Laurie got the Brewster Bus Company in Banff to give Eddie a free bus pass. However, Eddie often stayed overnight with Laurie when he missed the bus, and on those days Laurie took Eddie with him to school. Today, I tell Eddie, he was one of the first Indians to attend a school in Calgary.

When I asked Eddie what it was like living with Laurie, he told me, "He was the best damn man cook I ever knew," a typical teenager's remark.

Eddie's father, Chief Enos Hunter, was an honoured storyteller of his tribe. So, Laurie took to joining the young people who sat at his feet to listen to past history and legends of his people. Laurie realized that he was no Homer but he was determined to save these legends for these people with no real written language. Their past gods were rather like the Greeks. They could be mischievous, enjoy human characteristics like envy, and they too fell in love with human maidens who dance to the stars. Laurie the schoolteacher understood those values that were like ones of the clans of old.

Mrs. Hunter in turn saw in her young white listener the spirit of a son she had once lost in birth. She decided that he should inherit her dead son's Indian name translated as White Cloud. A great and sacred ceremony was prepared to include the other Indian families. To Laurie's delight he was the centre of this impressive and beautiful ceremony involving the four directions of the whole world's sky pipes, smoked and handed about, the sweet smell of incense, and drums and dancing. When they presented him not only with a new name but also with a beautiful headdress of tall eagle feathers and ermine skins and beautiful bead work, he realized that the expense they had gone to in time and money meant they almost had to go hungry, they were so poor. So, Laurie knew he had at last found a family of his own, one who truly wanted him among them. It was a sacred and secret thing.

Laurie's beliefs, like all beliefs, were limited by the times. He, like those about him, looked upon Indians not as individuals or as members of a given tribe, but as humans. Laurie thought about his new family a great deal. Fifty years ago he noticed there was little theft on the reserve despite the poverty. Instead, they seemed very willing to share with one another. There was no murder; there was no drunkenness. He knew there was some alcohol on the reserve despite the laws, but the Indians of his day despised drunkenness. There was little physical fighting; however, there was a lot of cruel jealousy based, he supposed, on the very principle of sharing. A person who gained more was not envied or admired if he didn't share. Sharing could build up just as much resentment as the individual fortune building of our capitalist society. He noticed their cheerfulness, wry humour, and their love of talking around the fire and listening to the storytellers. He noted the preciousness of words to them; they had, after all, no writing. Often a pause was meant to be as effective as what was said; silence meant "no," and "yes" meant action. Among them he attempted to do it their way, yet occasionally if they asked or showed interest he would show them the white man's way. Filling up time with talk was not Laurie's way.

The women kept busy with their never-ending chores of preparing food, clothing and baby care, but the men had so little to do. They held the ceremonies and dances to keep up their spirits and their wry humour was part of presenting a patient front; a shrug had become a way of life for them. What really angered Laurie was the lack of food, the lack of learning, and the lack of jobs to give meaning to life. He found the absence of hope for a better tomorrow almost frightening. Yet, he knew they had survived immense hardship on this reserve trying to keep themselves a healthy and strong people, even without always having faith and hope.

His reading had confirmed this. When the Europeans arrived, they had found a strong race. He had to find out why there was so little food now, why so little education or books and, most importantly, why was there this awful hopeless pall of idleness? There had to be a way to lift this grey pall of lethargy. He talked first to his good friend the missionary. He told Laurie that the schooling was difficult. No one believed it led anywhere.

There was the constant conflict of language, of culture to overcome, and there were no friends to help his overworked teachers. He had to fight continually with the Department and sometimes he felt that he was not a man of God, but just a beggar, always begging friends from the Church, and from the Department. When he had suggested a woodworking class or an art class, it had been turned down. But how could they ever improve their houses or fix their cars? He knew they had to write and read English to exist in today's world, but he knew as well that they could do little with a grade five education. No one wanted to leave the reserve. There were no jobs here. Laurie could see that farming offered a poor life on the reserve. The land was aptly called Stoney. The Indians claimed that name came from their way of heating stones to put in their water to cook and for sweat baths. Laurie wondered if it had come from all the stones on their reserve. Once a great place to hunt game, being part plain and part mountain, the reserve was now devoid of sufficient sources of wild food.

Without ploughs the native's harvests were often lost. Laurie's natives had told him how difficult it had been to train their skinny riding horses to pull a plough especially the eastern Canadian-manufactured McCormick, the only one sent to the reserve, while the Americans all used the sharper plough that could cut through the centuries-packed, hard prairie soil. There was also the tragic case Laurie told me about of the first potato experiment. The natives had not been told to cut out the eyes of the potato, so they put them in the ground and the whole potato rotted. A recent book by Sarah Carter, *Lost Harvests*,[1] confirms that the Indians did not receive unbound binder twine at first, just binders, so when they cut their crops, it laid flat on the ground and died.

On Laurie's first day on the Indian reserve, he awoke cool, surrounded by the fresh smell of his evergreen mattress. He enjoyed lying on fresh fir boughs under a fur robe and smelling their clean aroma. He got up and admired his glorious plumed headdress. How beautifully and carefully it was made.

This was the beginning of the growth of John Laurie's pride in his Indian family, the way they almost unconsciously shared time and whatever they had, the way they forgave others. He liked their soft voices, their laughter and the way they made him laugh with them at themselves and at their own weaknesses.

As he slept out in their tepee, he marvelled at the architectural perfection of its design. The sloping sides shed rain and snow. The ingenious opening at the top of the tepee could swing to catch any wind and suck out the smoke from the coals of the open centre fire, which heated the tepee. The whole design was so crafty that they never caught fire. It was the women's job to put it up and they could do it in a few seconds.

The Indians told Laurie how far they used to travel with a travois, the vehicle they designed so well, which consisted of two thin poles crossed and tied at the top, but separated at the bottom by a basket whose size could be altered easily. It was beautifully designed, so light and flexible that it could be pulled by a dog, a woman or a horse over the roadless terrain. He realized what clever intelligent people they were. They had thermal knowledge long before the white man, and knew how to produce heat. They knew how to freeze meat instantly in winter and how to preserve it in summer by cutting it, when fresh, in strips, smoking it slowly over the fire, wrapping the strips in fat with berries, and burying it in a clean bladder membrane to take care of hunger years later.

After breakfast he and his new father Enos Hunter sat on the ground with their backs against the cabin wall lazily smoking one of Laurie's cigarettes. Basking in the warm sun under a blue cloudless sky, John asked his father about the headdress. In his soft, slow voice he told him what his hat meant.

Tentatively, Laurie commented on how valuable the headdress seemed to him. Hunter explained that they had always been valued. In the old days they were worth 15 horses. At one time Norman Luxton would pay forty dollars for a fine short one.[2] Laurie thinks of the poverty all around him and he is in awe of the generosity of their gift to him.

To Laurie, the ceremony of placing it on his head had been very solemn. The Medicine Man had raised a long-stemmed pipe high above his head and made a great circle, then pointed it in each of the four directions. It seemed to Laurie this perfectly described in motion that little-understood word "universe."

These Indians felt that their lives had no limitations; they felt they were at one with the whole world. During the ceremony the circle was formed and reformed by dancers and elders to symbolize the unbroken unity of the universe. Laurie felt at home and oddly at peace with it all. He loved the wild energetic dances with the fierce beat of the drums. After all he was a Scotsman raised to the thrill of the Scottish fling and the skirl of the bagpipes.

John Laurie's adoption by his new Indian family resulted in a change to his personality. When comparing photographs of Laurie in his Indian headdress, and without it, he appears as almost a different person. This is also true of today's Indians. At their Association meetings they all wear white man's clothing. Once at a reception in Calgary, a young man, dressed in full Indian regalia, came over and stood beside me to make polite conversation. I asked, "What tribe do you belong to?" He replied, "Oh Ruth! I'm George Labelle." George was a Stoney from Morley and well known to me, but in his ancient native dress he looked quite different. All the old lost pride had been returned to him.

So it was with John Laurie. Inwardly he had become an Indian and proud of it. Today Laurie would say that Indians must retain their past culture, but not try to live it in today's world; instead, use it to remind themselves inwardly of their long magnificent history as survivors.

One morning Laurie awoke to excitement and the unusual commotion of swift movement. It seemed someone had spotted an elk up in the hills. With amazing quickness a hunting party was formed. They found a gun for Laurie who presumed they were honouring him by including him. Laurie had never hunted nor wanted to. For years his life had been guided by a memory kept alive through his lonely Oxford days: his beloved father placing a soft and small wild duckling into his cupped hands and explaining what a fine thing it was to hold life in your hands.

He was terrified to admit to his newly found family who had centuries of instinctive survival hunting built into their culture that he really didn't want to kill. Fortunately they were, as usual, short on equipment so Laurie relinquished his gun, but asked to come along. A lone elk was spotted high up, standing in a swamp pond. The Indians were disappointed that there were no other elk. This immense beast had probably been driven out after a fight with a younger, stronger male during the spring rutting season. He was now condemned to spend a lonely life in an aging existence.

The kill was quick and easy. Laurie was amazed at the skill with which the carcass was cut up and dressed. Laurie concealed his secret distaste, but shared the load of carrying the animal packs back to the horses. He reflected that this was no "idle dwelling in Eden." Even though it was a fine day, with no storm or blizzard, this was precarious survival. He marvelled at the joy with which his slow-moving Indian family completed the difficult job. A life dependent on hunting for survival was hard, hard work. Laurie wondered what it must have been like for the ancestors of his family in centuries past when they pitted themselves against the harshness of hunting, without even the benefit of a gun.

Laurie loved that first summer when he spent long, happy days with his Indian family on the reserve. He felt as if he was in a foreign country where by law, he should have obtained a passport each time he turned off the highway to drive across the dirt trails to his new family's forced-to-live-in area. All he had was a legal passport issued verbally by the resident agent representing the Department of Indian Affairs. The reserve was a foreign land where the people largely spoke a different language, practised foreign customs, lived in different houses and wore different clothes, all of which differed from those of the country Canada that surrounded them.

Their government was not the same as the rest of Canada, as they had no part in electing the Canadian government that controlled them nor did they receive the same service as other Canadians, and their governing laws were different. The only food they could get was entirely different. The reserve was a foreign country with boundaries. Even on the highway was a sign saying, "You are now entering the Stoney reserve." The Indian reserves were foreign lands, but foreign lands within Canada; to cross their borders was more startling than to enter the United States. If there was no entry to this foreign country, except through government officials, there were no maps or guidebooks for the visitor. It was a foreign, unknown country within Canada and in it lived an unknown people.

Canada's national anthem promoted the idea that we were united, strong and free – but all weren't. The Indians themselves blamed the frustration of their life on the agent, the missionaries, schools and doctors.

Laurie was concerned with the label "savage" that had been attached to his Indian friends. It could be traced back to Christopher Columbus. One of Columbus's men, observing the comely almost naked Indian maidens on the beach, had jumped ship for the beach. Like every sailor all over the world he was looking for a girl in every port. However, the Indian maidens had no intention of being raped and together they beat him to a pulp. The frightened crew, watching from the ship, explained his illegal absence to their Captain and that the maidens had killed him then eaten him. Whether this was true or even visible from the still-at-sea ship is not clear, but it titillated the Europeans.

It is a human weakness that we all are fascinated by monsters. Witness the duration of novelist Mary Shelley's *Frankenstein* and Bram Stoker's *Dracula*. The unknown people of the "new world" became monsters. German print makers made a fortune out of producing ridiculously savage monster prints, some headless, some mounted on ridiculous shoes that were actually snow shoes except that they showed the Indian stumbling amid summer flowers on them. This picture avoided the Church's ruling against depicting nude humans enforced by fines against pornography. The label "savage" was now permanently affixed to Native Americans. Laurie noted that it was still shared by some Calgarians.

He was concerned about the Indians' actual savagery or cruelty. Their historians, the storytellers, had recounts of ancient battles and of tortured prisoners. Radisson had entertained London audiences with accounts of his own tortures as a captive, but admitted that if he was brave he was free. He told it in a great English city whose own Tower of London still exhibited its own remarkable torture dungeon, still visible today.

Indian wars had been over invaded hunting territories. The Indians had not made war on the invading European explorers. On Canada's west coast, Captain Vancouver had been amazed when he was greeted at the spot where an arch stands today in the city that bears his name, that the natives had merely showered them with fine goose feathers, similar to the confetti we still sometimes use to celebrate weddings or victories. John Laurie saw that the Indians' reward for their kindness was confinement on small reserves.

When the Indians fought back it was always labelled a massacre or rebellion, but when the non-Indians attacked, it was merely called defence. There had been only two records of inter-racial massacres in Alberta: one in the south in Cypress Hills and the other in the north at Frog Lake. The Cypress Hills massacre had in reality been an ugly drunken brawl between Indian and white American criminals who were breaking the law by selling intoxicants to natives.

That first summer on the reserve had been a glorious one for John Laurie. Part of it he spent sleeping in the tepee behind his family's home as he now called it. He still took a few racehorses to local meets and went to all the local rodeos, sometimes taking his Indian family with him. It was then he discovered how many Indians could fit in one car, since neither the old, the young, nor a friend could ever be left out.

They had something that should be understandable in today's society, we who travel the world. They walked across continents and could move whenever they felt they wanted to. Laurie realized how cruel it was that they were now confined to a reserve, with "no going off" without the agent's permission. There was only one harassed agent on the large Morley reserve who, with cause, could deny the Indians permission to leave. To escape without his consent to them was to revive their once great scouting activities. Laurie discovered that the Indians had formed themselves into what they called a "moccasin telegraph system": each passer-by passed on information about where the agent was, so it was easy to avoid the agent.

By the end of the summer, Laurie felt he could now "walk in their past moccasins a thousand miles." He even attended one of their sacred sun dances.

Laurie never forgot that first summer he spent living with his new Stoney Indian family. He always referred to it, making a pun, as his "Indian summer." In the West we refer to Indian summer as that gift of a few more weeks of wonderful lush warm weather that follows after the first frost reaches and vanishes with the first snow. It is our loveliest time of the year and for John Laurie that first summer with his Indian family was one of the loveliest of his life.

As he sat around the campfire, where only the men escaped each night, he listened as they repeated the tales that often told what life was like in the days of the buffalo and the great skirmishes at Belly River, their ancestors' time. Laurie's family's ancestors had some short-lived skirmishes with the dreaded Blackfoot warriors who had tried to invade and hunt on their territory or tried to steal their horses. These skirmishes resulted in few casualties. These were different tales than the past legends he had written down to save. The legends that Mrs. Hunter had told him were legends about how one could live one's life and fight back evil gods, much like the Greek legends that Homer saved.

Laurie realized that it was now over fifty years since his Indian family had signed treaty and been imprisoned on this small reserve. This tribe had supposedly been among the last to have once roamed the great prairie plains that stretched from Lake Superior west to the Rocky Mountains, land that had been theirs, not for a few years, but for thousands of years. Laurie wondered if anyone around the campfire could remember that moment of awful loss. They would have to be over seventy-five years old or at least have been ten years old when the treaty was signed and their way of life had vanished in an instant.

The great hunts and wars were not really memories at all; they were just tales that they were keeping alive because they desperately needed them to endure the sad life they were now trying, with stolidity to endure. His heart went out to them in a rush of understanding.

However, there was in this circle of men some, only a few, old men of seventy-five years. Laurie resolved to talk to them. After all, their side of treaty signing had never been told. After his wonderful adoption ceremony Laurie had read a book his friend Alex Calhoun had found for him, a book called the *Treaties of Canada with Manitoba, the Northwest Territories and Kee-wa-ten*.[3] It was three hundred and seventy-five pages of small print so he hadn't read it till now. He resolved that he must read it, most importantly, to discover the Indians' reasons for agreeing to accept this confined and miserable life. What John Laurie would see for himself was what little was now left for them of their freedom of their past.

When Laurie read the Indian Act he realized that the boundaries of the reserve were like invisible prison walls and were legal. The government agents were like guards who patrolled this prison. Much later one of the students at the high school where Laurie taught, Morris Schumiatcher, wrote an article in which he commented that life on the reserve was concealed behind a "Buckskin Curtain."[4]

The reserves were each a foreign country, locked and concealed within the democratic country of Canada, strange circles sprinkled across an empty waiting land. In this foreign land the Indians wore different clothes, colourless and wrinkled as though just folded around the body. Here woman had no swirling coats with belted waists or shapely shoulder pads; some were merely wrapped in a blanket. The women wore no hats, only a fold of cloth on their heads. Everyone's hair was black, long and braided. With foreign clothes, foreign languages and dark faces, they had remained as different from their white neighbours as mountains are from plains.

As he listened, suddenly the dogs outside began to bark and they heard the horses hurrying as they neared home. The boys carried the packages in and Mrs. Hunter started to carefully check the rations. She carefully counted out each slice of what to Laurie seemed thick, not pink and white, but coarse yellow slices of salted bacon. She said, "The agent counted right this time, thirty-two slices for the four of us for this month." Next she carefully hefted a bag of flour and put it in a crude cupboard in the corner. Then came a small bag of sugar and one of tea leaves and finally a small handful of matches which she carefully put up on a high shelf. "It's all right this time," she said. Laurie asked if that was the week's rations. She said, "Oh no, it's for the next month for the whole family." Laurie looked around at the miserable pile that contained no fruit or vegetables at all. He felt like he shouldn't share supper with them, but Mother Hunter insisted he stay and began cooking on her stove, which consisted of an old, abandoned, empty metal gas barrel sitting on its side. Its two sides were flattened out so it could sit evenly on stones on the floor and flattened enough for the big iron frying pan and pot to sit on top. She fed the stove small dried sticks and somehow she skilfully kept the fire burning inside.

Enos Hunter and Laurie hauled hand-pumped water from the well and carried the full pails into the house. Mr. Hunter seemed quite proud of his squeaking, rusty hand pump and well. He explained that not many homes had a well. He said, "I like the river water better than the water the tank man brings around once a week, but this water is fine for washing and cooking. We are very lucky to have it. I've had it for four years now." Laurie had also noticed a rain barrel, another abandoned rusty gas drum sitting at each corner of the house. It held dark rainwater with a strange smell. Now that he thought about it, all they drank was tea – strong and black. Laurie also realized that there were no chickens or milk cows in this farmyard.

That night as they all sat around a small fire that the boys had built on stones outside the cabin, young Eddie proudly played his violin. Laurie thought how much better it sounded out there reaching toward a clear sky sparkling with stars. That night he fell right to sleep.

One day Laurie, Enos Hunter and the boys climbed a mountain and using a flashlight led him into a cave. Its entrance was a mere crack, just wide enough for one person. On the cave walls Laurie saw soft lines faded to a soft pink and there were painted murals of men with horned hats and masks. Father Hunter said this was done long, long ago, but we tell no one about it or we will lose it. The Crees up north had an important big black stone with a red painting on it of a buffalo head, a big elaborate serpent of stone, but the government survey crew took it away. So we don't show this to white men.

Years later when I published a small magazine, I got an Indian to lead a young poet, who once won the governor general's award for Canada, into the cave and he drew it and wrote an article about it for my readers. I still have never seen the cave nor do I even want to speculate on its location. Like Laurie, I feel that the Indians must have their own art in its own location for their special pleasure. I admire the fine collections, but I'm sure, although non-Indians enjoy them immensely, that to the Indian the original place chosen for the art means so much more to him than it could to any white person. Laurie told his family that night around the fire about the art he had been admiring for years of other Indian people created long ago in Mexico and on the deserts deep in America. He promised to bring them a picture of it on his next visit.

On the last day of his wonderful first holiday with his own family he went with them to the small McDougall Church to a funeral. Two small children, both from the same family, lay side by side in tiny homemade wooden coffins. Laurie's concern was whether they died as a result of a fatal infection. He politely inquired of the weeping young mother what her children died from. She said she didn't know as they got sick on Thursday. Laurie was afraid he was interfering with a taboo of some sort and waited until later to get an explanation from Hunter. Hunter explained to Laurie that the doctor came to this reserve of over six hundred people on Wednesday morning of each week only. The mother did not get a chance to find out what was the matter with her children because they got sick on Thursday and the medicine man's herbs had helped keep the fever down and let them sleep, but all the prayers had not helped. They had died before the doctor came.

An inner rage shook Laurie that this situation existed in the great age of public healing, hospitals and inoculations. On his way home, Laurie stopped and talked to his now good friend and school principal, the Reverend Staley. Laurie was certain the Indians were mixed up and just not using the facilities right. He asked Reverend Staley why no one had taken the dying children into Calgary to the hospital. Was it merely superstition? Reverend Staley explained, "No, it was not superstition. The Calgary hospitals would not take in any Indian from the reserve, but if an Indian lived in Calgary and was hurt they would. It was the Indian's fate, under the British North America Act that they were under only the support and control of far-away Ottawa and could use no provincial or city health unit. Ottawa makes the rules; they pay the shot. The Calgary doctor who comes to this reserve one morning a week is a good man. He even got a boy who was dying of tuberculosis into the special hospital that they had for tuberculosis patients near Bowness. However, when the boy died there the Indians became afraid of going to hospitals. One of our missionary schoolteachers, who had some nursing training, does try and treat the children in the school, but many of them have tuberculosis. Haven't you noticed the many coughs on the reserve?" Laurie was appalled. It had been a glorious week for him, but also a week full of shocks. It was shocking to realize that there were human beings in Alberta with not enough food or health care.

Laurie was to receive one more shock. Casually, Reverend Staley said with a grin, "Young Eddie is doing a lot better at school since he goes to Calgary for violin lessons. I guess travel broadens," and then added, "I will be sorry to see him leave school next year." This was news that no one had ever mentioned to Laurie. He asked what grade Eddie was in. "Well," said Reverend Staley, "Our grades are all mixed up, but I would say the equivalent of your grade six. He is a good student, but he is sixteen and the government won't let us keep Indians in school past sixteen. I've already squeezed Eddie in for an extra year without being caught by the government. Another year would make them suspicious. It's too bad, most pupils can't even speak English when they come to our school and it's a trauma for them to live in residence, so it's several years before they can even read or write or add. Not many get a good education before the government makes us turf them out, back to a life of idleness and no jobs on the reserve." Laurie was horrified at the thought of bright young Eddie's education stopping. All winter long he had given Eddie books to take home with him to read. Laurie recognized a good and curious mind.

Reverend Staley went on to explain to Laurie that the Church doesn't direct or control the missionary residential schools. The government promised under treaty that they would "treat Indian children like their own" and that, of course, in our country means free schooling. It was the early missionaries that opened the first schools. The Catholic Oblate priests were very dedicated about this and the Protestant Reverend McDougall built one of the first small day schools and brought a teacher, Mr. Sibbald, here.

Staley also explained to Laurie that "the government then decided we had to have residential schools, which made sense because on large reserves some children can be as far as forty miles away from the school and they couldn't possibly come. In the winter, even the ones who were three or four miles away couldn't make it. The Indians all hate the residential schools and no matter how hard I try, I can't make them like it. To the parents, it's like losing their children for a whole year. Sometimes the agent even has to send the mountie out to make the children come, but what else can we do?" "No John," he said, "don't go complaining about this to the agent."

"Once I got mad about the poor quality of the food, the poor ration amounts that they gave parents for the children and they are so poor. Well, Ottawa wrote my Church officials and said since I was discontent, possibly our denomination should be removed from the reserve. The Catholic Oblates were doing such a fine job on the education funds on their reserves and I got in all sorts of trouble. Now the church's mission funds send donations so we can quietly, on our own, buy better food for the children.

"I remembered your expression when I asked you to become one of my reserve teachers and named the salary. I can't attract great teachers here, just dedicated persons or teachers who can't get a job elsewhere and often I find there's a good reason why I can't – for a teacher it's a lonely life on an Indian reserve far from other non-Indians, shows and entertainment. Teaching in a residential school means long hours after school with dorm supervision." Laurie assured him that he understood those difficulties. It was why he had been so glad to leave Western Canada College and teach at a public day school.

Laurie left, having great admiration for how Reverend Staley managed on such meagre federal funds and best of all how he kept his good sense of humour and sanity. However, all the way on the drive home he wondered about Eddie. He couldn't live by just playing the violin, even though the boy was elated because he had been asked to play, and even been paid, at several barn raisings and dances in the Cochrane area. Laurie was unhappy as he drove home. It was clear that neither the agent nor the missionary schoolteacher could do much more to help Eddie. It was far-off Ottawa that controlled the daily lives of the families on the reserve and a poor job they were doing: not enough food, health care or education. He resolved to go back to visit his family soon and take baskets of food with him.

He was now embarrassed at how casually he had eaten up their generously-shared limited rations and rabbit stew. He also began to think about what a sacrifice the Hunter family had made to give him a feast and gifts when they adopted him into the tribe as their Indian son, White Cloud. He muttered to himself, "You better get busy helping your new family and bring some prosperity onto your very own family."

Laurie tried to understand his family and was disillusioned. Laurie's visits to the reserves had taught him what an admirable people his Indian family were, but he also realized that they had somehow lost the admiration of the white race they now shared this country with. He knew that like all problems this could be solved only if you understood how the problem had been created. In this case, that would lie in the distant past of the Indians and the mistakes that had happened since they first met the pale-faced invaders of their country. He would have to study history. The trouble was his Indian people lived in small tribes and without the necessity of trade forcing them to develop a written language, they had retained no history of what had really happened to them, either before the white man came or since he had. The storytellers had preserved only the history of their own tribe and the legends their people had created which, like the Greek legends, only preserved the way of life that a human being might be exposed to either through their own errors or the uncontrollable actions of some supreme gods. He would have to search the written history of the pale-faced Europeans, who had first come to this continent.

Once back teaching school in Calgary, he was due for another shock. Hardly any of his white friends, his good friends, shared his enthusiasm for his newly found Indian family. He was shocked at the words they used. They said Indians are hopeless people – dwellers too long in the Garden of Eden. None of them will do a full day's work. They are just lazy. A few even used uglier phrases, "They are heathen savages from the beginning and in five hundred years they haven't improved." Others said, "You've got to watch your possessions when they're around. I'm told they think everyone owns everything in common and they are quick fingered," and added, "They shoo them out of most Calgary stores." Laurie felt like shouting at them, "You don't even know one. How can you believe such dreadful things." Even his good friend Alex Calhoun the librarian wasn't too sympathetic, although he was a man of great sympathy. He was so involved with his own career that he could only guide Laurie to the history books he needed. In those books he might find the answer.

Laurie thought it strange that the white race could get excited about the poverty and injustice of their own people, but no one could seriously consider the tragedy of the red man. However, in honesty he finally had to admit that most white persons knew nothing at all about the conditions the Indians existed in. No white person was allowed to visit the reserve and see things for himself without permission of the Department's agent. To many whites, the Indians were still magnificent, seen only riding in a parade or written about in silly western novels, the most popular fiction of the day. Laurie got up and turned off his radio when the stirring tune of the William Tell overture signalled the start of the "Lone Ranger" with his poor Indian friend Tonto, who really helped that daring hero. The show travelled across the radios of America and Tonto's only means of communication when he was allowed to speak was expressive grunts or an occasional "Ugh, Me Tonto."

There were other examples of the distance between us. I recall how one Indian meeting broke up when a chairman observed, "There seems to be a difference of opinion and to talk about it would be rude." This attitude has created a breakdown in communications between Indians and non-Indians, which exists even to this day, whereby politicians tend to regard an Indian to have agreed if he does not continue an argument. In reality it just means to them that the solution has not been found.

There was also the difficulty of the language. Once, I was trying to explain to the Indians that they must be careful of foolish spending of their trust funds or they would lose the interest on these funds. An old Indian rose up and simplified matters by saying, "The principle is the cow, the interest is the calf, and if you kill all the calves, you will soon have no cows," so they understood.

The Indian way of learning was different. They understood the strange, loud sounds of the night, the sad howl of a coyote or a wolf, the sudden yelp of a small animal caught by an owl, and the rustling in the bush. A boy knew he must sit still, in complete control of himself, self-contained. George MacLean, the last real medicine man of his tribe, once laughingly told me, "I saw no vision. Once I heard a movement and in fear I followed it. It was only a horse loose in the woods. It was the solitary meeting with self that was all important." The boy could become silent and self-contained with a sense of pride in himself, his one defence against the fierceness of nature. The white man robbed him of that and left him defenceless in our strange world of today.

The ceremony of the sun dance and belief in it is gone. The Department never legally forbade it, although they did forbid the equally important potlatch ceremony in which an old Indian chose to hold a party and give away all he had.[5] The guidelines for the religious ceremonies were retained in small special containers, named the bundle or the pouch, making it easily portable for a nomadic society. Whoever held it had received it by heredity or as a gift from its previous owner. It was ancient and precious and handed on by hand.

Ceremonies were usually held at night in a special house or tepee or a sacred outdoor place. Special songs by designated musicians and drum music were an integral part of all ceremonies. Some included a mask of the god who was the central figure of the particular ceremony being conducted. Without written language the Indians handed on these rituals verbally, and they varied from tribe to tribe. The Indians regarded a ceremony just as we do attendance at church; some came from a deep sincere belief, some just to make a petition for a personal special need.

There have always been fine white persons who have had deep life-long concerns for the tragic circumstances of the Indian people, but they have approached it from their own personal viewpoint of the Indian's needs. John Laurie was doing it a different way. He was concerned enough to listen first to what their hurts as human beings were before he attempted to create changes in their circumstances.

While Laurie loved the wild exuberant release of the Indian sun dance, he also went on Sundays with the Hunter family to the McDougall's Methodist United Missionary Church services. There they softly sang the hymns in their native language and silently prayed. The Indians understood prayer, as they too had always prayed to their spirits in and out of their sweathouses. Laurie thought that in their soft guttural accents the hymns almost took on a new message.

Laurie had never been a religious person. The fierce assertive Protestantism of his grandmother and the proud ceremonial attendance she had made of going to church had made him a sceptic. Even his own mother was determined that he seek out the acceptable position of the ministry at the church college. His years with the "Angry Young Men" had given him a further sense of scepticism. Interestingly enough though, before he died, John Laurie had become a registered Anglican lay minister who spoke in Indian churches. But that was far from his thoughts now.

The Indian agent had shown John Laurie his only and well-worn copy of the Indian Act. He said, "It's all here, what I have to do and what the Indians have to do." The Act to Laurie seemed like a lot of legal gibberish. Laurie asked, "Who is their member of Parliament that passed this thing?" For the first time Laurie discovered, with real shock, that the Indian of all the people in the great democracy of Canada had no vote.

The government's agent explained, "Oh, they can vote if they want to, but they are so ignorant they are afraid to. They feel safer under the Department's protection. After all, about half of them still can't read and anyway what would they do with the vote?" Laurie thought, shades of Socrates, what couldn't they do with a vote? However, he learned with even greater shock when he tried to talk to father Hunter about it, that not only would his father not talk about it, but Laurie found his father looking at him with guarded suspicion in his eyes, a look that Laurie hadn't seen since he had first proposed giving violin lessons to Eddie. Indians had come to distrust any offers of gifts from white men as they, only too often, were the bait in a trap.

I recall Norman Luxton once said, "The idea of Indians voting is ridiculous. What they need is food. However, if he wanted legal advice, Laurie should go and see his brother-in-law, George Ross." Luxton himself had never used George as a lawyer, as he had his own lawyer in Calgary, my father, M.B. Peacock, and Ross got paid for legal cases. But his brother-in-law Ross, being a politician, was in the business of talking anyway so he talked to anyone. It turned out that George Ross had more important talking to do at that moment and he referred Laurie to a younger lawyer, Manley Edwards. Manley took his given name very seriously and Laurie found him pompous, if young, but he looked at the Act and said, "Well, yes they can vote if they want to, it says so here. See, it is under enfranchisement. There are two kinds listed voluntary and involuntary. From this it would appear that the Indians had just chosen not to vote."

9: A HISTORY TEACHER STUDIES HISTORY AROUND THE CAMPFIRE

On Laurie's first visit to the fine old Indian blacksmith who fixed his horse's shoe, he began to discover the past legends of the Indian. He also started to search for it in the few existing historical books but he found nothing there except the fighting between Hurons and Iroquois, the martyrdom of early Jesuit priests, the Riel rebellion and the treaties.

In 1864, a Peigan Indian named Four Bears predicted that future generations of Indians would live in padlocked boxes (which would be our houses) and travel around in black bugs (which would be our cars).

Laurie had majored in history in his first years at college. Continuing this pattern, native stories became his new study. Every night he sat up late with the male Indians around a glowing campfire and listened to the soft voices of the storyteller's tales of long ago wars and great hunts. The only barrier to his complete happiness was language: theirs was totally unknown to him and his little-known to many of them. To correct that, he carried around a pocket-size notebook and wrote down the translation of every unknown Indian word he heard. He was creating a pocket dictionary of the Indian language and before his death he prepared one for Calgary's Glenbow Museum, a full-size dictionary of the Stoney's language that is still filed there.

Language is so vital. Without it there can be no understanding of either hate or love. Often other visiting Indians faced a worse barrier than he, because their tribes spoke still a different language, neither Stoney nor English. They were from reserves where the only teachers had been devoted Catholic priests, who taught the Indians French only. Laurie as a historian understood that.

From the beginning, out of courtesy, John Laurie learned the language his new family spoke, just as they were mastering his. Indian languages all have a guttural pronunciation, which is difficult to acquire. He watched their lips and within a year he had practically mastered it. He also learned that the last syllable of their words was usually silent. Years later when working in Eric Harvie's Glenbow Museum, Laurie traced the roots of their language, by communicating with an American linguist near the Atlantic seaboard.

In Northern Alberta there were small tribes and a large one who spoke a similar language, so possibly that was the source of their first route to the prairies. Their own description of a word they then used for prairies translates to 'place without trees' so at one point in their distant past existence, they too experienced a phenomenal first sighting of the flat prairie land. Natives had once been great explorers who prepared from memory known routes for the new white traders and homesteaders who would follow later on.

Probably the Stoney Indian that Laurie most respected was the medicine man George MacLean. His broad face was different from that of other Stoney. They believed he was a Cree and had been exiled as a baby with his mother, and brought to the Stoney reserve. He was the last true native medicine man living in my time and was my great friend. He wore not a plumed headdress, but always one made of a buffalo head with horns on it which he wore when leading the Calgary Stampede Parade Indian section, where his appearance always met with resounding cheers from parade watchers. He never acknowledged the cheers and held his head high.

A native medicine man occupied a unique position, chosen like the earlier chiefs by mutual acceptance of the tribe. He was a combination of a today's medical doctor, psychologist and pharmacist. He had a vast knowledge of curing herbs. As a psychologist he was able to analyze and help troubled persons and became a trustworthy confidant. He healed using elements of hope and faith to encourage patients to help cure themselves.

I heard about an incident in John Laurie's life after his first severe heart attack when he was confined to the Calgary General Hospital. One evening just at the hospital's closing time, four Stoney Indians dressed in full Indian regalia including medicine rattles, sneaked quietly into the hospital. They went up the back stairs to Laurie's room and once in, propped a chair under the door barring the entrance. There, they stayed all night gently beating their drums and singing a soft soothing chant.

The nurses, on finding a locked door and hearing the chanting, in desperation phoned the hospital's administration head, Dr. Johnson, before calling the police. Dr. Johnson was Unitarian in his religious beliefs. His own church in Edmonton was under the direction of Mrs. Reta Rowan, wife of the head of the zoology department at the University of Alberta, so he had a special interest in this patient, John Laurie.

Through the locked hospital door he asked Laurie if he was all right, and did he want the Indians to stay. On the affirmative he wisely gave instructions to carefully watch the room, but not to interrupt the Indian's healing ritual. The natives stayed all night with their white friend and stole away in the morning. In two days Laurie was well enough to leave the hospital and he was moved to the home of the Sarcee chief David Crowchild and his wife Daisy Crowchild. They cared for him until he was well enough to return to teaching.

In his own writings Laurie speaks of his life being saved. He also noted that George McLean had what seemed to be an extremely hot black stone he placed on his bare chest. There was the smoke of sweet grass and the soft chanting of the drums. During the same time we non-Indians had begun to research the application of heat as a possible medical procedure for cardiology cases.

From his Stoney family's storyteller, Laurie learned how the Indians remembered their very first contact with a white man, the Protestant missionary Reverend Rundle, an amazing man who fortunately kept a diary. Between him and the Indians there had been no conflict at all. They had welcomed him and served willingly as his guides. He in turn admired them and even learned some of their language. He was as much an explorer as a missionary and he counted the number of people and tepees and even ventured into the Rockies with the Indians guiding him. Today the biggest mountain in Banff, Mount Rundle, is named after him.[1]

John Laurie, the listener, was much interested in storytelling. On sunny days Laurie would join the Indian children who gathered around his Indian mother's feet to be told their own fairytale-like legends. Soon, Laurie was recording these tales in a small notebook of his own. He was fascinated by these stories that reminded him of our own fairy tales and even Greek legends.

Laurie also came to understand the Indian burial ritual. In early years the Plains Indians had buried their people wrapped and placed high in the trees to save them from predatory animals. Far south in the American desert, we know that earlier Indians had a method of mummifying bodies by wrapping their hands around their knees and sitting them upright in the air and sun, but this was only suitable to areas of that dry climate. All natives believed in an afterlife, so they preserved the body clothed.

John Laurie's new viewpoint made him appreciate his new knowledge that native people had not only preserved this wonderful land for us to inherit, but they had influenced our culture by giving to us the names we would call it. For example, we call our beloved warm winter wind the Chinook. But we robbed the Indian culture by taking away their own names and giving them new names: i.e., Peter Moose Killer became Peter Wesley after an English religious leader.

Laurie learned about the winter count. Natives had a way of keeping a historical record of their past. They counted years by winters called the winter count. The earliest Blackfoot Nation's day count that had survived began in 1764 and lasted to 1924. Laurie found that five individuals kept records during that time. This is also told in the diary of Reverend Haynes who in 1912 saw an original count kept by Bull Plume, the last keeper of an Indian winter count.[2]

Laurie soon learned that the natives had a wonderful sense of humour – it was their first relief from the failures of their small reserves. Laurie realized that past centuries of training in endurance now enabled natives to apply the cure of "humour" to their lives. Even until this day natives have a distinct and marvellous sense of humour.

The Department of Indian Affairs drove personal bravery out of the Indians. Bravery was the most-admired quality that an individual Indian could have. Natives had held bravery high. These people whose theory of fearlessness had enabled them for centuries to resist the assault of a cold and destructive climate were able to successfully hunt dangerous animals that were bigger than them without weapons. But in Laurie's opinion, the Department brainwashed the Indian into believing that he lacked ability and drove out their instinctive fearlessness.

On the Hobbema reserve, the great priest Father Latour once told me about seeing a small Indian girl during her play hours sitting all alone in one corner of the playground. Being kindly, Father Latour picked her up and asked why she was not playing with the other children. She replied that they were playing 'Cowboys and Indians' and they wanted her to play an Indian. She was now afraid because according to the traditional rules of the game that meant that she would have to be killed. We had driven bravery, his most priceless possession, out of the Indian.

Laurie also studied herbs. An early trader's wife had met an Indian woman with a scarred breast who told her that she once had lumps there, but her medicine man had treated her and they went away. I asked the Indians if they had any past records of herbs for the galloping killer, cancer. When I was only seven years old, an Ontario nurse by the name of Rene Caisse had an Ojibwan Indian patient with healed scars on her breast who told her it was the Ojibwa medicine man that had given her a herb and the lumps had gone away. The nurse Rene Caisse was so impressed that she followed it up by writing the recipe down and took it to Banting and Best's laboratory to study it with Dr. Brusch. There, she was threatened with prison by the physicians in the area.[3] Today it is, if still unproven, a hope for the possible cure.

Much later Laurie and I together came to realize, although our historians and government people regarded our Canadian natives as small isolated ignorant tribes, that they were in reality villagers or separated areas of people who had occupied and shared for 6,000 years a continent and common culture. Like all of Europe, they too had divided countries and separate villages. This made it easier for the Europeans to conquer the small native tribes, one at a time, in Canada.

All across Canada natives had similar dances. In my younger years, I had watched a dance in far off Mexico City. I shivered because as they shook the bells and twirled their hoops I knew what the next movement to the drum music would be. I had seen it on a reserve, 2,000 miles north on a winter night in far off Alberta. The storyteller's plays were word-perfect songs memorized and carefully re-taught. They must be accurate and perfect. One man's music had a perfect beat. He played it with hands moving so swiftly they were like bird's wings in flight. The first native artists made giant pictures of a vision in the sand, as though seen by God in heaven looking down on the earth. On the American desert there were still pictures using different coloured sand that took hours of searching to find.

Laurie enjoyed the pictures of the great Indian art and buildings that the Indian once erected in a warmer climate where there was a full year of activity, not the three-month short summer of the Northwest.

Their designs on tepees and garments were individual and the artist drew them to suit the person. Even in my time when the Stoney gave me a fine buckskin beaded jacket, Leah Simeon, its maker asked me, "What is your flower," and was shocked when I said I had none. So she said, "I will give you one," and she beaded onto my jacket a symbolized design of the wild tiger lily which, strangely enough, even though I hadn't told her, was already my favourite flower.

10: A HISTORY TEACHER STUDIES HISTORY IN BOOKS

As a history major and teacher, Laurie had learned that history's changes were facilitated by individual great leaders. Laurie would never have believed that he too in his time would become an individual who by himself would make a change in his own country's history. How native people came to this continent is still being studied. Laurie and I always just accepted America's most popular newspaper columnist and movie star Will Rogers' version. When a very dignified American woman had said to him, "My people came on the Mayflower, when did your ancestors arrive here?" Rogers, who had some Indian blood in him which he had never been ashamed to admit to, replied, "My ancestors didn't come over on the Mayflower, but they met the boat." They are clearly our first people.[1]

A native once said, "Without a history we are like a field of grass that a great wind has blown over leaving no trace of its path." But natives had not found the way to write it out, to contain it, to preserve it in writing that would reach beyond their land.

When Laurie looked for the history of his new native family in our history books, he found there was little mention of the native people. His historical searches had found the creation of the still-persistent erroneous beliefs about the Indians.

The published fact was that two Spanish explorers, viewing the Indians on the seashore, had condemned them as naked heathens and savages. The Europeans showed this in their drawings, depicting them as ugly savages, some without faces. They were still perpetuating Columbus's 400-year old error in calling them Indians, believing that he had reached Asia's India.

Secondly, they described them as pagans, worshipping man-made idols. Yet, there was no record of any such native statues in Canada at all. In fact, it was the Europeans who brought with them statues of Mary and Christ.

More propaganda than fact, scalping had been the Indians' method of registering a win at war and creating a visible transportable medal for the victor to wear. Compared to past European torture that is still on display

63

in the Tower of London, Indian scalping was milder. Hair was a removable and portable piece of evidence of a victory before they learned to use the much swifter and crueller steel knives, and it was the Europeans that brought them to the American Indians. In fact, the victim could and did often survive. That the Indians used hair as a visible mark of the death of an enemy's surrender by conquest at war, led to the dread of a scalping Indian. The earliest record of human scalping is credited, not to the natives of North America, but rather to the Scythians of Southern Russia over 2,000 years ago. Scalping, Laurie discovered, was introduced to the American natives by the Dutch, who encouraged scalping by offering a bounty for each scalp turned over to them by the native warriors as evidence of their assistance to them. They used these scalps to calculate their payment and perpetuated the propaganda of fear. Scalping became a routine part of a European warrior's duties in the new world.

Europeans had been more fascinated by how natives had originally got to the new-found world than how they themselves had got to Europe. Alex Calhoun's Calgary library already had dozens of books on this. What divergent theories they had! The archaeologists of Laurie's time did allow that they must have come from Northern Asia, crossing that very narrow body of water, the Bering Straits, where today's Alaska points a finger of land to Asia's Siberia.

The history teacher Laurie read how Europeans, the people of the shores of the Mediterranean, had brought their long madness of cruel kings and burning at the stakes, and imposed it on the native people. Laurie traced their oppression of America's natives and the hardships it brought, and also how the native people had survived it all.

Laurie also studied what had happened to his native friends when they no longer dealt with a remote England but with a government elected by those pale and hairy faces in Canada. It began with Confederation in 1867. What had led up to that and what part had the Indians played in that? Their aid added to the wealth of the trading companies and the medical assistance they gave in the War of 1812 saved Canada from being conquered by the U.S.A. These were their connections to history with the first invading Europeans now resident in their country and who now outnumbered them a thousand times.

When Laurie studied the history of the time of Confederation, all the government was concerned about was 'could it be done?' Could French-speaking Catholic Quebec and the long-alienated and isolated three Maritime provinces as well as Ontario possibly unite and somehow act together? The problem was immense. After all, Ireland and England had never quite happily solved a similar problem. Unfortunately, the men assigned to solve

Canada's problem were totally unprepared. Most had just graduated from being small-town politicians who only had to make sure the beer got to the pre-election picnic. The majority had never even seen most of the country they now found themselves governing, except on a map.

Canada inherited all this as well as England's past policy toward the native people: keep them isolated and under easy but firm control, run their affairs not by the government, but by civil servants responsible to whatever elected government was in power. Canada also inherited the unfulfilled promises England had made, but not paid out, to gain easy conquest of Canada's natives, such as those in the Royal Proclamation of 1763.

England now traded off running and paying for control of the colony of Canada and gained instead strong alliances in a 'commonwealth of nations,' in contrast to a Crown-owned empire.

The newly confederated Canada had never run a country, let alone native affairs. But now suddenly a bunch of local politicians were given a giant country to govern as well as control over the lives of our native people.

Our father of Confederation and first prime minister, Sir John A. Macdonald, faced the difficult task of uniting Ontario and Quebec, the two large provincial bodies that had come from conflicting races. The people spoke different languages and had different religions. The Indians could not speak English or French, but had dozens of languages from their own tribes. In Europe, the French and English had fought one another in more or less continuous warfare during the so-called Hundred Years War that had, in reality, lasted 114 years. The Catholic and Protestant religions had been opposing one another for over a longer period, and both sides had been trading and exploiting the Indians. The English had been closer to our first people and the Iroquois of Quebec had usually chosen to fight with the British, both against the French and the Americans. Macdonald, with his immense charm and good intentions, was able to bring the two races, French and English, together in the new country of Canada, but had to leave out the Indians. The French were not prepared to include the Indians who from the time of Champlain had been fighting one another. The Indian people were completely left out of our constitution as participants, and were left as they had been during the empire building and colonizing periods under the direction and rule of bureaucrats. The Indians were given no power and had to rely on bureaucratic reports to government.

The empire was gone, but the highhanded system of controlling the Indians remained. For simplicity's sake, the new Canadian government left the Indians vote-less and on reserves where they were controlled by the Department of Indian Affairs. It was a case of moving bureaucratic control from London to Ottawa.

Victoria was Queen of Canada and she brought with her the hypocrisy of her age. The type of rule that prevailed was based on domination of the natives and strangely accompanying this was the hypocrisy that Victoria's government itself developed. There was the Englishman's great need for justification of empire and, if necessary, reasons had to be made up and created. In the case of Canada's native people, the justification was that they were hopeless and desperately needed the aid of the English, and so control and exploitation was justified.[2]

The Canadian government that was created in 1867 continued this hypocrisy. Laurie, as an 'angry young man' could not accept this. Mackenzie King, the prime minister, was able to lead even the best Canadians to believe it. All the good conquerors had to pray in the church and be knighted at the same time as they pushed down the Indians. They had titles to cover over the blight of the smothered Indians.

This hypocrisy created the secrecy that made it impossible for me to get government records about the natives, yet the government was going to convict some native people based on information in those records. Hidden in those government records were the records I would need of promises made and broken.

Canada became a country during this period of hypocrisy, resulting in what was most important to John Laurie: natives locked on their own land. The hypocrisy was minimized here. Non-natives had equally usurped their land as squatters and then legally imprisoned the natives for their own protection. The result was that native people had a fraction of what they had owned for centuries.

I remember in my adored grandmother's house a large steel engraving of a surprisingly slim Queen Victoria, backed by her entire governing cabinet. Kneeling in front of her was a half-naked Indian in a fine dark feathered costume. The Queen is quite solemnly handing him a copy of the Bible and saying, "This is the secret of England's greatness." There is no mention at all of all those armed warships or crack regiments. The Canadian Indian, however, as they well knew, had received better treatment at treaty time than his American counterpart. America herself had revolted from England's colonial status for less taxation and more freedom, but the government would later fight a long and terrible war. One of the issues in dispute was the freedom of the dark-skinned slaves they had imported to their country. Freedom is viewed sometimes as only a self-desire, not a necessity for others. Canada admitted Indians to English democracy, but not to equally share it, and it never had anything to do with us reading our Bibles.

At treaty time, the ~~Indians~~ were first exposed to bureaucratic rule. Bureaucracy had been a long-time policy of England's but not used in

English Canada extensively until Canada itself became a country. Canada's national anthem includes the words, 'the true North strong and free,' but not even uncrossing their fingers as they sang it, they whispered to themselves, "Well, except for the Indians."

Canada actually owns one-third of the entire world's land and a large portion of its inland water. Possibly that's an overwhelming responsibility. We have only been attacked by a foreign enemy – by our big friendly neighbour to the south, the U.S.A., especially during the war of 1812. It was a war we didn't know had begun at the time, and we didn't even know when it ended. We were indifferent to our own country's independence. We almost took for granted what we had, and so when it came as an unwanted gift we took it with almost total indifference to who governed us. That may be peaceful, or just sluggish. This indifference toward our fate, to our own destiny, made it easy for Canadians to be unconcerned also for the sad fate of the native people in our midst.

For twenty-seven years we were governed by Mackenzie King: five in opposition, twenty-two as prime minister. On his death, F. R. Scott wrote, "Truly he will be remembered, whenever men honour ingenuity, ambiguity, inactivity and political longevity." Mackenzie King would even say of himself, "It was probably more important what I didn't do than what I did do."

He was prime minister from 1921–1948, except for 1930–1935 – a long period of influence. Some people reached middle age knowing no other politician. During this long, successful political career he led a hypocritical private life. This kind of leadership inevitably led to ignoring any hypocrisy in government and its civil servants and had a profound effect on what the public got to hear about the true conditions of the Indians. The general public knew nothing about them. No wonder Laurie faced such strange views on the streets of Calgary.

In my time, the Liberal MP, Mr. John (Jack) Whitney Pickersgill was supervisor of the native people on all Canadian reserves. His last ditch effort to drive treaty Indians off their promised small reserves that they had so ungraciously been locked into resulted in the Hobbema trial. Mackenzie King also allowed that director of Indian destiny, Duncan Campbell Scott, to hold down for an equally long period a fine native people. These were men who understood one another's motives and were not shocked by them at all.[3]

Pickersgill had a brilliant academic record. Raised in Manitoba, he won a Rhodes scholarship from their university and even held a professorship until he moved to a larger, more lucrative field, which he did through his personal closeness to Mackenzie King.[4] How had he achieved this? I can only make a guess. He published several key books on the Liberal party and on Mackenzie King.[5]

I can imagine that that strange and lonely man was flattered by the attention of an attractive young man as he told him of his views. Mackenzie King, we did not realize until after his death, was a lonely man, and a man of secret vices. In photographs, he looked like the popular plastic cast of celluloid kewpie doll with his round tummy and his spare hair pulled over his almost bare head. King never smoked, he never drank, and he attended church twice every Sunday. He never married or had a lurid private sex affair.

Only after his death when he allowed his strange diaries to be read did we discover the true nature of this man. He had been obsessed with his mother after her death. He secretly kept candles and flowers before her picture. He built a garden to her memory. He admitted, this church-goer, that he prowled the streets alone at night in search of prostitutes and he totally believed in the readings of a psychic he secretly visited. Such was the hypocrisy that grew from Victoria's reign.[6]

It became Laurie's job to tear back this curtain of hypocrisy and reveal to all Canadians the sad plight they were allowing to be administered to their native people. Canadians are such nice people, which was why we suddenly got so many people behind us.

With the advent of Confederation in 1867, the Canadian government passed a special Act, the Indian Act, which dealt exclusively with Indians. No other Act in Canada separates out one racial group from other Canadians. By this Act the Indians became legal wards of the Department of Indian Affairs and, as such, they had no control over their own land, or money from the sale of their land. Their land and money was held in trust by the Department of Indian Affairs. The tribes had no legal right to demand money and the Indians could not access their money unless they first obtained consent from the Department.

Indians could not buy more land if they needed it, nor could they buy seed for crops or farm machinery, unless the Department allowed them to do so. Almost universally, Indian requests to improve their lot were denied by the Department of Indian Affairs. This was especially hard on a progressive individual who rarely, if ever, could obtain consent from the Department. All attempts at becoming self-supporting were discouraged rather than encouraged. Meanwhile in Ottawa the Department of Indian Affairs grew in size and wielded control over larger and larger sums of Indian money, while on the reserves the Indians were forced to live in idle semi-starvation.

From the moment that the government got their hands on the land that the Indians originally occupied, by paying them with a small fraction of that land which we call reserves, and promising that it would be theirs forever, the Department began to invent systematic legal avenues to break that promise and take back the land.

The Department tried to steal back reserve lands in five ways:

1. Direct sale of reserve land – the government gave land then bought it back for next to nothing, and then resold it for a large profit. In 1844, a New Brunswick law allowed the sale of Indian lands.
2. Allotment – the government attempted to sell several individual pieces of land in the middle of a reserve. A bill was proposed in 1857 in Toronto by John A. Macdonald to eliminate Indian reserves. The bill was called the "New Living Civilization Bill." In that bill a debt-free Indian who proved to be responsible for three or four years could apply to become a citizen and take his land out of the reserve if he agreed to relinquish his rights as an Indian. William Lyon Mackenzie King fought this bill on the grounds that its sole aim was to take land from native people.
3. Scrip – issuance of scrip land following the Riel rebellion.[7]
4. Expropriation – a further method of taking back reserve lands arose when Frank Oliver, a Liberal, placed in the Act a section which allowed the government to acquire by expropriation or forced sale of any reserve land that was close to a town whose population was greater than 8,000. This was undoubtedly put there to expropriate reserves in the wealthy mineral area of Sudbury, but would also have affected the Sarcee tribe reserve near Calgary in Southern Alberta. Frank Oliver publicly said, "Indian rights must be abolished. The object of the Department is to continue until not a single Indian in Canada has not been absorbed into the body politic and there is no Indian question and no Department of Indian Affairs."
5. Enfranchisement → A) compulsory B) voluntary.

This system by which the government of Canada, under the advice and direction of the Department of Indian Affairs headed by Duncan Campbell Scott, added to the Indian Act a section called "Compulsory and Voluntary Enfranchisement." The first Indian Act was said to promote assimilation. A sober industrious Indian could apply to give up his rights as an Indian in return for British citizenship and the right to vote, which no white person in Canada ever had to do. Western Canadian Indians were excluded from this provision as the government at the time considered them too uncivilized to be included in Canada. At the time, land in Eastern Canada was much more valuable than land in Western Canada. Today, the Department is still at it: they judicially delay Indian land claims. It is estimated that there are over 6,000 outstanding claims which will take many long and expensive court battles, and means that a whole generation of young Indians will grow up without the necessary land and its income that was promised to them over a century ago.

The reserve system was established 13 April 1830, before Confederation, by the British in Upper Canada, on the first transfer from England of the parts of Canada, Upper (Ontario) and Lower (Quebec).

Our Fathers of Confederation, as they were called, could have been more honestly labelled "Fathers of Confrontation and Confusion." That's what it all amounted to. Nor did they ever get compared to the U.S. who wrote a constitution accepted by their majority of citizens. Canada wrote its constitution 90 years after the Americans got their constitution, and was still happily entwined in Mother England's apron strings even though England had no real desire to take further care of their overseas child.

Canada, with no constitution and no vote on it by its people, began to try and run a country. In 1982, this country finally got its own constitution and that was not by election, but by Pierre Elliott Trudeau who designed it himself and prevented Parliament discussing it by threat of closure. He got it passed with a majority from only one political party who hadn't even been elected to pass a constitution.

One thing was clear, Quebec did not want the Indians to be included so they were left out completely of our government and continued under the empire-building system of their givers, the "trusted" politicians and their bureaucrats.

The only reason that the Canadian Indians were placed on reserves was so the Canadian Parliament could assure the Canadian Pacific Railway (CPR) that they had a title clear of Indian claims that had been clearly established in the Royal Proclamation of 1763. For this, the government needed a legal surrender of the land the CPR was expecting to receive free along the route. You will find no mention of this in any parliamentary report. However, Laurie, with his historical knowledge of dates of the treaties and the final payment to the CPR, was aware of what had taken place.

Strangely enough, proof of that land grab from the Indians is revealed by the actual dates of the rail routes and the dates of when and where Indian tribes were persuaded to surrender their legal claim and sign onto a tiny piece of land, a reserve. In your imagination, if you look at a map of today's vanishing railway tracks you can trace the original route the CPR officials were contemplating for their railroad. It wasn't the reserve lands themselves that were so important to the CPR. What was exciting to them was to obtain a free grant of a large part of currently unoccupied Western Canada's Crown lands that only the eastern Canadian government could give them with a good title to as part of the payment. They were paying to build a railroad that would belong not to the taxpayer, but to the CPR. The Eastern Canada government didn't wish to fight the Indians over a vague promise about their land that had been made to them by the British government previous to Confederation. The Canadian government wanted to guarantee the CPR payment for signing the contract to build the railway from Eastern Canada to the Pacific Ocean, land that the railway would then own.

Today, you can check out for yourself, just as Laurie did, the systematic signing of treaty Indians onto reserves by following the main route of the CPR. The dates and areas reveal and exactly conform and confirm the accuracy's of Laurie's studies. Laurie and I often discussed this.

It began in Ottawa with Canada's first national government. The fact that the railway would take the difficult and expensive route up into the area of the Laurentian Plateau seems strange rather than taking the shorter easier more southern route. But there was economic gain for the CPR in this too. Laying the tracks in that almost unpopulated area would be slow, difficult and expensive. However, the secret that the Canadian Shield covered a great mineral wealth was beginning to leak out to prospectors with claims in the area and was in our time revealed in the vast wealth that caused Sudbury, Ontario, to become a world-known location. The excuse that Prime Minister Macdonald made to Parliament was that it was essential that the railroad be remote from the American border. After all, the War of 1812 when the Americans attacked Canada was still fresh in everyone's mind. So, Macdonald was able to convince Parliament and the voting eastern public that the northern route was most desirable.

The cost of the CPR was entirely born by the government of Canada as was the cost of the surrender of free land and vast quantities of free Crown land still available in the Northwest Territories (NWT). The NWT were not yet part of Confederation and the taxpayer paid for land which was just handed over to the CPR. It was an unbearable financial burden on a small, new country that consisted of two Maritime provinces, Quebec and Ontario and had no money yet in its budget.

This financial burden started the Canadian taxpayer on his long march to increasing yearly deficits with high interest rates that soon reached the point where there would be no escape from debt forever. If the building of the CPR, the longest railway in the entire world, put a burden on the Canadian people, it placed a tragic burden on the native people of Canada by locking them onto small unprofitable reserves, small pieces of land they had a legal claim to, and placing them under the complete control of the federal government in Ottawa through the bureaucrats in the Department of Indian Affairs.

The Indian people, with no writing or reading in the English language, had no concept at all of the ancient English common law rights to property, be it 'my castle is mine' or 'my home is my castle.' Their idea of property rights was that the land belonged to nature and whoever was on it had the right to live and hunt there. Their idea was a sort of 'territorial rights' that bird watchers observe birds enforcing today. Legal title to land was totally alien and incomprehensible to the Indians. They were concerned with where they pitched their tepees and where they could hunt.

The fact that their rights had long ago been preserved by the British for them in treaties made in Europe and often as the result of wars fought in Europe was unknown to them. The government's guardians of laws were another civil service group, the Department of Justice, and because the Indians had never been accepted as equal citizens, that department felt no special responsibility to deal with their affairs at all.

However, this vast new country that became a reality as a separate entity at the time of Confederation inherited legal obligations to the Indians which were ignored. After all, they had too many other vital, vast and impossible problems to solve. The new country was a vast area to be governed politically and protected by armies with the smallest population per area in the world to pay for. The Indian problem could wait until it became serious.

11: A RED MÉTIS MEETS A WHITE MÉTIS

Until the arrival of the pale face immigrants, the Indian had no real need to organize in large units. For economic reasons they had wisely divided themselves into family or tribe units so they could live in economically sound and peaceful units. However, as a result, there evolved different languages and customs. Unity between them was unnecessary nor was rebellion or uprising a necessity. There had evolved a patriarchal hereditary chief system. Their custom was not to oust an unsatisfactory chief but simply to desert him and move away. Coventry of isolation by silence was their punishment for anyone who committed a crime against the tribe. There was no need for freedom fighters among Indians.

Surprisingly, the persons who would assist the Indians in organizing tribes of many languages into effective united groups so that they could resist the repressive dictatorship of a bureaucratic Department came first from persons who were experienced in organizing united resistance – the non-Indians. The Indians themselves were deeply aware of how they were being hurt. But the manner of solving it was alien to all their previous experiences.

In Eastern Canada there was a group known as the Six Nations of the Iroquois and in Western Canada a group calling themselves the Blackfoot Nation. Strangely enough, both groups' unity was reduced when the American revolution set the boundary between Canada and the U.S.A. and artificially divided these two groups' unity with a man-made border. The non-native outsiders who came to help the Indians organize were themselves unique persons. In Eastern Canada, to assist the Six Nations, came first from the American side a man who called himself Chief Niagara. Later came Frederick O. Loft and then from Alberta a Métis of English descent Malcolm Norris and, last of all, the Calgary schoolteacher John Laurie.[1]

The bureaucratic Department that was created to govern the Indians had one fixed rule: divide and conquer. So, from the beginning, they resisted violently any attempts of Indians to organize into effective groups for their betterment.

Probably the first Canadian organized inter-tribal Indians were the council of tribes established by Chief Thunderwater who also had the delightful name of Oghema Niagara. He came from across the border and had chosen a good name as Niagara Falls is still a well-known border crossing. He visited the Six Nations reserve and created his council in November 1914. When he held a rally on the St. Regis reserve, one that spanned the border, the chief agreed to investigate the Canadian complaints against the Department even to the courts of the land. He wrote the Canadian director Duncan Campbell Scott, Deputy Superintendent of Indian Affairs, to that effect. Scott didn't even answer him. Instead, he wrote the American Bureau of Indian Affairs and said that Chief Niagara was probably an impostor and possibly indulging in fraudulent activities. By 1919, Thunderwater had behind him over half the reserves at Caughnawaga and they made headway in Quebec and Ontario. So, in 1916, Scott tried to get immigration authorities to bar him from entering Canada. But the Department of Immigration refused.

In 1917, the *Ottawa Citizen* newspaper reported that the chief was in Ottawa to report to the Department of Indian Affairs on his association and they had refused to see him. The chief said he would seek incorporation and then force the Department to listen to the Indians. On April 3rd, a private bill did appear in Parliament signed by 176 Indians. Scott was furious. He wrote to Arthur Meighen, Superintendent-general of Indian Affairs from October 1917 to July 1920, saying that the chief was supported only by shiftless Indians and his Department was considering prosecuting him as "obtaining money by false pretences as he had collected hundreds of dollars in membership fees from the Indians." Alarmed, Meighen and Prime Minister Borden advised the withdrawal of the private bill and it was done away with.

The chief had been accused by a Canadian Indian of abusing her son whom she had given to Thunderwater to adopt and raise. And so Scott tried to get Immigration to act again. But again they refused. Scott then used this doubtful testimony. In 1927 in Louisville, Kentucky, on a request from an American newspaper, Scott maintained from Canada that Niagara was probably an impostor and most likely a black. A newspaper ran an exposé claiming he was a negro and bald. Chief Niagara sued the newspaper and summoned Scott to appear in the U.S. Court. Scott did not appear but sent a representative. The Court refused to convict despite Duncan Campbell Scott's exhaustive efforts.

Years after Chief Niagara left Canada, a man calling himself Chief Niagara held a meeting in far off Cleveland, Ohio, pleading for the Indians' need to organize and get more justice. One newspaper supported him. Their rival newspaper ran an exposé of the "so-called chief." They claimed to have hired a Pinkerton man and they produced a not too clear photograph of him. No one will ever know if poor Chief Niagara was an impostor or not.[2] Threatened and followed by Pinkerton men, disgraced in newspapers, he evidently gave up. But the Indians still dreamed of organizations for strength in their demands for just treatment.

When John Laurie was first visiting with his Indian friends at Morley he would hear the humming of the moccasin telegraph. It was full of concern. At Hobbema in the Cree territories and in the far north, Indians were being driven out of their land, promised to them for "as long as the sun shines and the river flows over land." Fear flared as they had so little of their homes, and their country that had been promised them. The poor frighten easily as they have so little. Further loss seemed impossible to face. Laurie would have to study this new threat: forced enfranchisement.

Laurie had always been intrigued by the story of a Mohawk, Frederick O. Loft.[3] Loft had seemed to him like a "shooting star," the one who had held the first great meeting of Indians and Métis in Alberta at the Cree's Hobbema reserve and then vanished. He first heard the name Loft when he had been researching the department of bureaucrats' role in bringing about the poverty of his adopted Indians. He had only really considered how the Indians had got locked by treaty onto the reserves and how the bureaucratic department in Ottawa with their special laws only for Indians had come to be, and how they ruled, suppressed, and half starved a so completely vulnerable race. I, like Laurie, was intrigued by a once great Indian leader who fought almost alone, and who had set the Indians of Canada on their route of forming associations for strength in their uneven struggle for survival.

The Indians remembered that Loft had told them they needed better health service. They did not need to be reminded of this. During this time the Indians were attacked with severe influenza and tuberculosis. With no sanitation on the reserve this had become severe.

Strangely enough, the very Indians who had come to the meetings had all received education, but the loss of small Indian children to residential schools was a contradiction to thousands of years of culture. For most Indians in that day, they could not foresee that it would lead to any jobs, but only remove their children from their homes. The care of their children had been the primary concern of every tribe. It was by their children that the strength of their tribe was maintained. Their mothers gave them exceptionally tender care.

There were no Indian women who spoke out at Loft's meetings. That would not come for another 20 years. It had been concern for their children's futures that convinced Indians to accept low treaty payments. The government stressed it would be the payments that would exist for "as long as the sun shines and the rivers flow." The hunger of their children was a worry, but was in conflict with the complete loss of their children who seemed to vanish from their sight into residential schools. It was the hope of possible strength in unity that made Loft's message so wonderful.

After the First World War, the government gave white veterans land for their service in the war. The Department of Indian Affairs made it legally impossible for Indian veterans to get the same. All Indian veterans could get was title to a piece of reserve land they already owned by treaty. The Department then deducted the payment for this land from the tribe's trust fund. So the veteran not only lost what land he had on the reserve, but also the money held for them in trust. This scam was even worse than those perpetrated by the earliest explorers who bought Manhattan Island for twenty-three dollars. The real disgrace is that this was done in 1920 by our Canadian government without the Indians realizing what was actually being done. They relied entirely on the advice given by the Department of Indian Affairs. Never was any Canadian, let alone a veteran, so ripped off by a government. However, once Loft and the League toured and revealed this matter to the public, Loft was able to stop this "blot on Canada's reputation." But the civil servants just kept thriving; no firing took place, no atonement was made.

In Alberta we can look to Loft as organizing and directing the very first Indian organizations and their attempt on their own to at least better their health. Education could provide the opportunity to grow and to now work beside the new immigrants who the government of Canada had brought onto their ancient land.

This new head of the Department, Campbell Scott, seemed to have as his life's work – stopping Loft's attempt to organize the Indian tribes of Canada, so that united they could take some effective action against the Department's domination. It was a battle between two dominant and independent personalities – the bureaucrat Scott, and the Mohawk Indian Loft. It was an uneven battle. Scott was a very bright ambitious man with an already big strong department behind him. He had influential politicians as speaking acquaintances and often friends. He had acquired, through his published poetry and his membership in the philharmonic society, a much respected image. In contrast the Mohawk, Loft, had to act almost alone. He was impoverished and began his crusade on behalf of the Indian people when he was already middle-aged without any reputation or credentials. It was an uneven battle.

F.O. Loft, a Mohawk born in 1862 on the Six Nations reserve,[4] spent most of his adult life working as a clerk in a Toronto insane asylum. In 1898, he married Affa Northcote Geary of Chicago, cousin of Lord Iddesleigh. He served in the Canadian Forestry Corps in the First World War, but because of age never saw active duty. On 20 December 1918, at the Grand Council of Ontario Indians on the Six Nations Reserve, Loft was involved in the resolution that a "League of Indians of Canada" be formed. Its first congress with delegates from as far away as Manitoba and Saskatchewan, held near Sault Ste. Marie on 24 September 1919, elected Loft as president.

After his spies discovered that Loft had held the first Indian meeting, Scott decided to strike back. The use of Indian band funds was denied. He figured that most Indians with no jobs and treaty payments of five dollars per year had no funds except those in trust. Loft's funds could be stopped. He immediately cut off access to the trust funds. Loft circulated a letter suggesting the Indians contribute five cents each to join the League, and five dollars for each band, so membership was possible for all Indians. Loft then planned a meeting in Elphinstone, Manitoba, on 20 June 1920. The agents reported his request to Duncan Campbell Scott, and it was denied. Scott advised Regina Indian Commissioner W. H. Graham to curb Loft's activities. Also soon after Bill 14 permitting enfranchisement became law.

The compulsory enfranchisement section in Bill 14 was dreamed up by Duncan Campbell Scott to get rid of Loft. Loft wrote a letter to that effect to Major Gordon J. Smith, Indian Superintendent at Brantford dated 8 October 1920. Loft again felt threatened in 1921 that he might be enfranchised and he wrote to Sir James Lougheed, Minister of the Interior from Calgary, Alberta, protesting this. But Scott replied that since Loft is not a ward and because he is so able then he should be enfranchised. Scott tried to discredit Loft as best he could. "He is shallow and talkative and he is endeavouring to live off his fellow Indians by collecting fees for organization." Scott added that Loft had no real active service in the war. In truth, Loft's education was equal to Scott's and Scott knew Loft was 55 years old and so was barred from active combat service because of his age. Scott himself hadn't even volunteered.

Early in 1921, Loft learned he was to be enfranchised; however that failed when Meighen's Conservative government fell in 1921. But Loft persisted, and a meeting of Alberta Indians was planned for the Samson reserve on 21 June 1922. Scott sent a patrol of RCMP to monitor. Fifteen hundred Alberta Indians attended – Blackfoot, Blood, Piegan, Stoney, and Cree. Late in July 1922 Loft addressed the Regina Rotarians. Favourable press again was received. However, the League declined while Loft was absent in the U.S. due to his wife's illness. He was scheduled to speak to Indians at Saddle Lake in July 1931 but did not appear. He died a few years later.

Loft's activities caused a fright. The Winnipeg strike of 1919 had caused suspicion of many meetings. Under the Criminal Code, section 98, attendance at meetings of this kind could be considered revolutionary.

His lifetime achievements were considerable and a western branch of the League continued, but even though it split into Alberta and Saskatchewan groups, it was the foundation upon which future Indian organizations in the West were built. I would be at meetings similar to those he held in Alberta with no funds and pursued by fierce attempts to arrest him. It was these meetings that eventually lead to the Indian getting the vote in his own country.

The Department of Indian Affairs felt free to communicate with the other government bureaucracies such as Justice and the RCMP whose main offices were in Ottawa, thus creating a solid and confidential partnership that reinforced each other's activities. This partnership was never abandoned after Scott's retirement as Laurie and I would later find out much to our chagrin when we were nearly arrested. As the Deputy Minister of Indian Affairs, Scott had effectively thought he stopped his department from being criticized at all by any Indian unless they were prepared to go to jail. He had made his department invulnerable from any criticism from Indians or whites.

Laurie would not learn in his lifetime of the activities of the Department of Indian Affairs. He could read certain records and laws that were passed but there was no way he could exactly follow how Scott tried to persecute Frederick Loft. The story of the magnificent struggle of Loft would have been lost to today's millions of Canadian people of Indian or Métis descent except for the vigilance of concerned journalists and a group of non-Indians in Regina's Rotarian service club. It was only they who helped to hand down a written record of a piece of our Canadian history.[5]

There are also the records of John Laurie's Métis history. In these one could find and trace this almost ghost story of the founding father of all of Canada's Indian associations. What a story it was. Like all freedom fighters, he would die without being remembered or knowing how his life's struggle finally succeeded.

If the half-breed Canadian's future had been set into a strange pattern by the Riel rebellion, it also had a profound effect on John Laurie's life and even my own. Laurie would almost die and I would have my life directed for seven years. It was the question of "scrip" payments that resulted from the Riel rebellion that would have such a profound effect on the Indians of Alberta in 1940.

For Laurie, his pity for the half-breed would be intense but it had to be kept almost secret. He was so moved by the plight of the half-breed that he secretly wrote a poem about it that I found one night among his papers. A line from it reads – "Why they should have been the ones left out of everything on earlier times is not clear."

The Hudson's Bay Company had directives encouraging their factors to make what they termed "farm marriages." They felt to acquire an Indian wife strengthened the alliances between the Indian tribes and the traders, and added that sometimes the best place to learn Indian culture is in the bed. They didn't have to encourage those lonely men frozen in five-year stretches to those outposts in a wilderness. The Indian girls were so beautiful. Many of these marriages were true love marriages and today some of Canada's most honoured families know of the Indian blood that flows in their veins.

Their generous Indian families usually welcomed them back into the tribe, but one of the first among the many vicious changes the Indian Department persuaded an indifferent Parliament to add to the Act was that they didn't have to pay these women treaty moneys. It wasn't until then that their rights were at last recognized.

Probably one of the great true love stories isn't Hiawatha, although Henry Wadsworth Longfellow based that poem on the life of a great Canadian Iroquois. What history must read is that it is probably the greatest of all fur traders, David Thompson, who as an employee of the Hudson's Bay Company, chose to marry an Indian named Mary Small. By her he had 14 children, and at the end of his amazing career, when destitute on the streets of Montreal he pawned his prized quadrant, probably the greatest quadrant in our history because it accurately mapped so much of Western Canada. He pawned it so he could buy bread for Mary and those fourteen half-breed children.

The Indians themselves at the time of treaty spoke with concern of their "cousins" as they accurately called them, as they had grandfathers of the same race. The Indians realizing how small their reserves were, and though still governed by their long-time belief in "sharing among the tribe," had to limit who was included in the tribe. Morris himself, who had been commissioned to sign the Indians of both Alberta and Saskatchewan into treaty, wrote also of the half-breeds or Métis. He had specific orders from Ottawa to exclude them, but in the book he fortunately wrote personal and fine tributes to a fine people.[6]

The so-called Riel resistance and then rebellion would be some of the first history-making moves ever taken by Canada. They were a sudden pricking that awakened the long peacefully sleeping giant, Canada. It was an awakening that suggested possible dangers to come. It came at the moment when we as a country were sloughing off all of our past and stepping in to a new future with its many problems. Until then, and ever since, we have only ever decided to fight a war about our country, we have gone only to aid our allies in wars they chose to initiate, and were already fighting. Unlike all other countries even comparatively new ones like the United States, who had a revolution or fought a tough long civil war to settle their directions, we had not.

The Riel rebellion would be our first and, to date, last decisively historical movement for change. Riel's legal hanging was justified on the grounds of the death by execution of a man by the name of Scott. This had come to light a length of time after Scott had been put on trial and convicted by an unofficial Métis Court. The decision of the jury was split.

J. Peter Turner, an ex-lifelong member of Canada's worldwide-known and best-respected Royal Canadian Mounted Police force, chose to write a history of his own force.[7] Each of the two volumes is amazing. He died shortly after preserving this great piece of history based on official records, not on theory or opinion. One would have expected him to write with some bias. After all, three Mounties, while innocently and without any even apparent opposition had been shot down in tragic Indian Big Bear's murder over at Duck Lake and according to court evidence their bodies were shockingly mutilated. In the Riel rebellion itself, the Mounties had been a large part of Canada's organized military opposition to Riel. Instead, Turner is amazingly sympathetic to Riel's leadership of the mixed Indian and French forces the Mounties had been forced to fight.

He saw Riel as a young man totally confused by the failure in his attempts to act legally within a written constitution that would see a democratically elected government, a minimum of lawlessness and violence and even trials by law. He saw a young man who was driven to fanaticism and almost insanity, but not quite, and then death by the failure of what he believed. He didn't allow himself to become involved with Eastern Canada's concern with Fenian plots, Canada's possible invasion by America, the fierce conflicts of avid Toronto Protestant Orangemen, or Montreal's priests encouraging anger at the loss of the "Little Quebec on the prairie settlement at Red River, Manitoba." He did recognize the new country's government needed to pay off the Hudson's Bay's corporate traders demanded price for the western half of its country, and pay the bills of another corporate body of financiers in the railway corporation, the CPR. He did not sit in judgment of the politicians of the time whose manoeuvres were motivated partially by re-election.

What can we say about Louis Riel? He was hanged by his country's official orders. That same country's Parliament has several times debated an official pardon to whatever was left of his rotting corpse. He was born in mid-Canada on the banks of a beautiful river called the Red, in a province we would later name Manitoba. In his always slim and graceful body he would carry all the conflicting differences of Canada of today – part Indian, part French and part English blood. He would be educated in one of Canada's largest cities – Montreal.

Before the Riel rebellion, Canada had been surreptitiously under Europe's control. The London-based Hudson's Bay Company owned, operated, and had total control of the then North-West Territories. Upper Canada was Ontario, Lower Canada was French-speaking Quebec, and the eastern seaboard provinces were named the Maritimes. Canada hadn't really settled the directions their future would take and vast areas west of Ontario's western border, called the North-West Territories, represented a comparatively unknown land.

The Riel rebellion in this area would be the first dramatic event in this unknown land. What a pity there wasn't a Shakespeare here to write about it. It had all the stuff he had built his tragedies on and even enough left over for several comedies too. It was not an imaginary play on an imaginary stage. It was a very real event. It could have easily been called the "Real Rebellion" instead of just being named after the fanatic Louis Riel, whose history gave it its name. The stage it was played on was located in the fertile valley land of the Red River near a place we now call Winnipeg.

This is an area fraught with tragedy. The Red River settlement was created by Lord Selkirk who, as the biggest shareholder in the Hudson's Bay Company, had been able to buy the entire area. This early evidence shows it pays to be the biggest shareholder in a company. The idea behind his settlement was to block the progress being made by the Montreal-based North-West Company, which was rapidly taking over the trading areas totally dominated by the Hudson's Bay Company. The settlement failed with tragic consequences for the settlers; however it resulted in the first peace treaty being signed in Western Canada with the Indians known as the Selkirk Treaty.

The next settlers to the area were largely descendants of the French 'coureurs de bois,' the great riverboat men called "voyageurs" used by the trading companies who married Indian women. Catholicism became their only religion and French the predominant language. They had developed an efficient and flourishing community. Agricultural holdings were developed along individually owned narrow strips of land that gave each holding a riverfront. It had been nick-named "The Little Quebec on the Prairies." Many people who travelled west to this "new land" experienced both farming and cold weather. They had to face total crops lost to locusts, early snowstorms, and grasshopper plagues. Due to these conditions, many of these new settlers emigrated south and some returned to Europe.

If this were a play the lead character would be Louis Riel – a man fleeing back and forth between two countries, Canada and the United States. Two religions, his Catholicism and allegiance to the Indian's great spirit as well as the conflict of the blood that ran in his veins of English, French, and

Indian all pulled in constantly changing directions. If ever there was a split personality it was his and if ever there was a confused action taken without direction or meaning it was this so-called rebellion.

There was not a single strong person that could lead either side anywhere. Riel, constantly torn between his desire to be rebellious and yet law abiding, could hardly be called a stable leader. The shots from the opposition side, in the so-called battle, were being called by a government at least 2,000 miles away and that was in an age of non-existing or extremely slow communications. Leadership was vague, confusion was constant but fear was everywhere. The Indians were now afraid of their so-called white friends and the few white settlers of the area grew terrified of the fact they were surrounded by a large group of Indians who might now possibly murder them in their beds.

The underlying cause of the rebellion sprang from the rapid necessity of the newly formed country of Canada's central government to find an immediate way to pay off pressing financial debts. The second underlying cause of the rebellion was the necessity of the new country, Canada, to build a railway that would tie the vast land together. Canada's birth had been tumultuous in attempting to unite into one country the French-speaking Catholic persons, and centralized the one province, Quebec, with the other provinces, Ontario and the Maritimes. They were predominately Protestant and of English descent, and had brought with them other well-to-do descendants from other European countries. For instance many German descendants remained loyal to the British Crown because once Queen Anne of England had provided them with an escape boat to her American colonies when they faced religious persecution. This vast wave of immigrants to Canada via the United States were on the whole the wealthiest landowners in the American colonies and largely occupied professional positions who were not touched by the roughness and violence of the ordinary Americans who had fought in the revolution. For that class of persons the revolution was as it has always been – a case of the downtrodden rising up against those who are wealthier and have more control.

These immigrants had turned Ontario and the Maritimes into predominantly an English-speaking race loyal to the Crown of England. For Canada's first prime minister, the problems of bringing these two distinct races together had faced him with a Herculean task. Canada had become a country without having to put up a single blow for freedom but it was also a country totally unprepared to govern its vast new inheritance in the sparsely populated northwest. In this vast area there was no survey of land yet completed, so no land could be safely and legally transferred or sold. It had no official government, and it had no system of justice. It had no police force to enforce

Canada's laws nor an army. Worst of all it shared a long undefended border against a faster-growing, stronger, aggressive country immediately south of it, the United States.

Fortunately drunk or sober, Sir John A. Macdonald, Canada's first prime minister was a man of vision. He understood, as had Caesar, that to control a country, it was essential that you have roads; but how could a poor country quickly build roads across two thousand miles? Even Caesar had never attempted that. The quick way was on steel rails. In the United States, which had settled much earlier, many small companies had built small connecting rail lines and these had made many new American millionaires. There was a company, however, which would call itself the Canadian Pacific Railway and for a great price was prepared to start building a trans-Canadian railway. Macdonald wisely understood this. He also understood its advantages as a political policy as Eastern Canada needed Western Canada's raw materials. Eastern Canada also needed a market for its manufactured goods and it would be the only way to attract new immigrants to Canada on a vast scale.

The problem was Canada, as a new country, had no revenue and also had to pay off the Hudson's Bay Company. A wonderful solution was found. Western Canada was expendable, so both commercial companies could be paid off with Western Canadian land. As a result it has never been totally revealed but clearly the Canadian Pacific Railway got one in ten sections of land along its tracks and the Hudson Bay Company got other land. In addition to the land, both companies acquired the mineral, petroleum and gravel rights on said land. Today's great wealth of both these commercial companies is based on these promises. However, Macdonald was facing several difficulties because you cannot transfer land unless by survey its boundaries are established, so that legal title to the land can be filed and legally proven. Nor does anyone want the land unless safe occupation of it is established and it is in a friendly neighbourhood.

Therefore, it became essential to complete the deal that Western Canada be surveyed and the Indian problem of land ownership be peacefully established. It was with that purpose in mind that Western Canada's Indians were signed into treaties and locked into reserves. It would be the signing of the Indians into treaty that would cause western unrest among many isolated or omitted Indian tribes. It would be these very surveys that cut across the land in the French Métis Red River settlement that would be the underground causes of the Riel rebellion. A simple dispute was blown up into a seemingly vital fray.

12: THE DEPARTMENT AND ENFRANCHISEMENT

The Department in its Ottawa tower has no one to check on its activities except the Auditor General who frequently reported questionable expenditures but only on the financial side. The Department had developed very fine concealment tactics. This continues even lately. They were unable to give me on request the exact dates or addresses of a specific past deputy minister although they maintain expensive archives they then conceal from being used. Secrecy was a way of life with them making it sad for an Indian seeking material on his own people's background or for me, a lawyer seeking material for a lawsuit as will be seen in the Hobbema Case.

Cases of individuals who had been evicted from the reserves in the past may never be found. Evictions began in Northern Alberta where the gold rush of the Klondike began. The wealth to be gained by reducing reserves or treaty Indians to the vanishing point began among the Northern Cree.

In 1976, Indian Affairs' budget was nearly $3 billion. One must realize that that sum also supports a bureaucracy and expensive but ineffective hearings, not only direct payments to the Indians themselves. As a service to their employers, the new government of Canada, the newly found civil servants' first duty was to protect the government, only after that the Indians.

The role of the civil service is a necessary one in a democracy, if we want to be free to elect any man or woman to our legislature. The chance of him having experience in a special cabinet post governing a special needs group is indeed rare. That isn't how we elect our MPs from across the country. It's mostly based on his attractiveness and his declared commitment to a political party we are already supporting, or anger at a past party's performance. So the cabinet members and MPs need specialized advice and accounts must be kept of government departments both in and out.

At England's Cambridge University with a twinkle in their eye, they point to a college as the origin of the civil service. There, Henry VII created the first civil servants in the Western world. A rather frugal man, he was shocked that there were no records of roads he had built or were needed or even exact amounts in his treasury. He was also shocked at the high cost of running his own palace. He noted an over-supply of so-called young courtiers. On investigation they turned out to be for the most part illegitimate sons of his lords who didn't quite want to abandon their blood. They would have positions.

There seems little hope for a violent change to ensure our government's better handling of today's Indian problems. Jean Chrétien, then Minister of Indian Affairs, drew up a new 'White Paper' that caused outbreaks of protest and resentment from Indians all across Canada led by Harold Cardinal of Alberta. Lloyd Axworthy was also a past Minister of Indian Affairs and Paul Martin is the son of the late Paul Martin, whose past action as a Minister of Indian Affairs was under review for a doubtful political donation he had obtained from the Indians. It was dropped after 7 years of serious investigation. The future is not full of hope for reform. A better approach will have to come, as in the past, from the Indians themselves. Duncan Campbell Scott is responsible for this creation – this department. He was a poet, but personally I think even his poetry was poor stuff, that despite the fact that in 1995 the Ottawa-owned Canadian Broadcasting Corporation did an extensive salute to it. I can't help but note he couldn't even rate in any of the top, long-established English magazines during his lifetime while an Indian woman named Pauline Johnson was in all their literary magazines. I find his poem called the Algonquin Madonna in which he pathetically describes an Indian woman as "the doomed mother of a doomed race," who sits beside a stream and hacks off part of her own breast to use as bait to catch a fish so she and her starving very small "in arms" baby can eat, simply ridiculous. Small Indian boys were taught to catch small fish in their hands. Besides, she would have understood that there were worms under the earth and that any passing insect could serve as fine bait. Oh no, Scott has to have her slash her bare breast for a bit of bait. Frankly, I think he knew the pornographic value of the bare breast just as past German etchers in the 18th century made a fine living in the pornographic trade of selling etchings of beautiful, if nude, Indian maidens. In Scott's age, bare breasts were confined to peep shows and good Ottawa matrons kept theirs proudly corseted so it made his titillating verse saleable.

His one worthwhile literary effort was allowing the remarkable Diamond Jenness[1] to do his fine study of the Indians of Canada. However, Scott labelled the original copy, which I have, as a pamphlet of the Department of Indian Affairs. He took the money to pay for it out of Indian funds, funds that were not spent on Indians with uncared-for tuberculosis and typhus, and in an almost semi-starving condition. But it did allow Scott to be able to hand it out to McClelland & Stewart to impress them with his ability to find his own money in the difficult field of publication. Scott also used his job to get paid for three newspaper columns in the best-read papers in Eastern Canada. In a newspaper interview at the time of his death his best friend said, "Well he rarely went near his office."

Today the autocratic rule of the Department is being constantly disputed by protest groups to our Canadian courts. Long ago that rare soul who did appeal had to appeal to the Privy Council because it was a governing legal body outside the reach of political influence of the government he wished to sue. Canadians have lost the right they once held to appeal legal matters there. Fortunately today, we have the creation of the world courts under the United Nations Charter of Human Rights. Indians are taking more and more cases there to overcome the Department or the Indian Act. Since Laurie's death and the cessation of my own association as legal advisor, there has been much additional criticism of the Department's Indian Act, and criticism of the Department itself.

In December 1990, the Alberta Human Rights Commission met at Morley to consider the Indian Act. That commission heard Lethbridge University professor and lawyer Leroy Littlebear break the present Indian Act down, section by section. The then Alberta commissioner of human rights, Mr. Phil Frazer, stated what I had always been saying since I first read this Act in 1944. In those 46 years there has been little improvement in this law governing nearly a million Canadian lives. Commissioner Phil Frazer has since been removed. Today's powerless hearing is the new occupation of the Department. These ineffective hearings have people begging, "please, no more!"

Today the Department's policy seems to be to hire more specialists at both Indians and Canadian taxpayers expense to present at hearings which have no power and whose key purpose would seem to be to assure the Department's continued existence. They claim integration is their aim, yet financial support like loans similar to those white students receive were cut. Indian students who wanted to be educated for their future were forced into sit-ins.[2] The situation on the reserves remains serious with over-crowding and limited economic opportunities. They have been locked in and semi-starved on a reserve and penalized if they leave – all strangely suited to ensure the Department's future employment. Likewise, both provincial and federal governments are desperately trying to find easy ways of quietly gaining more government funds from Indians by taxing liquor, gambling and cigarettes.

One finds it hard to find principles or even rational justification. We may be back to pre-treaty principles although the actual record of success among Indians is shown among the suicides. Youth unemployment on the reserve is a real fact, and not just talk, talk and more talk. The Department officials are by now super-specialists on talk. These "dinosaurs" from the past are still hiding out in expensive Ottawa offices. Neither Indian or non-Indian Canadians can rely on them. As advisors they must go. A federal accountancy branch is all that is needed and it should employ only well-trained personnel.

Did the Department save money by pushing bills owed under their carpet? What if native claims had been paid? They could have been settled for a fraction of what we now owe. But think of how much more improved would have been the conditions of today's Indians. The Indian unemployment rate would have been lower, and there would have been better living conditions, better health and better education. How much that could have added to our Canada of today. Those who did receive at least the pittance of treaty-promised payment have been successful despite these incredible odds.

The Department also did not manage the moneys held in trust for native people well. By 1948, there were $19 millions in trust which in the next ten years increased to $29 million. It is money that belongs to the Indians. The Department regarded this as a mark of success although the major source was the sale of land and timber. Out of this they paid their promised aid to the Indians. Yet the relief for the whites comes from the government's money not from the trust monies of the poor. They also used the trust fund money in aiding agriculture and supplying roads on reserves with the smallest amount of all going to houses. In other words they used the Indians own trust money to fulfill their treaty promises as payment for the surrender of Canada. It was not the government of Canada paying at all. The Indians were paying quite a large part of it from the sale of their own assets.

About this time I learned the true meaning of the "trust fund," the section in the Indian Act that had so confused me on my first meeting with the Indian Association of Alberta. The *Calgary Herald* was getting a new publisher, Basil Deane. The past publisher invited me to meet him for lunch at the Palliser. They wished me to write a book review. I had never even written for the school paper, but unabashed I accepted. They spoke of line length but I didn't understand that. The book I was to review was called *Tribe Under Trust*[3] and was written by the Hanks, an American and his wife, who had chosen to spend an entire summer on the Blackfoot reserve to study the Canadian government's trust funds system. It was a wise analysis of the trust funds on that reserve and showed how the Department exploited the Indian.

While the money created some industry, workers on a reserve received half the pay they would have off the reserve. Work off the reserve was restricted and permission often withheld. It did little to truly improve the

Indians' future, but it allowed him to exist. To this day few non-Indians understand the operation of Indian's trust funds, and when they see a fine architecturally beautiful centre or a fine residence on a reserve, they feel the Indian is being over-helped whereas in reality he has paid for this out of his own band funds – his money. Unfortunately it allowed for all sorts of patronage on the Department's part. Their friends or friends of the government in power frequently got too high pay for unneeded construction and real needs were ignored.

This was all in the book I was to review. I was so impressed, I wrote on and on about it and when it got published in the *Calgary Herald*, it wasn't as a book review but a full column editorial continued into two editions and it caused a commotion not among Indians, half of whom couldn't read a newspaper, or if they could never saw one on their locked-in reserves, but among concerned, decent non-Indian persons. I also began to explain to Indians the rip-off that frequently occurred in the unwise application by the Department of their trust funds.

When the *Calgary Herald* sent me an unexpected cheque for $35, it had been the first money I had actually earned since I left law and I celebrated it by framing the cheque, a fact that likely upset the *Calgary Herald* accountant on years end when they found they couldn't balance the books. The Department lay low about the article and never defended themselves, believing, I expect, no Parliament member in Ottawa would read it anyway.

When I first met with the Indians, I opened my mouth to try to explain that the system of trust funds and "wards of the state" had been created to protect insane people, people in prison, young children or women who had no older male to protect them. I couldn't say it. It was such an insult to these intelligent persons I was facing. Even their reserves the Department had promised would be theirs weren't. The land and all the buildings on it were still kept in title to the government, and the Indians were mere tenants subject to eviction by the government.

That book, one of the most daring and revealing to appear, had been written by Americans. It's out of print now and to some degree conditions have been improved, but the tragedy is Indian land is still under the control of a government. "My home is my castle" is not Indians' law. Rarely is it now enforced except when it is to the government's advantage and not necessarily the Indians. Legally and quietly they can just do it. Forgiveness will come from Parliament.

Success in the Department depended on one's abilities to shift their policies to match the ever-changing politicians whose first duty was to fulfill the hopes of their electors. The Indians were no-one's electors. They were non-existent on their isolated reserves. Even if there had been able heads in the

Department many didn't know Indians except by appointment in their own pristine Ottawa offices. The majority of them had never been on an Indian reserve, they had never walked through miserable homes, nor witnessed the idle frustration of the average Indian's days. In Ottawa, they awoke in their comfortable warm homes, they passed their days in neat, well-organized offices, efficiently filing clean papers they had written.

One can blame the Indian tragedy entirely on the deficiencies of the civil servants in the Department of Indian Affairs. Certainly one cannot blame the average Canadian who had been kept unaware of how the Indians suffered. Because the Indian had no vote, he had no chance of directing his own life, or to complain. The fact that the Department worked hard at depriving the Indian of the vote was its greatest crime. No progress could ever be made until that barrier was removed. Then like all the other persons in a democracy, they would have a chance to seek out reforms for a better life.

Because the Indians lacked a vote, the Department of Indian Affairs had been totally free from critical observation or effective control. The Indian lot could only improve when we have changed or eliminated this situation. I would like to see the day when all members of the Indian Affairs Department were Indians who understood their people's problems.

But getting the vote was critical. An Indian agent had explained to John Laurie how that section in the Indian Act gave him complete control over the Indian actions on their reserves. It would take John Laurie much longer to learn how the enfranchisement section of the Act worked. Enfranchisement as it was called was first considered in Canada in 1857 and incorporated in the Indian Act of 1876. Duncan Campbell Scott was a persistent advocate of enfranchisement as a means of removing Indians from a reserve and he became particularly concerned that there was no means of enfranchisement or taking away an Indians right to treaty land if they were not on the reserves. In 1918 he proposed and subsequently amended Section 122. This outlined the Indian enfranchisement process for Indians who did not follow the Indian mode of life and who held no land at present in a reserve even though they had a right to it. If there was evidence that the Indian was self-supporting, he would receive his share of the present band funds but relinquish all future profits owing him from funds held in trust, or future money gained by selling band property.

Up until then only 102 Indians across Canada had ever been enfranchised but when he changed the Act in the next two years, he managed to evict 258 persons from a right to treaty payments. What Scott wanted was a further change to the Act so that an Indian could be enfranchised against his will merely on the report of a person from his Department on the fact that the Indian should be enfranchised. He called it Bill 14, and it was presented to

Parliament in 1920. Unfortunately, few understood it. The *Ottawa Journal* welcomed it, believing it must give our Indians full citizenship immediately. But on the other hand, the Toronto *Globe and Mail* felt the Indians were not ready for a radical alternative to the reserve and needed the continuing promise of treaty payments. The committee looking into the Act held seventeen meetings and heard evidence from only thirty-five Canadian Indians.

The majority expressed distrust of the amendment, fearing it would destroy their communities. Scott however spoke to Parliament on the bill and said his desire was merely to turn Indians into Canadians, which should eventually lead to the closing of his own Department. This self-sacrificing speech was much admired by the press and as a result, the committee members supported the bill. MacKenzie King in opposition at the time appeared to oppose it – but it was passed by the Conservatives. There had been such a fear about the bill that the Department was careful not to enforce it until after the election in 1922.

The Indian organizations of Canada continued to oppose it, but without success. Scott had won the right for a small committee of three to force any Indian who resisted or criticized his rule off his reserve and into compulsory enfranchisement. For that, all he received was the right to vote in Canadian elections. Although it had been billed as enfranchisement and the granting of the vote to the Indians, in reality the Indian could also be forced from his reserve if he voted or asked for a vote. To the Indians who had never understood democracy's value, they thought it was a poor bargain. Few had applied before for voluntary enfranchisement. Now enfranchisement could be forced on them by Scott.

The general public failed to understand that this was not the giving of the vote to the Indians, it was in reality depriving the Indian of the promised land and treaty payments. Moreover the decision to so deprive them was solely in the hands of the bureaucrats in the Department of Indian Affairs. At last Scott had obtained a means of total control over all of Canada's Indians. If they criticized him, he could then on the pretence of giving them the vote or compulsory enfranchisement, rob them of their homes, their land and life with their people. Only a few of the highly educated Indians understood this complicated means of robbing them. The politicians on the other hand could now say no one has denied the Indian the right to vote.

The two sections were separated in the Act. One section dealt with voluntary enfranchisement and the other compulsory enfranchisement. In voluntary cases the Indian would lose his treaty and reserve rights, but he would receive a small cash payment that disguised the actual robbery of the Indian's rights to lands from the public. The result was that now if the Department wished to force any rebellious Indians off the reserve, they had only to threaten that Indian by enforcing the compulsory enfranchisement of the Act. They could then say to him, 'if we do that you get no money at all. However, if you apply for enfranchisement you will receive a small cash payment when you leave the reserve.' This brilliant manipulation meant that the records would show few forced off the reserve. Machiavelli would have certainly admired the Act and Mr. Duncan Campbell Scott.

Once MacKenzie King was returned to power he conveniently forgot his opposition. After all, the number of Indians who had a vote to give him were ever fewer in number, and he was an expert in being re-elected. This would be the law of Canada up until 1962 – the Indian was now in reality voteless – not a citizen of Canada.

Laurie wondered why Duncan Campbell Scott had worked so hard at putting this one section into the Act. As a bureaucrat what interest was it to him whether the Indian voted or not, and he had worked at this change harder than anything else in his career. True, it gave his Department more power, but it hardly seemed to be worth the tremendous effort he put into it. It would be later that Laurie would find that there was a motive behind this "enforcer" clause in the Act. The Department wanted to ensure that there would be no protests on the reserve. Agitators like Loft and his supporters could be removed. It was why the Indians never complained of their situation to him or even as a group to protest his actions.

The right to vote therefore had been turned into a threat. Only one who lived the Indian way of life could live on a reserve. The Indian past way of life contained no votes for government, so ergo they could vote but if so cease to be an Indian and then could not live on their promised forever reserves. It was a "catch 22" situation.

That was why Laurie's Indian father was angry with him for saying he should vote. Once when we had just joined some Albertan Indians at a meeting, one stood up and said: "Don't believe this white man. He is here to try and enfranchise you." After that meeting Laurie had quietly spoken to him and said there is a law of libel. You can't just shout out things unless you know them to be true.

The forcible enfranchisement section turned the bureaucrats into virtual dictators of the Indians' life on the reserve. No protests, no complaints against their action in public or off you went. At that time, that meant you left with no home, no money in your pocket, and no training for any job.

Today I can note that concerned Indians now speak or write of the change in attitude that took place in the 1960's. Many don't know that is when they at last got the vote by the Act of Parliament.

Initially if Laurie tried to get the Indians to demand the vote they would fear losing everything. Laurie knew that trying to get the non-Indian public concerned enough to demand the vote for Indians who weren't asking for it themselves would be equally difficult. It would be seen as a legal matter. Although each man is presumed to know the law, the average citizen only becomes aware of the laws that govern him when he runs into personal and direct problems. It seemed to me I would need the help and support of more prominent lawyers obviously mostly male lawyers. It seemed almost hopeless.

So with his genius for understanding the Indian, Laurie devised a simple battle cry they could understand – "We want bread, not votes!" Yet we both knew without getting the vote the Indians' future would be hopeless. We had had 100 years of failure of the Departments so-called "care" of the Indians behind us. The Department would only change if forced to – the only way that could be done was in the legislature. The Indian had to acquire a voice there. To date, there had never been any Indians' ballots in the box. The only voice they had ever had was of deeply concerned compassionate legislators and unfortunately there were few of those.

It had been Laurie and his formation and subtle direction of the Indian Association of Alberta that had taught the Indian anything about what we call democracy and the vital importance of each individual to a country. It was in the Indian Association of Alberta they learned the principal of each person is equal and has an equal vote. Chiefs had one vote, the medicine man had one, the councillors one, and so did the young boy of eighteen. You paid your money, you got your membership ticket, and you then had your vote.

The Second World War had created a spiritual vacuum by the loss of the world's finest of their young men's lives just at their prime. Europe and Asia's two great countries had lost their forms of government. Now, across the world, there seems a budding of growing new concern for not only things that grow, but concern for every living thing. It took us a long time to understand the sharing offered in a democracy, where each person has some small say in the forces that govern his life, whether he will starve, or die in a war, or suffer from ill health. As the winds of war blew in the first half of that century now near the end of it there is a fresh concern for the quality of human life. Concern for others is a goal. Its realization is another thing. It would be an age where at last a man of concern would be listened to, possibly even followed. If John Laurie had been born in the eighteenth century he might have lived and died known only as a fine man, the nicest man in his town.

When peace came, the victorious democracies threw up a tall, vulnerable glass tower in New York they called the United Nations and without even an army, only a police force and the sanctions of world opinion they placed their faith in the rights of each human person to live. It was a woman who had no power, just the wife of a president, the indomitable Eleanor Roosevelt, who hammered it into a Charter of Human Rights, and tirelessly carried the message around the world.

She toured to the most unlikely and remote spots to spread her message even to Calgary. The women's society that sponsored her was small in numbers and had no money to hire a big hall. With typical Western ingenuity, since there was no hockey game scheduled on the evening of Mrs. Roosevelt's arrival, they simply got the use of that. I will never forget seeing that tall, almost awkward, grey-haired lady slipping and sliding her way to the centre circle on the ice rink. The acoustics were simply awful, but the arena was more full than it had been for any hockey game. In the audience was John Laurie listening with fascination as he realized that at last world philosophy and his as a man with only a concern for things human were joined. He was, at last, a man matched to his times.

However, we must remember that even as the First World War was fought half our own non-Indian population, the women, were denied the vote. The struggle for women to get the right to vote was a long and painful one, requiring distraught women to fling themselves to death under racing horse's hooves, chaining themselves to fences, going to prison, and being force fed when they attempted to protest through fasting.

But the Indians' route to getting the vote would be even more difficult than the women's. For them it would be made illegal for them to even protest their lack of a franchise. The price of asking for the vote, protesting for the vote, was made not totally illegal but by law if any Indians attempted it the price would be so high he couldn't afford it.

The problem of getting the vote for Indians in Canada was extremely complicated. By the Indian Act passed at the recommendation of the Department of Indian Affairs by a non-knowledgeable Parliament, if the Indian even asked for the vote, he could instantly and without any trial be removed from the house he lived in, the land that was his on the reserve and his people, and not only himself but his children and his children's children. For the Indian who had never had the vote, the price became much too high. The only way the Indian could acquire the vote would be by the insistence of the voting non-Indians in Canada that the Act that had been in force for over a hundred years be changed.

13: THE HARSH REALITY OF ENFRANCHISEMENT

To Laurie and me, the dreadful two clauses in the Indian Act of compulsory enfranchisement and voluntary were, we realized, the way the Department of Indian Affairs controlled from Ottawa every single Indian on a treaty reserve. It was, however, more a threat than a horrible reality. We had heard rumours that in the far Northwest around Dawson and in the Klondike gold rich areas that quite a few Indians were accepting the small cash offer of voluntary enfranchisement. Similarly, around mineral-rich Sudbury Indians were now being enfranchised.

No records can be demanded or found of this because if the Department wished to drive an Indian off, they would first threaten him with instant compulsory enfranchisement and expulsion from his home and his people and discontinuation of the still-owed government's small but promised forever treaty payments. Or they would say to him, of course if you voluntarily enfranchise then we will let you take a share of your own trust funds with you when you leave. This money that the Department held out legally in every way belonged to the Indian anyway. The Department under law was committed to hold it in trust for him. Of course when the Indian accepted the voluntary payment then all the records would show was that the Indian had left the reserve at his own request with no compulsion placed on him at all. That explained why there had always been two clauses – voluntary and involuntary – the fact that had so confused me when I first read the Act.

However, no visible or provable enfranchisement was being exercised although we realized this section gave the Department total control over an Indian's life on the reserve. For a long time it seemed wiser to simply continually file by a majority vote in the Association a protest against Department control because we had no real proof to fight it with. The two sections in the Indian Act called compulsory and voluntary enfranchisement were still almost as much of a mystery to me now after ten years of working for the Indian, as when I had first read the Act to explain it to Laurie's group of

Indians in Calgary's Paget Hall. Nothing at all was heard about it. No Indians were protesting against it. No action was even mentioned.

I had analysed the enfranchisement sections in the Act and explained to the Canadian Bar that they prevented the Indian from voting because if he did so, he would be evicted from his reserve forever and the government would not have to maintain or live up to the treaty promises they had made so long ago that were to be the Indians' long-time payment for their peaceful legal surrender of most of the land of Canada over a hundred years ago.

Enfranchisement was the threat that bound the Indian not only to the reserve but also completely subject to Ottawa's bureaucratic control of his entire life. But evidence of the threat being used was never revealed. John's second Indian "son," the recognized artist from the Blood reserve called Gerald Tailfeathers was so threatened.

It seemed to Gerald until this time he had lived most of his life in confusion. He knew he had been born in the year 1925 on the Blood Indian reserve in Southern Alberta, but he always felt unsure about his birthday. His mother had told him it was February 13th, but when he was ten years old a new government agent on the reserve had announced the date would now be February 14th. At the time he felt like he had lost his birthday, but his mother just shrugged and said no, now you have two to celebrate. It really did not matter, except Gerald always felt stupid when he was asked for his birth date and he stuttered about it and then other people thought he was stupid too.

For a long time he felt he did not have a real name. His grandfather had a fine name. An old storyteller told Gerald his grandfather had stood tall and made his "X" beside his name, The-Man-With-Tailfeathers-Around-His-Neck, on Treaty No. 7 in 1877.

His grandfather had not believed the buffalo were really gone so he had taken his family and wandered the prairie for four years before they had to return to their allotted reserve, hungry for the rations of lard and flour, tea and sugar. The Blood reserve was the largest in Canada so the agent was always busy, and short-tempered with everyone. The agent was also not one for writing very much so he shortened Gerald's grandfather's name to Feather Necklet.

Gerald's grandfather had found an honoured position. He had become a Mountie scout. But it was this job that had led to his death. As a Mountie scout he got into a dispute with the head of the tribe, Thunder Chief. Thunder Chief pulled his gun and shot Feather Necklet, but before Feather Necklet died, he too pulled his gun and shot Thunder Chief – dead.

After that, Gerald's father, Fred, had decided to learn to farm. That had been a period of hunger as it was so long between crops and even longer before the government agent would sell the harvest. Fred had become a minor chief in the Bullhorn Band. He then insisted on having his own name, "Tailfeathers."

In his teens, Gerald had nearly lost his father's name. Gerald would go to the nearest town and sell postcards he had painted. One day a big fat man in a red shirt had laughed and laughed at his name. The fat man did not buy the postcard either! After that incident, Gerald signed his paintings "Gerald Feathers." One day, when he had sold a lot, he wrote Gerald T. Feathers. Then, he completed a really big painting and he firmly signed it "Gerald Tailfeathers," and took his name back.

Gerald Tailfeathers was not the only Indian to feel the bitter hurt of the robbery of his own name by a total stranger. It was extremely common in earlier days. There is nothing more personal than your own name. An early loss of a privilege imposed on women was to lose their names on marriage. Fortunately, today many refuse to, and widows and divorcees frequently shed the imposed name. Today, if women do this they do it by choice. In the early Indians' case, name loss was simply forced onto the Indian by the whim of a stranger because the government agent was too lazy to write the Indian's full name out in the longhand in use at the time.

Not only did the agents deprive Indians of their surnames, I discovered with great confusion during the Hobbema trial when I was desperately searching through old records for proof of descent that about half of the early Hobbema reserve women were all named "Nancy." The reason I finally discovered was that Nancy was the name of the agent's wife so he just entered all additions of young girls and wives under a short easy name he knew how to spell.

To the Indians in their tribe-hunter days, a name was very important. It might signify or commemorate a great event in their lives, a moment of bravery, and names were frequently changed by choice and the tribe's acceptance. Even today, Indians sometimes have secret private names given to them by societies or in a dream. Classic changes of names were those where Indians themselves chose to adopt the name of a man who had been truly influential in their life. The Maclean and the Wesley families are among some that the Indians had changed adopting a name to honour a once great white man who had helped their family. A classic example is the Samson family. Chief John Samson's (who went with me to Ottawa) grandfather once had a fine long name but an agent said his name was too long, that he was a big man, and gave him the name of another strong man from the old testament, Samson. One of the most tragic changes I have always felt was when lazy agents simply changed a whole tribes' beautiful significant name. One tribe had been named "The tribe who have only a blanket of the stars." An agent reduced that to Star Blanket, which signifies absolutely nothing.

A name is just a name but the Indians' names were sometimes earned and significant to them and the fact that a stranger of another race with a stroke of his pen could wipe it all out was a personal put down. In the case of the young Tailfeathers, not only had he lost his family's name but he had also lost his "roots," his directions.

At first Gerald hadn't felt he was meant to be a painter. It was his older brother, Harvey, who Gerald loved and always followed around, who was the real painter. Harvey had been taught to paint by their uncle, Percy Plainwoman, who painted under his personal Indian name of Two Gun. Percy Plainwoman came to live in the nearby Bullhorn coulee each summer and painted. He was a great painter of all Indians and their country and of the Indian pictographs. Gerald watched Percy while he taught Harvey to paint. Harvey was so good he went each summer to an art school on St. Mary's Lake in Glacier Park, Montana. This school was run by a white man, a German named Winold Reiss who was a famous painter of Indian subjects.

Then a terrible tragedy happened. Harvey fell sick and lost his eyesight. Gerald's mother had always wanted a painter in the family and she and Harvey felt so devastated that Gerald had begged to take Harvey's place at the art school, which he did and the teachers thought he was a very good painter.

Gerald's first home was a house his mother had dragged across four miles of prairie so her four sons would be within walking distance of the only day school on the reserve. She did not want her children going to the dreaded residential school. Gerald missed his old playmates and the cave and hills and having a well for water but he was able to go to day school. Eventually Gerald got too old for the day school and he had to go to the residential school. The school head, Canon S. H. Middleton, discovered Gerald's art talents. The Canon found Gerald a small room to paint in and he also wrote the Indian Department in Ottawa many letters begging for money to help Gerald buy art supplies and pay for an art teacher. But Ottawa never sent any money.

Then Gerald's mother died. He now had no home to go back to on the reserve. The Canon thought if he could get a scholarship for Gerald to a school that taught art, Gerald would have somewhere to go and also learn how to make a living. The Canon sent two of Gerald's pictures to Ottawa and requested help. There was great excitement when Ottawa wrote and asked for a third picture. But all was in vain – Ottawa sent a note saying, "Indian Department promises a small grant when the occasion arises." The occasion never arose nor were the pictures returned.

The dear old Canon didn't give up! He had heard of the art school in Banff. Without telling Gerald, he sent the Banff school some paintings and won a summer scholarship for Gerald. The only problem was the scholarship covered only tuition. The Canon went once more to the Indian Department for money to pay the room and board. Each Indian has ration money and each is owed treaty money so the Canon thought Gerald could have this money for his room and board. Thinking that there would not be a problem with money this time, the Canon sent Gerald off to Banff in a good dry-cleaned suit. It was the first time Gerald had ever been on a bus alone.

The money did not come in for three days. Of course, the dining room was not going to feed an Indian free so Gerald went hungry. Finally the money came, but only enough to pay the room and board and $10 to pay for all his supplies and any spending money he might need for the entire summer. Gerald had to stay at school because there was no money to go anywhere.

He spent every night after class walking alone in the woods on beautiful Rundle Mountain. It was there that he met Mr. Laurie. To Gerald, the teacher had just come out of the forest like a spirit. But, of course, he hadn't. The teacher held out his right hand, palm out, fingers spread in the traditional Indian way of greeting and said, "I have known many fine Indian people. My name is John Laurie."

After that they walked and talked many evenings. Gerald had found someone he could talk to. Since his brother's death he had lived in a world of silence; there had been really nobody. He had never had a need while his brother lived. He began by telling John about his brother. It had been all bottled up inside since his brother's death making him just aching there.

John Laurie took Gerald to concerts and plays. On one exciting evening, which Gerald always remembered, John took him down to Banff to a restaurant owned by a Greek. The three of them sat around a table and laughed and talked and laughed some more. The Greek treated them all to a large bowl of ice cream. Gerald had never known such happiness.

One of Gerald's art teachers was W. J. Phillips, who was very encouraging and felt he was a real artist. Near the end of the summer, Gerald began to worry about where he would go. That winter John spoke to the University Women's Club and they gave the tuition scholarship so Gerald could go to what was then the Provincial Institute of Technology and Art. This was a tremendous achievement for an Indian but the old problem was still there. Gerald did not have any money to pay for his board and no one would rent to an Indian.

John Laurie again came to his rescue and took Gerald into his home. John shared his food, Indian fashion. John had also insisted that Gerald take drafting in school as well as art so that he would be able to make a living. On graduation, Gerald got a job with an oil company in its drafting department. Gerald then got married and had a child. All this time he continued painting and living with John.

Gerald felt that he was imposing on John and that the house was too crowded. He wanted a place of his own. Because he had a good job, he thought he could rent a house – one with big windows for light. Rental houses did not have big windows and no one would rent to an Indian. At the oil company, one of his friends told him about the National Housing Loan mortgages. Without telling John Laurie, for he didn't want to hurt his feelings, Gerald applied for a mortgage. He had no birth certificate just a treaty card and number, so he sent that in. Now this letter had arrived! The white paper was like a bolt of lightning. It split him like he had once seen lightening crack a tree. He wasn't a whole person; he was a divided person like that tree, a man of nowhere between two worlds. He was an Indian. He got the letter at the reserve. It said, congratulations and they would be glad to agree. In fact they would even pay enough to almost pay his down payment provided he signed the voluntary enfranchisement form. If not, he would have to be compulsorily enfranchised now that he wished to own a home and work in the city. Gerald said just what so many Indians did: "I'll have to ask John about this." The teacher would know what to do. John read the letter slowly then, taking his glasses off and covering his eyes with his hands, he said very softly, "Gerald, this is not good news." John, the teacher, explained to Gerald that now the Indian Department knew he had a job and that as he thought he could live off the Indian reserve, the Indian Department could now do what they called "enfranchise" him. This meant that Gerald could never go back to the reserve that he would have to stop being Indian. This was the strangest thing Gerald had ever heard!

John went on and explained that enfranchisement meant that neither he, his wife nor their children or even their grandchildren could go back to the reserve. They could not claim their future treaty payments. It had been the law for 80 years that Indians could not leave the reserve to work or better themselves and then come back to their home. It did not matter if an Indian actually worked, or bought a house; it was enough that an Indian demonstrated the intent to leave the reserve that triggered the enfranchisement section of the Indian Act. Gerald said he would not buy the house or get a mortgage. John told him that it did not matter, the damage was done. Gerald had shown his intent to stay off the reserve just by making an application for a mortgage. John suggested that if Gerald took his family and went back to the reserve now, that the government agents may be too afraid to push him off, but that it was not certain.

John told Gerald that he had lots of experience with the powers the government agents had under the Indian Act. John went on to explain that the government used the enfranchisement power to control the Indians. They used it as a threat when Indians get rebellious or if they want a job off the reserve or if they want to get ahead in life. The government enjoyed having this power and did not wish to give it up. Because the Indians did not have the vote they did not have any power to change the laws. Gerald heard that as long as he was Indian he could not vote. If an Indian protests about not having the vote or about not having the chance to earn a living off the reserve, the government used the enfranchisement provisions of the Indian Act to punish them.

Gerald was shocked at the position he was in and the rules under which his people lived. If he went back to the reserve he would have no job; he would not be able to buy a house; he may not have a good house to live in because the Indian population was increasing much faster than the government was building houses for them; he would not have a good school for his child; it would be very difficult to sell his artwork; the government may still enfranchise him. On the plus side, he would be with his people; his child would grow up within his own culture.

John could not make the decision for Gerald and Gerald realized when he looked at him, the pale blue eyes looked grey – John was crying. For the first time Gerald realized that if he went back, that it would be the end of their special relationship. For nights Gerald could not sleep. Finally, he decided the reserve was where his heart was and where his art was.

Gerald went back. Life was as John had predicted: the house was poor; the school was poor. Fortunately one of John's students, Don Henderson, had persuaded the oil company he had worked for to build a service station on the reserve and asked Gerald to operate it.

But it didn't work. Gerald couldn't give credit because Indians did not own their own land or assets; they were held for them in trust. The oil company in order to collect on a debt would have had to sue the Crown. The Indians did not understand why Gerald could not give them credit even when they had no gas in their car and needed gas. Gerald was called apple – meaning red outside and white inside. He saw the Indians turn away from him. He sold few pictures. He struggled on and designed their fine centre on the reserve, basically a tepee shape, and made a trip to Ottawa in 1960 (he paid his own way) to try and get better schooling on the reserve, the kind that the teacher John Laurie had given to him, but he died at an early age and who will know what art was lost to Canada.

His family continued his example. In 1989 the medical faculty of the University of Alberta was the only faculty of medicine in Canada to establish an annual award for aboriginal students – the "Darcy Tailfeathers Memorial Award." In 1988 the faculty extended the 118 quota in medicine to include two positions limited to qualified students of aboriginal ancestry. Darcy Tailfeathers' life was one of the tragedies of today's Indian world. The first medical student at the university, he was killed two months into the programme in a car accident when he was showing one of his non-Indian faculty members his people' ancient way of life, hunting.[1] When Laurie died, Gerald Tailfeathers contributed to his memorial.

Hugh Dempsey in his book about his father-in-law, Senator Gladstone, states that Gerald was under a mistaken impression that he would have to return to the reserve. Mr. Dempsey's connection with the Indian Association of Alberta was through his father-in-law, Senator Gladstone, because Mr. Dempsey was the husband of his daughter Pauline. We had no connection with him except as Senator Gladstone's employee in Ottawa and later as a fine curator in a museum where one becomes a fine authority on artefacts and the customs connected with them, but is far and remote from the actual human conditions in which members of the average Indian bands live and their verbally retold history that Laurie and I saw and heard at every meeting. If Mr. Dempsey had attended the meetings he would have known what a serious threat enfranchisement was to the Indian people, a threat always available to the Department of Indian Affairs and which the Department with determination never intended to remove because it enabled them to so completely control individual protests unless done by such a large group that they couldn't identify an individual. Mr. Dempsey never realized what actual danger the Indians were always in from the threat of expulsion that as late as 1960, the Department of Indian Affairs was determined to retain.

The law preventing the Indians the right to vote in a democratic country, or rather making the penalty of acceptance so difficult it was impossible to accept, was concealed in Section 112 of the Indian Act. It had remained there almost unchallenged for a hundred years. The Indians didn't dare challenge it or they might be thrown uneducated out of their only home, their land, the reserves, because to challenge it meant intent.

Laurie would never know that what he had worked so hard for his whole life would be achieved – the end of mandatory enfranchisement. He would be dead almost two years before I would be allowed to stand in Ottawa and demand compulsory enfranchisement must go. But Gerald would know because he would be standing beside me. But for Gerald it was too late. The death of Laurie and the terrible struggle had broken his health and he died in 1975.

In Ottawa during the hearings, which ended enfranchisement, one of the old Liberal senators arose and started beating the old enfranchisement drum. Smoothly he asked, "Gerald, aren't you the Indian artist who returned to his reserve? Now, did you do that voluntarily?" Gerald answered, "Yes," and then when the senator said, "Now, wasn't it because..." firmly Gerald said, "No, it was because of the reasons you have all heard today." I went over and stood beside him and said he was afraid he would be enfranchised. I think looking at that man standing so calm, so determined, had a profound effect on the audience. There followed a period of total silence. Gerald helped put into force the teacher's impossible dream; now, the teacher was dead and gone. The Indian did at last get the vote.

14: LAURIE AND THE INDIANS FIND ME

The lives of John Laurie and I were poles apart. It was not just the male/female thing. Laurie was a confirmed bachelor all his life and I was a happily married wife and mother, age 29. Laurie was 43 years old. I had been born in a big Mount Royal house in Calgary. He had lived in a small rented house in Calgary for probably 20 years of his life, yet we had never met until he introduced himself over the phone one day around 1944. I believe Laurie first heard of me from his adopted Hunter family in Morley as the daughter of M.B. Peacock.

My father's first experience with the Indians was when he was sixteen years old, in the village of Stroud near Barrie, Ontario, where he grew up. When he came west he had learned about the Morley Indians from his law client, Norman Luxton of Banff. Possibly Laurie had also read about me in the newspapers. As one of only two women practising law in Calgary, my agitations for reforms for women were often reported upon. Laurie mobilized the Indians into action and then he mobilized me.

Laurie was a hard-up teacher and, for most of his early years, had led a lonely life. It was said of me that I was the spoiled, only daughter of a rich, successful lawyer and wife of another lawyer. I did not know how lucky I was to have had two parents that for life equally loved one another and me.

Laurie shared the lives of Indian families. He listened for long hours to their tales. He was one with them despite his high, pale forehead. He talked quietly as they did; it seemed to me that he even walked differently when he was with them. I was the alien. I could never stay, never visit. I had to hurry home to my white family. My time with the Indians was short and filled with answering their questions. I wanted to share my own world with them.

Laurie was different. He enjoyed and was a part of their own unique world and he didn't want them to ever lose that. He wanted them to keep their inheritance close to them – the inheritance he had grown to admire. Robbery of their customs worried him; robbery of their rights as fine human beings concerned me.

The Indians felt this. Once when that Saskatchewan Indian, John B. Tootoosis,[1] had come to an Alberta Indian meeting and stood up and said, "Why do you let this white man lead you? He is just trying to enfranchise you." An Indian leaped up and said, "John Laurie is not a white man; he is one of us." That was one example of how magnificently he had crossed those tough barriers of race.

Laurie's was the unique quality. His dedication was eventually the death of this rare human rights leader. I was the one who for free supplied the coaching and legal knowledge to obtain their rights, what they could and could not do. But I had no time to do it with them. I had a husband who never came with me, and a child I left at home. I missed so much of the Indians' way of life and their pleasantness. Not so Laurie.

Laurie had felt he had no living family at all after he was six years old. He found an Indian family when he was thirty years old, and he struggled to become part of his new family; their customs and their stories became his. The neat, tweed-covered schoolteacher who walked the streets of Calgary became a disguise assumed by the man inside who had found his true family.

The centre of my life had been my mother and father. I travelled with my family to what seemed in those days far places to live in fine hotels in California or Florida or Alaska and to travel through Europe in a private car. When I visited one of the large farms my father owned, I lived in the ranch house and rode my fine horse across the fields. I never sat on the corral fence. I met many famous people, but my family was a family that made no distinctions between persons of wealth and poor people. They were aware of everyone's unique abilities or talents.

When I came to the Indians, I saw them as just fine people. I had no inclination to study their differences, their uniqueness. I collected their fine legends and noted the workmanship of the lovely gifts they gave me. These were gifts from friends. I did feel for my adopted Indian family, the Samsons, because they were such fine human beings. I would become angry that they were being hurt just as I would feel angry about women I saw abused, or prisoners, or physically disabled persons.

My first meeting with the Indians when they asked me, "What does it mean that we are wards of the government," was a moment of intense shame for me, shame that I was a white person who, unconcerned, had let other white persons, namely the Ottawa bureaucrats, use the legal device of wardship which they had encompassed in the Indian Act to treat the Indians in such a despicable manner. I explained to my attentive Indian audience the legal meaning of the ward system. A 'ward' was a legal name given to a person who needed special protection, people such as orphans who had no adult to look after their money or welfare. In this situation a 'trustee' was

Ruth Gorman with her mother, Fleda Pattyson Peacock, and her father, Colonel Mark Bennett Peacock, KC, *ca.*1915.

created legally for them. This was a person who held money for the children, paid their bills and brought them food, homes and the necessities of life until they reached the age of 21. Then, both by wisdom and by law they were allowed to hold and administer their own money and property.

I explained that in earlier days women had been 'wards' of their male fathers, relatives or husbands and had no control over their money or lands. I said that wardship was also a legal system for handling and controlling prisoners' funds while they were in prison. I was just about to say that it was also a legal method for handling insane persons' funds and possessions when I looked out at those earnest brown faces looking up and listening so hard to me and my voice gagged over saying aloud the word 'lunatics.' Yet, that was the group the Department had publicly legally classified them into. I think that at that moment I realized how truly shocking our handling of

Indian affairs had been in the past. I never did finish my sentence aloud and say 'lunatics,' but I think that was a point where I decided I would like to put a stop to this unjust treatment of sane adult and able persons, no matter what colour his skin. When the white man first met the Indian he had given them the misnomer of savages. With the implementation of the Indian Act, we called them wards, legally classifying them with the insane.

We Canadians were the immature, ignorant ones who had allowed this to happen. The ward system had led decent Canadians into being unconcerned for the Indian people in their midst. If asked, the average Canadian would assure the questioner that we are applying excellent care and concern for the Indian people. One of the finest things I learned about my new native friends was their acceptance and great patience in the face of almost daily failure of even their hopes for a better future. It was the same hope and faith that Laurie had and which he instilled in his pupils in Calgary classrooms.

John Laurie, always the teacher, taught me that I must listen and receive from the Indians and that would be as much my job as aiding them. Behind every successful man there is always a great woman!

No man lives alone on an island. Even Robinson Crusoe had a "man Friday" to help him. But one thing you have to do all alone ultimately is make decisions in your life. My man Friday was my father M.B. Peacock. He came from a large Ontario farming family and revelled in that. He would have enjoyed a large family in his own life but unfortunately was sent only one small girl. Due to my mother's semi-invalid condition he mostly raised me. Fortunately my father admired women including his own mother, his mother-in-law, his wife and his sisters. He saw them as equals. He raised me with some male training. I put on my own small gloves and he taught me to box with him as self-defence was vital. I had to ride a four-reigned horse holding them all in by my left hand only so my right hand was free to hold a gun if necessary. And he subtly succeeded in overcoming my disinterest in following him in his, and three generations back profession – law.

Possibly I lived a lonely life. There were few other children near the big house I was born and raised in, in Calgary's prestigious Mount Royal district. I spent even my holidays, which included a great deal of travelling, with my family. When I escaped from home and boarding school to university, I revelled a little in the fine professor's opening instructions and the great collections of books in the stacks. But, it was living in a girls' fraternity and going dancing each night, preferably with a different good dancer, that I enjoyed most until I graduated with an arts degree.

Then my father subtly suggested that it would be unfair for me to work. So I could stay home and drive my mother about or go back and take law.

I got a degree largely paid for by the taxpayers, so I would not rob one of them of really needed jobs. That's how I became a lawyer.

Living with such loving parents allowed me to live a life of extended adolescence. However, the sudden death of my protective father and my exposure to the unearned hardship of the Indian people awoke me to the realities of the world around me. Fortunately I had training in law. The University of Alberta law school was not large and I was exposed to magnificent teachers. Dean John Alexander Weir[2] had exceptional abilities respected all across Canada. Dr. Malcolm M. McIntyre, the only other permanent professor, was Harvard-trained.[3] His book on torts became a classic and he became a professor of the University of British Columbia law school. Another exceptional teacher taught us courses in international law, and another became the first Western Canadian appointed to the Supreme Court of Canada. Probably most fortunate of all, a boy named James Constabaris, who was forced to work his way through law school and won every scholarship, chose to study with me. Unfortunately, he was killed as a volunteer pilot in the Battle of Britain and his talents were lost to Canada. Together these men gave me great respect for law and how it had been used in the past to either oppress people or free them for possible growth and a chance to realize the best possible chance for fairness for them. In the conglomerate mass of ambition and greed, the law was the most reasonable and successful protector humans could find.

As one of two women in law school, I was clearly a minority in what was the last bastion of male professions. Today's feminists would be shocked at my behaviour. I decided to simply charm them while keeping up with them, and it worked. They would all invite me to their morning coffee break and pay my way. Just to keep me in my place they would flip a coin with the loser having to pay for me. I in turn would every now and then prove my own scholarly abilities, and I rarely said, "What is more, I can also have the babies." Most of those boys who survived the Second World War were my lifelong friends, and provided some of my finest assistance in the legal Indian skirmishes I would be involved in. I married one of my classmates, John C. Gorman, after a short time of practising law in my father's law office, Peacock and Skene in Calgary.

During this period, Calgary's Local Council of Women composed of thirty-two volunteer women's clubs asked me to become their conveyor of laws, a polite title for their free and available lawyer. I would wave the roughly 3,000 strong women's votes I directed threateningly at city councils and in the press by speeches and I did achieve some success. I succeeded in enforcing changes and improvements in married women's dower rights, divorce laws, women prisoners and, most satisfying, I saved Prince's Island, opposite downtown Calgary, from becoming a second mid-city line for the Canadian Pacific Railway. Instead, it became the beautiful city park it is today.

Early Calgary had always been a comparatively tolerant place for women to live. I thought it was because in Western Canada we were still close to the pioneer era when the few women partners who ventured into the wilderness had earned the respect of males. In order to enforce the desires of Calgary's Local Council of Women I became a frequent speaker at the women's clubs which ran the school and the churches if not yet the business section of the city. My husband had moved into my spot in my father's law firm. Canada had entered the Second World War the day after my marriage and all Canadian wives including me underwent violent change. I now had a baby daughter whom I wanted to raise. Fortunately I would be free all my life from financial pressures – not quite rich, but possibly never in danger of being poor either. I was free to indulge in the privilege of using my comparative advantage in those times of being a law-trained woman to indulge myself by helping others.

At this point I met John Laurie. He introduced himself to me over the phone. He was obviously familiar with my past activities but somehow I hadn't yet become aware of John Laurie's constant efforts on behalf of Indians. He spoke at many of the same women's and men's volunteer service clubs, luncheons and evening meetings as I did but on different problems and at different times. Like most other average Canadians, I was unaware of the forced isolation of the Indians on the reserve and the deliberate secrecy practised by the bureaucrats in the Department of Indian Affairs. My ignorance was probably less excusable than the average Canadian's. My lawyer father had already become recognized and honoured by the Indians as a free legal advisor. As a young man he had taught with his missionary brother at George Peacock's Methodist mission to earn enough money to put himself through law school.

John Laurie, always the teacher, taught me that I must listen and receive from the Indians. That would be as much my job as aiding them. In the past so much well-intended support of whites had fallen down the gap created by centuries of different cultures.

Europeans, overcrowded and constantly at one another's throats over war and religion, were incapable of grasping the cultural development of a race of people allowed to grow in family groups without religious conflicts or power struggles who could survive in a vast continent that had been generously sufficient for all humans without the necessity of the labour of agriculture or the blood-letting of war or conflicts in the market place. Actually,

Colonel Mark Bennett Peacock, KC (second from right), being made honorary chief of the Stoneys, Morley, 1937.

by just listening to another culture's needs I gained a wider knowledge and understanding of the basic needs of all humans.

Those needs were almost lost under the conflicts in my own society. Power seemed to be gained only by the creation of personal wealth. This struggle had given incredible power to the banks, which controlled all deposits of money and credit. They had gained immense power over the government who had to wheel and deal with them while they went in debt to pay for their expensive re-election promises of give-aways to blocks of voting groups.

The Indians' way was something from the past that I had to study and relearn. This was what Laurie had done when an Indian family first adopted him. My route to learning was through John Laurie, one of the few truly concerned whites who understood the Indian world. Just as Laurie's high school students had found him a great teacher so would I. He made learning easy. He made it interesting. He made it understandable.

I never did record the date of my first meeting with the Alberta Indians or John Laurie. At the time it seemed almost a nuisance and a duty date among my commitments to speak to associations. I merely marked it on my throw-away calendar. I had no idea that it would mark a date that would change the rest of my life. I believe it had to be 1944.

Over the phone came his beautifully well-modulated voice. He said he had arranged for three young lawyers as volunteers to speak to a group of Indians about the Indian Act. Most Indians understood little of the law that governed their lives. As I watched my small daughter mount the side of her high chair and prepare to perform hara-kiri by falling to the floor, I firmly said no to him. I had too many commitments already. I was foolish enough to add that I didn't want to see any more Indians at all. As I later found out, John Laurie was not only persistent but sometimes he could make his listeners feel guilty in his efforts to aid the Indians. Calmly he went on and said, "But I understand that you have already received some fine gifts from the Indian people." This did not soften me up. It made me remember with distaste how I had received those gifts.

My father had brought an Indian case to the Court of Appeal and won.[4] He received no fee but got some wonderful and strange friends for life. When he died they ran behind the hearse. They made him honorary chief of the Stoney Indian tribe at Morley and to further honour him, they made me, his only daughter, a Princess of the tribe. At this age I wasn't proud at having to be made an Indian Princess. I remember that the ceremony took place in the green field beside the tennis courts of the Banff Springs Hotel during their much-celebrated "Indian Days." Without warning I got steered into an Indian tepee and found myself surrounded by very serious-eyed Indians costumed in great feathered headdresses and heavily loaded doe-skin suits. They looked at me coldly without batting an eye and said, "Take your clothes off." I said all I could think of, "No." After a quick consultation an Indian lady came in and said, "You can leave on your slip and I will help you." She dressed me in moccasins and leggings, a buckskin dress, a cape, and a beautiful eagle headdress that reached from a high point in my head to trail its feathers in the dust.

Amid much flashing photographers' lights I became a Princess of the Stoney Indian tribe and was given the new name of Mountain White Eagle. This was the name of the Indian Hunter "family" ancestors. There was, however, sudden consternation when everyone realized at the last moment that I was a girl and they had given me a man's name. They hadn't had a Princess before and that was quickly solved and I was renamed Mountain White Eagle Girl, Princess of the Chiniki Indian tribe. It made headlines across Canada and humiliated me greatly. I had no ambition to be an Indian Princess even if it was complete with a tepee, all the cooking utensils and arrows from each family of my tribe so that I could always stake a claim to sharing food. My father, however, was very pleased and the Indians seemed pleased and I just stored the gifts I received and went off to the University of Alberta and hoped everyone would forget it. It wasn't until my father died that I recalled the ceremony. As a lawyer he won back the ancient treaty rights for Alberta Indians to hunt for food on their reserves.

Laurie always had the art of saying the right thing at the right time, and said to me on his phone call, "Your father loved the Indians, so...." I felt I was almost being blackmailed. The night before I was to meet John Laurie

Ruth Gorman in ceremonial dress with Mr. Justice Clinton J. Ford, Morley.

and his Indian people to explain to them the Indian Act, I read a copy of the Act. I had never seen an Act like it. As I read through its complicated sections it became clear to me that the Indian owned nothing outright. We had given them the land on the reserves, but it was still in the name of the Crown, held only with their permission and under government control. The Indian owned neither the house he lived in, nor anything he produced on the land. He could sell that produce only when he obtained an Indian agent's written consent. It was also clear that no white person could go onto the reserve, or an Indian off the reserve for any length of time without the consent of the Department of Indian Affairs. Never had I seen an Act that gave a bureaucracy such power.

The Act had clearly been amended and added to at various times, and where in one section a liberty had been given, later in a revised section it would be diminished or withdrawn. Years later, as I interpreted the Act to an elite section of Canadian Bar Association lawyers, one member reflected my opinion when he repeated an old cliché: "Looks like even a Philadelphia lawyer couldn't interpret this." I wondered how I could stand up and explain the injustices of this Act to the people whose way of every-day living depended on it. So with reluctance I went to explain to the Indians what a disgraceful Act we had designed to rule them with.

I hadn't been surprised when Laurie said the meeting would be held in a church. After all I had spoken often to groups of whites in the basements of churches. Nor was I surprised that there was an Indian Association of Alberta. If I had only known that I was to be speaking to a unique group – the only one of its kind that has been able to survive in Canada. A group composed of Indians from all tribes who met, not as tribes, but as individual people.

It was a wet, spring day. One of those late last snowfalls had fallen the night before. The meeting was in the basement of Paget Hall, a three-storey red-brick building. It was a simple building almost fastened to Calgary's magnificent stone and glass windowed Anglican Cathedral of the Redeemer. The meeting room was in the basement of the hall, lit with bright electric non-shaded bulbs that harshly illuminated its windowless walls and wooden chairs. When I opened the door to the room, the first thing that hit me was the odour. It nearly knocked me over. I do not know if you have ever smelled wet buckskin. It has a smell like nothing else on earth. Nowadays I love the smell of my wet buckskin jacket, but then it was a grave shock to me when I opened the room because each of the probably fifty to seventy-five people who were sitting in the room had on buckskin moccasins, a few with rubber overshoes over them, but not very many, and all of them with buckskin jackets. They were literally steaming in this warm, stuffy basement.

More to the point, I found myself facing fifty to seventy-five stone-faced unsmiling Indians. I then started trying to explain the Act, which the Canadian Bar Association would later call one of the worst written laws in Canada. I knew that I shouldn't be there. Most of the Indians knew very little English, so I had to explain this extremely legal and complex Act slowly and haltingly through interpreters. By the end of the first day I was only half the way through the Act. I was also becoming increasingly and inwardly shocked at the dictatorial powers over the Indians and the lack of even basic freedoms contained in the Act. On the second day, I was relieved when noon arrived and I looked at John Laurie and said, "We will adjourn for lunch." Except no one moved! There they sat still looking intensely at me. Angrily I said to Mr. Laurie, "Why don't they have lunch?" Sadly he just said, "They don't have any money. They expected to come to Calgary for only one day and they have used up their money." "Well," I said, "Just how did they manage to stay overnight without money?" He replied that they had either stayed in their cars or in the bus depot as they really wanted to understand the laws governing them.

I looked at the Indians all stolidly sitting in their chairs looking at me. Suddenly I was appalled. Appalled that people could be so desperate to have explained to them the very laws that controlled and restricted their very lives. I just gave up. I opened up my purse. I didn't have very much money but I took out what I had and handed it to Laurie. He too had money in his hand and I shrugged and laughed and said I guessed we would have to have chocolate bars for lunch. He smiled faintly and after I had used the phone to plead with the baby-sitter to stay on with my daughter, we just continued. I continued explaining the Act that governed their entire lives.

At the end, although Laurie stood and said, "We all appreciate Mrs. Gorman's efforts," no one applauded. The Indians stretched their tortured forms and a few approached me. None really thanked me. They said their names and a few held out cards. Some were red cards and some were blue. Years later I realized that they were showing me their treaty cards or membership cards in their Association. It was their way of showing me that they were cooperative Indians. They had cooperated as they felt I had.

After Laurie's death I took a professor from the University of Calgary, from whom I was taking a course on the Aztecs, with me on a visit to the Morley council. I introduced him to my Indian friends and they had an interesting exchange. One question he asked the Indians was the Indian word for "thank you." He said he noticed they hadn't used one when talking to me. After much consultation someone said, "We don't really have an Indian word for that. If someone is able to help you, they are the fortunate one." At last I understood. All my life I had been taught that it is more blessed to give than receive. Deep down I never really believed it, but the Indians did. It was a way of life with them.

About ten days after this harrowing experience I received a thick envelope in the mail. In it were typed foolscap pages containing every word of explanation that I had given about the Act, every question asked by the Indians and my reply. That's what the white man had been doing for two days as he sat so silently. I decided he must be a tireless and good stenographer. Little did I know that he had no shorthand knowledge and that typing to him was a horrible chore. Nor did I know that a copy of those minutes had gone out to every reserve of each participant at the meeting in Alberta where they were translated, pondered over and studied by the Indian recipients.

The meeting haunted me. What I should have noted were the sections of the Act called "Trust Funds," the administration of which I couldn't understand, and the sections dealing with "enfranchisement." I presumed they had voting rights. It would be a year before I realized that, although I had spent seven years taking history classes, I did not know that Indians didn't have a vote in our democratic country. Those two sections that Laurie suggested I omit I spent the next twenty years of my life wrestling with.

I had no intention of ever repeating my unsatisfactory and difficult first encounter with the Indians. I had been too vain to wonder if it was because I was a woman that they just watched me, silent and unsmiling. Being almost alone among males as a woman lawyer I had long ago expected some resistance. I had often spoken to all male service clubs and never felt shut out. I had no idea what a long-time, male-oriented society I was with. If I had known, I would at least have been consoled that the Indians had listened for so long.

John Laurie had done what I would watch him do hundreds of times again. He turned my thinking toward the invisible Indians in our midst. He awakened the shame in me. It was a process I would see him repeat over and over again with non-Indians.

In the fall Laurie phoned and politely mentioned that the Indians were having a gathering at the nearby Sarcee reserve and asked if I would like to go. It seemed a rather nice venture so I agreed. I didn't have to speak this time, only answer an occasional question. I noted with surprise that Laurie still sat against a wall writing continually and that this time several Indians occupied the dais. Laurie introduced me to them saying, "This is the lawyer who discussed our Act with us." By the third meeting all my resistance was gone and I didn't even protest when he referred to me as "Mrs. Gorman, the Association's lawyer." He had made it clear that I could be party to this continued persecution or help him fight it. With thoughts of my father, I realized that I had to join John Laurie.

The American poet Robert Frost said, "Time and tide wait for no man, but time stands still for a woman of 30." He was wrong in my case. I was by now kept busy by women's rights litigation such as dower rights and woman prisoners. With the aid of Calgary's Local Council of Women, more and more of my time was taken up with the always in turmoil native peoples' abuses and their constant need for advice about how these abuses could be escaped from. Laurie got the complaints and then usually over the phone he relayed them to me for legal advice and eventually, too often, we ended up with a trip to the reserve if the problem was serious or immediate. It seemed to me that the pursuit of the native people by a well-paid Ottawa civil service department was never-ending.

From about then on I met with the Indians at least once a year for the next twenty years of my life. I have often thought about why Laurie and the Indians accepted my advice. I believe it was primarily because I was available and my services were free! My financial independence had been assured by an inheritance from my father and also my inherited philosophy that money was necessary but should not become our master. When Laurie wrote about me in the Indian Association of Alberta's records he carefully pointed that out. My fear of their "difference" turned to love. It culminated when, after winning an impossible lawsuit with some help from some law school friends, I assured their occupation of the treaty-given reserves and I was allowed to speak to our Canadian Parliament, both the House of Commons and the Senate, in Ottawa for three days. This resulted finally in the removal from the Indian Act the section that prevented Canada's original people from becoming equal citizens with us, the invaders of their country. Indians now would be allowed without restriction to vote and elect their own government.

I was always so glad we had in effect won the Hobbema Case before Laurie died – this justified his faith in me.[5] That did give him some comfort about his beloved Indians' future. In all honesty, it hadn't been my legal brilliance that brought about that victory. That case had been won by the vast wave of public support that had come from the non-Indians in Alberta, support that depended on the independent spirit and generosity of Western Canadian non-Indians that had been built up by John Laurie's life of sacrifice. His determined logic appeared in his writing and his frequent speeches to the two races living side by side in Alberta.

Laurie had rejected a position of honour and wealth to live his life much like the lives of those he was trying to help. Laurie was a man who never had great wealth and it is particularly difficult for a man who has little to have the courage to give up that, even for a cause. He had never been afraid of poverty but to lose honour would really have hurt him. It was the Indians' loss of self-pride that he had fought against for so long.

I guess this explains why, when I published a magazine, it had many Indian stories, artwork and sculptures. They are the real roots of man's life in this country and for all time they will reflect our future. We must build our land together on strong foundations. I've written a different way about our Indians because from them I learned a great deal. I remember missionaries and later Archdeacon Cecil Swanson saying to me, "I wonder why I plead with them to be Christians? They understand 'love thy neighbour' better than we do." I remember an Alberta Judge, a great Irishman, who once introduced me as a speaker to a Rotary club lunch and said, "Next to the Irish, the Indians are the nicest people I know." I'm grateful to my Indians for all they, as brave people, have taught me. They are in trouble today and it is trouble we as Canadians must solve, not in a quick-pitying way but in an acceptance of "here is a fine people we first exploited and then ignored." Now we must pay for these errors, not our errors, but those of the past so that we may have a "whole Canada."

At that first meeting I understood their questions but did not realize that they were without anger. I went through the sections of the Act that said that even the land that we supposedly transferred to them wasn't even theirs to do with as they liked. The government had kept the title and the Indians occupied it only as government wards. It didn't amaze them that they had lived with those conditions for years.

There are a few advantages to being allowed to live eighty years; one is the panoramic view you gain of life in your country. Years ago, women had jobs for economic necessity. They had no visions of a future career. They thrived largely in two fields – teaching and nursing. Their natural capacity for concern for those weaker than themselves shone in these fields. All of them had sublimated abilities. They directed these abilities to club work. In Calgary, thirty-two women's clubs united into a local council of women concerned with improvement of life in their community. These clubs included representatives of every political party and religious denomination. They were both a wise and formidable force.

When I came home to slide with ease into my father's law office there was only one other practising woman lawyer in the city. My rarity could have qualified me for the freak shows that travelled to our town each year and were gaped at for their novelty. To the thirty odd club women clustered for strength in their local council, I was a welcomed addition. Many of the serious reforms fought for involved local questions. They were desperate for free legal advice and counted on mine for thirty years to fight for reforms and advantages men would have ignored. These women's clubs would become great leaders in support for the cause of the Indians when the injustice of the Hobbema Case was publicized.

Today's feminists will sigh or giggle over my behaviour. I may have been a first in many women's untried places or in receiving honours, but I was mentally bound for the possible joy of a family. My own sheer luck had been so good. I wanted to hand on that feeling of security where slowly I had been allowed to grow. That meant I must try to keep my home, my husband and my small daughter. As a result, I spent my days walking on the edge of a razor blade and felt that if I leaned either way it would be disastrous. If it didn't work I would be out in the fall. My husband had no intention of sharing my job, this chosen unpaid job, of helping the Indians. I suppose I was touched with the superiority of the lucky. It was a compromised life and like those lives, it lacked the satisfaction of a total victory.

Laurie's drive, on the other hand, was amazingly beautifully clear and swift and cuttingly effective. Laurie didn't admire my attitude but he accepted it. In one of his notes he indicated with some concern that "Mrs. Gorman had to hurry home to her husband." Not that he wasn't cooperative; he just found it non-understandable.

15: THE BUCKSKIN CURTAIN

I believe that Laurie coined the phrase "Buckskin Curtain," although one of his high school students, Regina lawyer Morris Schumiatcher, later cleverly explained the phrase under that title in an article published in the Hudson's Bay Company's *Beaver*.[1] The phrase was a copy of Churchill's "Iron Curtain," which the communist government had flung around the Soviet Union so nobody would know what was going on in that country and, more important, so that the Russians themselves would not be aware of the prosperity and individual freedom that people in other lands enjoyed.

The purpose of the buckskin curtain was similar: it existed largely to conceal from both the government and the people of Canada the pitiful condition the Indians under their care were in. The buckskin curtain was made legally tight and unbreakable by the Indian Act that allowed only those with the consent of the Department of Indian Affairs onto the reserve.

To understand our dealings with the Indian and the Indian Act you must realize several things. The Indians were originally given no vote. When the Indians signed the western treaties most could write only their own names. Non-Indians in the western territories, as this area was known then, did not elect members to Parliament so why would Indians? The Indians would not have wanted the vote if it had been offered to them. They ruled by hereditary chiefs, not elections. To rid yourself of a chief you simply left him and joined another tribe. It was a precedent that worked well for the Department's convenience. Without a vote, who was there in the government who had a voice to complain about the government's treatment of those they considered "wards"?

Until the enfranchisement clause appeared in the Indian Act, the buckskin curtain was not enforced against the Indian at all. He was still free to wander from his reserve in search of elusive game or whatever he wanted. Uncomfortable in the white man's world whose customs and language he did not understand, the buckskin curtain created no hardship for the Indian. In those days Indians wandered over the medicine line, as they called the

U.S. border because it was good medicine depending which way you were running. They took jobs as interpreters as George Maclean did as a young man when he worked in Calgary. They went on long visits to other reserves, and married into other tribes and moved in. They came to Calgary to trade and often just for fun. Calgary's first civic parade consisted almost entirely of Indians dressed up in their beautiful costumes and camping out overnight in the tepees they brought with them on travois behind their horses. There was open space along the Bow and Elbow Rivers and on Nose Hill. In fact, the lovely Nose Hill, that is now a park, is supposed to have got its name from the fact that an Indian had split his wife's nose one night there, the traditional Indian punishment for adultery.

There were street drinking laws about selling liquor to an Indian but, after all, the Indians themselves had requested those laws in their treaties and felt no real restriction about this. The buckskin curtain didn't worry them.

The Department of Indian Affairs itself soon found the buckskin curtain a useful tool to use against the churches and their missions and thus could persuade them to pick up most of the cost of educating the Indians. It was totally defensible because of the amount of publicity that had already been spread about the visible fortunes in Montreal and New York made by the fur traders who had exploited the Indians. So the buckskin curtain was acceptable to non-Indians as well.

No one objected to the buckskin curtain. The Indians felt it made the land more exclusively their own so they could drive off non-Indian game hunters who wandered on to the reserve. Neither the non-Indians nor their government were even aware of its existence. Only the odd missionary dared tell, then almost in secret, so he could keep his church on the reserve.

But in reality, the buckskin curtain was used by the Department of Indian Affairs just as the Soviet government used their iron curtain. It kept the Indian unaware of his rights for better treatment and it concealed from the government the Department's sloppy care of the Indians, care which was the only excuse for the Department's existence and the reason why their wages were being paid. Later the Department found a better instrument to handle the reserve Indians' protests with more firmness: the Enfranchisement Act.

At first the Department of Indian Affairs did not object to Indians holding pow-wows and meetings to discuss their affairs. They were regarded as inexpensive means of keeping Indians content on their reserve.

In the early records that I had legally pulled out of Ottawa for the Hobbema trial in 1951, I read accounts of large groups of Indians whom the agent had noted passing through his reserve. Usually the large groups were escorted by Mounties with the purpose of seeing whether or not that reserve met with the Indians' acceptance and, if not, the Mounties led them to another reserve. The confusion of who belonged on what reserve in the West was unclear to the Ottawa lawmakers and the Indian.

In Ottawa, the government started enforcing the sections of the Indian Act that confined the Indian to a reserve once he was on it and to also give them control over any fault-finding non-Indian such as the press, the missionaries and the Mounties. And so they simply put in the Act the clause stating that no one but an Indian could be on the reserve unless they had the permission of the hard-worked Indian agent out on his isolated reserve. The government began enforcing the laws, which gave the agents concrete powers over the Indian on the reserve. For example, an Indian could not go off his reserve for any lengthy period without the agent's consent. If the Indian persisted in working off the reserve, even to earn a living for a time, the agent could then enfranchise him.

This clause in the Indian Act, the cruelty of which was disguised under a word the non-whites had always associated with freedom – enfranchisement – instead became the bars of the prison that confined the uneducated Indian inside the reserve. Robbing him of game outside the reserve, he had to be content with miserable rations and miserable treatment. The Department had created what Laurie called a buckskin curtain around the reserve where they could dictate over the Indians while shielded from the criticism of the non-Indians.

The actual firing of shots at the Riel rebellion alerted everyone to problems including the Indians. The unhappiness and discontent could explode into warfare and whether or not it was a just war, the Department used it as an excuse to place in non-democratic laws just as Trudeau, almost a century later, passed legislation such as the War Measures Act that affected thousands of Canadians because there had been an unfortunate kidnapping and murder of one diplomatic official.

The way was wide open for the Department to justify all sorts of ugly control on the reserves under the excuse of possible violence even though there was none really on the Alberta reserves or even on the part of Indians. If the agents protested to their employer in Ottawa about either the lack of success of Ottawa's program or its failure, they could be removed from their jobs. If the missionaries sided with the reserve, the Department would deny them the right to operate their church or their schools, control of these now came under the dictatorial control of Ottawa too. Even the Mounties were removed from any occupancy on the reserve unless with Ottawa's consent. As for the press, without a permit they were barred from the reserve. There was a language barrier so few if any complaints could leak out if any Indian complained to the agent when he applied for his now essential rations. The traditional Indian food source, the game, was diminishing daily on the reserve.

The government of Canada's only knowledge of conditions on the reserve was given in the yearly financial report made up by the Department itself. Or the Department gave the report a low profile and rosied up their report of conditions on the reserve. Department staff was guaranteed continuation of their employment and indeed expansion of their budget grant.

The Indian without a vote had no voice in Parliament at all and although a concerned and caring Parliament thought they were under some sort of duty to care for the Indian, the truth was that hardly a single member of Parliament had ever visited a reserve, or known an Indian. Why should they? They had a difficult enough time trying to get their own constituents' problems in the remote West before a Parliament that was controlled by the population majority of Ontario and Quebec. The cabinet post responsible for the Indians' needs was never filled by a member who had even visited on a reserve or known an Indian. In fact, by custom it gradually became just a temporary first posting for a brilliant future powerful person in Parliament.

At the time of Confederation that cabinet post had been assumed by the fine dramatic actor Sir John A. Macdonald himself. He and the public liked the generous appendage that he was the protector of the poor savage. He soon became bored with the position and transferred the post to other members of his party with its chance for a place in the inner circle of government, the cabinet, with its title and additional power.[2]

The only persons in control of tribes of Indians were a handful of men occupying a building in the City of Ottawa, men who didn't personally know a single Indian and usually had never visited a reserve and certainly none of the remote ones in Western Canada miles from any railway station or highway.

The world's most perfect dictatorship had been created. There could be no revolt from the people they governed, none from the agents who were dependent on them for their jobs and were isolated from even communicating with fellow agents so they could not present a unified protest. By the Indian Act, the Department of Indian Affairs controlled and totally governed a remote people.

And who created that Indian Act? Why, the Department of course! The rest of Parliament on their one day merely listened to the Department head's explanation of the justice and need for the laws that they suggested to Parliament be implemented. The dictators didn't even have to worry about an army revolt. They had Indian scouts on the reserve and could even remove the fair-minded Mounties from the reserve at will.

The general laws of Canada couldn't protect the Indian because under the semblance of being savages, they weren't supposed to understand them.

The Department had in the Indian Act created their own set of laws that did not include any real contribution from the Indians and prevented them from sharing in the laws which guaranteed freedom in the democratic country of Canada beyond the reserves.

This dictator didn't even have to raise money to support his dictatorship. He set his own price when he spoke to Parliament and the Parliament that he had deliberately kept ignorant meekly paid whatever the Department asked. There were temporary and isolated cases where the perfect dictatorship developed a slight fear but that was quickly concealed or plugged up by the Department itself, the only ones allowed to do it.

A terrible thing had been created, a concealed dictatorship completely supported financially and morally by a government struggling toward a better and better democratic system. The real joke was that this dictatorship was honoured and respected and even trusted by the very democracy that provided the ample funds for its existence.

Power breeds power. Every move the Department made increased their power and anything that even remotely could undermine it was quickly sought out and destroyed. The fear was that if the Indians became better educated they might revolt if they got beyond their reserve borders. The contrast of life outside the reserves might inspire them and if they improved the quality of life on the reserve they might even become more independent. This would make the Department's job more difficult. To keep the Indians weak and uneducated was to the Department's advantage. Don't let their numbers increase; instead any money going that way would enlarge the numbers of their own little power group and their income. If the Department improved the Indians' lot they were in reality reducing their own jobs and importance and even the need for them to exist.

It was a vicious cycle and the helpless Indian was completely enclosed and imprisoned within it. If he revolted, he had nowhere to go. Uneducated and untrained, his punishment would be dispensed directly by the agent who not only controlled his rationed food but on whom by law he was now dependent for consent so he could better himself by selling his own cattle and crops that he himself had produced. So even that route toward freedom was barred to the Indian.

The training and the schooling was controlled by the Department and was kept at a minimum. In fact, even when I worked with John Laurie the Department was confining most Indians' training to such things as bricklaying. This at a period when no brick houses were being built at all and certainly there were no bricks on their own reserves with which they could build for themselves. It took Laurie and me two years of bitter negotiations to get the Department to allow the reserve Indians, who for centuries had been the world's greatest animal hunters, to take the necessary cheap courses to become licensed hunting guides and earn a few dollars that way.

When I had the privilege of working with Laurie, this treatment of Indians had been entrenched for years. Generations of Indians had grown up knowing nothing more. How could they wisely seek out anything better? They didn't even know it was there.

Once in Alberta's North I visited a small Indian home. The family was clean and courteous and there was great grandfather, grandfather, father and son who had never had a paying job. A dear little baby was crawling around and I just looked at him almost with horror. How could that child ever be made to understand the importance of gaining even a chance to better himself a small bit? Yet the average Canadian had no concept at all that he was the one responsible for this. Instead he complained about the Indians' failures.

Laurie, a very intelligent man with a close friendship with the Indian, soon began to recognize the source of the problem and that the Department fostered this anti-Indian attitude. The year after I spoke to Parliament before a special committee, Parliament responded and again called a special committee to review the Indians' problems for Parliament members. Needless to say I wasn't invited and had nothing much more to say at the moment except, "you haven't implemented the majority of reforms I asked for."

I obtained a copy of the committee meetings. Judy La Marsh was making waves as the single woman member in Parliament and would soon rise to a cabinet position. She was concerned about the fact that although Parliament had voted the money for building houses on a specific reserve, three years had passed and they still did not have them.

The Department had the audacity to explain to Judy that she really didn't understand that the Indians had been nomadic people and still were and so the Department couldn't get the Indian people to stay around long enough to choose the desired location for their houses. This was over almost one hundred years after the treaty. We had carefully ended their nomadic life and locked them onto a small, almost houseless reserve. Yet Judy, unsure of her facts and unable to get them from the Department itself, had to accept the Department's public explanation delivered to her in this humiliating way. In all probability those houses would have been paid for, not by Canadian taxpayers at all, but by the Indians' own money raised by the sale of their assets and held for them by the Department in trust.

16: DEPARTMENT OF INDIAN AFFAIRS AND THE IAA

John Laurie, Calgary, Secretary of the Indian Association of Alberta, with Eileen Tailfeathers (left) and Gerald Tailfeathers (right) (Glenbow Archives NA-1979-1).

It is difficult for those of us who have always lived or at least are now living in a democracy to understand the vital importance of an association of like-thinking persons. When Laurie asked me to explain the Indian Act to a few Indians gathered in the basement of Paget Hall, he was careful not to call it an association. It took me a while to learn the reason for his secrecy.

Like the rest of us I was so use to associations that I was almost bored with the whole process. I had already spoken on women's rights and the United Nations charter of rights to probably twenty different Calgary associations. But that was the mere tip of the iceberg. Calgary, like every city in our democratic country, sprouts associations like weeds. With fervour we organize them for anything and everything and then they grow and split up and multiply. Or new ones come and like weeds they grow and never quite die. We have societies for cat lovers, societies for special and rare people with diseases, societies that still mostly hold parties and lunches and listen to speeches and drink teas, and each political party has a society of its own. So when Laurie finally decided to ask me to come as a legal advisor to an Indian Association of Alberta meeting I thought nothing of it.

Laurie never did explain to me how unique it was that in Alberta there was a strong province-wide association of all the different tribes. The very new concept to the Indian people of inter-tribal action by democratic vote was not without difficulties. The most controversial feature from the beginning was how so many tribes different in size, origins, language and wealth could operate efficiently as one unit. Also to be coped with was the fact that the southern Alberta Indians – Sarcee, Blood, Stoney, Peigan, and Blackfoot – had occupied distinctly different geographic areas and practised distinctly different forms of hunting and economic existence. The Crees happened to speak one language even though they were divided roughly into bush and forest Crees and they differed from the prairie-dwelling Crees.

By the time of the Indian Association of Alberta, Canada's Indians had been settled by treaty on reserve land separated by miles from other Indians and even other whites. I saw how the Indian Act had locked them into isolation. No white person was allowed to visit an Indian reserve without the Indian agent's consent. No Indian could really mix or consult with non-Indians without fear of being threatened with enfranchisement and thrown off his reserve forever. They had, since treaty, been effectively locked in prisons – miles apart.

I was totally unaware in the beginning that the number of people involved, the distances apart and the different languages spoken had to be taken into account everywhere. For the Indians it was all totally new and the genius of Laurie's patience made it all possible. The mechanisms and the intense concentration of detail that went towards uniting all Indians together in a society of their own were immense.

I am sure that Laurie who was a good scholar, knew the history and the fate of earlier associations and how they had been systematically broken up by the Department of Indian Affairs. That was at the base of his fears and explained his secrecy about it all until we had broken through the buckskin curtain the Department had so craftily hung around the reserves they administered.

By far the greatest thing John Laurie ever did was to be the first secretary of the Indian Association of Alberta and continue, not an actual recorder of minutes in his last years, but its behind-the-scenes secretary until his death. Laurie overcame the communication difficulties from the beginning by sending minutes on to every reserve following both executive and general meetings. He commanded immense respect from the Indians in the

Meeting of the Indian Association of Alberta, *ca.*1950. Seated left to right: Senator James Gladstone, Ruth Gorman, and John Laurie; standing: John Sampson, Albert Lightning, and unknown (Photo: Lorne Burkell; Glenbow Archives NA-4212-154).

Association. His selfless and wise directions were always respected and in any situation of doubt the members would turn to him for leadership, although he always sat quietly through most meetings merely recording their own decisions.

Laurie introduced me gently to the process. Carefully he avoided any past history of Indian associations. I think he was afraid it might scare me off. At first I just attended meetings with him at nearby reserves, such as the Sarcee, Blood, Blackfoot and Peigan. Meetings at these reserves meant I didn't have to leave home. Later, and often alone, I visited the northern reserves to attend meetings.

For years I was the Association's unpaid solicitor as Laurie respectfully referred to me. In the beginning, I had difficulty understanding the two sections in the Indian Act headed "Enfranchisement" and "Trust Funds." I thought it just good luck that Laurie stood up and said that there was no need to discuss the sections just now. Later I realized that John Laurie the teacher was easing me into the subject gently – simple things first. Those two sections involved my whole future with the Indians. My role was largely in an advisory capacity and, along with Laurie, I was often the only white person at many meetings.

The Indian Association of Alberta was just that – an association of only Indians. Whether this was a part of Laurie's design I will never know but there were few non-Indians invited or allowed into their meetings even as spectators or hopeful reporters. Even heads of societies or groups who were prepared to aid in "the cause" were somehow politely excluded. Now that I think about it, the only non-Indians really accepted were women, not men, with the exception near the time of Laurie's death when Hugh Dempsey came to help the ailing John take minutes.

IAA presidents were men who weren't seeking the leadership role but rather were concerned about the welfare of their people. The position offered no financial reward at all, was difficult and not long lasting. The constitution and custom placed a limitation on the length of time a president served. Presidents elected by IAA were never the chiefs of one tribe. A few were past chiefs, David Crowchild and John Samson. Others included Gladstone and John Calihoo.

Unwritten bylaws determined that the president and executive would alternate each year from the north to the south – as custom prevailed as it always does among Indians. It became customary to hold meetings alternately in northern and southern Alberta so the distances would not totally bar anyone's inclusion.

The immense job Laurie had undertaken was to maintain constant communications between Indians separated by language and local conditions. Despite several crises, they remained united and achieved amazing reforms. The funds held by an elected treasurer met the paper and postage costs of notices of meetings, reports of meetings and proposed resolutions prepared and circulated by John Laurie to the varied tribes who then were able to study issues in advance and sound out their fellow tribe members for opinions. In this way each tribe could share in shaping the future. This was not traditional. Laurie was daringly breaking new ground in a society where the chiefs traditionally held the power. Now an elected executive tactfully led the Association's deliberations.

Laurie never seemed to weary from it and never did I hear him complain. He must have had long hours of despair and frustration but they never showed. He was always the serene, patient and sure teacher. The IAA was a new huge class he had voluntarily accepted to teach as their unpaid teacher just as he had the white classes in Crescent Heights High School and earlier at Western. Each pupil was important, was different and unique, and each had a value and could be helped to overcome his own personal and society's difficulties. Of course, Laurie also had to teach another class and that was the other Canadians who not only misunderstood the Indian they had really never known but who carried that age-old prejudice.

What I found so difficult about the meetings was facing continual despair. The Indians spoke out their deep-seated grievances. The only highlights were the jokes told by the Indians themselves. I was always amazed at how their humour never left them even in tragic conditions. But mainly it was long hours of tragedies and failures. Sometimes my adrenaline would get pumped up enough to keep me going as we listened to the petty misery the agents inflicted on their reserves. The pettiness was never put to us in anger by the Indians, only the sad question, "why." To that there was no answer. I was always afraid of breaking loose and answering, "It's because they are miserable bastards strutting their small power." Laurie would have pulled me down instantly if I had dared. He never tried to excuse or blame the Department. He would steer the conversation to Indian unity, to the oppression, forming resolutions not of protest but of change that could eliminate these petty persecutions.

The IAA meetings served as a means of eliminating some of the Indians' misunderstandings about the necessary and unnecessary administrative functions and the services that were owed them by law. Laurie and I were careful to always speak the truth to the Indians. The truth for Indians is so often bitter but somehow truth alone spoken without emotion has its own consolations. Ranting and raving against the difficulties provides little relief. We faced the question of what way to proceed truthfully with them and then at least we were always turning forward and looking for a new way out of their troubles, not merely reviewing the troubles.

While I was there they sat me up on the platform and I would speak only when asked for the legal correctness of some point. On the whole these were extremely peaceful gatherings, orderly and pleasant. I don't remember a single meeting where a loud or angry voice was heard. There was often laughter and chuckles and solid, quiet understanding. When I thought of some of the raucous, almost ugly meetings of whites facing a controversial question, this quietness seemed right.

They all wore white men's clothes and I wore my best too. The Indians' patience was remarkable. These meetings often tried my patience but never theirs. They would sit quietly on rows of hard kitchen chairs and benches for sessions 3 to 4 hours long before there was even a walkabout or food and drink. I wearied but neither they nor Laurie did.

On one occasion this tolerance drove me to distraction. A small four-year-old travelled around on his obviously new and prized possession – a very small wooden tricycle. Child and tricycle got up to the small raised platform where I was speaking. The child proceeded to vigorously circle round and round me while I kept on with my remarks. As he came closer and closer to me, to my horror no one either scolded or removed the excited child and finally he withdrew on his own. I saw a few twinkles in the black eyes of my audience and sensed a general air of enjoyment of this distraction.

Never was an individual corrected on the floor or told he was out of order or told to sit down. The patience of the Indian with his fellow Indian filled me with admiration. Often an elder would rise and on occasion he would wander off the topic under discussion into the glories of the past as old memories took over. I was always tempted to get up and bring him back to the subject under discussion but the Indians never did. I caught on. If I found my impatience rising I would look out at the audience to see that about half the members had closed their eyes and managed a quick nap at these times. I never quite mastered that art.

Yet rarely were the attendees misled. An amazing amount of business was still thoroughly discussed and voted upon. They seemed quite capable of sifting the silly, the too-personal, from what was really important. Although the pace was slow, at the end of each meeting an amazing number of wise decisions had been reached.

There were occasional after-meeting conflicts, but these too were amazingly rare. Oratory on the part of the Indians was confined to the big campfires in the evenings, after the meeting, the pow-wows with drumming and dancing. What amazed me most was the careful following of democratic methods by the Indians. This had to have come from Laurie. Their chiefs' advisors weren't elected and they had been denied the vote in their country as well. Yet the Association's presidents and officers were chosen by a vote, usually by secret ballot so no one would be hurt. Laurie was teaching democracy to a group that had been ruled by hereditary chiefs for thousands of years. That was among the greatest things he did.

Without a lecture or a long printed pamphlet, they had slipped past the Department's rules of administrative control. They also became more daring in their demands. The Department couldn't easily punish a hundred Indians directly. They were forging themselves into a unit and confidence often lit their faces as they proposed resolutions in opposition to government policy. The annual meetings, usually of several days duration, were held on a different reserve each year, alternating, if possible, between the north and the south. I would note with amusement that frequently it was the tribe of the next aspirant president of the Association that would hold the meeting under his direction. They had learned politics of democracy. The host reserve would announce the location and issue the invitation to the annual meeting a year in advance. The invitation was invariably accepted. The custom of being host was part of their ancient tradition.

Where the meeting was held was a matter of great personal satisfaction. At the end of each meeting someone would stand and say proudly, "My tribe would like to hold next year's meeting on our reserve." Like the banished potlatches of old, offering to hold a meeting was a great act of generosity. To bed and feed up to two hundred visitors for at least three days and nights represented an immense project for the impoverished Indians. No money was ever voted from the Association's meagre funds. A kind of custom took over the manner of financing the meetings. To travel to a meeting often involved long distances and at least three or four days of time. To make it possible for the poor as well as the wealthy to attend, tribes took their turns, not automatically but as their funds permitted, to be the host of the meeting. To host a meeting involved considerable expense. The host tribe held events all year to raise the money to host the Association meeting. Usually well over a hundred attended and they had to be fed and housed on a reserve located far from any restaurants, caterers or even grocery stores.

Reserves do not have organized town centres. There was a church and mission and agency centre but those were non-Indian centres. Possibly the Department had deliberately planned it that way. Forcing the isolation of their homes would break down the ancient tribal gathering of tents and render them lonely and slightly confused. So to gather two hundred strangers to a reserve for a meeting was difficult and required immense organization. For instance, even on the large advanced Hobbema reserve during the meeting the Hobbema Indians had to operate a constant shuttle service back and forth that met every passing train and bus because the meeting place was twenty-five miles from the nearest train or bus for visitors without a car. Cars arrived completely full of people. There was no room for extra tents or luggage to be brought in.

The tribe who gave the invitation provided everyone with sleeping quarters. Extra beds in houses had to be found or shared in freshly pitched tepees. Often the ceremonial tepee had to be pitched to sleep the visitors. Some pitched the tepees they brought with them and invariably, as is custom, usually brought their entire family with them. I would go to a nearby motel at night.

The women of the host tribe would cook all the food for the nearly two hundred guests for three meals a day from food saved from their meagre rations. They spent months collecting food, cutlery and even that rarer commodity, money, and indeed each meal was a feast or banquet for the visitors. Proudly they bore into the hall great platters of steaming hot food and somehow they always found enough chairs to seat everyone.

And no meeting could be complete without a pow-wow, a ceremonial dance, each night with the beating of drums and chanting as they danced. Laurie never spoke of these largely male pow-wows to me, but I knew he participated. I never participated in the pow-wows and in fact would try to keep my visit to a one-day stay because of my home responsibilities.

The small hall was always overflowing and the meeting with three interpreters, so lengthy. Laurie did all the planning and sent out written notices to as many as eighty elected delegates, answered their enquiries and kept peace among the delegates. Laurie never seemed to weary from it and never did I hear him complain. He must have had long hours of despair and frustration but they never showed. He was always the serene, patient and sure teacher.

John Laurie was learning as much as the Indians were at these three-day-long meetings. He met a quiet intelligent Indian, a minor chief in his tribe, who confessed that his main source of income and his occupation was poisoning or trapping gophers and collecting the one cent per tail bounty the Department of Agriculture paid – some job. He saw a young Indian girl with a lovely shy smile and red ribbons tying her jet black braids who had been crippled from birth, either pulled herself on a pillow across the floor or was lifted by her brother – no wheelchair. She would never even read or write. His anger became a cold ache inside him. He was seeing what few other white men ever saw.

I learnt from those meetings with the Indians that the wide gap between our races must be closed. There were mistakes in communication when one must use interpreters for four different Indian languages. There was the gap created by words we had never taught them in their schools and by the business practices we had hidden from them. For instance, one time I was trying to restrain them from letting the government talk them into spending too much of their trust fund on unneeded fancy buildings and trips and I was trying to explain that by doing that, they not only reduced forever their own trust fund but also they were losing the valuable yearly interest on the fund. I was speaking to a people who had never been allowed inside our banks and I was having a difficult time. But they proved themselves more adept than most people in their ability to breach the communication gap with regard to explanations of actions that are foreign and unknown to them.

John Laurie did not sit at the head table of Association meetings. He would speak only on rare occasions when asked a specific question. He would sit near the back of the hall, his back planted against a side wall and his head down jotting notes for the minutes in a small stenographer's note book. I knew he had no shorthand and had invented one of his own. After each meeting he carefully compiled and sent at least six pages on scrap paper that I suspected he scrounged and paid for himself, probably at a reduced price. On these pages was an exact report of every action taken, what Indian had spoken and how they voted at each meeting.

These reports would be sent to every member of the Association, on reserves all over Alberta. Back on the reserves over camp fires, in homes or in church halls the Indians would discuss these notes for hours until they were thoroughly understood. They would then write John Laurie expressing their approval of certain items and their concerns and confusion over the undeserved treatment they received from Ottawa. Always they wondered what could be done to change their circumstances. Laurie would then mail each tribe's concerns to the other Alberta tribes. With further correspondence and conversation with delegates who would stop at his rooms or telephone, new problems and new resolutions for reform were prepared for discussion at the next general meeting. The Department never guessed such unpaid labour could be so effective between each yearly meeting.

We will never know the countless hours, late and early, that Laurie sat huddled over his ancient high, upright typewriter poking out in his one finger style the endless notes and minutes. In every spare moment from his large high school class load Laurie was forever transcribing and typing. His memory was excellent and I rarely found anything omitted when the typed and mimeographed pages arrived.

John had to be careful. Somehow when I would receive the typed version of the meeting I would be surprised at how careful he was. Rarely did the name of an individual Indian appear. We were always walking the tight rope. There stood the Department, able almost without reason to enfranchise involuntarily an Indian and throw him off his reserve, or even more subtly, to have him moved to a poorer house.

After his death most of those notes and minutes were presented to the Glenbow Museum Archives. Yet we will never know what other enormous quantities of materials he produced and distributed during twenty years of prodigious output.

My volunteer job was only to read and advise on the possible legal route to success in dealing with the Indians' problems. I advised on further resolutions or demands that would be necessary to reach their goals. Compared to Laurie's time-consuming, endless work of twenty years, my own efforts seem as nothing.

The great strength of the Association was going on right under the Department's watchful eyes. It was in the minutes that John Laurie was so quietly writing at the side of the room. They never did realize how he somehow got them typed out and copied and mailed to each member and, in effect, to each reserve in Alberta where they were read till they were crushed and dog-eared.

Each recipient of minutes handed them from hand to hand. The Indians carefully analysed the minutes and fitted them to their needs. Also, well before each meeting Laurie would again mail out any new resolutions that would be put forward at the coming meeting. This to the Indians, long subject to surprise attacks from the Department, was so re-assuring. It meant that when they came and voted there was no sudden dropping of surprise legislation or sideshows.

John's knowledge of the needs in health and education came from the Indians themselves. Some tribes prepared their needs in a resolution they presented with a new authority at the annual meeting and if it was voted on there was the consolation of other Indians' understanding and anger at least. Rarely did we even get an answer from the Department, and if we did it was written on the bureaucratic standard forms they used to fend off busybodies from outside their organization.

But Laurie carried the knowledge in his speeches to groups of Calgary non-Indians. His speeches were not mere rhetoric; they often included examples that would stir the thoughts of those at the meetings. Laurie also deliberately contacted anyone that he felt would help, by letter or by phone call. He was weaving a web, a network of available aid for Indians outside reserves.

It was accepted that this was the news Albertans wanted to read. Laurie's years of writing millions of words to his Indian and non-Indian friends had created a mass of supporters. It is a fantastic record of success for an unpaid volunteer, rarely if ever equalled.

Laurie found some surprisingly exciting persons. There was still a bit of glamour attached to the unknown Indians but also there was an amazing number of basically kind if confused persons out there beyond the reserves, shocked to find themselves playing the part of the ones who imposed this injustice. The Department would have been amazed at the status Laurie's correspondence held. To the Department, reports of the agent on the reserve were only of a simply dressed, quick, polite teacher who went to meetings and took notes and rarely, if ever, spoke. At the meetings there was often laughter at a joke and although the Indians would shake their heads, no muttering or angry words worth noting occurred. The agents would barely report the meeting.

Laurie would modestly recount to the Indians reforms that were achieved. Through his communications sent with meeting notices he kept the Indians' courage alive in a time when for fifty years they had so little to be hopeful about.

As Laurie patiently wrote on and on in these halls on far-off reserves and as later he slowly pecked them out late at night after a full day of teaching school, he was pulling into something real the broken hopes and dreams of a race. He was making them visible at last in words. It worked slowly like water on a stone. The Indians were now entering into the consciousness of other Canadians if not into that of the Department that had ignored them for years. Their needs were becoming concrete requirements that had to be met by decent persons trying daily to live reasonable, at least not unkind, lives. The miracle was that it worked.

Unfortunately the schoolteacher did not live long enough to see all of these resolutions become realities. But Laurie knew that this was so often the fate of the teacher. Occasionally a student from Crescent Heights High School, now grown up and out in the world, would come to visit him to share his success with the man who had helped him. Fortunately Laurie did see almost half of the resolutions he sent out so hopefully during his lifetime become a reality: schools were better; the tuberculosis hospital in Edmonton was created; new homes were built on the reserves; more and more Indian children were somehow making their way into high schools and graduating. Jobs were still few but Indians were leaving the reserves in spite of the Department's attempts to contain them there.

I've often thought how Laurie's activities never seriously alarmed Indian Affairs bureaucrats in far-off Ottawa. According to the "spying" reports Ottawa demanded from their agents, the Indians' efforts seemed totally ineffective. John Laurie was reported to be a teacher who had never even been promoted within his school. His only apparent helpers at Indian meetings were a woman whose husband was a bird watcher, a housewife-poetess who had published little and a woman lawyer who was unemployed and who "kept house." No wonder they could see little to fear from the activities and strength of an Indian Association of Alberta. Its only visible meeting was once a year on varied reserves and it had no employees or headquarters. Fortunately Ottawa never realized the Herculean activities of the soft-spoken schoolteacher.

Discovering concealment became almost a game that both the Indians and Laurie and I played with the Department of Indian Affairs. The Department revealed nothing, neither future plans nor past actions. Only by listening to what happened to the Indians could we find out their actions, their plans. At IAA meetings Laurie and I would listen, then draw up their objectionable actions and plans in a protest form for the Indians and the Indians would sign the document and we would forward it to the Department, or the Association would put the protest in the form of a resolution and forward that to Ottawa. Laurie was functioning as a one-man inquiry team reviewing the Department's actions. We were one long "judicial inquiry" and what we heard had to be factual and proven true and supported by other Indians.

Laurie never encouraged protest. He would continue to put forward a resolution on a matter that would outline how conflict could be avoided. The Indians loved the petitions. They were a form of action. If they had landed in this mess because they had been able to make only an "X" on the treaties, they were delighted now to boldly write their names in full in protest against.

No petition ever went to the government with a single "X" on it. They all proudly and daringly wrote their names, knowing their names would be noted and a copy would go to their own agent from Ottawa. Ottawa would instruct the agents to watch the signers and make them aware that it was not wise to behave this way. These were small but wearying punishments. The agent could inflict denial of a permit to sell hay or denial of extra medicine for the sick – petty but continuous.

The rebellion symbolized by signing a petition appealed to the Indians. They understood that if they got many signatures it would be difficult for any one Indian to be picked out for special harassment. This was also an action the Indians could take themselves. They would travel miles to get signatures and to discuss the problem and the possible solution that had been thought out at their last annual meeting. We bypassed the agents and even the directors in the field. The petitions were then mailed off to Ottawa.

Resolutions and criticisms of the Department's actions, and those were the majority, were carefully recorded only by the votes of the entire Association. So the Department had to pick on one individual or punish everyone. However, to step forward and sit on the executive did at first carry with it, to some degree, fear of reprisal. Near the end, as our numbers and their determination grew, it became an honour to stand up and be counted. Elections to the executive were heavily contested.

Laurie always carefully kept the appropriate officials informed of our meetings and the agent was invited to open each meeting. There were polite closures that assured his departure if he didn't leave on his own. Everyone was aware that always in the hall there would be an Indian who was a spy and who would report our activities to the agent for favours received. A RCMP officer in full uniform and his Indian scout always sat silently at the first meetings; we were clearly under police supervision. The resolutions were always sent to the provincial or regional director and to Ottawa. The replies were always the same. Sometimes I wondered if they just used form letters. Occasionally they would pull out a section of the Act to justify their actions and I would send back a contested reply that never was answered.

From the beginning, Laurie saw the need for the Indians to somehow speak to the Department at least first as a province-wide group and then, if refused, somehow to get at least one voice into Parliament.

Laurie was certainly aware of the disastrous tales the earlier non-Indians who had attempted to help the Indians to organize had faced. He mentioned them in his writings, but never to me. Possibly he was afraid I would back off but he was careful to assure that I avoid their failures, if possible. Never was I to accept payment for my work; like his work it must be free. He was aware of the helpers and lawyers of the past who had faced the threat of being charged in Criminal Court for fraudulently obtaining funds from Indians when they attempted to collect even the funds necessary for expenses. This lack of payment for expenses was no hardship for me but for the already impoverished John Laurie, it was a hardship. Also it was why Laurie was careful (except on two rare occasions) about confronting Department officials, even then never rudely. Indeed he always sought the cooperation of the agents on the reserves who for the most part were hard-working men doing a lonely underpaid job. But to do that also he had to watch he didn't lose the confidence the Indians had in him.

In his work with the Association Laurie chose to be led by the Indians' immediate needs for reforms. Even this was not easy because often the needs of each tribe were in conflict with other tribes. For years the Department had used this device to deny any reform for the Indians. Divide and rule had been their formula. As long as the tribes couldn't present a united need, the Department was able to deny it.

For example, if one reserve asked for a school, the Department would find another reserve that already had enough schools and were prepared to state that they wished that no more of their treaty money or government money be spent on schools. If a criticism of the Department's action ever did by accident reach an MP or the press, the Department would immediately counteract by producing the one tribe's rejection and piously say, "We can't enforce our will on the Indians; that would be improper. Clearly we have this statement that no more money is to be spent on schools." And the confused MP or newsman would beat a retreat and probably never again try to help the native people. The persecution by the Department of persons who helped Indians made it difficult for the Indians to obtain even advice.

The Department discouraged Indians from forming their own associations. The trust funds available for such associations were limited to twenty-five dollars. The rest of the association fees could not be paid out of trust funds that the Department held for Indians, which is really the Indians' own money the Department is merely holding. This means that poor Indians found it difficult to join an association even though they have lots of money for this use held in trust by the Department. In effect the Department was preventing Indians from joining associations that might outweigh them.

Laurie and even I, who was several years younger, had been raised by parents most of whom believed a woman's place was inside the home. The world of business was a man's domain where women occupied lowly positions of aides and servants. However, the words and thoughts of women were rapidly changing through the first half of the twentieth century in Alberta where adventurous wives of pioneers struggled for recognition and five women pushed the "Persons Case" to the highest court, England's Privy

Council, and secured a declaration proclaiming that women were actually "persons." In every law through the British Empire that gave a person a right, that right was now legally recognized as a right of women too. The Persons Case had been one of the really important achievements for women in the English-speaking world.

Fortunately my father always admired and respected women and their abilities. He was a second or third cousin to Canada's best-selling novelist of her day, Nellie McClung, one of the five women who had pushed the Persons Case. He saw no reason why, if he had no son, his daughter could not follow his beloved profession as a lawyer.

Women of my mother's time had, in their own way, organized themselves into harmless groups related to church, school, hospital or home where their unused talents shone. It was these women who focused their efforts on humane activities and who gladly gave John Laurie his first audiences.

Women's clubs in Calgary raised funds for their good works through cooking, sewing and voluntary activities. For greater effectiveness, women had wisely united their groups. The home and school associations were city- and province-wide. They gathered under the strong leadership of Mrs. Bertha Hanson. The Family Home and Welfare Association united under Mrs. Harold Riley, Sr., whose husband's family had given part of their homestead land to form today's Riley Park in Calgary. There was also the local Calgary Council of Women, a very strong and effective group of the thirty-two women's clubs in Calgary. The Council had functioned in Calgary since the wife of Canada's governor general, Lady Aberdeen, related to Queen Victoria, had spoken in Calgary. Unlike the counterpart men's association they had no membership barriers on religious, economic or political grounds. Its political strength was amazingly effective: it was responsible for incredible changes, not just for women but for the whole community as well.

I was a legal advisor to the Local Council of Women of Calgary for many years. We had taken on the Canadian Pacific Railway when our City Council was going to give the entire south bank of the Bow River to the railway to run a second set of tracks across Prince's Island. I had legally directed their actions but it was their own dedication that saved the riverbank. They were exceedingly strong. When I would bring an Indian resolution forward that I felt involved the government's action against Indians, the local council would pass it on to each of their thirty-two women's clubs in Calgary and to their National Council of Women.

In these women's groups John Laurie first found a receptive and activating audience for the much-needed reforms he advocated on behalf of Canada's native people. John Laurie had spoken to these groups and gained converts before I had graduated from law school. We designed and pushed needed reforms through the Calgary Council of Women, which represented over 2,000 voters.

Laurie's entry into the family welfare women's group had been by means of a quiet, ladylike woman, Mrs. Anne R. Downe. Her venture outside the home was through mixed poetry groups where she modestly published under the *nom de plume* of "Lynette." Her daughter, Cynthia, and son, Tom, both had John Laurie for a teacher at Balmoral[1] and Crescent Heights schools and she knew of his concern for the Indians.

A violent push from an unlikely human rights violator, Adolf Hitler, launched Mrs. Downe on her life-long, devoted and very effective support to Alberta Indians and aid to John Laurie. In pre-Second World War years we watched, more amused than terrified, Adolf Hitler's screaming and impassioned speeches to great hordes of well-organized German youth. Mrs. Downe heard Hitler say that Canada was in no way to criticize the concentration prison camps he was forcing Jews into because Canada treated their Indian people even worse. A very angry Mrs. Downe hot-footed it over to her children's' school and inquired about the truth of this. Her enquiry was directed to John Laurie. When he assured her that there was a close similarity, she became a life-long and very effective supporter of Indian reform. She championed the Indian Association and carried the Indians' problems into her Anglican Church, the home and school groups and Mrs. Riley's Council. She got their endorsements to send petitions to the Department in Ottawa. These were voters and their views could influence politicians and their employees. She would also encourage various groups to invite Laurie to speak at their meetings. Mrs. Downe was quietly enraged by injustice and she took to battle with relish.

Mrs. Downe was president of the Crescent Heights Home and School in the early 1940's and represented them at the Calgary Council of Home and School Associations. Besides endorsing the Indian Association of Alberta's resolutions about the necessity for more schools on the reserves and the abolishment of the so-discouraging-to-Indian children residential schools, she carried the Association's message into every group of concerned mothers of school children in the city. The resolution protesting the Indian residential schools became a brief before the Cameron Commission on Education in 1946 and reached all across Alberta.

Mrs. Downe became a president of the Calgary branch of the Canadian Authors' Association and served three terms, and all over Canada our front thinkers' polls found themselves endorsing resolutions about the needs of the Indian people.

She involved church groups everywhere. I remember Laurie saying to me with a twinkle in his eyes as he climbed in the car one day: "There's hope that Mrs. Downe is now carrying on a spirited correspondence about the Indians with the Archbishop of Canterbury and that he's replying and sending it out to those in high places."

Hitler lit up the gentle mother and poetess. Her daughter amazed me when she told me: "I don't expect Mr. Hitler ever thought he would inspire a quiet lady like mother who wrote poetry in far-away Calgary to become a pro-Indian fighter of an entirely different sort."

The Germans, to my confusion, have a strange, unreal affiliation with the American Indian. Even today some of them spend their summer holidays dressing up in phony Indian feathers and living in tepees rendering their version of a pow-wow. I discovered this strange fact when I put out my small quarterly magazine called *Golden West*. Each time I wrote something on Indians a German came in and bought large quantities of magazines. Out of curiosity I asked him what he did with them and he explained that he resold them in Germany for suitable profit to these groups. He couldn't explain what kept these phonies going; I never discovered the reason. Possibly there had been very good German translators of the penny dreadful cowboy and Indian books that had so misled earlier English readers and done such harm in creating a fantasy literature of the American cowboy hero.[2]

In addition to Mrs. Downe and me, another sympathizer was Mrs. Reta Rowan who came to the Indian Association of Alberta meetings from Edmonton. Her husband, William Rowan, appointed chair of zoology in 1920 at the University of Alberta, was known for his important study of the migration paths of crows. I don't know what led Professor and Mrs. Rowan to start communicating with Laurie, possibly through reading one of the many articles and speeches he was making. The Rowans formed a group of intellectuals from among various church and university people in Edmonton called "Friends of the Indian Society" and they served as the Northern Alberta conduit for assistance to the Indians. The group was amazingly effective as speakers and correspondents on behalf of not only their own beliefs but of the desires and needs of the Indian people.

Mrs. Rowan had written every faculty club across Canada and had them forming study groups. They spoke at women's clubs that had fifteen members sometimes driving into the country to speak to the farm women's institute. But the Department didn't know about such a group – letters went out all over the country. They gave courses to young Indians, courses where the Indians had fun and acted out how to talk to the agent and be listened to. They persuaded church women to quit sending barrels of used clothing to the reserves that were filled with high heeled shoes and fancy hats but instead to get warm work clothes for them. It began with used clothes but when needed it ended up later with angry votes. They persuaded university women's clubs across Canada to organize study groups on Indians, and faculties and campuses to be ready to welcome young Indians. Their hard work brought tough and effective results, and produced understanding. In reality it was a groundswell that made cool intellectual discussion pale in comparison.

I used to watch these two women – Mrs. Downe and Mrs. Rowan – at the male-only annual meetings of the Indian Association of Alberta throughout Alberta. If there was one word to describe these vital assistants to the Indian Association of Alberta, I would use the word 'genteel.' They always sat together near the back of the hall, so neat in their matching twin sweater sets and sedate tweed skirts. Frequently they knitted, never once spoke out, but quietly and constantly made notes, as did Laurie. They would go back to Calgary and Edmonton and distribute these notes at any meeting at which they could get a hearing.

Fortunately the Department of Indian Affairs never knew of their actions. The Department misjudged the IAA assistants determinedly making a stand for Indian rights; we were sorry ineffective-appearing aides from the Department's viewpoint. Enquiries about my participation proved that I did have money but had to be a sort of dilettante more to be laughed at than feared and really one of little success. Although a graduate lawyer, I was a rare and doubtful bird. When I was called to the Calgary Bar there was only one other practising female lawyer in Calgary, Helen Steeves. To make it worse I was even an unemployed lawyer who had voluntarily chosen to abandon my profession and to return to keeping a home for my husband and daughter. But more and more service clubs, always anxious for an after-lunch fill in, were asking me to speak. I was willing and every time an amazing and promising woman or man emerged from the audience.

Since the beginning of time the Indians had been a hunters' macho society. It used to surprise me when I saw that I was often the only woman in the room until Mrs. Downe and Mrs. Rowan began to come to the meetings. Rarely was an Indian woman present. They came sometimes when their cooking chores were over and sat silently at the very back of rows. I think the Indians had come to look upon me as an asexual creature. On occasion one would say, "my brother I differ with you" in reply to an explanation. Patiently I would explain that I'm proud to be a blood sister but I am a sister and they would all laugh. I'm sure that is why I had the titles Princess and Queen placed before my Indian names, to explain my peculiar position. In fact the name the Stoney Indians had given me when I was young to honour my father and before I had gone to them, translated as Mountain White Eagle Girl. They explained that I had been given the name of an honoured dead Indian but since they gave only men names they had to tack the girl on to make it suitable.

Up to this time Daisy Crowchild was the one exception. A few of the chiefs and councillors' wives came and sat with their husbands for brief periods during the meetings. At one memorable meeting a woman attended as a representative of a band in the far North. Her husband had been killed and she was raising her two sons by digging some sort of a root out of the frozen tundra that she sold to a chemical company. Her hands were torn and dyed a bright orange and she had glowing eyes and fortunately spoke enough English to manage. Her tribe had chosen to send her for that reason. I realized she might have a difficult time finding a "bedding down" place so I asked her to stay with Mrs. Rowan, who had a motel room in the nearby town. She and I talked half the night and I learnt so much from her. But the IAA meeting was the biggest adventure of her life to date, she who faced polar bears and blizzards, often daily.

Nowadays Indian women are taking a fine position in their society. They have been great all along but in recent years they have found a way to use their hard-working ability. Many prominent chiefs are now women; one is the business director of her tribe. They have come a long way since it was suggested to the Indian Association of Alberta that it was time they admitted women as members of the Association and, slightly reluctantly after a debate, the men voted them in. On the next resolution after their admittance, which was by hand counts, I noted that the women as usual were sitting immobile in the back row. Finally I said, "Come on girls, you get to vote" and with much giggling and laughter they flung up their hands and voted. Now the Indian women are proving very able councillors and chiefs.

17: NEW ACT AND THE "MAN BEHIND THE THRONE"

Until the new Act Laurie and I had been helping the Indians fight the ungenerous restrictive control of this civil service department, a control the Department was always sneaking through Parliament as improvements for the voteless Indians. It came like a ghost, silent into our lives, not clearly seen or definable, a totally new Act regarding Indians and, like a ghost, it floated through our Canadian Houses of Parliament in Ottawa, was passed and left without even any exciting debate by the unconcerned majority Liberals, and disappeared. How Parliament had been coerced into actually passing such an Act had never been explained. Its consequences were never revealed to Parliament. It was totally different from all of Canada's past Indian Acts. It would rob children from future support that had been promised them. Fortunately Calgary's long-time Conservative MP Doug Harkness sent a copy of it to his past fellow teacher and present friend John Laurie. John Laurie's face was whiter than I had ever seen it. He just handed the copy of the new Act to me and said, "Read this." It was exceptionally long for any Act that passes through a Parliament. It was eighty-seven printed pages and its index took up one page and had even proved inaccurate. I couldn't find listed things I was looking for.

The timing of the new Act's arrival and passage into law was fiendishly clever. It had arrived in the last week before Parliament's long summer, 21 June 1951, one week before the final closure date for the spring session of Parliament. This was the day when all members of Parliament were planning their summer holidays, most of which included a visit back to their own electoral constituencies so they could contact, placate and listen to their electors if they hoped to continue holding their jobs. For western Canadian members of Parliament, it meant a long trip home, possibly packing up and moving their families, clothes and personal necessities, and arranging to close their Ottawa residences and open or rent a place in their constituency while their children were out of school. So it was difficult for the party in power to find a voting quorum on this day.

Most opposition members regarded it a waste of time to be in the House on this day as well. In any case, because the Indians had no vote and were not any MPs' constituents, Indian concerns were not really vital to the MPs. Newspaper reporters were unaware of the existence of the new Act because there was no debate about its passage into law in Parliament. The Indians whom it primarily concerned had in no way been consulted so across Canada nearly all were totally unaware of, let alone alarmed by, its existence.

The proposed changes in the brilliantly designed Act were so subtly worded that their true intent was concealed. The government would offer the Indians a right to vote, but not federally, only provincially. At the same time, if the offer was accepted, the new sections in the Act could be interpreted by the Department of Indian Affairs as a reason for forcing Indians who accepted the vote off their reserves, an action that would appear to be unconnected to the Ottawa department. The right to vote in provincial matters and to have liquor on the reserve would be the province's responsibility. If there were negative consequences it would be the province's fault, not the federal government's. However, a native could vote only if he signed a waiver to be subject to income tax. Natives would then, under the Act, not only enable the federal government to collect money for their own federal coffers but also to threaten them, the natives, with eviction from their federally-supported, long-term, small, promised payment of their land. If the Indians protested the Act, it would look as if they were seeking to avoid sharing the taxes the whites paid. If they didn't vote, under threat of the penalty of eviction, they were not really worthy citizens of Canada.

It was a cruel joke on the Indians and would once more up the political game we always play in Canada of having the federal government release us from a tax only to find out it has merely been transferred to the provinces, so that the taxpayers' burden has not been reduced at all, just shifted.

For the untrained, uneducated Indian, to be banned forever from his people and the land he regarded as his land and the home he had been raised in was a desperate prospect. Thrust off the reserve he would be left to wander to our cities and become a civic and provincial welfare responsibility. The aim of the federal civil service Department of Indian Affairs had always been to present a low budget to Parliament to justify their positions. Now they were seeking a legal loophole to escape any responsibility at all for the present and the future of the Indians. But the Indian, caught in this tossing about of his way of life between province and federal government, was condemned to a dreadful life in our cities. Without much education, no adjustment to city customs or life, no job training in any way, a different-coloured skin and poverty he was condemned to a terrible future. In my opinion it was a prospect of a lingering death of misery and poverty and unhappiness. The federal government in the process would save thousands of dollars by not having to pay the price they had promised for the peaceful surrender of half a continent and by at last permanently transferring to the provinces responsibility for the Indians.

For years I had been concerned about some strange sections in the Act that said that one was not a treaty Indian: 1) if not legally married; 2) if of male white descent; 3) if did not hold a treaty ticket; 4) or if ancestors took scrip. When I had first questioned the Indians and Laurie about my concerns they said, "The government doesn't enforce that. They never have. We have other things to protest. Let's not rock the boat."

But then we got a new Liberal Minister of Indian Affairs, the Honourable Walter Edward Harris, and he added new sections to the Indian Act. Laurie was greatly disturbed when he announced that by an amendment to the Indian Act the government was going to create new treaty Indian reserve lists to register the Indians as treaty Indians, especially because the Indians were already enrolled on reserve lists and all carrying their little cards so defining them. They held treaty tickets – red ones or blue ones – and they were always showing me their tickets to prove they were treaty Indians. Registration, however, was to be different. A time limit was set and all had to register. Within a certain number of days after registration any ten members of the tribe could protest the registration of one of their tribe's members based on one of the four grounds in the Act listed above that previously could have legally barred Indians, but had never been enforced, from being treaty Indians. Treaty Indian status meant sharing treaty payments and tribe trust funds, and the right to live on an Indian reserve. Any Indians successfully protested would be driven from the reserves promised them for life as part of the peaceful settlement of Canada without Indian resistance.

Laurie immediately saw the possible consequences and had been fighting the proposed changes in the law as soon as the bill was made public. A witless Parliament with a majority merely voted following the minister's direction.

Laurie was right to be alarmed. No one understood the new Act or was concerned. Having got it passed, the Department lay low for quite a while before beginning very quietly and without the public's awareness to enforce it.

It was a cunning scheme. Laurie and I always gave the Department credit in that. The list of existing treaty Indians was to be posted in the agent's office on the reserve. Then other Indians could, if they chose, sign a protest against the presence on the reserve of any Indian on the list. By getting ten to join him in the signing (and that was easy; most Indian families have a relation base of at least twenty on the reserve), the luckless Indian whose name was protested would be removed from the reserve and he, his family and his future family would lose the house they lived in and their only land, the reserve, forever. Imagine if such a thing were done in every city block. But of course in the Indian's case, it was worse. Not only would he lose his property but he and his future generation would be banished forever from the place he now regarded as his own, the reserve.

The Act seemed such a ridiculous proposal that I could hardly believe it could be passed in its first reading nor could I believe that this could really happen in Canada and be accepted by a democratic government. I had had no training in this type of investigation at all. But I fear that I had not fully contemplated the disastrous permanent consequences if the bill was passed into law. I could not envision Indian people without homes, without training or money, dispossessed of all they ever had.

The timing was to prove most fortunate for our long fight to better the reserve Indians' conditions. The prairie provinces, Alberta, Saskatchewan and Manitoba, and the coast province of British Columbia had been a long time without a true voice in the government of their country. In the entire period since Confederation, strange as it seems, it was a Liberal, a former dean of the University of Alberta, now elected Minister of Indian Affairs, Walter Harris, who was instrumental in passing the disastrous change to the Indian Act.

This new Act that I thought could eventually remove every Indian from their promised payments and reserve land could not have come from the Department. If there were no Indians on reserves there would eventually be no department and they were too smart and too experienced to advise on anything that would totally rob them of their own jobs. I had written a legal brief to the Indian Association of Alberta advising them to fight it and warning of its legal consequences.

That still left unanswered why the Act was passed at all. Laurie found out from Doug Harkness that it had been introduced to Parliament by a Liberal member from Newfoundland. If I had known the man I believed conceived it and how smart he was, I would have been terrified to take the case and tangle with him.

His name was Jack Pickersgill and his electoral district had no interest in native people. The original members of the tribe once on that island, the Beothuks, had been systematically wiped out. Why would a member from there concern himself with Indians in any way?

A study of the man Pickersgill who brought it to Parliament was revealing. He was brilliant. Born in Ontario at about the same time as John Laurie, he had attended not one of eastern Canada's prestigious universities but the newer University of Manitoba and he had even lectured in history there once before becoming a civil servant. Laurie and I would come to call him the "man behind the throne."

Pickersgill, with his shining record in the civil service, had been picked to succeed the aging Prime Minister Louis Saint-Laurent. For that purpose, he had run as a member of Parliament from a tiny village in Newfoundland called Twillingate, a sure-fire election spot where anyone could be elected who built even one new road in the poverty-stricken village. However, such a brilliant man had nothing to fear, being groomed for greater things. With full knowledge of the Department of Indian Affairs' operation from his quick rise in the government, Jack Pickersgill had designed an Act so that neither the Department nor the federal government could be blamed for what was done to native people. Pickersgill's plan would create big savings for the federal Liberals, which could affect taxpayers and assure a Liberal re-election.

Years ago, following the Riel rebellion, three men had come back to Hobbema who had been married to Cree women and the generous Cree had taken them onto the reserve. It was these men's descendants and their children who were to be removed from the new oil-rich Hobbema reserve. Of course, if the first hearing was successful, friends of those evicted would probably lay charges against those who laid the first charges and then they too would be evicted. Eventually the federal Department of Indian Affairs would be free of over half the natives on reserves in Western Canada. It would return to the government a fortune in land, plus all the money saved in paying small treaty payments and the accompanying support of schools and health, as promised in the treaty. It was a grave injustice.

The new change in the Indian Act, designed to remove natives from their homes, was a diabolical act. In desperation, when I saw how impossible it would be to prove what anyone's great, great grandfather or grandmother had done when there were no documents, or if there were any documents, they had been transferred to the Department of Indian Affairs, I decided to appeal to the newly elected prime minister of Canada, Mr. Louis Saint-Laurent.

I wrote a letter explaining the injustice, and that I had the Canadian Bar behind me. Saint-Laurent had been a highly respected Quebec lawyer himself and I was sure that as a fine member of the Bar he too would not wish to put this Act in force. I received a most courteous answer back assuring me that if my facts were correct, it was an injustice but he would need advice on it. That was followed a week later by another from his office, signed by him but the tone was entirely different. It said, "Mr. Pickersgill has advised me that your facts are lies and also points out that you can't even spell Ottawa correctly and that is the last we will hear from you of this matter." Well, he probably was right about the spelling of Ottawa.

With the new Act, Canada entered a new era of Indian affairs. Until then the only interference with and rules for Indians on their reserves were made by the federal government through a special civil service group in Ottawa, the Department of Indian Affairs. This group's overall aim was to increase their own Ottawa-based department and reduce the money owed Indians thus giving the civil service group assured employment and sure funds under their exclusive management. No one in the Department regarded our natives as the original people of Canada but only used them as pawns in a political and money game. The Indians could never get away from this total control by Ottawa's civil servants until they got a vote and had a voice in our country's government.

This sudden unasked-for new Act introduced as Bill 268 in Parliament was a new way for the federal government, through manipulating Indians, to steer more money into their coffers by recovering the oil-rich reserve land and by no longer having to pay the annual support solemnly promised and still owing to the Indian people. Nor would they have to continue supporting a by-now expensive Ottawa-supported large group of civil servants called the Department of Indian Affairs.

At least I could see the ultimate result of the Act but why had this long Act come out of nowhere? Who would it really benefit? In Alberta, one of the wealthiest reserves had become the three tribes at Hobbema. Fortunately for them, oil was discovered under land given them by treaty – more fortunate because such land was given for as long as the sun shines and the rivers flow, according to the treaties, and was given tax-free in exchange for a fortune in land claimed and sold by the Canadian government to its increasing numbers of settlers.

The Canadian government said that if a native surrendered his right to the future payments owed to him on his federal reserve, he could then move on and farm on free land that would just be given to him. From the native's viewpoint, here at last was a chance to escape off his now semi-starving reserve, a chance to own and raise horses or cattle on a piece of his own land. If anything was to be given to him, he would take it.

The federal government would be able to shed the federal promises of payment made by treaty and reduce the treaty payments owed, those deferred payments still owed by the federal government to the native people, easy payments to be made by a minimum payment to Indians but still costly to the government. The secret was to not publicly drive the natives off the reserve. Too many religious groups, also fair-minded Canadians, might be shocked at that procedure.

Pickersgill felt that his plan would not be opposed by anyone except some Indian descendants whose ancestors were a minority on the reserves. He thought that the Indians' opposition would be minimum as they could point out that by evicting some people from the reserve, the natives left would get more land and a larger share of band funds. He thought that the plan would be more successful because it would not be whites driving Indians off reserves but rather those chosen by the Indian people themselves. If anyone was to be blamed for the eviction, it would be their fellow Indians, not the whites.

But Pickersgill's brief service in the Department of Indian Affairs and the fact that he had never visited a reserve meant that he had no grasp of the ancient native culture base of 'everyone shares.' He did not seem to know that natives were not anxious to remove friends and fellow reserve dwellers.

18: I TAKE THE CASE

I took the case at the request not only of the Hobbema Samson tribe that were ordered evicted, but on behalf of the Indian Association of Alberta to protect all their members and other Indians on reserves who were not specifically even members of the Association.

My first objective had been to save the Hobbema Indians from eviction and after that, win or lose, my intent was that the Association would once more attempt to get Parliament to change the new Indian Act. I hoped that through court action Parliament would see what an injustice the new Act was despite the Department who had designed it and the politicians who had pushed it through by presenting it as desirable legislation. In reality it was against all treaty promises and previously passed and approved actions in Indian law, and was a cruel and basically unjust Act affecting all the Indian people of Canada.

I first heard of the expulsions in John Laurie's rented house. John Laurie had phoned on a mid-afternoon with his usual, "There are some people here who would like to talk to you." When I arrived at his house there were about twelve Indians sitting in a circle on the floor of his small living room with its few chairs. They had left a space for me so down I sat cross-legged in the space. Once more I faced the black inexpressive marble eyes and unsmiling lips that I had first seen when I met John Laurie and the Indian Association of Alberta almost ten years before.

The result of me simply, quietly joining the seated circle would bring a whole new cycle and years in my own life. Laurie's face was white and drawn. There were no formal introductions, no happy jokes. They launched immediately into the problem. Slowly and haltingly in low voices they told me how after the Indians had registered their names under the new Act the government men had arrived and consulted with some tribe members secretly. Now that they knew petitions had been signed, something terrible would happen soon and those whose names were protested would be driven from the reserve. It had already happened at Morley where the agents found ten

Indians willing to sign and now the agents were at Hobbema doing it. Laurie explained to the people that what would happen would be that friends and relatives in turn would in anger sign a petition against those who signed the first one and eventually every Indian would be driven from the reserve. And then the government who only held the land in trust for the Indians, having no Indians left on the land, would take it back, now a very valuable asset, and eventually there would be no reserves left in Canada.

This of course had not occurred to the Indians who were only frightened and angry with the Indians who had signed against their fellow Indians. The signers said they were just angry over a little something and to get even with the Indians they were angry at, they had signed the protest petition. I wondered if greed was somehow in the mix. There would be more for those left on the reserve when they drove off the others. I understood the federal government's coveting the land but obviously they had found a way to motivate greed in the Indian people too.

The Indians said that already some of the Indians who had signed the document asking for the removal of other Indians felt bad. They claimed they didn't understand what it meant when they signed. They didn't understand the banishment was for all time and would include all the person's relatives and babies. They felt that the Indians at Morley who had signed were the weak Indians, stupid people, not the important people in the tribe. They were against the signing. Laurie said, "I will go to Morley and talk to them. If they all say that they will say they didn't understand what they signed, the government will be afraid to go ahead if the witnesses won't testify or if they say they were misled."

Laurie rushed off to Morley and with his immense influence with the Stoney, that stemmed from his long association with them, he had managed to persuade the Morley people who signed the protest to go to the agent and demand it back telling him that they wouldn't testify against their fellow Indians. He successfully convinced some of them to tell the government that if they went on with the hearing and attempted eviction, they would stand up and say that although they had been persuaded to sign the protest form, they had not understood the concept of what they were signing. The result of Laurie's visit with the Morley Indians was that the protest form that initiated the eviction order had to be torn up. For the moment the Stoney Indians were safe. It was a small pre-trial hearing victory stopping the eviction of Indians from the reserve. It's strange now to remember that one of their chiefs today, Chief John Snow, would not even be on a reserve if that petition had been allowed to reach Ottawa.[1]

However, the Hobbema Crees' story was different. On the oil-rich Hobbema reserve with a couple of real grudge fights already in action, the Cree were not going to withdraw and we would have to face a hearing before a commissioner. There, the new chief of one of their three tribes, the Samson tribe, had signed a petition against three families of his own tribe. They said it began because his son had been sent to jail for drinking, they thought. So one of the families they were driving off was the man who had been the RCMP scout on the reserve who had arrested the son.

In those days the RCMP as federal police were responsible for policing the reserve. They had found the best way to do it was to appoint a reserve Indian as an agent. They paid him and called him not a policeman but rather just a scout and he was responsible for keeping peace in minor problems on the reserve and reporting any unsettled problems to the nearest RCMP police station. Chief Saddleback felt that the scout should not have reported his son and as a result of his reporting, his son had been sent to jail, a terrible disgrace. So he was determined to drive the Johnson and Lightning families off the reserve to punish them. The Indians believed that the chief would not reverse his decision even if he did understand the terrible punishment that would result because he would lose face if he didn't defend his son.

I didn't say any of the dreadful thoughts I was having to those quiet people. I looked across at Laurie and saw that I didn't have to say it to him. He knew. His face was quite grey and the eyes I rarely noticed behind the glare of his eyeglasses had turned a hard blue. And worst of all, when I looked down I could see his hands were shaking. All he had done was about to be lost. He had fought so long to raise the quality of life on the reserves and now his beloved Indians were in danger of losing the only home, the only country they had known.

Talk was very quiet in the circle. There was one moment of a flash of excitement. One of the Indian ladies very excitedly leaned across and laughing shook the hand of another Indian. I couldn't understand so I turned to an Indian who I knew spoke good English and asked, "What is that all about?" and he said, "Oh, she just discovered he is her cousin when she heard his name." All I could think of was, my God, they don't even really know who their relatives are. They are all intermarried even beyond the tribes and here they are being accused because of an ancestor's action long ago. I tried to remember the date of the Riel rebellion but it had just been another date I had heard in school and also I remembered all the red-headed Indians and young Indians I had noticed on reserves, and a priest who with a twinkle in his eye said, "I think we must have had a very virile early trader in this one area." I even remembered that Thompson, the great mapmaker who we early Westerners owed so much to, had loved, married and stayed loyal to an Indian maiden and wondered if his fourteen descendants would go too in this great purge? I grew more terrified by the moment and I noticed that

Laurie had calmly gone into the kitchen and returned with two great brown belly teapots with steaming strong tea and cups and I thought, "We're like the English." My father had financed a mobile tea unit so the Salvation Army could serve tea in the 1940 London blitzed areas. It had seemed ludicrous he had done so till we got letters from some of the persons, thanking us. Laurie, like the British, was going to serve tea in the midst of disaster.

After we had quietly smoked and drunk our tea Laurie looked at me very directly. This time his eyes were fixed and piercing through his glasses and he said, "Ruth, we must fight." He was pulling the old trick, not appealing to my pity but accepting that I wouldn't allow an injustice. There really was no choice. That's why I took the case. Later the journalists would dig up the money motive behind the expulsions. Thousands of dollars in oil rights would come under the exclusive control of the Department of Indian Affairs without the Department being obliged to explain their actions to Parliament because the voteless Indian had no way of protesting the Department's actions. The protest lists were being revived at each birth and each registration until eventually all Indians would be driven from reserves and Canada would get back millions of acres of land.

I got home late for supper too subdued to even let myself think about it. At home my fear came. I who had no court experience had just agreed to take a law case vital to almost four hundred people's lives. Although the actual number of ancestors who had lost scrip was only three, now there were actually twenty-seven adults whose names had been protested. If we lost, their wives and all their children and in some cases grandchildren as well would also be evicted from their reserve. Laurie said nearly four hundred persons, not counting their in-laws and their children, if we lost, could also be protested against and removed. Every day a new baby was born and the number of clients I had to defend grew.

I needn't have worried. Male lawyers, all from my own old law class, volunteered to aid and fortunately by now they had turned out to be the brightest ones: scholarship winner William (Bill) Morrow, Robert (Bob) H. Barron, and later my husband and his friend William (Bill) Major.[2] But on that first day I felt very alone and very scared.

Immediately Laurie sent out his letters to the members in their far-off reserves and that resulted in many phone calls, even visits from Indian persons. I advised all members that I thought they were unwise at present to sign any of the lists put up on their reserves enabling them to protest against any other natives resident on their reserve, no matter what the reason. I told the Hobbema Indians to send me any notices of the charges against them that they received, and I would handle them. There would clearly be a trial on the Hobbema reserve.

19: THE FIRST HOBBEMA HEARING 1951

In the newspaper it was announced that the first hearing by a commission at the Hobbema reserve would be on 29 March 1951. Across Canada, in the United States and even in England, the newspapers labelled it "The Hobbema Case." Legally, it is reported in (1957), 7 DLR (2d) at 745 (Alta. Dist. Ct.), under the title of "Reference to Section 9 of the Indian Act re: certain members of the Samson Indian Band, Hobbema Alberta." The Hobbema Case spanned over seven years from its opening to its final closure. That is a long time and to me it seemed the most continuously stressful time in my life.

The actual court hearings were comparatively short, only about six hours, but nearly every day between sessions Laurie and I were searching for evidence or consulting not only with our clients, the Indians threatened with eviction from the reserve, but also with all Alberta Indians, searching files and talking to the Alberta tribes. When he took into account three generations of each family, including in-laws, Laurie figured that nearly four hundred persons would face dire poverty, homeless and untrained, if we lost the case. We were at Hobbema because Laurie had insisted we fight the case.

The Hobbema trial was like no other trial I ever read about in law school. It was based on a recently passed Act of Parliament on which little law had been built. It was not a trial in an established court of law. It was only a hearing before a temporary government-appointed commission. The rules were set by the commission and not established on centuries of laws of justice. The commissioner was a special appointment with accompanying lucrative fees from the same government whose ruling we were opposing. Somehow I had to record this so that when the Hobbema Case information got into a court of law, if it ever did, this hearing would be evident for what it actually was. It was a case of the government against those it governed.

John Laurie and I would only appear before a commissioner chosen and appointed for this one purpose. We could not get to a court of law unless we lost the commission hearing. I knew my Indians would worry about why I was not pleading how unfair and unjust the new sections of the Indian Act were and I am sure they must have been very nervous about the direction in which I was going.

The only comparable thing to the hearing that I had ever heard of in the past was the Spanish inquisition. In the Hobbema Case, the hearing consisted of one person simply pointing to another; instead of declaring them a heretic they declared that that person's ancestors had done something wrong.[1] At least in the Spanish inquisition the accusation was based on the actual knowledge of a witness. In the Indians' case the ones who pointed the finger could in no way do it based on what they knew or saw. What they were accusing the person of was some act, done by their ancestors before any of the accused was born. It could be based on mere gossip or rumour. The only written obtainable proof lay in the hands of the inquisitors themselves in far-off Ottawa at the Department of Indian Affairs, records accessible only on consent of the Department. The poor devil who was accused was denied access to that information before the trial, and anyway it was cloaked in legalese.

One of the fine things that did happen during the fierce propaganda period before the Hobbema trial got to court I received from Robert Felix Battle. He was the Alberta Superintendent of Indian Affairs that so long ago had firmly ordered John Laurie to his office to account for John's first daring letter revealing how far Canada was behind America in the health care of our Indians. He had watched Laurie's fierce efforts for a long time to improve the Indians' life. He was now quite high up in the Ottawa office of the Department. He came to Calgary and privately met with me in a restaurant. There he surprised me by saying, "I am so shocked by the eviction process that the Hobbema situation has revealed that I have decided I just have to resign from the Department. Possibly that will shock the public and aid you and John Laurie. I just can't stand what's going on." I was filled with admiration for this conscientious, sincere man and I begged him not to resign. I explained that the Indians desperately needed intelligent concerned men in the Department itself. Laurie was ill but holding his own and if I lost, the Indians would need more than ever, honourable men like him in Ottawa. It was reassuring to know that there are great civil servants out there, ones not just lulled into assuming the superiority of their protected position. Eventually he didn't resign.

Later, after my Ottawa visit, Mr. Battle was made a chief by the Stoney and, best of all, Colonel Jones, Deputy Minister of Indian Affairs, would retire, and Mr. Battle, the boy born in the small town of Delia, Alberta, would become the Deputy. The long cruel reign of Colonel Jones and his staff was over and better times would lay ahead for all Canadian Indians.

With Mr. Battle, better times would begin for the Indians. The Stoney tribe gave him the fine name "Chief Mountain Chinook Wind."

The commissioner appointed by the government to hear the hearing was Mr. Grant, a highly respected Edmonton lawyer. After all the Indians had voted that I was to serve as their lawyer, I phoned Mr. Grant in Edmonton to tell him that I would be appearing on their behalf and to request copies of the natives' notices. I asked if there would be a court reporter and he said yes, if I paid for the services, and I agreed.

It was a wet, snowy day in spring when Laurie and I slid along that icy highway to Hobbema to hear the case scheduled to begin at 10 a.m., 29 March 1951. Fortunately we didn't know how many times we would have to repeat the drive. When we arrived at the schoolhouse situated well out in a field near the centre of the big Hobbema reserve, vast quantities of cars were parked around it. We opened the door of the school to go upstairs and the stairwell was jammed with native people very quietly trying to listen through a crack in the doorway at the top as they waited hopefully to hear their fate. They all broke into big silent smiles when they saw us and in their quick Indian way, without speaking, somehow made room for Laurie and me to squeeze up between them.

At one end of an oblong room at a table on a platform a foot higher than the floor sat Commissioner Grant. Also present were the superintendent of the reserve, James R. Wild, and Malcolm McCrimmon who was in charge of the membership and status division, Department of Indians Affairs. He was the man who was now touring the reserves and speaking to the Stoney Indians and the Hobbema Indians about the possibilities of signing the protest forms to evict other Indians. Out of twenty-three previous inquiries about evictions from the reserves, only one had been appealed and it had been set aside. He was present at Hobbema as assistant to Commissioner Grant and was constantly keeping in touch with Ottawa, then finding fresh evidence, if possible, to override the little we had from the files they had down East and were withholding from us.

Laurie and I had left our coats in the car, determined to indicate that we had come to stay, and we unpacked our stuffed briefcases. We marched up to the platform and I introduced myself. I wasn't sure how to address Commissioner Grant but I settled for a bowed head and a very servile "Sir." I noticed that his chin rose slightly at that and thought, well at least we have one advantage. The proverb "Pride goeth before a fall" is almost older than courts of law. He gave a studied nod of his head for consent. Two Indians in the front row on kitchen-like chairs, without being asked, vacated two front centre seats for Laurie and me to sit on. Poor Laurie had to write his record on his knee.

I asked if there was a sworn interpreter present as some of my clients spoke little English. The assistant Indian agent named one. The interpreter was the Saskatchewan rebel John B. Tootoosis,[2] a sincere but bitter man who was helping relatives who had signed the protest against the other natives. None of the signers realized what would really happen to those they signed against – they were just settling an old grudge when they signed. Joe Deschamps, the Mountie swearing in the interpreter, was chosen by the Department of Indian Affairs because he was the man on the reserve who could send the interpreter to jail.

At one point during the hearing I noted that as I asked witnesses in the box their questions, the Indians in the audience seemed quite excited. Then one ran back and said to me, the interpreter is giving another interpretation. He isn't asking the witnesses your questions when he translates to our language. Instead, he is telling the witnesses to tell that white lady what I tell you. I objected and got a new interpreter from another tribe.

At another point during the hearing, I looked over at the so-called court reporter, Commissioner Grant's own redheaded secretary from Edmonton, Thelma M. Fraser, and saw that she was not taking notes when I spoke to the witnesses or the commissioner. So, I pointed this out. She turned to the commissioner and said, "You told me that what she said was not important." I was furious and wanted that remark included in the record. Of course it wasn't. So the value of those so-called records is questionable. Poor John Laurie was trying to take notes in his shorthand and was obviously very upset while doing so. John Laurie's report of trial is on file at the Glenbow Museum, in Calgary.[3]

During the hearing the Department revealed that they couldn't produce the vital list posted on the reserve by the agent according to the Act and on which were the names of those selected for removal by others protecting their own presence on the reserve. The Department's Mr. Wilde testified that someone had removed it. It turned out that the crucial protest list had just disappeared or been removed by parties unknown. Now there was no original written list on which to base these proceedings. I always believed that the Department was ordered to destroy that list as it was in their care and always filed in the carefully locked department agency.

During my questioning I asked every native who had signed a protest how he knew that the ancestors of those about to be evicted from the reserve had actually taken scrip in the past. Not one knew. Everyone said something like my dead grandfather used to say he took scrip or, even worse, that it was known around that he took scrip. In law, one of the prime rules of evidence is that you must have seen it yourself. The evidence can't be mere gossip that is an exculpatory statement and hearsay. As I questioned them, not a single one of the persons who had signed the protest to evict my clients from the reserve actually saw or knew anything for themselves. Yet the commissioner took no note of my objections at all.

The commissioner questioned the first signer for removal himself, finally asking the witness, "Did you know he was removed?" After asking his age he realized that the signer was only three years old when the scrip was issued so he couldn't have seen or known anything.

The commissioner prompted the next witness by saying, "What did you know about an ancestor taking scrip when you were kids together?" That protester blurted out, "Nothing at all." The commissioner's questions to the second witness revealed that he too really knew nothing about the man he protested against for taking scrip and the commissioner concluded that, "All you know is that he has been on the reserve."

The commissioner's questioning of the next witness ended up with the witness saying that he didn't know the man he protested against.

The fourth signer of this protest said that he heard by word but knew nothing himself: "We heard he had taken scrip," but the witness didn't even know the name of the person's father he was protesting. One witness said that he believed that someone being protested changed his name to Lightning because there were two young Lightnings, but he didn't know which one.

There was no evidence produced at this hearing, except hearsay, that anyone charged took scrip. No one had first-hand knowledge but only had once been told that their ancestors believed they were half-breeds or had once taken scrip. The only facts established were that the persons charged on the Hobbema reserve were the descendants of persons who were treaty Indians on the Hobbema reserve.

In mid-trial, Mr. McCrimmon approached the commissioner saying he had just spoken to Ottawa. They had located a scrip document that proved an ancestor of the Johnsons had applied for and received scrip. I remembered from law school that you couldn't submit referrals to a document if the document is available. I phoned Calgary to check with my old legal mentor, Mr. Skene, about whether I was correct about my law and he assured me that I was right: if first-hand evidence is available, it must be admitted. So I demanded that the Department produce the actual document allotting the Johnson's scrip. This meant a delay but legally the commissioner had to permit it. The next day, when the document was wired from Ottawa and I examined it, I noted a hand-written note on left lower side signed by Colonel MacLeod (the famed Mountie who gave Fort Calgary its name), one of the scrip commissioners "Application denied as I believe this person is a treaty Indian." How I secretly blessed him; gone was the proof the government had claimed to have. This incident never appeared

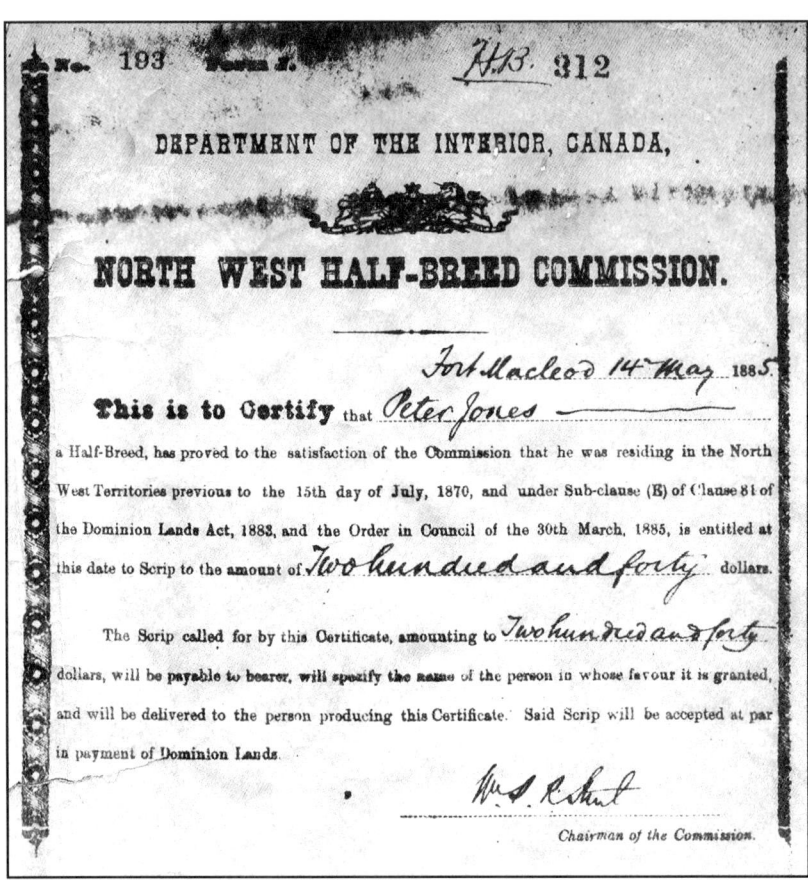

Copy of the scrip of Peter Jones, May 1885.

in the report or in any evidence again although they continued investigating the Indian concerned as having received scrip. As well, there was never any direct evidence that Jones in Fort MacLeod was the same as Johnson on the Hobbema reserve.

In a law trial a lawyer can ask to have a pre-trial discovery; that is, the person accusing your client must give the defendant a chance to find proof that he couldn't or didn't do what he is being accused of. Because it was based on a new addition to the Act, this first hearing was not a law trial, it was being heard before a government-appointed commissioner instead of in a court of law and I felt that the general rule that protects all defendants should apply. So I wrote the commissioner demanding copies of the documents they would be using in the case against the Hobbema tribe members.

The government held in their possession in Ottawa all documents relating to scrip, and they were protected by secrecy. So I had to get the documents out of them and trace their authenticity and then determine who were the descendants of scrip holders. The Department of Indian Affairs, however, refused to send any documents unless I could name a specific person and date for the 800 descendants of the original three men who had returned to the Hobbema reserve. I would need to show that the Indian they had paid scrip to was not the ancestor of the person they were attempting to evict. I had to prove that the ancestors of the three men had either been signed in treaty before the Riel rebellion was fought and had remained treaty Indians and that none had acquired this small document, none had taken at the government's invitation, a piece of paper that had to be turned in to be legal. Actually, it was impossible for me to produce exact names and dates at all.

There were thousands of scrip documents over one hundred years ago, and since they were transferable, they might have many owners' names on them, both white and native. The native people had no idea even of the name under which their great, great grandfathers or grandmothers had obtained the scrip documents.

The only proof that the ancestors had even been paid scrip was a document they had received saying that the bearer had received it, and if he sold it or used it to receive land, he had to file it in any land office in Western Canada. His name had never been on it anyway and then he had to surrender it to claim his land. Besides, if there were any records to prove it, they were all in the government's locked archives in Ottawa.

My job was to first trace the descent of my one hundred and two clients' lineage back – carefully. I was dealing with a people who had no registries at the time of their births. There were no Indian birth certificates, no proof of parentage at all. The Indians frequently on occasion, out of honour, took another person's name or chose a new one for themselves, just as they had "given" both Laurie and I Indian names of honour despite our own birth names, and referred to us by our newly given names. Secondly, I had to prove a legal marriage had taken place to make the children legitimate. Only three persons in the entire West in these earliest times could perform marriages and because no civil marriage was provided for those with Indian status, the Indians' marriages would be recorded only in the church records in Hobbema. The Protestant Church had burnt down, taking in its flames all records and the Catholic Church records had passed through about six missionaries. Their handwritten notes, if I could read them, were in French only.

In order to prove that my numerous clients had a right to remain on the reserve, I had to prove that all their ancestors back about three generations had been accepted as treaty Indians. The only treaty lists existed in Ottawa. The only record the Indian had confirming that he was a treaty Indian was the note the agent might handwrite in his record book, the daily reports he kept in a large journal. The daily reports were not a summary of events at all, so each report had to be read through to find any information. The journals were big, leather-bound ledger books with ruled pages and behind each page was a piece of onionskin paper. The reports had been written long before there was carbon paper to copy documents and they were copied simply by placing a damp cloth between the page and the onionskin paper so as to have a faint brown-coloured copy of the report. He then tore out the reports and periodically mailed them to his Ottawa bosses in the Department of Indian Affairs. When a book was filled it was sent to Ottawa and stored in their archives. So the only records that were continuous were in these large 19″ × 18″ ledger books, on thin onionskin sheets, the faint brown colour almost totally unreadable. Under the Official Secrets Act in force in Canada at the time of the trial, I required a court order to see these books.

The journals had a date column for treaty payments but, due to the fact that many Indians had no transport and the number of Indians to be paid were large and meant payment on a fixed day, the custom grew that the agent paid the annual treaty payment of $5.00 on whatever day a family could get to the agent's to pick up his rations.

I decided I would at least put up a fight so I demanded the right to inspect before the trial all records in connection with the Hobbema reserve from a year before the Riel rebellion till after scrip was cancelled. They obliged! How they must have laughed when they did so.

I received a phone call from the Canadian Pacific Railway (CPR) to come down to the train station, as there was a freight car full of documents in my name waiting to be unloaded. With my order in my hand I asked the railroad agent if I could examine the contents to be sure they belonged to me, and he consented. The inside of the unlocked freight car was half-filled from ceiling to floor with immense ledger books in no particular order containing the non-indexed names. Finding relevant facts in them made the task of finding a needle in a haystack easier. The old documents looked like someone had just shovelled them in.

In desperation I phoned my friends and the women who had worked so hard on behalf of the Indians from the Calgary Local Council of Women to ask them for help down at the train station. Eric Harvie closed the Glenbow Museum and sent his entire staff over to help me. I gave them a list of names who appeared anywhere in the books, any reference to Indians who had received scrip. For two days (which was as long as the car was allowed to remain at the station) these volunteers sifted through boxes looking for any of the 800 names in the documents. If we found any, we would still have to prove a direct relationship with the natives charged in the Hobbema Case. We did find a few cases showing a possible ancestor had been paid as a treaty

Indian during the time scrip was issued and afterwards, and also my best friend found one wonderful letter from the past. We also found a few good facts, but, of course, they told only of the actions of the agent at Hobbema, not the actions of Ottawa.

The CPR phoned me to find out if I was the one the freight car had come addressed to and I said yes. The bill for an entire freight car from Ottawa was enormous. When I had first looked in the freight car, the pile of jumbled and non-filed documents had looked so hopeless to sort through that I had told the freight station agent that it wasn't what I ordered and I was rejecting payment. They could sue me for it. However, a lawsuit and its publicity had never been the way of the civil service Department of Indian Affairs. The Department simply paid for the freight bill out of the Indians' own funds which they controlled, and forgot about it.

At noon of the first day of the trial we all retired to the school's dining room to eat. The commissioner and the Department's men sat at the head table and a young priest herded Laurie and me carefully to the bottom of the table. By the second night of the trial I had sent a tired Laurie home for a needed sleep and all alone I faced the two-room long full tables of copies of undated records and agents' handwritten books that the Department of Indian Affairs, in Ottawa had with tongue in cheek sent me when I demanded to see any relevant documents. It seemed such a hopeless task. How was I going to trace three Indians' ancestry, maybe even under different names, in them?

Getting very discouraged I finally looked at the pile and decided I may as well dive into it by chance. A funny thing happened; I actually found some defence evidence to examine in this way. Later Father Latour told me that they had held all-night prayer sessions for me in the church. Who knows, maybe some prayers worked.

One of my happiest memories of those dreadful trials was of Father Latour, the Oblate priest who ran the school and was admired by John Laurie. The Catholic missionary was a magnificent giant man, over six feet tall, a Montrealer who spoke seven languages. On the first day of the trial he came up and handed me one hundred and two dollars in one-dollar bills. I had insisted that each of the natives give me one dollar to represent them so that I would not be challenged and removed as not being their official lawyer. I always suspected that the priest had paid some of that money.

On the second to last day of the trial the commissioner and all of us had spent several hours at the little church where Father Latour read and translated from the French the old handwritten church records of baptisms and marriages. Natives had no birth or wedding certificates, so to identify the 102 Indians' ancestors and prove their births we had to use the Catholic

Church baptism rolls. The Protestant Church with its records had unfortunately burnt down and this was all there was.

That night I was again working late going through what documents I could find searching for the Indians' ancestors among the strange names recorded. I hadn't returned to town to eat and Father Latour appeared at the door and said, "We have some food for you at the priests' house if you would come." Father Latour drove me over to the priests' house. They led me into a room I will never forget. At a round table on a white table cloth under silver candlelight was laid out a meal for one. On fine china, with sparkling wine in a crystal glass, what a meal the two priests served me as they stood carefully behind me: steak and potatoes and a super dessert. I ate and they never said a word. It seemed, amid that weary day, almost a dream. When we retired for coffee to another room and they quietly asked me how I was doing I admitted, "Not too well, your records aren't helping much." The evidence from the baptismal certificates could probably convict one family, the Lightnings, because the gender, ages and names of their three children baptized by the priest matched names on a written application I had seen for scrip signed by that priest. I was gravely concerned about this.

Next morning in the schoolroom I listened as the commissioner said, "Now we will read the sworn evidence of the church from the baptismal records we saw yesterday." Father Latour got up to give evidence of the names found in the baptismal book. As he read, Father Latour was translating from the French. I suddenly became alert when I realized I didn't hear the name Lightning. He simply did not translate their surname using instead the name Leclair, which was lightning in French (*l'éclair*).

I, like so many of today's women, was always walking on the razor's edge dividing family and career obligations. A phone call from my husband informed me that my daughter Linda's eye had been injured and he thought I should be home. Laurie insisted that I go. We rehearsed all that he would need to ask and questions he should object to then he put me on the midnight train to Calgary.

The next day he phoned saying he was frightened at the way it was going – so I came back. The train got into Wetaskiwin at 10 p.m. It was blizzarding and standing alone on the platform was Laurie. He said there was no night taxi. On the walk back to our hotel, he looked so cold that we stopped for coffee at an all-night truck stop café.

Laurie had a heart attack early the next morning, the third and last day of our hearing on the reserve. In the morning he didn't knock on my hotel room door to wake me like he usually did. When I knocked on his door, there was no answer. I got the chambermaid to open the door and saw Laurie having a violent heart attack on the bed. Death had walked beside

Laurie for many years. Even when I first met him he knew about his bad heart, but I didn't realize it was serious until I actually saw him there in a spasm on what we thought would be one of the most important days for the Indians. He had left rows of medicine bottles out of bed reach. I held each one up before him and when he nodded I read the directions that seemed to leap off the bottle at me. Carefully I got the pill and liquid somehow in the twisted mouth. Slowly the face smoothed out.

I got the chambermaid to stay with him while I ran downstairs and asked the clerk for the name of the doctor in Wetaskiwin where we were staying. I phoned and explained. I could tell that the fact that we were hotel guests, a single man and married woman, and were here in connection with native people was not making much of an impression. However, the doctor did say he had a surgery that morning and would come as soon as it was over.

I saw Commissioner Grant heading for the dining room so I told him what had happened and asked for an adjournment of the trial. He refused. He said he wished to finish up and there wasn't much more anyway. I rushed back up to John. Although he was still in pain, he seemed calmer but he looked very ill. I said, "I'm not going to leave you." Laurie struggled to get out of bed and said, "I'll go if you won't." So I hired the chambermaid to stay with him and went downstairs to wait for my ride to the reserve. Never did I feel so blue looking out at the grey day and the snow. I joined the commissioner's party for the seventeen-mile ride into the reserve where the trial was held. As we waited for the car, I said bitterly that I wished I had at least seen a copy of the scrip document that caused all this trouble. To my horror Commissioner Grant said, "Oh, I have one, in the safe in my office. Years ago, I bought one and was hoping the price would go up but instead the government called them in and I lost money." I was so shocked I was speechless. He not only knew how scrip had been turned into a scam on the poor Indians and half-breeds but had even taken part in it, and yet he was being well paid to pass judgment on this case. His disclosure was, I think, the lowest point in my spirits.

As soon as we reached the Indians I told Father Latour about John and he arranged for nuns from the school to be taken back to take care of Laurie in the hotel. He promised to take Laurie to their mission to be nursed by the good nuns after the hearing. Now he drove me back to see Laurie. I assured Laurie that no evidence had been found against the natives yet, but that Commissioner Grant was holding his judgment in *sine die* which meant that a decision would come later. It seemed we had won. Until two years later, that is, when I received in the mail a judgment saying that Grant had decided that all the natives charged were guilty and would be evicted from the reserve.

20: AFTER THE HOBBEMA HEARING/ I GO PUBLIC

Ten months later, on 29 February 1955, the commissioner claimed he had received fresh evidence from Ottawa. And so, without a hearing and without me being given a chance to see it or cross-examine on it, he had accepted that evidence and reopened the hearings on 7 July 1955. Four years had passed with the Hobbemas living happily on their reserves when the notice was delivered to my office. Laurie was still very ill so I went alone but my husband John was able to fly in his airplane and assist me on the last day of the hearing.[1]

The original signers of the protest led by Chief Saddleback had had time to realize the actual implications of their signing of the protest and had employed a lawyer from Wetaskiwin, Mr. K. Leathem, to represent them. However, part way through the hearing, he withdrew, asking to be excused.

New evidence, copies of scrip documents, were produced by the commissioner. The one on the Johnsons did not include the handwritten note, "it was refused." We objected; however, the commissioner refused to accept our argument and said he had decided to accept the copies because someone in Ottawa swore they were originals.

He found that Lightning had two other names: a strange one no one had ever heard of before, David Thomas, and also Weyawasa. Of the three named, he had possibly married an Isabelle Piché in 1882, by Indian records at Cypress Hills, although the commissioner admitted the records may or may not have been accurate.[2]

It was decided that I should meet with the northern tribes possibly at Edmonton. The Hobbema people were getting angry and harassment of them was beginning. Laurie decided we must have a total commitment from the Indian people through the Association before a legitimate-seeming counter-campaign could be launched by the Department. In a way, it was wonderful. This was a western case; the problem was in the West. Ottawa was not yet totally alarmed. But already, Laurie was talking to his old friend, the teacher Douglas Harkness, with whom he used to smoke the forbidden cigarettes behind a furnace. On such small rebellions long friendships are often made. Harkness was now the member of Parliament for Calgary North and in Parliament, he and John Diefenbaker, leader of the opposition, began asking questions from the floor of the House. The Department of Indian Affairs was now becoming alarmed at the unexpected commotion and resistance.

Laurie had no trouble convening the southern Indians, but I was terrified of my meeting with the northern ones. I had never met many of them and I was not only going to have to get their united and total backing but also money to help the Hobbema Indians to last out the three months we still had before I had to legally file an appeal or throw in the towel. I took the night train to Edmonton and, when I gave the taxi driver the address where they had arranged for a hall, he was most solicitous. It seemed it was the Alcoholics Anonymous' hall. I explained I had other business there and just for fun said, "Have you been reading the newspapers about these Indian problems and if so what do you think?" "Lady," he growled, "I figure we stole the country from them in the first place and now we're trying to steal back the little we paid for." This was the most reassuring pre-trial statement I heard. With great relief I knew then that even if we lost the case maybe public opinion would change the Act. If a taxi driver understood it, clearly the average Canadian did too and they would win it for us.

To my amazement the meeting was well attended. It was in a way a bleak meeting where they faced a possible sudden bleaker future as relief recipients in the big unfamiliar cities. I looked at those serious Indian faces, faced with possibly more future tragedies, and I felt as unsure as they did. I explained that we had lost. I went through all the details carefully, letting them ask questions using interpreters. The loss meant that possibly there would be fresh protest forms that someone might sign from just greed or revenge and therefore more treaty Indian evictions. If we chose to continue to fight the Hobbema Case in the Court of Appeal I would need their consent to direct it and to employ better lawyers than myself, male lawyers, to present it at court. This would require more money.

Also I felt that I needed time for this so we could see what further could be done and this meant that the Hobbema Indians would be cut off rations right away. So if they were to be encouraged to wait to go to court we would be wise to raise enough money in addition to feed these Hobbema Indians during the allowed time of three months to appeal. Probably that would have to come from money raised by the Indians.

Also if I hired male lawyers more learned than myself in court work, we would need money to pay them for their service and in addition for their actual expenses in case we lost the case and the costs as well. The Indians voted to raise the necessary funds not only to pay out-of-pocket legal fees but to feed the hungry about to be cut off – the Hobbema Cree. We called it the defence fund and all tribes agreed to collect the money.

It was a very sombre time. Finally an older Indian rose and said slowly, "Well, I have known some good women." I got the message. They needed to discuss this without me being present so I said, "Will you excuse me? I have to make an important phone call home right now," and I went out and sat on the steps of the building in the sun. I never will know what they said but eventually I was quietly joined by my friend, the chief from Hobbema who, although never threatened himself with eviction, had chosen to fight for his tribe members that were. All he said was, "Can you come in and talk?" The money would be raised. I was to go ahead. I received a properly signed letter signed by Chief John Samson and passed by one of the three Hobbema reserve's bands called Samson, requesting that I act as solicitor for the native people in his tribe threatened with removal.

During the meeting one old chief had stood up and said, "I think we should ask the Queen to help us." I was aware that the Queen's powers in Canada were now restricted to only advising not interfering, but looking at the Indians I thought, why put down the little hope they had. To the Indians, Queen Victoria was the "great white mother" whom they thought they had signed treaty with, and now in their troubles they were hoping she might bring them justice. They all voted their approval of petitioning the Queen, Victoria's great granddaughter.

Victoria had been Queen of Canada when it became a country and to the native people it had been to this woman chief of the country or Queen, that the Indians called their "Queen Mother," that the Indians had left their vast lands and had signed treaty with, and agreed with, due to starvation, to go onto the small pieces of that land called "reserves." I had seen the letter poor Chief Bobtail at Hobbema had insisted the agent write to his Queen saying that he must leave soon because soldiers had searched his tent to find his son whom they suspected of returning from the Riel rebellion, and had tried to poison him with the bacon rations cured in saltpetre. In that letter Bobtail had also said if the Queen ever needed his defence, he would come to her aid.

I looked at their faces, knowing all their possible futures were threatened. I hadn't the heart to tell them that by a law – the statute of Westminster – the present Queen now had no real power over the Canadian government. So I just agreed to write a letter for them and I asked for her aid for her always loyal Indians who had signed treaty with her. The Calgary Public Library helped me. When I turned my query about form and custom when writing the Queen over to them they had a great time and even located a copy of a past acceptable form. What amazed me was that you didn't begin "Dear Queen," you began "Greetings Madam." I knew it had to go through the line of command, her representative in Canada, and Vincent Massey was the first Canadian-born governor general we had had.

Hopefully I sent it off, care of him. He consulted the prime minister's office where Mr. Pickersgill was and they just decided not to bother her majesty with this matter. If I had been in Pickersgill's position, I think I would have just sent it off to her majesty on a slow boat by China. I told Mr. Diefenbaker that I had sent it. This was the kind of stuff he was well suited to use. He was elated. Always a rabid supporter of the royals, he got up in Parliament and thundered out asking how dare the government interfere with the Queen's mail and Canadians' right to write to their own Queen if they wanted to.

A whole new group of Canadians were now actually listening to the plight of Indians being driven off their reserves. This was something the Canadian public could understand even if the complicated legal sections of the Act were beyond their clear understanding. Canadians hold their Queen in deep respect and for anyone to take away their own right to write her was clearly wrong. Strangely enough that gained more support than the injustice to the Indian people.

I hadn't told my Indian friends but I had no idea how this case could really be won. I had made it very difficult for the commissioner to decide against me. He had even had to say in his finding, "They are evicted because they are the descendants of either X or Y and either X or Y." That seemed clear injustice but how could I either clearly prove who they were descendants of except by hearsay evidence when all the documents were locked in Ottawa under the Department's tender protective care for themselves? Also, even if we won this one special case, wouldn't there just be hundreds more, each with varied circumstances for each Indian that could be easily lost or won? It was a bleak future. I think it was then that it came to me that there is only one hope. This terrible amendment to the Act had to go. That was the only way. That involved government and the non-Indian persons who elected them.

Poor Laurie had put up an intense campaign to try and fight the new Indian Act's passage. He had had such a short time. The new Act had been literally railroaded through Parliament by a Liberal majority with its necessary readings following in such rapid succession that there had been no time to organize even an explanation of the consequences of such an Act or organize any real effective opposition to it except by the Alberta tribes.

Now time was all I had. It could be a thirty-day delay before the forced expulsions if I didn't file. Till the last day I would be free to discuss the case.

Once the matter was before the court, official publicity is limited to publishing and speaking about the facts only. I decided to go for delay at least, and stopped at Hobbema to instruct the Indians not to sign their notices to appeal when they received them, no matter what the agent said. They were to carefully collect each one and bring them all to me in Calgary.

My one hope was not in Parliament but in its electors, the non-Indian population. I had always had faith in the eventual common sense and a common goodness of people. Anyway, it was all I had.

I GO PUBLIC

I had been a rather lonely shy child and one of my mother's favourite sayings was "fools' names and fools' faces too often appear in public places." A glimpse at today's many publicity campaigns hasn't changed my opinion much. However, if it is the only tool available that you can afford you would be amiss to ignore it. I knew that only public opinion, the ancient principle behind England's great common law, could help me. Statute law concerning Indians had been designed by their employer, the bureaucrats, for government benefits. Statute law is a rigid, unalterable, codified law, the type that had governed most of Europe and passed by dictatorial conquerors like Napoleon, which incidentally still forms the civil law in Quebec. Common law is based on cases heard in court, specific situations which are examined. It was only an appeal to that law formed by commoners, public opinions' pressure, that could help us in the Hobbema Case. I finally decided that I couldn't win under statute law, but maybe I could possibly influence common law. I hoped for a common law decision, for a change based on today's people's attitudes.

I had been determined to depend on the public's opinion in a democracy. It was the only instrument that could rectify the injustice the Indians were being subjected to and I was actually proven right. I had the great good fortune to have the support of a fine, sincere individual, the *Calgary Herald* publisher Basil Deane and young reporter Richard (Dick) Snell. However, the floodgates of public opinion when opened became at once terrifying as well as reassuring. My home phone was constantly ringing. There was the odd bigoted person who seemed to need so desperately to believe in the supremacy of his own race as a self-protection that he would phone to belittle me. On the other hand, Basil Deane phoned to say the newspaper had never seen anything quite like it. Unsolicited money was being sent into the *Calgary Herald* to help the Indians fight. That part was very clear to me so I insisted, I guess to his relief, that it be sent back with thanks. The women I had known for years in the Local Council of Women were prepared with great practicality to duplicate and mail out the letters necessary to be sent to Parliament, clarifying the fact that the Act was being used to perpetrate a breach of treaty. I had some phone calls, and even aid offered, by some who were soggily sentimental alcoholics who felt maudlin sympathy with the underdog. I had ministers who felt it was merely a matter that prayer alone should solve. My life became one of constant confusion.

The Indians, bless their hearts, at least had a sort of stoic faith in me and were content to let me carry on. Often at night I would have nightmares about all those people, 102 of them not counting those being conceived or born out of wedlock, and what would happen to them when thrust homeless into the cities' slum areas.[3] I was really neither cut out nor trained for what I was doing, and even as a lawyer I was deeply aware of my years of lack of practice that had preceded Hobbema. I decided that at least when I went to trial I must rely on experts. Although I understood the strange machinations of the Indian law that had been created by the Department of Indian Affairs through the years, I had practically no experience at all in a court of law. I also knew that the sections to evict Indians from their reserve were now statute law. In a court, I would always be backed up against that harsh wall of reality. All I could hope for really was that public sympathy of the justice of common law would reach through and sway the judge to find a technical loophole that might save those 102 innocent persons from eviction or stop the Department continuing their actions.

Laurie had built up a marvellous network of non-Indian supporters for the Indians' cause through his years of devoted speaking and writing on their behalf. I also now had my followers in Calgary women's clubs and men's service clubs, but what we needed was to quickly convert many new non-believers – to awaken the giant pull of the common persons toward justice. That was all I could do, but there had been lots of intolerance built up against Indians through the years. I desperately needed someone impersonal to pre-judge our case, and that could only be the press. This impersonal group could reach and convince many new supporters.

I had thirty days before I had to file an appeal. Once I filed our appeal, I could not then talk to newspapers without endangering by deliberate influence a court of law's decision. But I did have those thirty days and I was at least in control of when I would file our desire to appeal after which the ban of silence would fall down.

When I arrived back in Calgary from Hobbema I went immediately to Basil Deane, the *Calgary Herald*'s publisher, and said, "I have a story to tell you about what I believe is robbery of Indians' rights legally by an unjust law." He questioned me and I will never forget how he calmly lifted his phone and said, "Give me the *London Times* editor," and told him my story before he waved me out of his office.

The next day he sent a bright young journalist, Dick Snell, to interview me at my house. The young reporter from the *Calgary Herald* was evidently disappointed at my elegant furnished home with its fountain and goldfish and attached sunroom. I just didn't have the correct freedom fighter look! In the dining room I had my women friends and the always-supportive women in the thirty-two clubs from Calgary's Local Council of Women all copying by hand letters of protest to be sent to every MP and senator in Ottawa. One was my best friend Florence Harington, an ex-Mountie's wife; another was Grace Stonewall, who was president of our thirty-two women's club groups, Calgary's Local Council of Women.

I had written out by hand a short, simple, one-page letter that outlined the Hobbema Indians' plight and explained the injustice to the Indians. They hand-copied the letter and bought stamps and mailed copies at their own expense to every person and organization in Canada they knew was truly concerned with the state of Indians asking them to also protest and get others.

Poor Mr. Snell. Hopefully he said, "Do you have any files I could refer to?" and I hauled in a wooden apple box I had been flinging each paper into on top of the last. Later in his life at his farewell banquet from *The Toronto Star*, Dick Snell said that his most exciting and satisfactory assignment had been the Hobbema Case. Actually, the four-day newspaper coverage earned him and the *Calgary Herald* a nomination for the American Pulitzer news award.

What Dick Snell produced amazed me! It was a series of four articles, each approximately two columns wide and a full page in length and they appeared day after day. As I had insisted, Laurie's name, which was better known and respected, was used and the articles were written so clearly that even a child could understand the injustice of the Act. There was even a fine cartoon of discouraged Indians on their horses under the title, 'Treaty Rights For as Long as the Sun Shines and the Rivers Flow.'

In the first article, dated 14 January 1957, was a fine picture of Chief John Samson. Many persons would never understand that John was not one of the persons threatened by removal, but in the general tradition of his people was only protecting and leading his tribe. I allowed no picture of me, but in the later articles there was one of John Laurie, whom Snell also carefully interviewed.

The publicity campaign was a killer. My phone never stopped ringing, all too often from long distance spots. I made speeches, it seemed to me, at absolutely every Calgary club including the male ones who wouldn't let women even join them. The Calgary women's clubs in the Local Council were writing their national organizations and the farm women were up in arms.

Chief John Samson.

Dick Snell's articles were magnificent. They were being picked up off the press line across Canada. Gradually they appeared not only in all the Southam papers but in others as well and in dailies across Canada. The phone was ringing from Indians, non-Indians and newsmen, and for radio interviews from all over Canada. I was amazed and pleased at their reactions. Clubs across Canada signed in and gathered supporters. Individuals were taking their own action. The ill Laurie was equally frantically busy. We began to worry about whether the Indians would dislike the publicity and what pressure they would be under.

Laurie was doing the most vital part of the work. Using the moccasin telegraph system the mails and the phone he was linking together every Alberta Indian and every Canadian Indian into presenting an unbroken front of opposition to the Act. The Department of Indian Affairs' old trick of finding an Indian they could bribe or coerce or even just convince to support their policy in this case was broken. The Indians of Alberta and even beyond presented a solid unbroken front.

In no time letters came back to go to Parliament. Questioning newsmen bombarded Ottawa members of Parliament. They were asking questions of the old Minister of Indian Affairs, Walter E. Harris, and of Mr. Pickersgill, who had designed the Act. John Diefenbaker, leader of the opposition Conservatives, recognized that the Liberals had made a mistake even if they, directed by the so-able Pickersgill, still didn't.

The Conservatives were being fuelled by Calgary North's member of Parliament, Doug Harkness, Laurie's old fellow teacher who was all too familiar with Indians' needs. He had been the very first MP who had ever stood up and protested the Indians' status under the Indian Act.[4] We couldn't have been luckier. Fate was on our side.

During and after the Hobbema Case we got another break. The New Democrat Party (NDP) in Saskatchewan had joined in the protest because their Premier, Tommy Douglas, had as his special advisor Morris Schumiatcher. This came, as so often it did, as a direct product of Laurie's long years of work. He had had in his class at Crescent Heights High School, Morris Schumiatcher, son of a Calgary lawyer, and whose mother was extremely active in Calgary's musical circles.

I think the funniest protest that was sent to Parliament was from Calgary's Women Liberal Club. The women were long-time members of Calgary's Local Council of Women who had for years before supported John Laurie in his Indian work and later me who was also their convenor of laws. And believe it or not, they sent a protest out of Calgary against the action of their own Liberal party, the party in power in Ottawa.

I could keep up the protest for only three weeks this way and then I had to agree to go to a court of appeal after which newspaper reports of my statements could be claimed prejudicial to evidence to be used in our case.

The Conservatives kept questioning Pickersgill and Harris. "When were they going to test their Act in court?" I at least enjoyed one retort that Mr. Pickersgill made. He forgot himself enough to shout out in a reply: "Who knows what that woman will do!" I figured it was nice to know that I didn't need a name and that his remark at least brought pleasure to those of us who were grouped as outspoken, presumed inferiors. I'm sure it helped the case!

Even *Time Magazine* decided to carry the story.[5] Mr. Luce had changed the formula for new magazines and his two weeklies, the largely photographic *Life* and more journalistic *Time* magazine, became best sellers. *Time* was the only one to make the Hobbema Case their feature of the week for Canadian news.

Time Magazine, then an American magazine with several pages devoted to Canadian news, thought the Hobbema story vital enough to send a crew for special coverage. Their Canadian representative, Mr. Bob Ogilvie, phoned me in great excitement explaining that they would be flying in a plane full of their own cameras and staff for the interview. On arrival, however, their idea was to photograph me in a frilly apron at my kitchen stove stirring a pot in a story to be titled, "Housewife defends the Indians." It was a shock to them when I said, "No way will I allow you to do that! I will only give you an interview if you fly up to the Hobbema Indian reserve and feature a photo story of the poor houses those poor people are losing and find out how destitute some of the people there are and yet how their reserve life was necessary to them and preferable to being cast jobless and lonely into city streets." *Time* photographed the impoverished Indians and published a picture of a tiny Indian girl looking sadly out from a shawl hanging over the rafter in a bare, almost unlit cabin. Under Ogilvie, they did a good and emphatic job of describing what loss of the case could mean, and at the same time describing the failure of the Department of Indian Affairs' case for the need for reforms on the reservation rather than their threats and persecution.

Time magazine's investigation revealed a whole new aspect of the Hobbema Case. Laurie's and my only concern was about what would happen to those Crees at Hobbema when, still untrained and financially broke, they were faced with a largely unknown to them world beyond the reserves.

Time figured out in exact figures the fortunes in future oil rights the evicted Indians would lose and that was something readers could understand. They pointed out that the Cree would be robbed of hundreds of thousands of publicly promised oil revenue that went with their still-owned natural resources under the treaty. Oil revenue from the nearby successful Leduc oilfield would soon be forthcoming. It's amazing, when a loss is translated into dollars and cents, how much easier it is for the public to understand than to envision the mere slow suffering of other human beings. *Time*'s coverage opened a whole new dimension and, best of all, brought in concern from American tribes south of our border.

I had hoped for some aid, but I never expected what I got. I had support from Basil Deane's the *Calgary Herald* and through Deane, the two top newspapers in England. This spread to the Southam chain of publishers who joined Basil Deane. Even the opposing papers leapt in, the *Albertan* and the *Lethbridge Herald*. Then via Radio Europe it even began to spread across Europe. Our local station was terribly excited about it. They hadn't done anything like this before. In those days overseas broadcasts had to be done after midnight due to the time gap and then in three-minute intervals, with a minute rest, and on again with another three-minute section for a total of about an hour. Not too familiar with radio techniques, I found that tiring. The broadcast had to be done from the top floor of the *Calgary Herald*, then our highest building.

One night after doing a broadcast, I was so tired that when I went to push my way out the big, heavy revolving glass door at the street entrance, I gave such a weak starting push that the revolving door stopped only part way around, and I was pinned between two heavy glass doors and a wall. I didn't seem to have enough strength to push ahead at all. The old Herald building was full of offices but they were completely empty, as was the dark, cold, snowy street outside. I thought sadly, "they are going to come down in the morning and find me still standing up pinned frozen stiff between these heavy doors." I don't think he even saw me, but fortunately a man rushed in off the street. He gave the door such a vigorous push in his rush to get in that I got whirled around and spilled out onto the street in glorious freedom. It goes to show it's often those unknown to us who even inadvertently save us.

The pressure began to get to the Liberals. There were other signs too. Pickersgill's picture had appeared on one of the local movie theatre newsreels we enjoyed in pre-television days. Someone in the audience hissed. I wasn't there but the good old Calgary audiences who always enjoy a good fight joined in and the whole theatre rung with hisses. I'm sure Mr. Pickersgill couldn't hear them but I have no doubt he did hear about it from Calgary Liberals.

Finally I got a phone call from a fellow law student whose father was the rumoured Liberal 'bag man' from Alberta. To stop the publicity drive I had an offer to pay my fees. He said that the government was concerned that I hadn't filed a defence to the Indians' case. I knew what that was about – they were beginning to suffer from the fun the opposition were getting out of pestering them with questions about the Hobbema Case in Parliament, and I even suspected from the phone calls I had received of sympathetic support from long-time loyal Liberals, that they were probably getting letters from their own party members and it had become necessary to shut me up. The way to do that was to get me to file the appeal papers and once before the courts, any newspaper or speaking comments would be improper and endanger the case. So I stalled and said, "Well, with little help or money I wasn't yet ready to go to court." Then I got a direct call from the powers that be at Ottawa: "When was I going to go to court?" Very sadly I said, "I might never get to court. After all it takes money and paid lawyers to do that." Then I heard the lovely words, "Well, we would be prepared to pay your costs if you file the appeal," and then I had the great fun of saying, "Oh,

I could never accept anything as legally and ethically improper as that. I will let you know as soon I'm able to file." At least we had them on the run. I phoned Laurie the good news and we both had a long laugh.

But the problem of going to court was still very real even though the court case looked impossible to win. My time for filing an appeal had almost run out and I would lose by default if I failed to file on time.

21: THE APPEAL

Finally my time was up. I filed the appeal and three wonderful helpers appeared. Mr. William G. (Bill) Morrow, our law school classmate, had already won cases in the Supreme Court of Canada and would finish his very distinguished legal career as the first Supreme Court Justice of the Northwest Territories where he developed a whole new attitude towards law based on what he learned about the needs of the Northern Indian and Eskimos. The second helper was Mr. Robert (Bob) Barron from Calgary, another law school friend, and the third was my husband John Gorman. All three agreed to act with no assurance of payment. However, one week before the trial, Mr. Morrow got notice that a big case he had been waiting to have heard in the Supreme Court of Canada was scheduled for the exact same date as our appeal. A delay would cost his client a fortune. He did arrange for, as he called him, one of the finest trial lawyers in Edmonton to act in his place: Mr. A.F. "Spud" Moir, who turned out to be a great strategist.

The case is reported in the Dominion Law Reports (1957), 7 DLR (2d) 745 (Alta. Dist. Ct). The Reference to Section 9 of the Indian Act re: "Certain members of the Samson Indian Band, Hobbema, Alberta" didn't give a report reader much of a clue unless he already knew what Section 9 said. The trial was held in the court of the District of Northern Alberta, judicial district of Edmonton, on 1 March 1957. It lacked the usual lawyers but it did list A.F. Moir, J.C. Gorman and J.P. Brumlik as solicitors for the appellants. Strangely enough the Crown was represented by my very able university law instructor, the eminent solicitor George H. Steer, Q.C., his son, A.C. Steer and K.J. Leatham.

The morning of the trial was the same morning Bob Barron's first baby chose to be born, so my husband John, who was to fly Bob to Edmonton, was also delayed. J.P. Brumlik replaced Bob Barron. They arrived just as the court opened.

The Judge mounted his huge stand looking very severe. I sat at the defence table handling papers. Once during the trial I muttered a barely audible startled objection and the judge instantly said, "We don't wish to hear from you, Mrs. Gorman, at all." So I could hold only a "listening" brief.

The entire back part of the courthouse was filled with native people, in addition to the eight hundred waiting outside to hear their own fate. The courtroom was overcrowded with press and the twenty-seven named Indians plus nearly all their relations who added an additional two hundred people into the courtroom. Some of them couldn't even get into the courtroom. The judge sitting on the case was Chief Justice Nelles Buchanan. He had been a past and very able Edmonton lawyer before his appointment to the court. He was obviously not happy at having to take this controversial case and took note that it was obvious that the Indians didn't understand the protest, for one Indian protested against his own mother who took scrip.

I went to Edmonton alone three days before the court trial and stayed in my mother-in-law's house and met Spud, the new lead defence lawyer. Bill Morrow was right: he was a brilliant litigation lawyer and, like all good ones, he had the ability to get to the kernel of a case – whatever it was that the case would turn upon. For two days Mr. Moir and I shuffled through the facts and the evidence I had produced at the earlier commissioner's hearings, and the two decisions that were almost a complete reversal of the case. Spud said, "Our government opponents have to have you win this case, or face it in the next election, and it may be a decisive factor against them. We just have to give them a hook they can hang their hat on and make it easy for them to lose a case they now want to lose." We went over the case looking for something. We noted that the original protest sheet had not been filed in two places as it had to be. In fact, someone, probably in anger, had torn down one of the original sheets and it hadn't been replaced. Spud was delighted to discover that in part of my first case I had shown that one Indian unknown to himself had signed against his own family because he wasn't familiar with his own ancestral descendants.

Then the funniest one of all turned up over the spelling of the word "scrip." I've always had a twinge of guilt over that. I am a notoriously poor speller and I suspect that on my own defence papers I might have misspelled the word as "script" and a government employee had copied my misspelling. Anyway, the dictionary turned up several different meanings for the way it was misspelled and so Spud argued that the charges were in error and unclear.

During the trial, Mr. Moir chose to focus on the Department's method of posting the protest form on the agent's office in Hobbema. I had never seen the form – it had never been produced. Mr. Moir's plea was that 1) the protest slip had been posted in the wrong place on the agent's office, and 2) it had been posted on the wrong date. Therefore the protest had never been properly filed and no native people could be removed. As Moir predicted, the court was happy to follow such a simple excuse and Chief Justice Buchanan read out his decision and announced that he was throwing out the case. What this meant was that all the Indians who would have been evicted under Commissioner Grant's decision were free to now remain on the reserve.

The Hobbema Case was no triumph for me as a lawyer. When Judge Buchanan gave his judgment, he opened with a demotion of me as a "troublemaker." He had great sympathy for the long period of anxiety the Indians had had to suffer while waiting to have their future settled and he added that that was because of me. I could have added that it was terrible for the Hobbema natives waiting in their homes in fear of being evicted but at least they still had the security of their own homes for the period rather than being out homeless on city streets. But one does not interrupt a judge. He then reviewed the Act in its entirety and went into a lengthy tracing of the Indian Act clear back to the treaty signing time of 1868, and went carefully and accurately through how often the definition of an Indian had been changed, inferring that the new definition in the Act that could now drive Indians off the reserves was nothing unusual for a government to do. He continued that argument for two-and-a-half full pages of his response, his printed judgment. This, as he suspected it would, went into future reports.

My husband, John, had to be back in Calgary immediately after the court case and as a result I missed the Indians' Edmonton celebration. According to the newspaper accounts and pictures, there were probably well over a hundred of them inside and outside the courtroom who after the victorious verdict flowed out into the busy street in front of the courthouse and broke into a joyful dance. The victory dance went on for almost an hour and stopped up traffic and resulted in quite a few non-Indian Edmontonians joining the Indians in their joyful impromptu celebration dance in the streets of Edmonton.

When we got to Calgary, John let me out at the bus stop across from the *Calgary Herald*'s downtown building. In those days the *Herald* had introduced to Calgary a running electric sign around their building that spelled out vital news, a copy of the one in New York that had for years dominated Times Square. There, racing around in lights, was the message: "The 102 Hobbema Treaty Indians get to stay on their reserve." I guess it was then that I really felt it was over.

When I got home I put through a phone call to the Parkers' ranch at Cochrane. Those people had been wonderful to Laurie and had been keeping him there nursing him back to health. I had warned Mr. Parker to not let John Laurie see any newspapers or hear any radio reports until the trial was over or I phoned. I feared for extra strain on Laurie's so-damaged heart. When Mr. Parker answered I asked to speak to John and I told him that we had won. He answered with a great whoop of joy and kept saying, "Oh-oh-oh."

What else is there to say when there's victory at the end of a seven-year struggle? For Laurie the fear and the work had begun seven years ago when the changed definition of an Indian had been recommended by the Department of Indian Affairs and accepted by their new minister, Walter Edward Harris. All that time Laurie had been writing letters daily to white groups and Indians. He had at his own expense attended two lengthy conferences with both the Indians and the Department of Indian Affairs in Ottawa. He had met with individual Indians, tribal chiefs and quietly warned them of the dangers that lay ahead for them.

I was tired. It had been seven years since I had first taken my place in the circle of Indians sitting on the floor of Laurie's house and I had said weakly, yes, I would help them in their case. I was glad to be home again. About ten days later, I received a telegram inviting me to a dinner in my honour that would be held at the Hobbema reserve. My family would be welcome and any friends I cared to invite.

Laurie was still recovering slowly. My only family was my husband, John, and daughter Linda, and John's sister and brother-in-law. There had been many good friends to me and the Indians, but I didn't like to impose on my Indian hosts, so I invited just Basil Deane and Dick Snell of the *Calgary Herald* newspaper. Later I remembered almost with shame that I had warned them that there would be no need for elaborate dress. It would be a simple Indian meal. Fortunately I at least wore a good silk dress to visit my Indian friends.

My shock was fierce when I completed the 140-mile trip once again and stopped in front of the Cree's large community hall at Hobbema. Again there were parked cars everywhere. John Samson was standing on the steps looking magnificent in full Indian regalia, his eagle plumes blowing in the wind. He looked at me, laughed and said, "You are going to be queen for a day," a parody on a well-known radio program of the day with that name.

He led me down to the hall's basement and, to my amazement, the immense room was filled with long rows of dining tables running across the back and front and down the sides, and in the seats about three hundred Indians. John Samson, still laughing, led me to the head table. It was covered with a white linen tablecloth with lighted glowing candles and flowers in bowls and set up in fine bone china and silver and even sparkling wine glasses. Someone must have once eaten at the Palliser Hotel in Calgary. The food they served everyone was the traditional hotel chicken, mashed potatoes, green peas and delicious apple pie. The wine turned out, to my relief, to be pop!

Behind me stood four Mounties, magnificent in their red coats, and in front of the table at least four microphones representing all the national stations. I glanced over to Basil Deane's table. Afterward he said, "There I was an honoured guest, surrounded by reporters from all the other papers and I didn't even have a pencil." But I was caught, too. I wasn't sure I had my lipstick on!

John Samson got up and welcomed the Indian guests who had come from all over Alberta, some from Saskatchewan and some from Montana. When the meal was over, and the dishes removed by the smiling, hard-working Indian women who had cooked and served it all, John led me upstairs to a room full of Indians, many in Indian regalia. He placed a plain wooden chair in the cleared centre and sat me down and said, "Anyone who wishes to give a gift to Mrs. Gorman can do so now." I felt rather foolish but slowly, one by one, the women of Hobbema came forward and placed their gifts, without a word but shy smiles, in my hand. They were so varied and all handmade. I still have all of them. There were moccasins and beads, purses and gloves. One had exquisitely embroidered a pair of pillowcases made from flour sacks; one had tatted cotton doilies; one was in the Indian fashion like a buckskin scroll with dates important to them and me on it in beads. Such thoughtful gifts I had never seen before.

Then John led me back to the end of the hall and all the lights went out. A spotlight suddenly shone on the shining eagle feathers of a headdress lying on the floor on a fur mat. The drums began their low, exciting throb and grew and grew and to their beat a lone dancer in a beautiful costume came out of the circled darkness in a spotlight, and bent and whirled around the headdress with reverence, sometimes touching it. I had never seen such fine dancing. John softly said, "He is a great dancer and has starred in Hollywood. He belongs to the Saddleback family." That was like a miracle in itself. He was the son of the past Hobbema Chief Saddleback who signed the protest against some of the Indians of his tribe that had set in motion the awful expulsion and the seven years of pain. The fight was over on both sides, regrets were buried and forgotten, and peace had prevailed. The Indians had already healed their wounds from the fierce accusations and my own angry cross-examinations.

John Samson picked up the headdress and, just like all things the Indians had ever made for me, it fitted exactly. Then he spoke in Cree and as a concession to my ignorance, he said, "Your name shall be Morning Star – the first good thing we see after a long night. You are now the Queen Mother of all the Cree."

I was given the great name Morning Star. The morning star had always held an honoured place in both South and North American native cultures.

Celebration at Hobbema after the appeal was won, March 1957. Left to right: Hereditary Chief Samson, Ruth Gorman, Chief John Samson, and John Lightning.

Even Custer, that strangely cruel and ambitious American cavalry officer, had chosen to enhance his chances for a U.S. presidential nomination by giving himself the Indian name "Son of Morning Star." It hadn't fooled the natives, but did impress the newspaper reporters. The title "Mother of the Cree" was confusing to me at that time as I had not had time to study the position it held in native culture. The Cree women were most honoured, and rightly so, for being the source of life.

I had tears and I didn't know a proper reply. Finally I said that I had never expected to have so many children to care for and that I would try to love them as a mother should.

The lights went on. Everyone moved and stretched and the soft throbbing drums grew. John arose and said the first dance is for our new Queen Mother. Ten beautiful girls all in white buckskin beaded costumes whirled into a circle in the centre. Each one was carrying a small child or a baby. They were delightful. The mothers were all smiling and the children obviously loved the dancing and music and lights. As they circled past me, each young woman paused and lifted her child high in the air. John explained to me, "These are the children born to those protested against who will now always be Hobbema Cree." Then I remembered.

During the long seven years while the case was not lost or won but unsettled, I had privately spoken to Father Latour the Catholic priest and to Mr.

Macleod, the United Church minister. I had explained that if I lost the case all the children born of the accused in that period would be barred forever from treaty and their reserves too and I suggested that if they could see their way until the case was won, to please not marry any of them because a peculiarity of the Act would not bar them from treaty if they were the illegitimate children of men from the tribe but if legitimate children, they would be barred. It shook these two good men of the cloth but to my delight they were prepared to save the Indians, if possible. I heard that, the day after the Hobbema trial, two mass weddings were held in both churches of the young couples that could wait for marriage. The babies and children in the dance were the children born during that period, now all Cree members of the Hobbema reserve. It was indeed aptly named the mother's dance.

I had to drive home that night. Finally, I told John that I must leave and he explained to the assembly and added calmly that the pow-wow would continue all night and maybe tomorrow too if so desired. Later I heard it had indeed. Now over 30 years later I continue to receive, on Mother's Day, flowers or a plant.

Later they had Spud Moir down to the reserve and gave him an honorary name and headdress. Years later he became an Alberta Supreme Court of Appeal Chief Justice. When he retired from his long service at the Bar as one of our best, successful court lawyers in Edmonton (judges said), at his farewell dinner he said that when he looked back on his long and successful career his greatest legal case was the Hobbema trial. Today his headdress lies in the museum at Fort MacLeod, donated by his widow.

The true value of those seven long years of effort, effort that truly shortened John Laurie's life, was that there must of necessity be justice for our first Canadians or we fail as a fine country. That was the only permanent vital effect of the Hobbema Case. After it, any political party would have to be careful that we shared the equal rights of our native people and if we denied them, we truly lowered our real pride in being a Canadian. In a way, the Hobbema Case did what law decisions must do: it set a precedent, not in courts of law but in common beliefs, including common law, that we must try to preserve and hand on.

The case was settled on no great legal principle at all, but merely on the technicalities that the government's notices were posted in the wrong number and on the wrong date according to the terrible Act. There had been no understanding on the part of the Indians who had been pressured to sign the protest to drive their fellow Indians off because one Indian had unthinkingly just signed, not realizing his own mother was one of the people he had signed to get evicted, and that if the protest he signed was successful, he himself would be homeless.

Looking back at the Hobbema Case, I can see what a strange case it had been. It was hardly a legal triumph. As law professor Sanders said in his article – it was not the first case tried on eviction under the Act. The Indians had won one other. One had been tried almost without a defence and dismissed in Saskatchewan. Were those a trial run for the Department?[1] The stakes in the Hobbema Case were financial stakes as *Time Magazine* carefully discovered and as is so often the case, based on the millions of dollars of oil money involved.

When I look back, I realize it had even been fortuitous that we had lost the first round of the case. I realize we could not trust our judicial system. We had to go back to the real lawmakers in Parliament who make the law. Elected politicians are always more loyal to the party than to their constituents (at least until pre-election time). Courts of law did not have precedents yet to deal with racial tensions and racial law. There was no easy escape from hired bureaucrats whose own jobs and salaries hung on creating under them native persons totally dependent on only bureaucratic decisions.

Why was the Hobbema Case so memorable in an able reporter's and a brilliant judge's long careers? Why did such a case lead on to open the way for the Indians to at last share in the most basic right of their own country, the vote, and become a benchmark for a change in their history? I will never totally know why. It seems to me that it became a vital case for two reasons. One, it was a sign to the Indian people that they could fight for justice and win. The Hobbema victory returned to the Indians a little of the pride we had taken from them. It also gave them a belief that their side of the case could be heard not only in court but by decent common people across Canada. Second, the publicity campaign revealed to the public, who had secretly long felt guilt about the past treatment of other humans they shared this country with, just how low that treatment had been allowed to continue to sink until innocent people were threatened with being deprived of their homes, their income, everything.

As for my part, well maybe the fact that I was small and a woman but would fight anyways made other non-Indians realize that they too could begin to act on their better impulses and rise up and undo Indian injustice, and join the Indians in preventing further abuses.

22: SENATORSHIP

As author James Gray pointed out, Diefenbaker was aware of the value of the "Hobbema Case" to his own party's election.[1] So when a vacancy by death occurred in the Senate I got a phone call from Calgary's long-time favourite local politician and John Laurie's lifelong school friend, Doug Harkness. To my surprise he said, "There is a Senate vacancy and your and John Laurie's names are being considered. What are your feelings on the matter?"

I didn't have to think. I said John Laurie. After I hung up and went to wash the dishes, I confess that I tried on the label "Senator Gorman" for sound and that I shouldn't have. Then minutes later, Laurie phoned. He began by saying, "I just got a phone call from Prime Minister Diefenbaker and it sounded like his voice." Impatiently I said, "It was Diefenbaker and you said yes?" To my horror, he said no. I couldn't believe it! Then he went on and told me it would be easier on everyone if it were an Indian. To my question of what Indian, "Why," he said, "the president of the Indian Association of Alberta, of course." Because those were alternate choices in north and south Alberta, I couldn't in my confusion remember who that was, so I asked. Laurie responded, "Jim Gladstone." I thought I would faint. The pale-faced Gladstone, the only one not really an Indian!

Gladstone's grandfather had been a white employee of the Department as a carpenter and proven very efficient, but his daughter had left home and come back to her father for shelter with a tiny boy baby and then had left him in her father's care. The agency and missionaries taking pity on his plight had generously moved the boy so the kind missionary women aids there could take care of him. Little is written about those lay missionaries' great work. Despite the Department of Indian Affairs' reports to Parliament, no young Indian, unless he could get experience with a machine, could qualify for a job off the reserve. On Gladstone's return to the reserve, he turned out to be a good farmer and had the good luck to marry into one of the finest and most respected Blood families, the Healys, and been generously accepted by the Blood tribe as one to get a share in their land and meagre payments. But I knew and you could see he was a "pale face."

When Laurie was tired he could act without as much thought as he normally did. When Laurie had chosen Gladstone he had no reason at all to believe that he would support liquor on Indian reserves. It was this that would so trouble Laurie. What other Indian could Laurie have stepped aside for? His first choice had always been Ralph Steinhauer. But unfortunately Ralph had already chosen to run and been defeated as a Liberal candidate. And no way could the Conservative party accept not only an Indian but also a Liberal. Both his dear friends Dave Crowchild and John Samson were now at last chiefs of their tribes and were needed there. Gladstone had seemed so pliable and agreed to Laurie's plan when Laurie had made his choice and consulted him. After he had suggested Gladstone as a substitute to me, Laurie had told me how it had been agreed that he would go as Gladstone's secretary to Ottawa, taking the inferior salary but serving as a wise and knowledgeable advisor to Gladstone who had never had the advantages of schooling above that of a charitable-run industrial school or the knowledge of government that comes with having become an elected chief. This arrangement never came to be.

Laurie forgave Gladstone for this. I didn't. I had Gladstone and two of his family to my house and I tried to shame and argue him into accepting not just the salary but the conditions of his receiving it – all in vain. He quietly listened and never answered except with, "Just my own family" and that was how it had been. Gladstone would later have a different recollection of these events. His son-in-law, Hugh Dempsey, a distinguished author and long-time knowledgeable friend of the Indians who saved and preserved the Indian culture in Eric Harvie's Glenbow Museum, wrote a biography about Senator James Gladstone.

Gladstone believed that John Laurie was a harsh Calvinist bachelor who couldn't really understand family needs – a strange accusation. John Laurie had never been a Calvinist. He was, as Gladstone had to know, a lay minister of the Anglican Church. He was a man who deeply understood the needs of a family. He may out of poverty have to be a bachelor, never marry, but he had taken into his own home, raised and cooked for, two Indian boys with their wives and children. He also brought through those difficult adolescent years, two Indian sons, Eddie Hunter, the Stoney, and the Blood artist Gerald Tailfeathers. He had, despite his job, cooked for them, paid their bills, and steered them successfully through to adulthood. What more of a family man can you ever be?

Gladstone himself had known only too well the value of a family. As a son abandoned by his mother, he had been raised by a grandfather who had to flee the illicit American drinking post, Fort Whoop-Up. He had found sanctuary and a job on the Blood reserve and it had been only Gladstone's own marriage to that fine Indian woman, daughter of a great and honoured Blood chief, that had caused the Bloods to generously adopt the homeless boy and even vote to share their funds and land with him.

During his years in the Indian Association of Alberta, Gladstone was never seen drinking. He had as a member and president voted with the Association and it was because he was president of the IAA that John had deferred his offer to be senator, his own appointment, to Gladstone, and the position Gladstone had held in the IAA may have explained his sudden rise to honour and wealth.

The angry letters Laurie had written Gladstone, and the defiant vote of the Indian Association of Alberta against being forced to be exposed to liquor on their reserves had clearly and emphatically demonstrated to Gladstone that liquor on reserves was unacceptable. It had been, except for its glorious pay and honour, a lonely life in Ottawa. There I believe Gladstone fell under the influence of the Department of Indian Affairs.

Why had the Department chosen to legalize alcohol? There is no visible evidence except that they were the ones that chose it. Was it another attempt by the Department to keep their own jobs as caretakers of weak and ineffectual wards? In the beginning they had tried starvation and the Indian had somehow survived. Then they tried leaving him uneducated and untrained and jobless, a beggar for the rations they dolled out. And beggars can never be choosers. Gladstone was probably used by the Department, sent to Manitoba to speak out for the acceptance of liquor. On whose doorstop can today's Indians lay the blame?

For centuries they had chosen voluntarily to not follow an alcohol-strewn path. In their very first legal and official agreement with white persons, the Royal Proclamation, liquor had been a forbidden route. It had been part and parcel of their first treaty negotiations.

They, like all human beings from the beginning of time, had known about the seductiveness of alcohol and as always, the same with us, there are persons who desperately seek man's first-found tranquilizer, alcohol. That tranquilizer had been a large part of the newcomers adjustment to this harsh land's tough life. There were no shows, no televisions, no books, and parties often were a year apart. The bar was the only club for hardworking settlers and it thrived. It thrived until it became an apparent barrier to further progress. The poverty it created for families had given the first impetus to the temperance movement on the continent of North America.

It did, I think, bring great grief and fear to Laurie near his death. Today across the country the Indians, those great survivors for centuries, are fighting back against the old and long-recognized enemy. Now on every reserve there is an active Alcoholics Anonymous group that tribes are financing.

The Bloods, Gladstone's old reserve, have chosen and supported the first woman chief of police in Canada. She is a deserted wife and mother who, with a university degree, returned to her own tribe. She signed up for every job listed and available on the reserve and to her amazement found herself chief of police. She studied her list of criminals; drunken names topped it. She deputized Indians and on one night they threw about a quarter of the tribe in their small jail charged with drunk driving. Today her tribe has not only kept her a chief but built her a larger jail.[2]

The Indian, always a warrior at heart, is fighting back the new enemy after measles, chicken pox, tuberculosis, starvation and idleness. I only wish Laurie could have lived to see the justification of his faith in the Indian people. The Indian has become a tax source for the government. By one act the government increased alcohol consumers by over half a million persons.

Certainly, this had not been consciously planned by Gladstone. As a senator, he was himself free to drink. At a reception with his father, his son Fred was shocked when he was offered a drink by a mounted policeman in full dress and not punished for drinking it. Gladstone's grandfather had certainly drunk at Fort Whoop-Up. His mother had left him with her "wild friends." His early and final friends on the Indian reserve had been the so-called "wild bunch." But despite that, he had survived to find an honoured place among the Indian people, never as a Blood chief, but at least as the elected president of the Indian Association of Alberta with Laurie's blessing.

23: LAURIE'S DEATH

I wasn't remembering well. It had been only confusion since I opened the telegram that said, "I regret to have to tell you that John Laurie died. Please come." Gentle Dr. Harry J. Crosby Johnston, executive director of the Calgary General Hospital (July 1956 to May 1972), a tough Unitarian (a founding member of the Unitarian Church of Calgary) who had for so long been a tower of strength to John Laurie, had sent it.

In the last fifteen years, Laurie had suffered four heart attacks yet I was still unprepared for his death when I received the news in Edmonton. He had seemed almost indestructible. I flew sadly back that night to Calgary. I acted as his executor, although John C. Gorman and Gylman J. E. Liesemer were the official executors.

Alone on the plane down from Edmonton that night I thought of my daughter and husband I had so suddenly left with their Edmonton family. The winter gas flares, bright evidence of Calgary's prosperity at the time, were like a torchlight parade below the path the plane was following to Calgary. How John Laurie would have loved them, loved all of Alberta. I wondered which of those flares shone up from the Indian reserve at Hobbema where Laurie had fought his great last fight for his beloved Indians. It would mark the beginning of the end for him, but also a victory.

During Laurie's poor health there was no quick surgery or aids, except drugs, and limited activity or any extra strain. Laurie's own magnificent courage and his disciplined patience had made possible the seeming impossible prolonging of his life. It had developed in me a belief that he would always succeed. His death shouldn't, by reason, have been a shock to me but still I could hardly believe it had happened.

When I drew his will, John Laurie had asked that he be buried near the McDougall Church in Morley. He had been fixing the small cairn in front of the church when he first met the Indians and that led to his adoption by the Indian family, the Hunters.

When his father died, John McDougall asked the missionary society of the Methodist Church for a burial ground high on a hill looking down on the Bow River. After treaty in 1877 it became part of the reserve. In 1876 he placed there the body of his father, the famous Reverend George McDougall, who tragically froze to death near Calgary at age 54. Ten years later a child of David and Annie McDougall's died and was placed there by his grandfather.

Up to the end John Laurie continued his life as he always had. On the last visit I had with him we didn't discuss too much the brief that was settled. It was to include all the resolutions through the years built up, clause by clause. He did it all one week while he lay so shrunk on the narrow bed of his one-room apartment. When I knocked on the door I thought I heard a voice. I pushed the unlocked door and hesitantly peaked around it. The light had that basement type of light trapped underground. It's light but it has an unreal colour of its own. When I looked at the bed, I could see Laurie. His eyes were turned to me and lit for a second and there was a half smile but his face was so white in the strange light produced when sunlight is bent through basement windows, almost as white as the sheets on which he lay. There were only two bright spots in the room: the bright painting by Gerald Tailfeathers of a sun dance at the Blood reserve and the bright green oxygen tank at his bedside.

Sitting in the corner of his room was Laurie's ancient Underwood typewriter. For over forty years his fingers had pecked out the words that had united two races. The last heart attack before his death had convinced Laurie he could not go on with his work. His only strength was his great emotional concern for the hardships that had been imposed on his Indian family. From his bed he wrote messages of encouragement to the Indian people. These letters were to individuals and he also carefully edited letters to the newspapers. He was a warrior to the end of his life.

I knew I would have to do the talking so I chatted along – silly, disconnected. I talked about the brief, how long it was, how the Indians were agreeing with the sections, where I was going. He seemed tired so I told him I would be going away for a week or so with my family to Edmonton.

He smiled and said, "Gorman, there is something you must do about the proposed route of the new highway. There is an old man named Peter whose people have been there a long time. You must save their place from the highway's invasion." I knew that to change the route of a national highway would be a five-year effort at least. "I will promise to help if you promise to get better," I said. Peter was an old Indian who had written him. He had lived all his life in a cabin he had built in the wilderness smack in the middle of where the new highway was being built with approaching bulldozers. I must of course stop that. Sometimes I think that if I see Laurie in afterlife, his question won't be, "Did you get rid of the enfranchisement section?" It will be instead, "What about Peter's cabin?" His had been a life built on never losing sight of small things, doing them for each person each day. These had piled up into achievements he himself had rarely taken time to look back and review. Even at the end there was so much in life he could see to achieve. He just never gave up, even on his deathbed.

Laurie died in his sleep alone and I'm sure it would have been peaceful. He was a deeply religious man, raised in his early days in a strict Scotch Presbyterian Church and in England by an equally church-conscious woman. He grew up in Oxford, one of the most religious of all towns in England, where nearly each of the twenty-two colleges has a chapel that's as beautiful and ancient as a small cathedral, where you awaken to air full of church chimes. Maybe because of this Laurie in later life had become an Anglican and a lay preacher. He revelled in designing sermons that suited Indians and making the long trip to preach on reserves in their small halls. One evening he phoned me up and did a rare thing for me. He said, "I have to tell you my sermon for the Sarcee. I'm going to tell them the story of Peter. I think Peter is the Indians' apostle. He was always blundering. He was the one who denied Christ thrice and regretted it. He often doubted Christ's wisdom but despite this he was Christ's most-loved apostle."

As illness came closer to overtaking him, Laurie wondered if he should enter a seminary and become a priest. With his deep religious beliefs that didn't fuss much with either denomination or exact gospel interpretation, he had gained an immense faith, one he never imposed on others. He also acquired the Indians' wonderful belief in fatalism. Once so close to nature, they accepted death as a natural thing that there was little one could really do to avoid it. It would come as it always did in nature.

Laurie had no money as I well knew when, acting as executor, I had to look for it. The only real home of his own he had near the end of his life, a small cabin built by his friends the Liesemer brothers on land beside the river near Canmore, land that because the river had changed its original route had never been surveyed and was obtained cheap from the province. Even that home had been battered by vandals. He had no clothes, hardly enough to cover him. One of his students and friends, Don Henderson, told me that one time in Banff he thought he saw Laurie from the back because he saw someone in John's old brown coat and hat worn so often by him that it had become like a second skin, sagged and form-fitted to his slender frame. But to his delight he discovered that it was worn with pride by Eddie Hunter, the first young Indian that Laurie had arranged schooling and music teachers for. Eddie was proudly wearing it on a warm day.

Laurie had no furniture really, and what he had was so plain, so old. He did have two fine pictures that Gerald Tailfeathers had painted for him as a present. He never had a car in all the time I knew him. He pretended he didn't like to drive, he who loved the trips to the reserve with me and had once flown aeroplanes. He earned a good salary but not once had he taken money from the Indians for any service. At the beginning he couldn't have taken any pay without being legally charged. At his own expense he had made three trips to Ottawa to present the IAA's fine briefs of demanded reforms. These were based on years of difficult and long meetings on reserves followed by Laurie typing out the lengthy minutes of the meeting and mailing them to each reserve to assure that the Indians were working together on their desired needs, to protect them from being divided and conquered. He financed it all – the paper, the stamps, the endless trips – and it had taken everything he had.

Laurie's early retirement pension had been very small. I remember how surprised I was when he seemed so frightened when some lower minion in the school board office had threatened him with non-payment of his pension because they were not certain that his illness had occurred because of his occupation – teaching. I phoned the school board office and explained to one of the heads that I would be speaking about that injustice every time I gave a speech and I had almost a full calendar of speeches. Quickly Laurie's meagre pension was paid. It was such a small amount that I wasn't sure what I was fighting about. When he died I learned that it was all he had had for the last few years of his life.

John Laurie died when he was only 59 years old. No one would have ever known anything about the important formative years of his early childhood, if in the last four months of that life he had not deliberately chosen to do something totally out of character, totally alien to anything he had ever done before. John chose to write his own biography. He had been ill for months. He had already survived four heart attacks, his survival a small miracle, and he was almost continuously in bed when he chose to write about himself.

About seven years before his death, one dreadful night around two or three in the morning that seemed unreal and nightmarish, John Laurie had telephoned and in a very soft controlled voice had said, "I can't seem to get my doctor, could you get me one?" Laurie had had another heart attack. He couldn't get an answer at his best friends' home, the Liesemer brothers, and he had rung my number so often it was almost an automatic action. I don't think he knew the time but he so rarely asked that I had to go. My husband John got up and insisted on driving me over and we went into the dark little unlocked house in Hillhurst. I knew the door would be unlocked. He did this so that any Indian too late for a room in the Salvation Army's hostel or a ride back to the reserve could find his way to John's home and just come in. In those days at night, Indians were picked up as vagrants and without money for the fine, hustled off to jail, a place they hated and were so ashamed to be sent to.

We found Laurie lying still and breathing with difficulty in a darkened room so I held his hand while John rounded up doctors and ambulances. Laurie said to me, "I haven't got a will." To calm him I said, "Don't worry, I can draw you up one right now if you want to." After we had got his doctor, I found a paper and thought, to keep him unagitated, I will do this. "First I have to have the names and addresses of your family, your next of kin." There was a long silence when suddenly out of the semi-darkness there came a weird wail "I have no family, no family at all." I was really frightened. This excited person wasn't the Laurie I knew at all. I reached for him but he turned his face away. To calm him I said, "Oh Laurie, it's only for legal reasons I have to know. Didn't you once tell me you had a sister?" After a long silence a quieter voice said "She can't come. She's too old – too sick." So I said that all I needed was her name and address but suddenly he seemed so alone, so withdrawn, this man who was usually surrounded by friends, either in his thoughts or beside him.

Then trying to be nonchalant, I said, "Will you need an executor?" So he said, "Will you be the executor?" Thinking that we could draw up another will later, I said, "Yes, that will do for now."

He pulled himself together. Obviously he had been thinking about the will because he knew exactly how he wanted to be buried, that his one possession, a broken-down summer cabin by the Bow River on the outskirts of Canmore, should go to his lifelong friend, Aylmer Liesemer, whom he had taught beside for twenty years and Aylmer's brother, who together with other friends, had helped him build it.

He shocked me when he said that he wanted all his papers burned. I knew there were boxes of them. The Indian legends that he had collected and saved by interviewing the elderly would be gone, as well as those lengthy minutes that told the story of the Indian Association of Alberta. I said, "Laurie, they can't be burned, they are history." He said, "They will cause trouble and might hurt the Indians. I don't want people to see them." I said, "Laurie, you trust me. I will destroy any papers that hurt anyone. I'll tear up the personal ones and see that the others go to Mr. Harvie's Glenbow Museum."

I knew the papers had to have very great historical value. Laurie had no home, no furniture to leave but in those papers there had to be something of value because they were the papers of a man who had filled a strange niche in history. So he had left them to me to do with as I thought fit and we signed the will before the ambulance arrived.

He recovered from that illness and I even forgot the will but at his death I had to act, contact his sister, get the papers. Laurie was right. When I phoned his sister and told her Laurie had chosen to be buried out on the Indian reserve but we would hold the funeral till she could come, she said she couldn't and she asked me questions only about money. As to the papers, Laurie's friend Aylmer sorted out the personal ones from the typed histories and I phoned Eric Harvie, who was very upset and he sent someone to come and got them quickly out of the empty apartment before I even saw them.

The private papers I was to burn turned out, as his friend Aylmer said, to be all in one battered briefcase, all IOU slips from Indians. Laurie must have lent money to every Indian he knew and who got in real trouble where money was all that could save him. There were bail payments, payments to save the lien on the car being called, some just cash for a bus ticket. To teach the Indians the strange way of the white man, he had carefully written the IOUs out and made them sign but Laurie had never collected, at least the great pile here. I tore them up and wondered what there was left in the bank accounts. And sure enough there was little money in the bank, a mere four hundred and some dollars, not even enough for a decent funeral. I knew Laurie would never want me to accept gifts or ask for aid, even from friends. So I worried about it. But I needn't have.

I never saw Laurie's attempt to write a biography until after his death and there it was in his papers. It was unfinished, a mere seven and a half pages typed by Marjorie Bond. Laurie could no longer write in the last months of his life. This man who had been active all his life and had worked for almost twenty hours each day had been laid low, immobile in his small basement room where the green oxygen tank, the bottle of pills and the nearby telephone were his only constant companions. His two lifelong friends, the Liesemer brothers, took excellent care of him from their upstairs flat and the Indians had voluntarily agreed to let him rest.

Most of us have few real memories of our early age, and the ones we have are based on anecdotes told to us by our family. Laurie had no family to tell him anecdotes. He must have dug deep inside his mind to uncover those almost submerged early years of his life. Why he decided to try to deliberately look into a past he had concealed all his life even from himself, I'm not sure.

Laurie opened his memoir with the title of John Buchan's then recently published biography called *Memory Hold-the-Door* (London: Hodder and Stoughton (1940, 1950). Laurie was a great admirer of the writer John Buchan. He had some of the clan Buchan's blood in his own veins. Buchan had been poet laureate of England before he had been chosen by the king to be his representative as governor general of Canada. He was the first one who had no royal blood in him at all but he had been raised to Baron Tweedsmuir before the appointment.

In his biography was something that Laurie during his entire life suppressed. I think he had even blocked it out from his own memory as just too painful to face. John Laurie had been a rejected child. Today we recognize the terrible trauma of rejection as a child. In our courts it is often given as an excuse in the defence of criminal acts. The strange part was, as I read and re-read his biography, that in John Laurie's case he had turned the rejection into the makings of a most unusual man.

He had so very little of what this world judges success on. I think he was always aware of the friendships he had and the love. He was so careful to never use his friendships either socially or as a help. However, so often when we were stuck with an Indian problem he would say, "I think maybe I know someone who could help us now we're stuck," and invariably they did. But I don't think he ever understood the universal love and admiration he was held in.

Laurie spent long hours, usually alone, working far into the night, through the hours he could have spent with friends, getting out the literally thousands of letters it took to hold together the remote, once enemies, tribes of Indians. His typed minutes had been sent out to not only every reserve but also into any club whose endorsement might help to get the Indians' concerns listened to. His worn old battered typewriter's keys could be heard clacking far into the night until he arose once more to get to school.

Laurie was a dedicated teacher. He didn't just teach students the school curriculum. He helped them publish their first papers, their yearbook, and to put on their first and then yearly play. I knew how often discouraged students came to him with personal problems and, just as he did with the Indians, he would drop everything and listen. And how that man could listen. He listened with every pore, not just his ears, and his empathy alone often solved what could have been a life-distorting problem for a young person. Laurie knew he was appreciated, I think. He never stopped to think how much or how deeply. He was always too busy facing another problem.

Someone once described Laurie as a lonely bachelor. I thought of his small rented homes. He often had a whole Indian family living with him – young people going to school, families with their children with nowhere to stay overnight. He was probably the most unlonely person I've ever known. If friends weren't underfoot, his thoughts were far away, always with them.

24: LAURIE'S FUNERAL

The morning of the day we were to bury John Laurie I awoke before dawn, one of those strange awakenings where you don't know if you are awake or still asleep. This was the day Laurie would go down into the cold dark earth gone from us forever. My thoughts were disjointed; flying bits and pieces of long-forgotten poetry flitted in and out of my mind like tiny shifted bits of coloured glass in a kaleidoscope. I looked out into the still dark at the greyness that surrounded and smothered me and thought, even though I couldn't remember who wrote it, "First comes the grey." Strange too how leaden and slow our body becomes when the body of one close to us has lost its movements forever. I felt I moved to the slowness of a funeral march. I felt almost anger: Why had you done this, Laurie, gone and died when we still needed you so much? Without guidance I was afraid, and I also hurt from losing such a close friend to confide in and consult with.

So many things needed to be done and yet none were really important, nothing could bring life back to the now quiet schoolteacher. Today I was supposed to be in charge of the last of all we could do for that stilled body and I panicked. I knew nothing. I'm poor about funerals. I just don't want to believe in them.

At the funeral home, to the funeral director's dismay, I bought the cheapest coffin. Rather sadly he said, "I suppose it will be a small funeral?" I said, "No, there will be two." The Indians, I knew, must have theirs at the McDougall log church in Morley, 60 miles down the road from the large funeral in the cathedral.

I began to worry. Was Laurie's body even in the funeral home? Where was it? Late in the afternoon the day before I had had a frantic call from the undertaker. His voice was squeaky, high with alarm. He said, "Come, Mrs. Gorman. You must come. My place is full of Indians and they say they are going to remove Mr. Laurie's body." When I asked "who were these Indians?" he said, "I think Sarcee," and in reply to who seemed to be leading them he said, "I think it's David Crowchild and he is adamant and they are just getting ready to move the body, casket and all. Come." I said, "Well, put the leader on the phone," and sure enough there was the low, firm Dave's voice, soft with sorrow. He explained that they wanted to take Laurie's body out to their church on the reserve. He belonged there. He had preached there. I agreed with that but quietly reasoned that Laurie in his will asked to be buried from the church at Morley and that many Indians, the ones whose loss was so great, were determined to all come to his funeral. The cathedral would hold them all. And I thought that Laurie would really have liked that. He quickly explained, "We just want to pray with it, be with it all night. I'll get it back in time for the funeral." It seemed so reasonable and I said yes, to the undertaker's horror, and then wondered, was it a criminal offence to just take a body? So the morning of the funeral I phoned the tired-sounding nice young funeral director, Murray Jacques, and he confirmed, yes, the body was back.

Then I began to worry about the Mounties. They had phoned two days before, the head of the Calgary division, to politely request permission for the Mounties to serve as a guard of honour. They would accompany the body to the cathedral and then down sixty miles of highway to the McDougall Church's small graveyard.

That one silenced me. I was so long in replying I think the poor man thought I was trying to reject the offer. He pleaded how they really respected Laurie and wanted to honour him. But I was not quiet because of rejection. I was thinking back to the time that Laurie and I nearly got arrested, to that young Mountie who so long ago at the locked entrance to the Stoney reserve because he might have to arrest us. I was painfully smiling to myself and saying to somewhere up there, "Laurie, we have come a long way." Finally I blurted out that Mr. Laurie would indeed be honoured. But I had no idea what you were supposed to do with a bodyguard. What was I supposed to have told them?

Then I began to worry about the ceremony. When I drew Laurie's will I knew his religion was Anglican and that his long-time friend was Calgary's loveable Archdeacon Cecil Swanson. Laurie had thought it would be nice if he wanted to do the service. But a few days ago the bishop himself phoned to announce he would take the funeral service and it must be in the cathedral. Lamely, I explained Laurie's fondness for the archdeacon and finally we worked out a compromise. They would both speak. But then I worried about what happened when there were two speakers. Would this be awkward – the last thing Laurie wanted. I decided that since I couldn't do anything about it anyway, I would leave it to the church. They had functioned successfully for hundreds of years and Laurie had great respect for his church.

Suddenly I wondered about pallbearers. Had I asked the right ones and how many? For days the phone had never stopped ringing. I believed that two cabinet ministers and two senators were coming from Ottawa as well as a representative of the prime minister. And representatives of the premiers had requested to serve. A millionaire pleaded to be honoured as a pallbearer. And then the Indians, the ones Laurie would really want. So many close acquaintances seemed suddenly alert to their loss. After my lonely vigil at the undertakers coping with the poverty of the situation, this citywide concern seemed almost confusing to me. What ever would I do? I had been so disorganized.

About then I began to worry, had I even written an obituary and put the date and time of the funeral in the paper? I remembered starting one. I had looked in past newspapers and saw that I must first give his address. A now empty 2-room basement apartment suite seemed pointless to mention. Then, his relatives. Laurie had only a sister, much younger than him, in Ontario and he had felt she might not even wish to be notified. But I again was insistent as you have to have some living relative to at least notify. I had phoned her and, although she was sad, she had not asked how he had died but only if there was any money. She told me not to delay the funeral for her arrival, she felt she could not make the long trip to see the brother she had hardly known. So Laurie had no family at all, one thing else he did not have that in our society we regard as so vital. One has only to look at the massive lists in the paid obituaries to realize how important we regard families as a measure of success. That's what most obituaries consist of. Yet here was this quiet little man so universally mourned once we all realized he was gone. And, of course, the honours. But I had an awful feeling that Laurie wouldn't want me to mention those. He didn't himself when he was alive. As to profession, all I could really say was, he had been a schoolteacher. He had had only two jobs: a teacher and a secretary to the Indian Association of Alberta.

But when I opened the next day's papers I needn't have worried about the short obituary. In every single newspaper in Alberta, editors had written a column about him. The newspapers were full of John Laurie's death. Editorials were written from the heart by hard-boiled newsmen who felt compelled to write about their loss. It was almost strange to witness the sudden fuss over this quiet man, this man they had apparently come to accept as part of our way of life. I was not prepared for all the fuss. For so long we had carefully gone our inconspicuous way.

I realized more than ever that John had lived his life carrying around among his few actual possessions a series of brief bags, compartments. It was as though they had labels on them. One was school and it was full of all those pupils he had loved and whose problems had become his. Those were all carefully held there, separate but carefully saved. Only rarely had he let me glimpse into the school compartment. Then there was another bag labelled Indians. That was the one I was tucked away in somewhere. And then there was another labelled John's life, a small one and I had never really seen within it. John himself was the man who had so carefully compartmentalized his own life. We who knew him only really knew the contents of whatever compartment he had chosen to file us in.

John Laurie's essential simplicity came through with great force in his quiet manner when he chose to encounter you. This constantly amazed his pupils and those he deliberately sought out to aid in his great aim to liberate a race. This was so evident on his death, which came as a shock, a great sense of loss, to all those who felt about this quiet man that each of us alone had discovered.

Each person's death is a small death inside you. Something is gone, left forever. For sixteen years John Laurie had been a big part of my life. Laurie will be irreplaceable not because of death but because he was so unique, so only just one. Laurie had been such a real person. You felt that reality once those almost hard eyes peered out from the glinting spectacles questioning into yours. He had carefully and deliberately wiped away all false efforts to create impressions that the rest of us cower under. There was no imitation in him, no desperate seeking to impress, no unsureness. As a result he had stripped down life to simplicity for himself.

Laurie had received honours before his death. First was from the sincere young men who chose him as their citizen of the year. I remember that he had phoned me concerned about whether he should accept and he was a little relieved I think when I was insistent that he accepted this, although he had a great fear of honour. His natural humility and modesty made him feel that he was not quite worthy enough. Also he knew that honour was so often short-lived and could sometimes promote envy. He had loved the doctorate from the University of Alberta in 1956. He rarely called himself doctor but as we used to say, it comes in handy when you are being insulted by lower minions.

With trepidation I dressed and drove to the cathedral. The day was April 9th, the year 1959, the place the Cathedral Church of the Redeemer in Calgary. The Anglican Cathedral was a lovely stone building. When it was built it was fashionably west of the city, midway between the early big homes down near Fort Calgary and now fashionably further west. Throughout the years the less fashionable east end had crawled up and surrounded it. Still one block west of the once central city hall, the cathedral was now surrounded by more seedy establishments.

I was amazed at the vast numbers of people who had turned up to share my grief. All the honorary pallbearers were there: honoured citizens, government representatives and Laurie's closest friends, both Indian and white.

John Laurie upon receiving his honorary degree from the University of Alberta, *ca.*1956.

There were equal numbers of Laurie's personal Indian friends. I could see my Indian friends. Nearly every tribe was represented and as always they sat together in their own tribal groups dressed in business suits like the ones Laurie had always so carefully worn at IAA meetings. Laurie had saved his Indian finery he so loved for the Indian times and wore only his best suit to the meetings.

As I sat alone in a front family pew, it seemed sad to me that John had no family here. I looked around the cathedral filled with people and there sat representatives of the political leaders of our country. Mr. Diefenbaker had sent a most appropriate representative, the Honourable Douglas S. Harkness, Laurie's old school teacher friend and a former Minister of Defence, who was now Minister of Agriculture. Provincial Premier Ernest Manning had sent the Honourable Fred Colborne, his cabinet minister, as his representative. There sat Mr. Eric Harvie, the millionaire, beside the Liesemer brothers. The church was full of individuals into whose lives John Laurie had somehow reached. Suddenly I realized that Laurie did have a family and it was all here: in this full and overflowing cathedral was the family of man. When Laurie died he had hardly enough money left for his burial but with the right Reverend G. R. Calvert, Bishop of Calgary, presiding, his was the most overcrowded funeral the cathedral had ever held.

The sun shone through a beautiful stained glass window and its red beams found the cheap wooden coffin in front of the church altar, its only decoration the flaming red of his university doctorate hood and his Indian chief's head dress with its elegant eagle feather glowing in the sun's beam. The sweet voices of a boys choir faded and the solemn ritual of the clergy moved along. The Bishop of Calgary held his cross high and looked down on the coffin box that seemed so small. "And God sent a man and his name was John." The bishop's strong sonorous voice rolled above like a slow wave in flood through the still, sunlit cathedral. That was right; that's what it had been. Together all these people were burying John Laurie, teacher.

When Laurie's empty body was loaded into the ornate hearse and started to pull away, I noticed all the Indians running down the street after the hearse on its way to the Morley cemetery. It wasn't the colour of the costumes that was startling; it was the grief so evident on their faces as they ran on foot after the hearse. They were hurt as much as I was.

Morley. Such a poor little cemetery ground on the Morley reserve but at least his choice and it stood with the great pillars of majestic mountains about it. He is buried as he requested in the cemetery of the McDougall Church built by that great missionary and in the shadow of the mountain now called Mount Laurie. Well over two hundred Indians had come. They had made that long trip, one hundred and twenty miles return from Calgary, for the majority of Alberta Indians who couldn't come. It was a sight to see, that poor cheap coffin lowered into the ground. At least I had hidden the cheapness by covering the coffin with the glow of the bright red and white of his university doctor's cowl and the gleam of the eagle feathers in his Indian chief's headdress. The Indians liked that. One should go prepared to the happy hunting ground.

Norman Luxton had once told me how he had come upon the bare frame of a tepee on top of a cliff and in it, propped up, was a skeleton still dressed in his fine chief's costume with all the paraphernalia he would need – arrows, knives and pipes. The Indians no longer did that but they would understand and be comforted.

The day they buried John Lee Laurie was one of those perfect days we sometimes get in Alberta just as a gift. It seemed right to me that it would be a perfect Alberta day, one that John so loved and one a great Indian poetess Pauline Johnson had once written of:

But what are these, compared to one of all her perfect days?
For naught can buy the jewel that upon her forehead lies
The cloudless sapphire Heaven of her territorial skies[1]

John Laurie's burial at Morley cemetery, 9 April 1959.

Laurie had a jewel in his crown. The mountains too stood high, majestic sentinels that would eternally guard the place. It was the place Laurie had told me he wished his mortal remains to go to, but the hole looked so small, so small to hold all the giant and soaring thoughts that were always gathered around Laurie. How could one small hole dam those and hide them!

I was suffering great confusion, the confusion of the shock of a sudden death and the flood of loss and grief. My eyes weren't functioning. They felt like hard marbles in my head. I hadn't had the relief that a shriek of pain brings or the soothing tears. There hadn't been time – so much to do so suddenly. I knew everything must be done correctly. Laurie was such a stickler for correctness but I had never understood funerals and this one was not an ordinary funeral. It was an Anglican ceremony in a United Church graveyard. But the burial had to be as much an Indian burial as possible but done by whites.

I tried to look about but I really only saw that small ugly hole and the people there who seemed endless. Many of them had driven over 60 miles just to be here and I didn't even know their names, just a few faces seemed familiar. Even among the Indians I could only see a few faces I knew. But the quantity of them was overwhelming. Everywhere I looked I could see more and more trailing toward this small hole, trudging across the bumpy prairie so gaunt and poor with their grief wrapped lightly in the dull blankets, the old coats they hid themselves in.

24: Laurie's Funeral

The bishop was praying with his cross raised high, giving a small blessing. He had preached a fine sermon in the great Anglican cathedral in Calgary that had been so full of grieving people. The silence and solemnity of the orderly Anglican service for the dead in the high walled church had been just right for John Laurie. The sun glinted on the cross the bishop held up and his great majestic robes looked too black and white blowing in the slight wind off the mountain. Beside him I could see Laurie's dear friend Archdeacon Cecil Swanson but his lesser role seemed overshadowed by the dreadful grief on his grief-pinched face. The light caught the red uniforms of the Mounties and the blowing feathers of the odd Indian headdress like bits of sparklers. But the dreadful too small hole seemed to dominate it all and I remember thinking, don't put that great free spirit there. It can never hold him. I felt like almost calling out and saying, Laurie, don't go, don't leave me here with so much still to be done to finish your magnificent unrealized dream. And then I was so ashamed. He had already worked so very hard to realize that dream, why should we expect more? But more was to come. It would all be based on Laurie's magnificent efforts up to the date of his death.

The sun glinted on the colours on the coffin. There were no flowers by request. Instead I had arranged on the coffin his university robes. He was secretly so happy and proud of the fact that the University of Alberta had given him a doctorate. Laurie's profession was in the field of education and to be recognized by that near the end of his life had been a great source of pride to him. Although he had great inner pride he had no outer so I knew what it had meant to him. Beside it lay the feathered chieftain's headdress the Indian chiefs had given him when they had first honoured him by adopting him as a blood brother. Three tribes had given him that great honour and given him names he was so proud of.

Indian names are important because in the old days the name you were given was revealing. Frequently you had one at birth, maybe significant to that birth time, another you chose and were given with consent at puberty, and a third name, an honorary name, you had earned somehow. The Stoney had given him his first name, White Cloud. The Hunter family who had adopted him believed he had the spirit of a son they had lost in birth whose Indian name translated was White Cloud. I thought the name so suitable for John Laurie because he was white, so high and near heaven like the saintly person he was. The Sarcee had named him Sitting Eagle, and the Bloods gave him his honorary name, Chief Red Crow. These names, these other persons, we were burying too. But I thought that maybe the names would not be lost. Some day another fine young Indian might choose one of them as an Indian name. I thought there would be no more John Lauries but I was to be wrong about that. In the future a child of the first great Alberta Indian painter Gerald Tailfeathers would be called Laurie Lee John Tailfeathers. But I didn't know that then.

Then my wandering mind returned because they were lowering the frail school teacher. We were to that part of the Christian burial where it is "dust unto dust." The archdeacon bent and placed a handful in and then slowly the mourners were bending and picking up bits and walking by and looking in sadly as they flung their handful down. When the bishop picked up a handful of that poor reserve's earth there had been the rattle of small stones on the coffin lid, so symbolic to me of what a hard land the Indians had to cope with. It wasn't dust we were flinging as the grave really was surrounded by the stones of this reserve.

I remembered the time when I was a small girl and my father first brought me here and asked me if I knew why it was called Stoney. When I told him that was because all they had was miles and miles of stones my father laughed and told me the story of how this tribe who were Assiniboine really had a different custom from other tribes. They just heated stones in hot water pots and cooked and kept their food and water warm this way. So the other Indians called them Stoney. Laurie, when he was doing the vast research for the first dictionary in the Stoney language, had been corresponding with American archaeologists and had found out that they were probably once located as far east as Kentucky. Their word for prairie was translated to "a place without trees," showing their surprise on finding such a place. He believed the legends that the warlike Blackfoot Nation, jealous of their great hunting grounds of buffalo herds, had driven them off into the mountains where they were safe because there was a legend connected with the Ghost River that threatened death if they crossed it. I being a sceptic had said that it was probably because there were no buffalo and it was too far anyway. The Stoney name Laurie believed like my father was connected with either the mountains or the way of cooking. But here he was now being buried within the shade of his beloved mountains and near to the first Indian tribe that had adopted him and we were all throwing the harsh hard stones sadly into his grave. I noticed that a few Indian women threw a wild flower but how hard it all seemed, how hard his life had been.

After the funeral was over everyone stood around. The archdeacon who knew Laurie had come to stand by my side and so the bishop formally bid me farewell. I guess because there was no family there, that was a visible sign to others to express their grief to me. The line was so long that there was no time for names or even conversation but I couldn't help but notice how many there were who stood with tears streaming down their cheeks and simply said, "He taught me; he was my teacher." I realized what a truly great teacher he must have been although he had never talked of those days to me.

Old Chief John Samson, nearly 90 years old, who had come over two hundred miles to be here, said with tears in his eyes only one thing, "He ate with us." Suddenly I realized how true that was. Laurie was the one who had chosen to share their food, the rest of us thought of it as "we ate with the Indians." I realized that all the chiefs of those tribes and other tribes were here too. They had travelled much farther than their non-Indian friends to commit this body to this remote spot. As I watched these many people strung out over the prairie making their way slowly back to their cars for the long drive home, I was amazed at the impact the humble school teacher had made on so many and such different people.

I was also amazed to find that the official representative from the federal government, one from the provincial government, a federal cabinet minister and four senators and at least three well-known millionaires, had made the long trip to the grave to honour Laurie. Most amazing was the presence of several quiet Indian agents, our traditional enemies, whose faces I had noticed in the crowd. Nearly all tribes from Alberta were represented. All these were at the simple funeral in a remote place for a man who in his lifetime had nothing our civilization considered important. He may have been a beloved schoolteacher, and I remembered that he had felt honoured once to be asked to give a course at Mount Royal College, but he hadn't even been an assistant principal of a public school.

I had been afraid that there would be no money for a marker to the grave but the legion phoned and said that because Laurie was a veteran they would provide the soldier's white cross marker. A few years later Daisy Crowchild decided that a white wooden cross would not do. She went around and with the same persistence she had used to make members divvy up their fees at the Indian Association of Alberta meetings, she got enough to start negotiations for a marble marker. Fortunately the monument carver misspelled Laurie's name and Daisy refused to pay the total. From the Indians' viewpoint, John Lee Laurie wasn't his real name anyway. His real names were the three that the Stoney, the Sarcee and the Bloods had given him: White Cloud, Sitting Eagle and Red Crow.

I awoke very early the morning after the funeral. My face felt swollen as though full of uncried tears. I had been tired on the ride home and the yellow line on the highway, all that was visible in the darkness, seemed to lead to nowhere forever. My thoughts kept going back to that small gravely hole where they thrust in John's body and covered it up. But it was as though no such pushing away could ever stop such a free soul functioning. Would all his work be lost? Those hours and hours of patient listening, later nights of tap, tapping at his typewriter sending out messages across a land of racial understanding, were they really stopped and naught to come of them now? A failed endeavour that could never be achieved? Was it all just to stop?

Somehow those meandering streams of people slowly leaving the grave kept haunting me. Then I realized, no, they were clearly carrying something away. So many had their arms wrapped around their bodies in the traditional gesture of grief where we hold it close to us. Were they also carrying away your now-silenced message? With relief I realized, no, I had a schedule to complete to go to Ottawa and speak a message, really a message from Laurie, you who were no longer here. I would go to Ottawa and these people who had loved you so, they would each go on. So I said, with this memory fresh on my mind, "okay John Laurie, when do I have to be there?" The force of John Laurie's spirit moved us on after his death until what he wanted to do was accomplished: free the Indian from a cruel bondage.

25: LAURIE'S MAGNIFICENT RECORD OF CHANGE

Laurie's death brought an end to joyful plans and a sudden realization of loss to all Calgarians and many other Albertans, a realization of how by his own visible total dedication to the Indian people he had brought so many effective and real improvements to all Albertans', Indian and non-Indian, lives. They realized that his unselfishness and his dedication, even to the extent of impoverishing himself and hastening his own death, had not only made major and concrete improvements in living conditions for the Indian people but, equally important, had changed the viewpoint of many Western non-Indians regarding their own past wrong impressions and attitude toward that race. The rare dedication of this man to a unique cause had become apparent to all. Editorials about his contribution were overwhelming and magnificent and appeared in the major papers all over Alberta. A few of the editorials and columns written about him attributed his early death at fifty-nine to his Indian work. Certainly the intensity and the frustration of those nineteen years since he had taken on as his own not only the Hunter family defence but the majority of Alberta Indians' protection and assistance had been exhaustive. To John Laurie its compensation had far outweighed its cost in his physical health.

When John Laurie died, all those around him realized they had lost a rare person. They had watched his persistent kindness to another race, and some realized at what personal cost. Western Canadians still close to their early pioneers have always been "people respecters" and they realized that one of theirs, a great individual, had passed. After his death and his magnificent funeral a monument was erected on his beloved Morley reserve adjacent to the Trans-Canada Highway. The citizens of Calgary named one of their city freeways John Laurie Boulevard and the Province of Alberta and the federal government renamed one of their loveliest mountains Mount Laurie.

I still don't know in whose mind the idea formed to name a mountain after John Laurie. It certainly wasn't mine. Laurie had always kept himself so rigid and remote from honours it never occurred to me. Whether it was an Indian or students, I just don't know. The mountain idea, as so often happened, ended up on my doorstep. First I visited the Morley council and asked their thinking. They chose the mountain, one on their reserve, a magnificent one. We all walked out in the field to look at the fine mountain in the quietness of sun and mountain and sky. Eventually, I broke the silence by asking, "What did you call it before?" and they said one of those difficult guttural words "*Yamnuska.*" So I asked, "What does that mean?" After consultation, the chief said, "Flat Face," and then he added, "like Laurie" and passed his face across his hand. We all knew what he meant. Laurie with his owl face seemed almost expressionless as it was rarely marred by his own emotions. When I nodded my head we all laughed. Such a tribute to Laurie, thinking of him even in death, brought merry relaxation. My next trip was to Edmonton to visit Premier Manning as I would need consent and money for a monument. After I finished my request, he was silent for quite a while and then he said, "I admired him and I wish I could have lived a life like his. You can have what you need." The value of his life's work was recognized but its creator was gone and his story untold.

As I hurried home from that mountain-naming ceremony, how much I wished John Laurie could have seen how today the Indians had shown how they loved and appreciated his friendship. I also wished that I could have told them of his final gift to them and that it would be accomplished. I had only a politician's promise and I was old enough now to know promises are a politician's stock in trade. If the promise wasn't fulfilled, I would just raise their hopes once more that so often in the past we whites had betrayed. I could have told them that not only had he changed their history but for his fellow non-Indian Canadians he would have added a permanent honour to Canadian history too.

As I thought of a historic change this seemingly most ordinary of men had achieved, it seemed in retrospect hard to believe it had been done. I realize now that he had been able to achieve it because John Laurie had been just "the right man at the right place at the right time."

Few really realized the total accomplishments made by this man, how his actions led to changing the history of Canada, a change for the better. It was John Laurie's lifelong efforts that led to all Canadian Indians being given the vote after almost two hundred years of stubborn resistance. At last they were accepted as equal citizens with every other Canadian, and not as wards of a government bureaucracy.

When one considers the tragic violence that went on in the United States over giving the vote to southern negroes, and the ongoing horrors in Africa, the fact that this could be done peacefully with quiet dignity in Canada without a single angry incident makes one realize the stature of this man and what he achieved in his lifetime.

In reality, Laurie's great contribution to the Indian race had not quite been completed before his death. He died before the peak of his achievement had been attained: the Indian at last getting a voice in the control of his life. Laurie had laid the groundwork and he had helped fight and win the long Hobbema Case with me but still, the one great bar to the Indians' chance ever for equality and justice would not come until that awful compulsory enfranchisement clause was removed from the Indian Act. As long as it was there the Department in private could suddenly deprive an Indian of his reserve property, his treaty money. It was the big stick they held to always threaten an Indian.

In his lifetime John Laurie had done what no one else could do. He had torn down the terrible buckskin curtain that for many years had concealed from his fellow Canadians what a few people in an all-powerful bureaucracy had concealed from other Canadians: the dreadful conditions in which they were keeping the Indian people of Canada. Only after his death was he able to give his beloved Indians back the gift of freedom, the freedom of the individual who lives in a democracy. That priceless small act, the right to share in the government that rules your very life, is a short four-letter word called the vote. Even its name is small. In action, it takes a second in a private spot and requires nothing but a small mark. Yet for that, millions of young men have died. It's the spot twentieth-century history has led us to painfully and now it dominates our way of life. Although the Indian vote had not been achieved completely during his lifetime, it was the schoolteacher's efforts, almost on his own, that made it a possibility.

Laurie's actions were almost unique. He had not fallen into the trap: he had not chosen to act for one race against another. He had chosen instead to believe in the dignity of human life and how that belonged to each person whatever his or her skin colour. He truly had a vision of lifting the buckskin curtain and he was able to do it so swiftly and so peacefully.

It was Laurie's patient persistence that most amazed me. No one who has not worked closely with a large group of Indians of different ages drawn from tribes that speak different languages and have conflicting problems can faintly grasp how difficult it was. In our audiences were old men whose fathers had hunted the buffalo sitting beside young men who could not speak the language of their fathers but who spent their time fixing and trying to drive broken-down automobiles.

The Indians had been told such lies. It wasn't exactly lies the Department of Indian Affairs told them but it was lies by omission. By never really answering their questions the confusion of speculation grew and was gently fanned by the Department's "maybe" or "soon" hints. Then there were the Department spies. I'm being too dramatic here but on every reserve there was an agent's favourite, one who received subtle gifts of a little better home or the chance of a paying job. Invariably they leaked what the Association was doing. Invariably they brought back a denial or counter-suggestion, and always the implication about what Laurie and I were getting, and questions about why we should be believed. Over it all was the pall cast by a hundred years of failure that made Indians question and doubt.

John Laurie would not want to be remembered just as a man who cleared the way for the Indian to get the vote. He regarded that as only political recognition of a battle in finding equal rights for individuals, so they could live out their days as best as possible.

Laurie aimed all his life to hand over respect to life in each person. He was always the teacher. He ran a classroom without favourites where he respected each student's needs and tried to enable each of them to reach their needs without artificial barriers being flung in their way so they could attain their highest potential possible in their few days of permitted life on earth.

The fact that he could teach us is how he revealed racial misunderstanding between people and smothered its persecution. He had been able to break down the past barriers in the dialogue he created between individuals of two races so they could freely work to help another. This was his great achievement. The getting of the vote was merely clear dramatic evidence of growth of the acceptance of this achievement, one that we can see and measure.

From John Laurie's viewpoint he felt his life had been a happy one. The poverty it had imposed was tragic, the only mistake he had ever made in his carefully planned strategy. That his Indian work came at the end of his life when he was physically very weak was the result of the biggest personal sacrifice he had brought himself to make on behalf of his Indian people. Laurie had spent his lifetime like a giant spider who had slowly and meticulously spun a web over all of Alberta that put him in touch with every Indian that had ever been torn asunder.

Attaining the vote for Canadian Indians was in part due to the success of the Hobbema Case and the fact that the Conservative party under Diefenbaker while in opposition had so vigorously and with much publicity fought on the Indians' side, which no doubt, at least in Western Canada, aided in a small way after years of Liberal rule of Canada.

Now I realize that all we buried that day in April was Laurie's worn body. His spirit had somehow escaped the earth and gravel shovelled and thrown down on it and it would dwell forever in that place of high mountains and in men's minds. Laurie had changed the history of Canada and never again would anything be quite the same.

The amazing part was how he did it. He did it almost alone – just one man, not high born or with a place in society or wealthy or a leader of an organized group or part at all of a ruling government. All I can see that he ever had was a compassion for things human and a strange determination that they were worth any effort. We can't afford to lose this part of Canadian history in an almost history-less country. Nor can we afford to lose the hope that each person can add to the life of all. I like the Webster dictionary's definition of history. It is the story of human affairs. John Laurie changed the human affairs of Canada, not only for its first people, the Indians, but also for today's people. In that a wrong was righted, progress in the human march was made.

John Laurie left behind at least fifty published articles, pages of resolutions, and twenty years of building the Indian Association of Alberta into the only truly representative Indian association.[1] He was a publishing miracle for dwellers on the wide lonely plains. They came out weekly in the *Canadian Cattleman* that was delivered to remote areas. It kept alive the spirit of the West that the ad-overstated dailies were ignoring while they pumped for more tourism and investment. But their contributors' columns now read like classics. Laurie published the really authentic Indian legends. He would spend hours with the oldest Indians on the reserve and quietly listen with an interpreter and write their stories. Of course he interspersed them with articles on what a danger the Department concealment of their treatment of the Indian was permitting to happen. Sometimes he would write articles for both sides on the terrible danger to the future existence of the Indians the changes in law were. He wrote those articles as though two Indians were talking, and not as scholarly criticism, so readers had a real look at the dangers of the enfranchisement sections that locked the Indian on the reserve in poverty and gave him as an only alternative slow starvation in a city. And later Laurie wrote about the evils hidden for the Indian race in the seemingly harmless new Indian Act of 1951.

From the beginning Laurie's was a Western Canadian thrust that included the Western-born students he taught who carried a sense of brotherhood out from his classes. The old timers were part of it: pioneers like the Crosses and the Luxtons and all the other old lives that backed him because they were somehow associated with the thrust, such as a business person like Eric Harvie, the Junior Chamber of Commerce, the Law Society and the Rotarians, in fact nearly every single service club in Western Canada. And best of all the women's clubs and the Local Council of Women, and Mrs.

Downe, Mrs. Taylor and Mrs. Rowan. The Western churches of all denominations spread the Western identity.

It was a magnificent effort. I think the effort could only succeed in one man's lifetime because he lived his life in the free air of Western Canada. Laurie came West and fell in love with Alberta, its ranchers, its city schoolchildren, its Indian people. The still almost pioneer land allowed his dreams to be fulfilled.

26: THE BRIEF / I GO NORTH

John Laurie in Stoney tribe ceremonial dress (Glenbow Archives NA-2554-2).

Laurie had won several things over his twenty years with the IAA including pensions for old age and the blind, and the children's allowance that had to be fought for because it was not included in Indian rights as it was in white Canadian citizens' rights. He had worked hard to get better schooling grants, health services, and the Charles Camsell Indian Hospital in Edmonton to treat the Indians so seriously infected with tuberculosis. Many Indians had no hospital services available to them on their reserves at all except for the once a week doctor's visit. And as the Indians used to say with their gentle humour, "It's hard to get sick just on Wednesday."

If all the tribes in Alberta voted on the brief with one voice the Department wouldn't dare enfranchise that many of them. This was proven by the unprecedented uproar over the large number of Indians the Department had tried to remove in Hobbema by the protest system. After Hobbema, the Department had broken all previous treaty promises and initiated giving liquor to the Indians against their own will which convinced Laurie that at any cost the Indians must get out from under Department domination. This could be achieved only by a united Indian vote. This had always been my opinion too but Laurie had held back, hating the thought of how many individual Indians would just be removed if we acted too soon and without solid arguments.

This was the first time we would speak with political support in Parliament. The Department had always successfully won over the Liberals during their long reign in power but John Diefenbaker and the Conservatives were now in power. We knew that the two minority parties, the CCF, and Social Credit, would be on our side.

John Laurie had been so careful as to never fall into the legal trap of having the Indians ask for the vote, get it, and then lose their reserves. Without actually asking for the vote he had spent twenty years training Indians to be ready to move from the hereditary tribal chieftain form of government to the democracy that surrounded them on the borders of the reserve. In the Indian Association of Alberta one membership was one vote and it carried equal weight in electing presidents and executives to lead them. There was no executive of chiefs bringing with them their confirmed power from their own reserve. The poorest Indian on the reserve, if he paid his dues, got a vote equal to any chief's. In the Association, John Laurie had directed them concerning their needs, taught them to elect an executive and to demand that the executive follow the majority or face not being elected at the next annual meeting. He had squelched the ancient and accepted for centuries Indian belief that leadership hung on personal generosity alone, but rather taught them that it hung on general welfare. He also had to teach the polite Indians that they had to be voluble if criticism was to be heard – merely turning away from a leader was not enough. He had prepared them for democracy. The only question was, if it failed, if we asked for the change in the Act and lost it, would the Department just quietly start legally removing Indians one by one from their reserves?

Laurie regarded the whole problem as he always had, from the personal, the human viewpoint of each Indian, and I was viewing it from the legal viewpoint. Unless the section went from the Act we would face years of guaranteed losing battles against bureaucratic decisions that considered a bureaucracy's function equally important to that of an individual's right to choice in forming his own life. We both worried about how an Indian who had never been given a choice by vote would be able to handle it. The whites who had had a vote ever since they landed in this country all too often blundered. It would be an immense leap for the Indian people. The Indians, even if they got the vote, would be in such a minority, spread so thinly over such a vast country, could they even protect themselves sufficiently? For so long jealousies and the tribal differences had seriously divided their steps of progress. Would the vote only increase the division? And then there was the terrible thought. Suppose after all these years of gently preparing them for democracy the Indians' well-established fears would cause them to just rise up and totally reject the idea of voting even if the way was cleared by Parliament amending the Act? Then the Indian would once more be labelled a savage, unprepared for democracy, and still necessary to be kept under the dictatorial paternalism of a poorly motivated bureaucracy. Was it too soon?

The brief could seem to take a compromising attitude by just taking out the compulsory section of the Act and leaving in the voluntary one. That could win at least Parliament's support even if it would infuriate the Department of Indian Affairs. But that still left another battle to be won. Could we get the Indians, who for so long had understood the terrible things that could happen to them under any enfranchisement section, to even accept that they should support our request to leave the comparatively harmless voluntary section to them, provided they themselves didn't choose to use it? To agree to support a brief to Parliament that even contained a mention of the word enfranchisement was going to be difficult and would require a great deal of explaining to the IAA members.

We would face still a third danger and that was all sorts of uninformed well-wishers in Canada could start to pressure the government when they heard the brief and demand that the government give the Indians the vote immediately. If that happened before we could get the compulsory enfranchisement section out of the Act, it would mean that the Department under law would still be able to remove any fault-finding Indian or Indian rebellious of the Department's tight hold on every aspect of their lives while they were treaty reserve Indians, and even quietly and secretly force them out of treaty and off their reserves. The Tailfeathers tragedy would be repeated over and over again.

Moving ahead with the brief had been a daring decision for a tired, ill Laurie to make. When finally he made it, we got busy putting in place the list of requests we would now have to get all the different tribes of Alberta to consent to.

Laurie designed a petition about the acceptance and endorsement of the brief to be signed by individual Indians. The Indians loved petitions. I could never figure it out after they got so severely burned after marking "X" on the treaties. Possibly they felt that a petition at least represented some personal participation and was an action they could take after interminable talks and unanswered letters to the Department.

Laurie had great fun making up a poll. It had questions such as: How many people live on your reserves? How many are children? How many milk cows are there? How much land? How many children are in school and how many have passed? Where is your nearest sickness assistance? How many of the heads of households have jobs? Are jobs available? Is training in any off-reserve jobs available to you?

Laurie always said that if the Department hadn't been able to legally discourage other Canadians from seeing conditions on Indian reserves, the reserves would have been removed years ago. But the hope of dragging Parliament from reserve to reserve was hopeless and we knew if left to the Department the choice of visiting representatives who might arrive already biased and see only what was wanted to be shown. We hit on the wise old solution that if the mountain would not come to Mohammed, Mohammed would have to go to the mountain. Take the conditions on the reserves to Parliament with photographs of conditions and people on the reserves and with a collection of real information. To my delight the Indians took to this with a relish and at their own expense. The photos when they started coming in were delightful. I'm sure the Indians had carefully photographed the worst houses, the most broken fences and bridges. I pasted the pictures in a cheap scrapbook and stapled the surveys of the reserves together. Laurie laughed and said, "all's fair in love and war." What else is politics if it isn't love and war?

They did prove effective. While I spoke in Parliament I could hear the rustle and see them circulated from spectator to spectator. Possibly they were too effective. They asked to keep them for a few days and they never did come back. A record of cringing pictures and the survey is in *Hansard* (Parliament's daily published report) but I never did get them back despite numerous requests to the Department. There was not to be a recorded pictorial history. But at least they did their job for this one hearing before they disappeared.

And now alone, without Laurie's wise aid, somehow I had to complete the legal brief John and I had worked on together for hours. It was the culmination of all Laurie's and the Indians' plans and requests through the years, some which I had advised on and some which Laurie had prepared three times already and taken to present at special meetings with the Department and to a commissioned hearing at Winnipeg. He had paid his own way out of his so-limited funds to go with the Indians to assist and speak along with the small Indian delegation that was approved and paid for.

Ruth Gorman's trip to Lesser Slave Lake to speak to Indians before she went to Ottawa, April 1960.

Laurie was determined that every Alberta Indian should know what was in the brief and vote his approval. There was to be no more swift confusing surprising things pressed onto Indians with no reason behind them as had been done the past. The Indians had to be prepared and as always totally informed of what we would be asking for before the brief was finalized. That meant visiting each reserve.

Laurie had been much too ill to visit the reserves as of old but we thought that first we would begin to deal with the three large southern tribes that could send delegates to visit him in Calgary. Fortunately their leaders frequently called on him and by such messages and letters and talk he had alerted the southern tribes to the presentation of the brief. Then he could write and then phone the northern tribes. However, the northern tribes had not been consulted when Laurie died. It would be left to me to travel to the northern reserves. I had never really visited most of them, just met their representatives at annual meetings.

I didn't really want to, but I followed Laurie's plan. The meetings had to be set up. I wasn't sure the Indians would listen to me with the same confidence without Laurie's advice. First I made a trip to Edmonton carrying the consent of the southern tribes. I met not only with the executive of the Association but also with whatever locals could make it to the meeting. I felt a poor substitute but the Indians, as always, were polite. In order to get approval from all the Alberta Indians for my Ottawa brief, it was necessary that I meet with the Villeneuve northern Crees. I asked for an interpreter and they arranged for it to be Albert Lightning, an official interpreter from Hobbema, one of the members of the family that had been threatened but saved from expulsion on the Hobbema reserve.[1]

The rains had made the roads almost impassable. That northern brush country land under the spring thaw turns into slimy gumbo. For one mile, almost crab-like, the bus could move forward only by grinding sideways with a terrible roar. We stopped and picked up Indians all along the road. Laughing, they greeted Indian friends already on the bus but no one stared at or spoke to me. I thought what a shock it's going to be to them to discover this white lady in her fur coat is who they are going to meet. Possibly they knew but were too polite.

When the bus did stop at a small, abandoned school building and they all got out, so did I. Fortunately there were some to meet me. As I stepped down into the mud down went my rubber boots, both sucked in, and I couldn't pull them out. They all laughed and someone just lifted me out of there and carried me in and then went back to wrestle the boots out of their muddy grave. Well, we were all introduced anyway.

That little school house was almost filled with serious-minded Indians, most of them representatives from out-lying tribes. With my Cree interpreter by my side I started in, clause by clause. They questioned me and voted on what they wanted me to tell Ottawa about their needs. They were so intent and concentrated. After a long evening of questioning, they came to understand and finally sign the brief.

About mid-morning it happened – I needed a washroom. One of the hardships of being a woman venturing alone into a man's world is that no one ever mentions the bathroom. In Calgary in the courthouse, I shared one small unit with the women jurors and policewomen and the three of us would play musical chairs in a cubicle. Here I was out in the wilds with not a woman in my audience. Obviously the schoolroom had no extra door in it. I consulted with Albert Lightning and after much consultation he led me out the back door and silently pointed down a dark path leading into the woods.

When I rounded the corner I came face-to-face with four very serious Indians. Without saying a word they separated and behind them was a tiny wood outhouse – but it had no door. The four Indians, with the methodical precision of an army on manoeuvres lined themselves up shoulder-to-shoulder and closed ranks to create a living door, their backs to me in the outhouse. When I made a discrete cough my human door swung open and I marched down the path ahead of them. I couldn't resist a giggle and soon I heard giggles behind me too!

I have never forgotten with what tact, what ingenuity and what politeness they had so quickly solved the problem of the lady lawyer and a doorless out-house.

The ladies who gave Ruth Gorman their only hamburger
while everybody else had whitefish! April 1960.

At noon we all moved to a nearby partially built house for lunch. It had no partitions and all the Indians were able to sit down at long trestle tables. The air was filled with the marvellous smell of fresh whitefish being fried. I had eaten whitefish only once in New York where with pride I had read at the restaurant, "Whitefish fillets from Great Slave Lake, Canada," and I was really looking forward to the meal. I was served first in my middle spot in the *U*-shaped tables. However, when I looked down at my plate I saw two small hamburger patties. It took me a moment to realize that they ate white fish every day and I was to get the big treat. Everyone else had that delicious smelling whitefish. No treat for them; they had to live on that which they fished through the ice holes all the long winter. I, as the honoured guest, was getting the only meat. After the marvellous dinner with home-cooked pies, I went into the kitchen to thank the laughing Cree ladies who had worked so hard to produce it. I assured them I really liked whitefish and asked if I could also have it at the next meal.

I will always remember that first visit with the Northern Crees. In the Saddle Lake area Ralph Steinhauer took care of me and fed me in his fine home. Ralph was a past president of the IAA and a future Alberta lieutenant governor.

Today as I near eighty years they sent me from Giroux the newspaper notice in their own English of the death of the past head chief. I realize he was probably one of those eight-year-old children running up and down the aisle during that meeting.

27: I GO TO PARLIAMENT

In 1927, thirty-three years before I appeared before a parliamentary committee at Ottawa, the British Columbia Indians, united in the allied tribes under Andrew Paul and Peter Kelly, asked that in British Columbia where native people had no treaty rights, that Indian rights to land be recognized. Their request was refused. Thirty-three years later, I appeared before a parliamentary committee, this time asking that the Indians not only have their land rights recognized but that their rights as Canadians to all civil liberties also be recognized.

When Laurie and I were fighting for the Indians to get the vote it was in an age where communism had grown to the height of its power in the Soviet Union, an area larger than our own Canada. Canadians had never really understood that our vaunted democracy actually in a way had created communist communes on our Indian reserves. We ran them just like Russia was run, by bureaucrats. In the Soviet Union, their bureaucracy consisted of only those high in the party system, "the cadres" of their party. In Canada our bureaucrats were not political appointments but they had been turned by our system into servants to assist the politicians temporarily in power in Ottawa "to do what they wanted done" rather than civil servants, meaning servants of the people seeing their country run as efficiently as it could for the benefit of those who lived within its borders. Laurie in a joking way used to call them "uncivil servants" claiming they didn't know how to be even civil to the public anymore. They were too superior in their power to even be polite.

Yet I could never in public compare Indian reserves to communist cells. There was a red panic abroad in the world. If the public ever attached the label communists to Indians it would be harder to get rid of than that awful label "savages" attached to them for centuries. It wasn't that Indians were political communists. They had for centuries lived with an equality of the individual within the comparatively small tribes. But the equality had been there by mutual endorsement, not imposed on them by one person in a strong leader position. In Canada, the Department of Indian Affairs' bureaucrats were the enemy and the Indian people had to fight.

I had no training in politics, nor had Laurie. It was Laurie's personal friendship with his fellow teacher, and in my case admiration for his courage and honesty, that had attracted us to Calgary's Conservative MP, Colonel Douglas Harkness. We had both been approached after the mammoth publicity attached to the successful Hobbema trial and been courted as possible candidates by all the different political parties looking for candidates that had had successful public exposure. We both had cowardly declined preferring the more human-related route of helping individuals. The Indians' enemy, we both realized, had not been the politicians, who because of the Indians' lack of the vote had been cut off from dedicated concern for their fate, but the bureaucracy of the Department of Indian Affairs.

Laurie had spent a lifetime hammering for reform from that Department. During his lifetime he had made three trips to Ottawa at his own expense. His first trip had been extremely successful. Since that time we had never been able to overcome the Department's barriers that they carefully maintained so no one but them could give a report to the government on the true conditions of the Canadian Indian people. When Laurie had forced two meetings with the Department, they had manoeuvred them out of Ottawa, far from the centre of power, to Winnipeg and other locations.

Laurie had spent hours preparing those long briefs that detailed the Indians' needs. He had also carefully gained the united opinion of Alberta Indians and even some non-Indian Albertans' support for the cause he championed, and had even gained support beyond Alberta's borders from some other non-Indian associations and churches. But the Department had somehow never mentioned these requests or they had watered them down before giving them to the government in Ottawa.

The Department was well ensconced with the eastern and Liberal Parliament that had for so long dominated Ottawa. The defeatist attitude of Quebec toward the Indians had assisted in this. French-Canadians had never forgiven the Quebec Indians' support to the English on the Plains of Abraham that had contributed to their defeat. They were also aware of the Indians' consistent support of the English both through the war of 1812 and in two world wars in Europe toward which many French Quebecers, but not all, had opposed. In both wars they had refused to be conscripted.

It was not until the last years of Laurie's life and, indeed, until after his death, that the great opportunity came, because of the surprising and overwhelming election of John Diefenbaker's Conservative government, to speak to a Parliament that was at least sympathetic to the Indians' reform. The Canadian government was at last prepared to accept a direct appeal by the non-voting Indians rather than relying on the able and familiar report of the Department who simply passed over the areas they had failed in and carefully emphasized their few successes, such as their penny-pinching success in reducing the cost to government of aiding Indians, over half of which had gone to their own salaries or to projects where non-Indians could be well paid.

When Prime Minister Diefenbaker's government surprisingly swept to power, Diefenbaker recognized that his support of Canadian Indians was responsible for the assistance he received from the electorate because of the general public's change of attitude toward the Indians' situation. The changed attitude had enabled him while in opposition to pound against the Saint-Laurent government about the injustices revealed in the Hobbema trial. Prime Minister Diefenbaker had once confessed to me that although there were other powerful forces such as the Trans-Canada pipeline, the Liberal support of the Department's advice to try and eject treaty Indians from the reserves that had been so publicly exposed by the vast publicity of the Hobbema trial had materially contributed to his surprising election. That publicity had really originated in the *Calgary Herald* under publisher Basil Deane's direction. It had come "out of the West" and exposed Canada's Indians' cause in the trial.

And now at last, on that morning of 10 May 1960, I was in Ottawa carrying a brief that summarized years of Laurie's preparation and the amazing united support of a large group of Indian people. I was also going to be able to get this brief before the government, not the legislature itself but a parliamentary committee whose membership came from all political parties who had members elected to Parliament.

Long after the hearing in Parliament I found the history of the chairman of the parliamentary hearing, Diefenbaker's newly-elected Noël Dorion, who was appointed by the Diefenbaker government. He had been born in Quebec City in 1904. Educated in law at Quebec City's Laval University, Dorion was president of the Bar committee of the province of Quebec by 1944 and elected to the House of Commons as a Conservative just two years before his appointment as head of this parliamentary hearing. It was, I suppose, a politically expedient appointment. It would please Diefenbaker's small group in that French province and prove a financial reward to a Quebec Conservative member even if the man knew nothing at all about Indians.

I knew I had a good brief. It was succinct, only fifty-eight typed, double-spaced pages. It had a chance of being read, understood when listened to and I would be giving it to a government in power who were at last sympathetic to the Indians' cause. It covered a history of the Canadian Indian relationships, treaty rights, the need for self-government, education, health care, employment and hunting rights. The brief covered the multiple needs and solutions the Indian people felt were necessary for the Indian people. The brief was the collection and summary of John Laurie's lifetime work with the Indian Association of Alberta.

I also had brought signed petitions of the backing of this brief by over 2,000 Indian people of Alberta stating that this was their desire and I was backed by two great Indians – John Samson of Hobbema and Howard Beebe of the Blood reserve – who the Indian people of Alberta had chosen to stand beside me.

I had with me the survey of the poverty on the reserves that showed the Department's failure backed by a photograph album. So at last members of Parliament who had never visited a reserve would receive a true glimpse into the reserve conditions the Department had never really revealed existed.

But I knew that the most vital part of the brief was to remove the legal barrier in the Indian Act, the compulsory enfranchisement section that meant the Indians could lose all treaty rights and their homes if they dared to vote or even ask for the vote. Unless the compulsory enfranchisement section could be removed for all time, Indians would be barred from demanding reforms or rights except if the Department wanted them and the last thing the Department wanted was Indians' voices replacing their bureaucratic ones in reports to Parliament.

Laurie and I had at last been able to explain to the Indians that it was only the compulsory enfranchisement section in the Act they had to vote on to open a way for them to speak directly to Parliament. The voluntary section we could still leave in the Act. By leaving it in we would overcome the belief that Indians had no interest in governing themselves through the Canadian government. The Indians, like myself, well understood that any Indian who was angry enough or ready to leave his reserve did not need protection. What was needed was the right to demand participation in Parliament. At last the Indians had understood that if they could get that compulsory section out of the Act, the enfranchisement section, they would break the Department's total threatening power over them. With the compulsory enfranchisement section in the Act removed, then could follow an actual voice into Parliament on their own behalf.

I knew by getting this brief into Parliament we would get some knowledge and understanding into the government of Canada of the Indian peoples' needs. There would be possible some future reforms in all those desperate needs in health, education, self-government and job training, but it would still be by courtesy only, not right.

Like every other Canadian, the Indians had to have a vote. If the threat to voting was removed by removing the compulsory enfranchisement section then eventually their right to vote could be passed by Parliament. But what was equally important, the right to vote would be accepted and exercised by the Indian people themselves without fear of punishment for either voting or asking for the vote.

To reach this point of acceptance by the Indian people had been a long and painful route through many years. Laurie and I had to fight their real, well-grounded fear all the way since if we advised the Indians to ask for the right to vote before the Act was changed, we could condemn them to enforceable expulsion from their reserves.

It was now one year after Laurie's death. I had come to Ottawa and was going to speak to Parliament, not through the Department's voice but through an Indian's voice, about the need for the removal of this little-understood section of the Indian Act – the compulsory enfranchisement section – that barred them from being a part of Canada's beloved democracy.

What was even better, at last I would speak to a government that, if they didn't exactly understand the legal technicalities of the Act, were at least sympathetic to the Indians' need to vote. Furthermore, when Laurie and I had been approached with an offer of a senatorship by the newly-elected and triumphant Mr. Diefenbaker and Doug Harkness, we had been assured a chance to put this to Parliament. The chance had at last come when I arrived in Ottawa that morning of 10 May 1960, and I was full of both hope and confidence.

At the train in Calgary, John Samson was waiting for me on the steps. Indian style, he had put on his best to go off to fight. In this case it was a new hat and overcoat. My teenage daughter had given me a corsage as that was a young girl's symbol of success, and I was, as usual, hoping I had remembered to turn off the stove. I didn't notice the flashing photo bulbs nor had I the good luck to see the *Calgary Herald* newspaper as we sped eastward. On its front page in only slightly smaller print than the one that flared out was "Mrs. John Gorman Takes Indians' Brief to Ottawa." It ran to two columns of print on the front page and then was continued in a full page in the second section in detail. They had summarized each of the sections of the brief. They knew how many Calgary readers had endorsed the brief, even had read it, and wanted to be sure I had included their concerns.

A half hour en route we stopped at the Gleichen station and Howard Beebe, equally debonair, joined us waving goodbye to his friends on the small railway platform. Our funds were limited and those two big men somehow tried sleeping three nights in a lower berth and me in an upper. We persuaded the porter to provide us with a card table and I distributed a copy to each of my Indian associates and clause-by-clause out loud we reviewed the brief. I knew we had to be letter perfect before we faced a possibly unsympathetic Parliament's committee.

We gained a small audience from the other passengers who hung over the back of our railway seats or stood in the aisle. Occasionally, carried away with enthusiasm, they would offer to buy us a drink. But we would have to rely on the porter to find out if we were passing through a province that allowed Indians to drink. Drinking laws were not yet uniform. And John Samson would make and win small bets by looking out the window at an unmarked land and say "we are entering an Indian reserve." When he invariably won the bet he finally revealed the houses had "backhouses." They have now almost all disappeared, an outdoor toilet whose lingering presence at an Indian home had become almost an identifying symbol of the Indians' way of life.

As the train had approached Ottawa, I looked across at the magnificent panorama of Canada's Houses of Parliament high on the hill, and I felt a surprising surge of pride. Here was our democracy, Canada's real source of power.

However, that joy was very short lasted. When the train drew into the station Senator Gladstone and a nice young man representing the Department met us. Thoughtfully reservations had been made for us all by the Department in a good hotel. I noted it was a long way from Parliament, so I said I would prefer to make my own closer to Parliament, and since I was paying my own way suggested I would prefer the Chateau Laurier I knew was just a few blocks from Parliament, the scene of the action. Senator Gladstone took care of my two Indian friends and they were all happily talking Cree and the nice young Department's man offered to drive me to the Chateau. While we waited in line at the reservation desk, aware that I was paying my own expenses in this expensive hotel, he kindly said, "You will only need reservations for at most three nights." I said, "Oh, no, I begin tomorrow morning and am to give my brief for three days and that's till Friday." "Oh," he said, "You can't speak on Friday at all. Your committee is composed of senators and MPs. You need a quorum each day from the Senate and from the Commons to be allowed to speak. You can't get a quorum on Friday. The Senate doesn't even sit on Friday and most senators go home on Thursday, so you can only speak before the committee probably for one day, at most two."

I was shocked. My brief had been timed and prepared and I had been promised three days. Already the Department had succeeded in making our presentation just a minimal appearance. Suddenly, I realized that I had been outmanoeuvred already by the Department. I was so mad. I said I came to speak for three days and somehow I would. He shrugged and then said, "If you can hurry getting into your room I will wait and drive you back with me to the Department's office as the director, Colonel Jones,

Ruth Gorman and Chief John Samson at the Calgary train station en route to Ottawa, 8 May 1960 (Glenbow Archives NA-2557-17).

wishes to welcome you to Ottawa and it's a long taxi ride." He was right. It would be a long taxi ride. The Department of Indian Affairs had not only isolated itself from Parliament by the Indian Act, but it was isolated even in physical location reigning in isolated power far from the Parliament buildings too.

The director's office was not too large. It had a large cleared desk and I immediately noticed only two pictures: the compulsory one of Queen Elizabeth and almost but not quite as large as was not permissible, just barely within the statutory restrictions, a fine coloured photograph of Mrs. Ellen Fairclough.

Mrs. Fairclough, a Hamilton MP, had training in insurance and accountancy and had the great distinction of being the first woman cabinet minister in Canada. Like all her predecessor ministers of Indian Affairs, she was "A Comer," a token cabinet minister, but at least picked for her ability. She too had no knowledge at all of Indians' affairs but would need political training by the Department. She had made the fine gesture of visiting the Sarcee Indian reserve in Calgary after she was appointed Minister of Indian Affairs. I had been directed to go down to her private railway car and accompany her and introduce her to the Sarcee tribe. She had come as a gesture of goodwill and I appreciated that. The Indians were not so appreciative. They had come to the meeting loaded with questions and complaints. She opened her speech by complimenting them on the great beauty of their reserve with its view of the beautiful mountains. In fact, she added, with a politician's charm, "Your reserve is so beautiful, I am tempted to marry an Indian so I can share in its beauty. I realize," she added indicating that she had carefully read their Act, "I am unable as a white person to share this beauty with you." Her political charm, however, didn't go over with the Indians. In reply Chief Dave Starlight said, "Madam, you have ignored one thing. You would first have to be asked in marriage." I couldn't help but laugh at the subtlety of establishing the Indians' few rights, and to Mrs. Fairclough's credit she wasn't too taken aback. The visit hadn't been a total success but I was delighted with her attempt and was hopeful.

I considered Mr. Jones's large portrait on his office wall as the wise feathering of the nest of his political boss. Colonel Jones himself was a large, exceedingly handsome and imposing man. He asked if I was content with my hotel accommodations and when I explained I had my own at the Chateau, he seemed to reassess me and the carefully chosen best clothes I wore, and then asked me to lunch at his club. I knew because it was an affiliate of my own Calgary's Ranchman's and it was one of Ottawa's finest. However, mindful of my need to pare down my presentation or hopefully to discover how I could expand the presentation, I thought I could safely and quickly get right to the heart of the matter. So I said, "Colonel Jones, I think you should understand the heart of my presentation is my desire to get the compulsory franchise section removed from the Indian Act and that I have been partially promised will become a reality." There was a long silence. He placed the fingers of his hands together to form a steeple and thoughtfully tapped them together and raised his eyebrows so they too formed an inward arch that met high over the centre of his nose. He regarded me in silence a long time. Finally he said, "I think there something you must understand, Mrs. Gorman. It is my contention that the time is not ripe for the removal of the compulsory enfranchisement section from the Act and fortunately," and here was a long pause, "in advance I have the full confidence of my minister." And he turned and looked at Ellen Fairclough's picture over his shoulder. I think I might have kept my calm if he hadn't added, "And fortunately she accepts my advice and does as I say."

Then I lost control of the situation. I stood up and said, "Well fortunately Colonel Jones, you are not elected by the people of Canada and possibly it will be those people who will make the decision this time." I had blown it. I turned and like a child in grade four marched angrily out of the principal's office. I didn't stop till I got closed out in the building's corridor. Then I came to. I had blown it. I had let his arrogance push my pride. If only patient Laurie had been there he would have as he had for years gone on manoeuvring and manipulating for at least some favours for his Indians in the face of the impossible wall he knew had his Indians imprisoned, rather than protected on their reserves. I leaned against the wall well aware of my foolishness. I had blown a chance for discussion and peaceful manoeuvring. On thought I realized that I had come to Ottawa full of over-confidence in political promises. However, on the long taxi ride back to the hotel, this time one I had to pay for myself, I reassured myself. If I could just get the brief cut down in my mind to a day's presentation, I could still win. The brief would be to Parliament and I still had the backing of the government in power, never mind the director and my lack of knowledge of parliamentary procedure.

Next morning I arrived early at the door where I was to speak when friends and Senator Gladstone arrived. He took me over to a dapper Frenchman and introduced me to the chairman of my hearing, a Liberal. Then came the second shock. He casually said, "It's too bad, but the minister, the Honourable Ellen Fairclough, won't be here. She has been suddenly called to Nova Scotia to unveil an Indian monument. However, she assured me she will be here for just a few minutes to extend a welcome to the committee." Suddenly I thought, Laurie, you weren't paranoid when you said never, never trust the Department especially when like the Greeks they come bearing gifts. I should have known if they paid our travel we would get a hearing that was mostly only a token ceremony.

I decided my only hope was to speak to the minister before her public appearance. I stopped her in the corridor explaining that it was vital at this meeting that I convince the committee they should recommend the hoped-for removal of the compulsory enfranchisement section from the Indian Act. Charmingly she explained that Colonel Jones said "it will be more effective if I announce in Parliament that now the Indian can vote."

I had high hopes that I could convince the minister before the committee to express support for the removal of the compulsory enfranchisement act. The advantage of convincing her to commit herself before a committee composed of her political opponents would assure that after I was long gone, if she didn't do it, they would taunt her with this in Parliament thus assuring its passage.

Now not only would she be absent but she had even been seduced by her deputy into merely announcing that the government would give Indians the vote before the enfranchisement section was gone. If that happened, as the Department well knew but she didn't, the minute any Indian dared vote he would be open to being evicted at will anytime by the Department on the grounds that he had clearly shown he no longer wished to continue the life of an "Indian" as defined by the Act.

I had to stop this happening. There was not going to be the removal of the compulsory enfranchisement section, the law that placed the Indian under the total control of a Department whose basic motive was to keep the Indian undeveloped, a failure requiring and allowing for their total domination. That domination was to keep and make easy the Department's own lucrative jobs.

I had failed despite getting all the Alberta Indians united and agreed that this was what they needed. Despite getting the party in power prepared to give us this chance to present it to Parliament, I had missed out on getting the understanding and backing of the minister, Mrs. Fairclough. Colonel Jones had outsmarted me. I hadn't gone and talked to Mrs. Fairclough myself. I thought that Mr. Diefenbaker's belief in removing the section and its very rightness and need was enough. Now the minister was never going to hear our needs and desires here. Colonel Jones had manoeuvred her on the great need to dedicate a monument to have her beyond hearing the reasons for removing the compulsory enfranchisement section before the committee. And with no past real understanding of the effects of that section of the Act on the Indians, she would just leave it in and think how great it was for her and her party to announce in Parliament that they would give the Indian the vote – an announcement like that would be welcomed by the press. To many whites and Indians it would be a great thing to do.

The minister had no knowledge that if she did that without first removing the section that said if an Indian indicated he no longer wanted to lead the life of an Indian, voteless and locked on a reserve, then he legally ceased being a treaty Indian and the country was under a firm legal obligation not to pay him as promised over the years for surrendering peacefully (with no down payment or real advantages) a country which by occupation and defence he had held for years. He would just in good faith sign a treaty of surrender. Indians would now be legally driven off their reserves cheaply and whenever it was beneficial to do so.

I knew Harkness understood that, and so did Diefenbaker who had been raised in St. Albert, Saskatchewan, and as a lawyer acted free for some Indian clients. But Mrs. Fairclough from Hamilton who had never really seen an Indian didn't. She had to rely on the advice of Colonel Jones and he wasn't going to advise her to remove a section that would reduce either the need or the power of his own department.

I had made a serious mistake by not writing the new-to-her-post minister whom I didn't know personally. Somehow she had to be shown suddenly the error of following the Department's self-motivated advice. I knew nobody in Ottawa except Doug Harkness, Laurie's past fellow schoolteacher and my own MP, but Indian Affairs wasn't his department to control; his was defence. Since he was the only one I knew, I must somehow get help from him.

I just started running down those high-ceiling, seemingly endless corridors. Fortunately a guard stepped out and firmly stopped me and said, "No running here, Ma'am." In desperation I said, "I have to speak immediately to the Minister of Defence." Firmly he said, "Go back to where you entered the Parliament building and they will phone up and see if they can get you the necessary permission." I knew that would take at least half an hour. Hopefully I said, "It's terribly important. Why don't you take me there and go in and ask if he will see Ruth Gorman right away. It's terribly important and can't wait."

Maybe the guard got weary telling tourists where the elevators were but keeping a firm hand on me we ran. To his surprise Doug said, bring her in right away. He arose smiling and holding out his hand but I blurted out, "Doug, Mrs. Fairclough isn't going to remove the compulsory enfranchisement section. The Department's convinced her."

Doug had won his distinguished George Medal on being able to make a quick decision and turn it into action and save many of the troops under him when their ship was torpedoed.[1] He hadn't lost the training. He said, "Go back," picked up the special phone and said, "Give me Mr. Diefenbaker." And my now curious guide led me back through that maze of corridors. I felt like Alice in Wonderland. The ceilings were going up, the walls closing in.

Mrs. Fairclough was speaking, telling them the usual, the concern the government felt for their Indian people which she carefully avoided calling voteless. But suddenly a young boy entered, went up to her and handed her a small folded note. She paused, read it and then looked up and said, "It gives me pleasure to announce in this session of Parliament that my government will ask for the removal of the compulsory enfranchisement section from the Indian Act." I couldn't resist it. I looked across at Colonel Jones flanked by his assistant and his mouth had dropped a trifle ajar. So, impishly, I raised my finger to my forehead and saluted the colonel.

After her speech we adjourned for lunch. I was so excited and exhausted I felt I wanted a moment alone in the fresh air. So I asked at Parliament's entrance desk where I might find a nearby coffee shop. I was told there was a new outdoor mall nearby with plenty of little eating places. At that time I had the old phobia of a woman eating alone in a public place when I happened to look up and noted on one of the buildings a brass plate bearing the name the *Ottawa Citizen* and I remembered a boy at college who, I had heard, moved to work there. I thought it would be nice to see a familiar face so I went in and asked if they had a reporter named Frank Swanson. The lady asked if I had an appointment, which I thought was an Eastern formality for a newsroom. To my amazement he turned out to be the publisher. He came rushing out, glad to see me. When I explained, he said "Let's have a sandwich." He had noted a big spread in the *Calgary Herald* about me bringing a brief to Ottawa. We discussed what was happening and to my amazement the next day, the *Ottawa Citizen* carried almost a full editorial column on the importance of the Indian committee hearings. Once more a Westerner had ridden to the Indians' side and for the next three days of the hearing, the hall was overflowing with MPs and reporters.

I returned to the hearings after that lunch. I don't know if it was fear or the adrenalin rush I had got running down strange Parliament halls that seemed to go on nowhere the faster I had run. I settled down on my heels to talk. I didn't have the written brief to follow. That was now gone into the clutches of the system, maybe to be actually published in *Hansard*, the daily report printed in the evening after Parliament. I realized most members only read it to send quotes of their own speeches home to convince constituents during the great pre-election drives that they had desperately tried to act on their behalf. The Indians would need the continuous support of Parliament for years to come if big changes were to happen. I knew I probably looked awfully small in that room full of semi-bored men. I had noticed with delight that the only four women senators Canada had in their Parliament had trooped in and conspicuously were sitting together in front row seats, elderly and well-dressed ladies who kept smiling at me. I also knew they were all Liberal appointments, as were some members of the committee and audience.

On the morning of the last day just before the hearings opened, a tall man had come up to me and said, "I am Senator Gershaw." I well knew Dr. Gershaw. He was the long-time Liberal member from Medicine Hat, Alberta. My father, who had once unsuccessfully tried to be a Conservative speaker on a platform against him, once said, "Dr. Gershaw is the kind of member of Parliament that everyone, no matter what their politics, wishes they could elect."

The criticism I was voicing was of a department under the Liberals who had been in continuous power up to Diefenbaker's surprising election. But he very determinedly had left the Senate and come to give me support. Laurie had a respect for senators that I didn't share. The senators at least

THIRD SESSION—TWENTY-FOURTH PARLIAMENT
1960

Joint Committee of the Senate and the House of Commons
on

INDIAN AFFAIRS

Joint Chairmen:—The Honourable Senator James Gladstone
and
Mr. Noël Dorion, M.P.

MINUTES OF PROCEEDINGS AND EVIDENCE

No. 3

WEDNESDAY, MAY 11, 1960
THURSDAY, MAY 12, 1960
FRIDAY, MAY 13, 1960

WITNESSES:

From the Indian Association of Alberta: Councillor Howard Beebe, President; Chief Johnnie Samson, Northern Representative and Mrs. J. C. Gorman, B.A., L.L.B., Legal Advisor.

From Blood Indian Reserve Protestant Group: Mr. Gerald Tail Feathers, Delegate.

From the Department of Citizenship and Immigration: Honourable Ellen Fairclough, Minister of Citizenship and Immigration and Superintendent General of Indian Affairs; Mr. H. M. Jones, Director of Indian Affairs; Mr. R. F. Davy, Chief, Education Division; and Mr. R. F. Battle, Chief, Economic Development Division.

From the Department of National Health and Welfare: Dr. P. E. Moore, Director, Indian and Northern Health Services.

THE QUEEN'S PRINTER AND CONTROLLER OF STATIONERY
OTTAWA, 1960

23087-0—1

Cover of *Hansard*, 11 May 1960. IAA members (Beebe, Samson, and Gorman) are listed at the bottom of the page.

replied to his letters and actually many had proven to be the only friends Indians had in Parliament. They of all parliamentary personnel were the only ones who had shown some concern for the Indian. From my viewpoint the Senate was hopeless. In an attempt to create a second House of Parliament so there would be a measure of counterchecks so necessary for a democratic government, the Canadian Senate had been created as a hybrid. It lacked the *noblesse oblige* and education for rule that the not elected or appointed House of Lords' aristocrats had who also represented the wealth and capitalists of England. And it lacked the regional representative quality with teeth that the elected American second house, the Senate, had. It fell somewhere in between and fell down into a spot of nothing but a pool, the politicians finding a spot where the politicians could exercise patronage by offering a dignified title, high salaries and privileges with no responsibilities except to the political party that appointed them.

28: THE VOTE

It was Albertans, both Indians and non-Indians, who were able to act together and break down the last barrier to freedom for the Indian people – the right to be free voting citizens in a free land. Getting the Indians the vote was an all-Alberta effort. It included the Indians in their Indian Association of Alberta; John Laurie and myself. It also depended upon the earlier contributions of George McDougall, the first permanent missionary to the Stoney Indians; Norman Luxton with his Banff Indian trading post, his final gift of a first Indian museum; George Ross, the first Calgary MP to stand up and speak for Indians to Parliament; Calgarians; and other non-Indians in groups, church organizations and individuals.

The catalyst, the schoolteacher, the one who put together that valuable alliance of whites and Indians, was John Laurie. In life he hadn't done it. But he had prepared the way and so it had to happen. After his death it was completed by the persons his life had inspired and benefited. It was a feat of magnificent proportions. Laurie's army was the people of Alberta and they were an army of Indians and non-Indians, every one of us of different political beliefs and religions but with one thing in common: we all came from Alberta.

The editors of a Calgary-based magazine, *The Canadian Cattleman*, first gave Laurie a larger platform to speak from and it was the *Calgary Herald* that led the whole of Canada to give the needed publicity. Calgary's Doug Harkness first introduced it to Parliament and another Westerner, John Diefenbaker, made the Indians' right to vote the future law of Canada. It was an all-Alberta effort that I would like to continue.

When the Indians first got the vote, they were terrified to use it. For generations they had been told, "If you exercise your vote you will lose your reserves, your homes." They were not even sure that the vote would benefit them. The very first time they had a chance to exercise their franchise they sent for me to explain it to and discuss it with them.

The Indians' questions made me think hard about the weaknesses in our democracy. They were quite right. Why would we vote for someone to represent us who we didn't know was a good man? In their small tribes it was quite easy for the Indians to discover the flaws in a chosen leader but in our enlarged society everyone was so obsessed with the image of a candidate, who could restyle his hair, get a good speech writer, and, above all, an experienced public relations representative and a professional campaign man, that with little more than image, he could get elected. The job we were electing him to paid him much higher than his past one, including hidden benefits, and this could easily be his incentive. Canadians had it so easy in such a fine unoccupied country that even blinders couldn't totally deprive them of their land. Canadians had fought for and inherited freedom so long ago that today's citizens had almost forgotten about this history. I wondered if democracy could really work officially in today's world. I placed before the Indians two aspects they understood: a people who respected warriors and a people who had suffered hunger. I wondered if going to the polls was probably a waste of time anyway.

In Quebec where the Indians had not participated at all with the Alberta Indians' request for the right to vote, the announcement that they now had the vote was met with distrust. Who can blame them? The last time they had marked a paper with an "X" was at treaty-making time and look what they had lost.

I had asked Parliament, as in the U.S.A., to give participants voting instructions but Diefenbaker was defeated and as expected the Department of Indian Affairs felt it unnecessary. What the majority of Indians failed to understand, not having a grasp of our parliamentary system, was that the biggest dividend in obtaining the vote was that they now had their own voice through their elected MP who would communicate their needs to Parliament. Without a vote, they could only complain to the Department as they had no representative on the floor of the house, and Parliament would listen to the bureaucrats' annual report but not to the voteless ones who had no legal right to speak to Canada's Parliament.

The vote freed the tribes from the total dominance of the Department in all their affairs. I know, as did Laurie, like all of Canada's minority groups, their demands were reduced to a mere whisper against the majority who had assured the election of the MPs. But no vote at all meant not even an assured whisper by a politician. He saved those for his next-time-around-possible electors and contributors. The vote gave a minority at least a legitimate whisper in making the rules that must govern their and our lives. It enabled tribes to criticize the past total rule of the bureaucrats in Ottawa with a voice that was beside the sympathetic, who by law must be unpaid, non-Indians. They were now equals at last in one important field with the white invaders.

If one looks at the violent changes and improvements of life on the reserves of today's Indians, one can date most after 1962 and the getting of the vote.

Non-Indian Canadian voters often turn out in pathetically indifferent numbers at elections, unlike the English or Americans, or Australians who even get a tax penalty if they don't vote. However, with few Indian candidates running and their constituencies split with white neighbours, it is difficult for Indians to struggle to the polls just as it is for white voters. I would like to see the possible reform of the process whereby natives voted on their own for the cabinet minister of Indian Affairs and a council from each province to advise him and communicate their needs. The Department could then be returned to the mere accountants, their proper role, and not policy makers, and all the employees of the Department of necessity should be of native origin.

But that was only a beginning of a long and alien new road for Indians. At first they were still afraid from those years of agents telling them they would lose their treaty rights and their own reserves if they voted. At the first election they phoned from Morley saying, "Ruth, you must come and explain." It was a long evening. They asked so many questions that I could not answer clearly but I remembered Laurie and I answered them truly. When they asked, "Do you know the man personally you must vote for?" I often had to say no. When they said, "Does he do what he promises you before he votes?" I often had to say no. After many wise questions, I began to wonder why the vote was important and I said that we have found this is not a perfect way but the best way. At least the individual's needs and dreams are listened to and the majority control the direction our lives should take rather than power or fear or hunger. They thought about it carefully and then the chief said, "All right, Ruth, who do we vote for?" and I said, "That's the best part of all. You are allowed as an individual to go in the booth alone and your ballot goes in a box and no one can really punish or reward you for making your choice for the kind of life you dream of for yourself, your children, your tribe." After the election, the Indian chief phoned and said that over eight hundred Indians voted.

Laurie's dream had been completed. Almost alone in his lifetime he had moved the Indian from where he was almost starving, concealed behind a buckskin curtain in a closed place, the reserve, into a new world for him, a democracy. But of course, one does not easily change the centuries' old tribal system. Nor can the hunter in his rich forests- and plains-oriented tribe suddenly become a small cog in the highly structured, and maybe even too swiftly moving world of technocracy. Even those of us who have had centuries of preparation for today's world, so often find it confusing, frightening and a strain.

After Ottawa and the Indians voted, I hoped my job was done, but without Laurie the Indians lost direction. In the Association, the Cardinals, Crees from the North, became presidents and the meetings were held there. As for myself I was into a wild venture of trying to publish a small quarterly magazine I had named *My Golden West*, publishing and writing because it turned out I couldn't afford writers for the articles I wanted in it. I hoped to make Albertans aware of the fine history we had. This was a full-time job.[1]

The effect of that is still daily changing Canada's history. In 1989, the first treaty Indian to be elected to Parliament in Ottawa came from Alberta – John Wilton Littlechild. He was a fine athlete who had earned his law degree with an athletic scholarship. He was elected by seventy-five percent non-Indian and twenty-five percent Indian constituents. Laurie would have glowed and laughed to know that Johnny Littlechild came from the Hobbema reserve where Laurie had suffered a heart attack when he and I had done legal battle to prevent his family's eviction.[2]

In Manitoba, another Cree Indian, Elijah Harper, also made Canadian history by simply standing up in the provincial legislature all alone and saying "No" to the Meech Lake agreements that federal politicians and provincial premiers were trying to force on Canadians who had never been given a chance to vote on them. Mr. Harper did it legally and properly. He took advantage of a law giving Manitobans the right to have a public hearing before any constitutional amendment was voted on by the Legislature. To introduce constitutional amendments in the Manitoba legislature required unanimous consent from its members – Mr. Harper refused to give his consent. Then, a thousand other Indians, to make their previously impossible-to-be-heard voices heard, signed up to speak before the proposed public hearings – if the amendment was accepted by the legislature – thereby delaying acceptance of the amendments beyond the deadline. In the event, the number of people wishing to speak before the public hearings and Mr. Harper's continued denial of unanimous consent forced the legislature to adjourn before the deadline imposed by Ottawa for passing the Meech Lake constitutional amendments. Thus did Meech Lake die on the arbitrary date set by Ottawa and Quebec City.

A poll had shown that the majority of Canadians who had been denied a chance to vote on the Meech Lake Accord did not want Parliament or their provincial premiers to impose the accord on them. An elected Indian, with a vote, had now changed the history of Canada in a democratic way. Laurie would have chuckled with delight!

Ruth Gorman at her desk, editing *Golden West* magazine, Calgary, *ca*.1970.

The publicity of the Hobbema trial and the parliamentary hearings had revealed to a shocked Canadian public the hypocrisy and failure of the Department's past treatment of their so-called wards, the Indians. A sharp reversal of attitude to the Indian and his shocking condition that had been smouldering away behind the buckskin curtain all these years resulted in an amazing period of action by concerned Canadians.

All over the place groups formed and cities opened friendship centres, and Calgary was no exception. The friendship centres were financed by concerned non-Indians and semi-volunteer non-Indians who gave freely of time, money and effort. On the whole they were able, concerned, unselfish individuals who were meeting for the first time the difference between a culture based on different principles and trying desperately to adjust to the terrible gap of time and the isolation between those who had dwelt on the giant island, the garden of Eden, and those who had followed another crushing route in overcrowded Europe where the focus was on more production, more money and more war.

The group of volunteers that tried to help the Indians was usually high on warmth and desire and low on actual knowledge of the Indians and their aspirations. The Indians who joined such associations were not usually the majority of treaty Indians still living isolated on their reserves, but Indians who had ventured off, many of them with a bitter sense of persecution and failure. Those Indians had little real concern for the reserve Indians. They also mainly suffered from terrible inferiority complexes from their difficult exposure to a totally alien population. Those Indians were seeking recognition, money and power within the white man's world that had been so long denied them. The generous Canadian people wished to make amends but the tragedy was that by now the problem was vast and their true knowledge of it poor. They approached the problem with the zeal of the early missionaries but they lived largely not on the reserves or even visited them but held dedicated meetings in elaborate buildings and conventions. The thousands of meetings saw little action or results.

Most whites, like John Melling, an Oxford graduate and Quaker, struggled desperately with the problem. He wrote books and the Indian-Eskimo paper.[3] The Department was delegated to finance the whole thing. This gave them a public image of enlightened, struggling helpers. They didn't really have to cope with the problem. Just as they had left the schooling to the missionaries, keeping control of their money, they financed and seemed to aid the multitude of concerned groups that like mushrooms had appeared overnight. There was activity and guilt and pettiness but actual improvement was totally missing. The Department still sat secure in the centre in Ottawa like a spider weaving a web to keep feeding itself and maintaining its own existence. They gave money to expensive cultural centres on reserves. This was a visible effort and flattered the Indian but the money contracts went to their white friends for the fabulous expenses and created neither training nor jobs for the young Indian.

They financed Indians to go to university, but there was neither a future for them on their reserve or in the city, and they were even parsimonious then. Witness the students' pathetic sit-down strike to get money for maintenance while attending university.[4] Educational loans were available for whites, even the newest of immigrants, but not for Indians to live while going to school in cities far from their reserve homes. Was it any different than before? They had once trained them as bricklayers when there were few jobs for bricklayers but refused to give them the short training required to obtain a hunting guide license. They continued their old, so easy and good for their Department's, policy. For instance, Lethbridge University graduated Indians as teachers and yet few were ever employed. Conferences and studies were easy to give grants to but where were the results? They financed Indians to interminable discussions and meetings but no action. When young, confused Indians rebelled, they just handed out grants for more temporary useless studies. An image or aura of hope was created and with nowhere else to go it was welcomed.

The one concrete move the Department had made giving him unasked-for liquor privileges was doing to the Indian what their earlier starvation policy had done. They were being driven into the slums of the city as drunken beggars or committing suicide and drunken murders on the reserves where still, with no hope of a permanent job, they grew up. The ambitious Indians formed societies to get grants and invariably failed with no concrete opportunities. These so-called off-reserve leaders were invariably locked in a power struggle against one another as they scrambled for the crumbs in rations, now renamed grants, the Department flung out.

Ministers came and went. In the Department men were developing careers and training ministers who knew nothing about Indians and who were totally dependent on their advice. Many of these ministers became disillusioned; a few even threatened to disband the Department but the well-trained civil servants handled them too.

What Colonel Jones had said to me when clutching my unfinanced but well-researched brief that I would present to Parliament, "fortunately I have a minister who does what I tell her and respects my advice," continued to be the reality. Given that Indians were a minority political group, Parliament facing a million other problems for the country, and all too often just to get re-elected, hadn't the time or the energy to fight the Department.

Able ministers would criticize and fight with the Department, but when able they invariably moved on. Ineffective ministers were content to just accept the Department's own version of affairs. What else could they do? The Department continued to go down wrong routes and put into force damaging policies, just as they had done under Harris and Pickersgill.

Today in Alberta, on their own, the Ermineskin tribe owns property in British Columbia and a Ponoka lumber company, and the Samson band owns a trust and insurance company, apartment buildings in Edmonton and condominiums in Vancouver. The Sarcee own a golf club and have another planned, a gravel company, and were employed by the Canadian Forces base in Calgary before its closure. The Siksika have a pottery business, a supermarket and a commercial complex. All of them have cultural centres where their arts and crafts not only preserve their history but also bring income to Alberta.

EPILOGUE

I had functioned at the Indian Association of Alberta as a group lawyer representing not one Indian or one tribe of Alberta but all tribes. I went as an unpaid volunteer and never was in the normal client/paid-lawyer relationship. I advised them as a group at their meetings only on matters that were causing all Indians on all reserves problems. I never acted for one group of Indians who were opposed to another group or tribe opposed to another's action. I fought the common opponent to all Indian people and that was usually the dictatorial actions assumed by the Department of Indian Affairs, a bureaucracy not elected and who, although like all civil servants, presumably were responsible to their cabinet minister.

But in reality the Department served as mere advisors to a minister who, unfortunately, because the Indians had been isolated on reserves, and their activities concealed behind a buckskin curtain, usually knew nothing about Indians' problems at all and even possibly had never known an Indian as a person. They knew only that a long-established Department had been selected to be responsible to Parliament for what that Department chose to tell them and, needless to say, their reports to the concerned minister were slanted to present their own actions in a favourable light.

I had watched a young Alberta Cree native, Harold Cardinal, make a fine speech at an IAA general meeting. I had asked Laurie during it and he said that Cardinal could possibly be another Louis Riel. He was sincere and, from his session in Carleton University and talking to Ottawa bureaucrats, believed the Department. This was the platform he had run on to get elected as the new president of the IAA. He said our Association would have officers, stenographers and grants if we go about it the right way.

I knew what the Department was up to. Now the grants they would give out of Indians' and taxpayers' money to "chiefs" were a new form of "rations," this time money to control the Indians and to isolate them into ineffective, small groups. Joint associations were dangerous for the bureaucrats in the Department. Isolation and rationing had held Indians down for so long.

Why not continue the practice? But I had no desire to become part of either internal tribal problems or conflicts between tribes. Unity for strength had been Laurie's success and I would follow that.

The defeat of the bureaucrats' Indian Department's old system had forced the Department into a new route. They would now "drive the donkey" by dangling a carrot on a string before his nose. The carrot would be cash grants. That was easy for the Department to do; it wasn't their money, it was the taxpayers. For the so long hungry losing Indians, it would seem at last a victory. Laurie had tried to warn them.

It was only two years after my successful trip to Ottawa and the vote that I would choose to leave the Indians as their voluntary lone solicitor. I had had over twenty years of it. Times all over the world had changed in those twenty years. At least colour discrimination was vanishing, a kind of world government was looming on our horizon and it was attempting to incorporate the rights of individuals, not just power groups, in each different country. The bureaucrats at Ottawa understood this too. Now they would attempt to still keep control of their Indian subjects by grants not laws and this was an unknown field to me. I too had branched out and was enjoying publishing a one-woman quarterly magazine about Western Canada, the area I had always lived in and had given me a good life. By 1964, I had only an honorary position with my Indian friends and their still-thriving Indian Association of Alberta.

Incidentally, in 1992 the IAA elected a woman president. Regina Crowchild is the daughter of Howard Beebe, a Blood Indian and one of the two chiefs who had made the trip with me to speak to Parliament at Ottawa and clear the Indian people's right to vote. The other Indian that made the trip that got the vote for all Canadian Indians was the great Cree chief John Samson of the Samson band at Hobbema, Alberta. He is still alive and an honoured elder of his tribe.[1] At Christmas for the past 30 years I receive a gift to "Our Mother Morning Star." He calls me "Mum." If they ask, I occasionally speak to them. Before the Alberta Indians went east to fight as we all did on our unvoted constitution that Trudeau had alone imposed on Ottawa, they asked me to speak to them. I told them, "Keep it simple. All you have is your reserve land and the democratic laws of Canada to protect you. Don't give up your rights. Fight for equality and Canadian rights." Today white people complain about the payments, but the reality is they are no higher per Indian than the poor whites on welfare receive, the free schools and the health services. "Yours were promised for land voluntarily surrendered and you are still the poor, the jobless and less educated in our country. You are not beggars, just persons having to fight to get proper repayment of a promised debt."

My jobs, after Laurie's death, that seemed too difficult to do while trying to keep the small first of its kind *Golden West* magazine alive at the same time were varied but time-consuming necessities. They varied but one that I will not forget was the fight for compensation and safe underpasses with the Alberta Government over their section of the new Trans-Canada Highway across the Morley reserve land. I lost my temper during the battle when their minister was pleading they hadn't enough money, by unfortunately blurting out one of my own chosen swear words (chosen for its explosive sound, I never did know its meaning, of that one swear word "Balderdash"). I brought newspaper headlines that the actual theft of Indian property had not. The strain on me was showing but it was with the election of a new young idealistic IAA president, Harold Cardinal, which made me decide that now that they had the vote, they should "swim on their own." He had attended Carleton University in an age populated with the "Flower Children." He wanted to fight for his people. The bureaucrats got him in and made promises of new grants and new aid in an IAA office and secretary. To Harold it must have seemed a real victory with possibilities.

Although they recognized that the Department of Indian Affairs had a record one could hardly be proud of, Jean Chrétien and Pierre Elliot Trudeau's white paper offered the Indians a message that pleased most Indians. But they tied it to doing away with any special status the Indians had under treaty or past laws. As usual, if anything was offered to the Indian it had a fierce price so naturally it was not acceptable on those terms by the Indian people. The negotiator for the Indian people was Harold Cardinal. I found some of his policies extremely disturbing. In contrast to the all-important work done in open assembly of all Indians involved, Cardinal was transferring business to the executive with decisions being made behind closed doors. He pushed two interesting resolutions through the Association: one for a much-enlarged new office and the other for expenses for himself. I could not help but think of John's policy that everyone shares all.

In my opinion, the vast sums the Department is slyly sliding into promoting Indian culture is in a class with the cheap glass beads the first Indian traders exchanged for valuable furs. Taxpayers' money should be spent on settling legitimate Indian land claims, supporting Indian self-government, aiding in creating reserve industries that make money and create jobs, and, most of all, higher education and job training for young people. Because of our past lack of promised education, we owe the Indians special funds set aside by the federal government for higher university education, and especially job training, which could be a combination of academic and paid apprenticeship.

Why would we deny Indians the free schooling, the health care, the protection from starvation that is the proud mark of Canadian democracy? They should receive equally every benefit that every other Canadian receives. In Canadian society we have always recognized that certain groups need special aid – children, widows, the old. The Indians are crippled because we allowed the Department to shirk its duty for many decades. The Indians need special aid, not because they are inferior, but because we crippled their progress. This is why we owe the Indians special funds set aside by the federal government.

It is much easier and cheaper to direct the money to promoting culture and eat it up so real aid can be avoided. And this from the very Department of Indian Affairs that spent the same taxpayers' money destroying the magnificent culture the Indians evolved to fit their almost perfect way of life. There are memos to them to stop the dancing and drumming and pow-wows. Their original culture need not be lost entirely; indeed, pride in one's heritage adds pride to oneself.

Fortunately there are already many fine books about the Indians' early culture, many of them that the Indians can't afford, and in some tragic cases can't even read. There are fine Indian paintings in museums that Indians can't see. This should be rectified by building lodges and museums to house cultural items on their own reserves. But building vast cultural halls designed by whites is just another joke played again by the Department.

For the Indian, his past one hundred years, created by mismanagement of a self-serving bureaucracy, offers him little to imitate or follow. Before the last hundred years, Indian history was based on living in a land of plenty and now plenty is gone. Even scientific advances cannot promise plenty: the numbers are too high to share in the production pot of a global village. The Indian has to build anew in the twenty-first century. The reserves are too small to support future Indian populations. Their young people will have to make plans to move into the cities. But to replace rations with welfare is not enough. They may, if given opportunity, find a new place, bring a new flavour to our world. Already they have been proven successful writers, architects, singers, dancers, and actors. They have proven with their warmth and laughter to fit well into the humane fields of people dealing with people. But their success will depend in the future on the Indian people themselves.

Democracy is only a form of government, not a way of life. It's only the frame around our way of life that holds back tyranny. When Laurie brought the Indian the vote, democracy was all that the Indian received but he had to be accepted as one of us, as a Canadian. Now the question is, is the privilege of citizenship of any value if we allow a dictatorial group of bureaucrats to continue to control the Indians' lives and the Indians have to spend their lifetimes defending themselves against their control? Or are the Indians and us ready to remove the dictatorial bureaucrats and clean up the Department for real democracy in this land?

We have wasted vast sums on a Department of Indian Affairs. They and their errors have cost billions. The money set aside annually for them by the federal government is divided proportionally between each Indian in Canada, not by tribe, but by individual in the tribe. There are no tribe trust funds controlled by Ottawa. That money is returned to the tribes now and in the future with one stipulation: only 20 percent can be spent in any one year. So one untrained council's error cannot lose it all, until their training in handling their own money is caught up.

The tribes must elect their own councils. The government must hire and pay accountants who every six months present the expenditures, gains and losses of the councils across Canada to a public meeting of all members of the tribe. Any loss of fifty percent proportionally requires a new election or re-election of council by ballot. At the end of the six-month period, the council can hire all personnel on their own reserves and pay council and chiefs' presented expenditures. It all could be run by Indians except the accountants who would report to the auditor-general who then reports to Ottawa.

The Indians are one of Canada's great assets. They are naturally conservationists in a world now desperate for them. In the U.S., the government has set aside large funds to train Indians for executive work on their own reserves and those jobs should be theirs exclusively. Let us have no more political appointments of civil servants.

None of it will work, of course, or succeed, unless we can see, as Laurie always could, the Indians as fellow travellers in life, human beings, not merely persons we travel through life with, with a label hanging around their necks. The Indian people have so much to add to Canada's future. But we must first gain the benefit that can come only with the desire for its success and the knowledge that is based on careful and deliberate study and knowledge on both sides of that invisible fence, still around our Indian reserves.

Never must we take back one foot of the land we promised to the cooperative, friendly, first tenants of this land. Promises cannot be seen to be broken ever without damage being done. Our payment was so low; what we got in return was so great. We must allow Indians to grow in the way of their own choice. It's quite possible these people, the world's greatest survivors, can still help us to survive.

The reserves are Indian land by treaty and were paid for long ago. We should leave them the ones they were given and give back to them the ones to which they have a proven claim. We will be disgraced forever as a

University of Calgary's first convocation, where Ruth Gorman received an honorary degree, 26 May 1966. Stoney Indian Elder Tatanga Mani (front centre), flanked by Dr. Ruth Gorman (left) and Dr. Herb Armstrong, the first president of the University of Calgary. Back row: Daisy and David Crowchild, Howard and Mabel Beebe of the Blood Reserve (Photo: Neil Crichton).

country if we renege on the treaty promises. Because reserves are their own land, Indians are the only ones who can decide on taxes and on production of that land.

Our first Canadian government had little money and no tax funds and could make only small payments to the Indians for the surrender of the vast original land to which the Indians had uncontested claim by long-time possession and occupation. Our impoverished first Canadian federation of Parliament did not have the money to pay properly for the surrender of land occupied by Indians at the time of Confederation. So they struck this cheap bargain for land title to Canada by promising exemptions and assistance spread out forever as interpreted by the phrase, "for as long as the sun shines and the rivers flow." Canada, now a wealthy nation, would be most amiss if it ever attempts to renege on those small payments. Today's generation of Canadians have to assume the cost of the promises our first impoverished Canadian government made so they could get a free uncontested legal title to Canada and which Canadians have used ever since as a great source of profit, both in sales of land and in taxes.

The Department is always threatening reserve Indians with the elimination of the penny-pinching payment due them from the treaties, and their

Indian Act, which actually is a reduction in many cases of treaty payments. The government has used this dual quality of the laws governing Indians to keep them impoverished, and until we have Canadian statute laws passed by Parliament that confirm that all Indians have a legal right to their treaty land and any claims to treaty land, the present Act remains one of the few legal defences Indians have. I hope that in the future, by law, there will be passed a Canadian statute that does not chisel away Indian rights but clearly confirms owed or claimed reserve land and treaty rights, and thus eliminates these constant and expensive legal court fights that cost Canadian taxpayers billions of dollars and keep Indians in dreadful suspense about whether or not they will receive their properly owed amounts.

The Department must go. At least that would represent a saving for Canadians each year in administrative fees, an amount with interest could be turned back annually to the Indians for them to establish a heritage fund for their own future.

In 1969, Jean Chrétien, then Minister of Citizenship and Immigration which also included all Indian Affairs, tried to pass a law he labelled the white paper in which he suggested assimilation of treaty Indians and the elimination of the Indian Act. As Chrétien hoped, the only part that had any appeal to Indians generally was the possible dissolution of the Department of Indian Affairs. However, this would deprive Indians of present minimal services and provide no future or payments at all.

There was no uniform treaty or reserve land in Canada at all, and to suddenly eliminate the Department of Indian Affairs by law recognized in the Indian Act and all treaties and the administration of treaties was to face chaos. Loss of existing rights would require a whole new set of governing rules to give uniform benefits to all Indians and these have never been estimated by Indian people acceptable.

A disillusioned young Harold Cardinal, past president of the IAA, who had been hypnotized by government grants for studies and payment to individual Indians and groups, in anger attempted a reply in a published paper of his own, the red paper. The red paper was not accepted by authorities because, although Cardinal condemned the treaties, he also wished them confirmed. The treaties were a very cheap land bargain struck by our early Canadian governments but at least they did give legal title to the Indians in their reserve land.

Cardinal brought a copy of the red paper to my magazine office, with apologies, and wanted me to return to the IAA. But I had given them twenty years of my life and I could foresee that the Department's new policy of paying large grants to Indians, often for worthless studies, would create, as the Department intended, jealousy among the tribes. I couldn't face a future of helping Indians fight other Indians that was being created by this large grant system.

The grant system was new policy that is still being continued and it divides Indian unity and power but still keeps a Department paying out large funds to individuals and bands. This destroys Indian initiative in meeting their chosen needs. It creates temporary prosperity for a period on reserves often in building projects that bring no permanent improvement in employment, education or in solving the alcohol problem. So I did not go back to my old position of being a free legal advisor in the all-Alberta Indians' Association. If Laurie had been alive, together, we might have made some small inroads in the government's new policy.

It was only after Laurie's death that I came to understand the burden he had carried for twenty years. I received literally hundreds of letters from Indians with problems and nowhere to turn as their complaints were usually against the Department. I will never forget the letter I received from that Indian woman from whom the Department had taken her child as she had not enough money to care for it. They had sent the child back to a reserve where she was not welcome as a tribe member. Included in her letter was a crumpled one dollar bill as a payment but I knew her case would take at least a year of hard fighting and then without a happy solution. Regretfully, I returned the one dollar bill with the name of some authority she might see. Without a determined individual fight, her small tragedy would never be righted and, even so, too late for a proper solution. This flood of tragic letters made me realize how many of these Laurie had received every day of his life and how many problems he had averted. No wonder he had four heart attacks. He died at the age of 59. With no Laurie to go on with and carry on the majority of the fight, I could not face the struggle alone with any hope of success. A new kind of approach was needed and fortunately now the IAA that Laurie and the early Indians created was still functioning.

In 1992, the IAA was the only Indian association still province-wide. It is still an organization where each Indian's vote, be he chief or young brave, has an equal value. It is modeled on the very democratic lines John Laurie insisted on from the beginning. It is the only Indian association that has openly survived as such for over fifty years, a tribute to John Laurie's founding and to the patience and perseverance of Alberta Indians themselves.

Since that time you can almost draw a line from 1960 (when Aboriginals were given the vote) on when Indians of Canada and their despair ceased! This small weapon – pushing an unseen ballot into an election box – had given them the desire to fight the government. Now if they protest the Department's action, they face no danger of eviction from their homes. Now like other Canadians they can stage marches or sit-down strikes without facing the loss of their own identity or land.

The Indians' problems are vast. You cannot replace three hundred years of poor colonial administration overnight. It may take yet another one hundred years before that is achieved. I am confident, as was Laurie, that the Indian, if given a chance, will choose a way that suits all Indian people, yet does not continue the old policy of dividing the tribes. A solution will be found.

Originally, largely to benefit two large corporations' desire for land and land speculators, we rushed the Indian, uninformed and starving onto reservations with no time to give them to study and establish not only their needs but future needs of their children. We must now adopt the patience of the Indian who has always been loyal to this country.

But the future of the Indians on over-crowded reserves living in almost slums will require major moves of careful improvement. I am certain that the kind of unity that John Laurie himself found in his own life with his Indian adopted family can eventually be achieved in all of Canada.

Recently, I searched over five general history books, and not one of them mentioned the date of when or how the Indians got the vote. The reality is that the federal vote, with no penalty when exercised, was given to Canada's native people when Conservative John Diefenbaker was prime minister of Canada.

A student of Canada's history quickly learns that in the past 80 years, Canadian policies have been largely guided by the Liberals. It was during this period that the government of Canada denied the Indians the right to vote without being penalized. In fairness to those Liberal leaders, I must add that I do not believe that any effective group within their party was aware of this deliberate omission of a special people in this country being denied democratic voting privileges. They were not aware because the Indians themselves did not ask to have this injustice removed. They wouldn't have dared to ask because by law the price they would have had to pay was too great. To gain the vote would have meant losing their homes and being forced to leave their reserves, thereby depriving their children of their rightful inheritance. Only a small group of Indians took action. They had no colourful leader to speak for them. The federal vote came to the Canadian Indian as silently and naturally and as unnoticed as breathing. Only a few newspapers commented on it. Since then hardly a single history book mentions it.

How can a story so important to a whole country go untold? The story about why Canada's native people were the last Canadians to be allowed to vote has not been well documented. Recorded histories are often only of our successes. We tell over and over again the stories that we are proud of, but omit those of which we are not proud. The story remained hidden because the long denial was unpleasant both for those who originally omitted it and those who continue to omit it.

How the Canadian Indian got the vote is, however, a credit to many Canadians. The greatest credit goes to a modest, unassuming Calgary schoolteacher, John Laurie, and the friends who believed in him. I am one of his friends who fought this battle for freedom for Canada's Indians beside him.

At the time of the Hobbema trial, Calgary's support and aid to the Indians threatened with eviction from their reserves was almost total. It involved citizens from all walks of life. Without that support it is possible there would never have been the changes in the sections of the Indian Act that were designed to keep Indians powerless and without the most basic democratic right – the right to vote. Long after that political victory, the closeness between the city and reserves continues.

The facts mentioned in this book are true and documented. The thoughts attributed to John Laurie are probably an intermingling of his thoughts and mine. He was, after all, for twenty years my mentor.[2] He was a shy and very private person. He was primarily a teacher all of his life. A good teacher, as history shows, often speaks obliquely in parables, or by his own actions and life.

I have only one advantage over John Laurie – I survived him to write this book. This enabled me to complete the lifetime jobs he had set for himself. Sadly, it was after his death, and so unknown to him, that, based on his lifelong efforts and writings, the Alberta Indians and I achieved his goal by gaining the right for all Canadian Indians to vote without being punished for doing so. This allowed Indian people to cut free at last from bureaucratic rule and become citizens in what had always been their own country. The Indian people were the first people here but were the last Canadians to get the right to vote.

Appendix I:

TIMELINE OF EVENTS CONCERNING RUTH GORMAN AND JOHN LAURIE'S INVOLVEMENT WITH THE ABORIGINAL PEOPLE OF CANADA.

Date	Event
1899	John Lee Laurie's birth certificate states that he was born on a farm in Oxford County, Ontario on 23 October.
1914	Ruth Gorman (née Peacock) was born in Calgary, Alberta, on 14 February.
1915	John Laurie attends the Collegiate Institute in Galt to complete his final two years of high school.
1917/1918	John Laurie attends Trinity College at the University of Toronto for his first year of study, specializing in English, history, and languages (Latin, French and German).
1918	John Laurie joins the Royal Air Force in Canada as a cadet on 27 August. He was then decommissioned on 13 January 1919.
1919/1920	John Laurie attends his second year at Trinity College, again specializing in English, history and languages.
1920	John Laurie comes west searching for an 'adventure.' He first goes to Medora, a small town in southwestern Manitoba and then moves to Calgary, Alberta.
1921	John Laurie moves to Evergreen, a small hamlet between Rocky Mountain House and Red Deer, Alberta, where he first taught at school.
1921–1927	John Laurie probably first meets members of the Stoney Band near Morley while moving horses in the summer from Priddis to Eckville. Later, he assists the band with the rebuilding of the old, original McDougall Church and is introduced to Reverend J. E. Staley, who invites Laurie to teach at the residential school; Laurie politely declines.
1923	John Laurie completes, via correspondence, the requirements for his B.A. from the University of Toronto.
1923	John Laurie begins teaching at Western Canada College as English and Latin master.
1927	John Laurie accepts a teaching position at Crescent Heights High School, Calgary, teaching English and drama.

Date	Event
c1930	John Laurie attends a meeting organized by Reverend J. S. Woodsworth concerning the creation of the Cooperative Commonwealth Federation (CCF) party of Canada.
1932	Ruth Gorman's father, M.B. Peacock, litigates the 'Wesley Case' for the Stoney Indians, successfully fighting for a clarification of their hunting rights.
1937	Ruth Gorman is made an 'Indian Princess' by the Stoney and is given the name 'Mountain White Eagle Girl' in a ceremony at Banff.
1937	Ruth Gorman receives her B.A. degree from the University of Alberta.
1939	Ruth Gorman receives her LL.B. from the University of Alberta.
1939	Ruth Gorman is made Convenor of Laws for the Local Council of Women, Calgary, a position she held until 1963.
1939	John Laurie is invited by Reverend J. E. Staley to judge a music contest at the Morley Residential School. There he meets Eddie Hunter, a violin player. Laurie invites Hunter to board at his house and attend Crescent Heights High School. Later he would also invite other children, most notably Gerald Tailfeathers, to live with him and attend school in Calgary.
1940	Ruth Gorman is admitted to the Alberta Bar.
1940	Chief Enos Hunter of the Wesley Band adopts John Laurie into his family. Laurie is given the name 'White Cloud' by his adoptive family. From his new family he learns the Stoney language, traditions and spirituality. It is from his time spent with his adoptive family that he takes a true interest in Indian affairs.
1944	John Laurie is nominated (in absence) by the newly reformed Indian Association of Alberta (IAA) to become its secretary, an unpaid position he delightedly accepts.
1944	John Laurie contacts Ruth Gorman for the first time asking her to help explain the legalities of the Indian Act to the members of the IAA. She reluctantly completes this task in the basement of Paget Hall in Calgary.

Date	Event
1946	Ruth Gorman agrees to act as unpaid solicitor for the Indian Association of Alberta.
1944–53	John Laurie travels to Ottawa to attend business concerning the Indian Act (all trips were financed with his own money).
1948	John Laurie's first of a series of heart attacks.
1951	Department of Indian Affairs revises the Indian Act making it more difficult for natives to register on their reserve. In particular, four conditions are laid out that could prevent tribal members from being registered: illegitimacy in their ancestry; non-native blood in their ancestry; people who did not join the correct band at treaty time; people who had accepted scrip for land after 1870.
1951	Under the new Act, members of the Hobbema tribe protest the legitimacy of other members against whom they had been holding a long bitter grudge. A hearing date is set for March 29.
1951	The first hearing lasts only six hours but would consume almost seven years of Ruth Gorman's and John Laurie's lives. Labelled the 'Hobbema Case' by newspapers, it is held before a government commission. See (1957), 7 DLR (2d) 745 (Alta. Dist. Ct.).
1952	John Laurie has a serious heart attack that would eventually force him to retire from his position as teacher at the Crescent Heights school.
1954	After finally being allowed to review the material that the expulsion was based on, Ruth Gorman and John Laurie prove that some of the natives did not accept scrip. The Commissioner takes the evidence and adjourns the proceedings sine die (without specific date).
1955	On 29 February, the Commissioner announces that the case will be reconvened on grounds that new evidence has been found supporting the eviction. The Commissioner sets the date for the reopening of the hearings to 7 July 1955. Ruth Gorman appeals this decision.
1956	John Laurie retires from his teaching position for health reasons. John Laurie also resigns his official duties as the IAA secretary.

Date	Event
1956	John Laurie receives an honorary doctorate from the University of Alberta.
1956	The registrar reverses the Commissioner's stay, and the originally named Aboriginal people are set to be removed from the band rolls. They are given three months to leave the Hobbema reserve.
1956	Hobbema Commission hearing resumes. Beginning with a petition sent to the Queen from the Hobbema tribe, Gorman successfully solicits newspapers, magazines, interest groups, and parliamentarians to her cause. The campaign brings pressure onto the Liberal government of the time and arguably helps influence their final decision.
1957	On 4 February, Ruth Gorman files the appeal and on 1 March, a decision is reached. The judge bases his ruling on legal technicalities and reverses the 1956 ruling of the registrar.
1957	Shortly after the ruling, Ruth Gorman is invited to a celebration by the Cree and is named 'Queen Morning Star of the Cree.'
1958	James Gladstone is appointed as the first Aboriginal senator by John Diefenbaker.
1958/59	Ruth Gorman tours Aboriginal communities in Alberta to prepare for her Indian Association of Alberta brief to the 1959/60 Joint Senate and House of Commons Committee on Indian Affairs. Before the Joint Senate, she collects petitions, pictures and other information to present to the committee.
1955–59	John Laurie accepts a position at the Glenbow Foundation compiling information on the Stoneys and a dictionary of their language.
1959	After years of heart problems John Lee Laurie dies on 6 April.
1960	On 10 May, Ruth Gorman with Howard Beebe, president of the I.A.A, and Chief Johnny Samson, northern representative and Gerald Tailfeathers representing the Blood Indian Reserve Protestant Group take a fifty-eight-page compiled brief to Ottawa and present it to the 1959/60 Joint Senate and House of Commons Committee on Indian Affairs at Parliament Hill.

Date	Event
1960	Ellen Fairclough, Minister of Indian Affairs, announces the Government of Canada's intention to remove Section 112 regarding compulsory enfranchisement from the Indian Act. This in effect allows Aboriginal people to become enfranchised and vote without losing their treaty rights.
1961	Mount Iyamnathka is renamed Mount Laurie (Iyamnathka) to honour the work of John Laurie with the Aboriginal people of Alberta.
1962	Ruth Gorman resigns as official solicitor for the Indian Association of Alberta.
1966	Ruth Gorman receives an honorary doctorate from the University of Alberta at Calgary.
1965–75	Ruth Gorman publishes her own magazine, My Golden West, where she is publisher from 1965 to 1970 and editor from 1965 to 1975.
2002	Ruth Gorman dies on 10 December.

Appendix

NOTES

Author's Introduction

1 Ruth was first to admit that when it came to dates and specific recollection of time periods, her memory was sometimes less than perfect. The references to both the age difference between John Laurie and Ruth, as well as the number of years that they were together, would appear to be an example of this inadvertent type of error with respect to dates, since John Laurie was 14 years older than Ruth Gorman.

Chapter 1: The Mountain

1 Aphrodite Karamitsanis, ed., *Place Names of Alberta*, vol. I: *Mountains, Mountain Parks and Foothills* (Calgary: University of Calgary Press, 1991), p. 136. It should be noted that, effective 15 December 1984, Mount Laurie (*Iyamnathka*) is the official name of the feature. It is the first dual official name in Canada.

2 This information contradicts an earlier statement where Mrs. Gorman claimed to have first met John Laurie when she was almost 28 (see above, p.6). If they had first met in 1942, as is stated earlier in the text, John Laurie would have been 43 or 44 years old and she would have been almost 28.

3 Enos Hunter, a Stoney elder, and his family adopted John Laurie.

4 She initially had to be persuaded to become involved in the enfranchisement issue by John Laurie.

Chapter 2: The Stars Shone Bright

1 Donald Smith, "John Laurie," in Max Foran and Sheilagh Jameson, eds., *Citymakers: Calgarians after the Frontier* (Calgary: The Historical Society of Alberta, Chinook Country Chapter, 1987), p. 265, indicates Laurie was born 23 October 1899 on a farm in Blenheim Township, Oxford County near Ayr, Ontario.

2 Ruth Gorman saw herself as a "freedom fighter" and certainly behaved as such in various Calgary civic controversies, i.e., the CPR railway relocations.

3 Ruth Gorman often used "narrative" to emphasize a point. It is believed by some that her "narrative" here is a device, or a story to emphasize a romantic early life.

4 Ruth Gorman was aware of the way the words "our" would be construed by 2006 readers. However, as she indicated, this was symbolic of how people in the 1950's and 1960's thought; consequently, the word has been left in the manuscript.

Chapter 3: Strange Omission

1 Why John Laurie would state this is a mystery. Professor Donald Smith clearly indicated in his article on Laurie that he never went to England. Laurie's sister was puzzled by John's fantasy as well.

2 According to Smith, the family had moved to town to ensure that John went to the best school available.

3 It is true that his grandmother did come to live with the family.

4 This was probably related by John Laurie to Ruth Gorman on one of their car trips.

Chapter 4: The Winds of Change Blow across the World

1 In 1916, the Non-Partisan League, largely a farmer's organization, elected a majority of the state legislature and the governor in North Dakota. The Non-Partisan League was to contribute both members and intellectual content to the United Farmers of Alberta.

2 Gerald Friesen, *The Canadian Prairies: A History* (Toronto: University of Toronto Press, 1987), pp. 410–11.

3 See Bob Hesketh, *Major Douglas and Alberta Social Credit* (Toronto: University of Toronto Press, 1997). Clifford H. Douglas was born in Scotland in 1879 and spent the rest of his life in

England. Once famous, he went on a 1933 world tour that included Australia and New Zealand. The newspapers made much of the Australian tour.

4 Barbara Nicholson and Donna Lohnes, "Alexander Calhoun," in Max Foran and Sheilagh Jameson, eds., *Citymakers*, p. 149.

Chapter 5: An Angry Young Man

1 John Laurie actually joined the military in late August of 1918 and was demobilized on 13 January 1919. Donald Smith, "John Laurie," p. 266.

2 Approximately 4,000 Canadian Indians enlisted between 1914 and 1918. See Janice Summerby, *Native Soldiers, Foreign Battlefields* (Ottawa: Government of Canada, Veterans Affairs (1993), 2000), pp. 3–6.

Chapter 6: Laurie Finds the Right Place

1 John Laurie first came West in 1920 and Alberta in 1923 after completing his second year at Trinity College in Toronto. Donald Smith, "John Laurie," p. 266.

2 The Palliser opened 1 June 1914.

3 MacRae was born in 1869 in St. John's, Newfoundland, and received his BA at Dalhousie University in 1893. He was mathematical master at Pictou Academy, Nova Scotia, for a few years, then studied theology at the University of Edinburgh, spending several years at Leipzig and Jena universities in Germany. He received his PhD from Jena and studied for one year at the University of Paris. He moved west to take up missionary work for the Presbyterian Church. MacRae was founding principal of Western Canada College where he taught from 1903 to 1923. He left to take up a position at Royal Rhodes Military College in Victoria, British Columbia. Interview with Gloria Dingwall, Historian of Western Canada High School, Calgary, 28 November 2005.

Chapter 7: A Horse Did It

1 P. K. Page was born 23 November 1916 at Swanage, Dorset, England. She left England with her family in 1919 to settle in Red Deer, Alberta. She was educated in Calgary and Winnipeg and later studied art in Brazil and New York. In the early 1940's, Page moved to Montreal to work as a filing clerk and a researcher. Her poetry was first published in 1944 and she also wrote short stories, novellas, a romantic novel, and *Brazilian Journal* (1987), both a travel book and an autobiography. From 1946 to 1950, she worked for the National Film Board as a scriptwriter and, in 1950, she married and has acquired a reputation as a painter under her married name, P. K. Irwin. Some of her books combine her poetry or prose with reproductions of her drawings or paintings. Excerpt from the biographical section of "Canadian Poets Online," Department of English, University of Calgary, Alberta, at *www.ucalgary.ca/UofC/faculties/HUM/ENGL/canada/poet/p_page.htm*

2 Born in Rapid City near Brandon, Manitoba, on 31 December 1896, Gladys McKelvie's family moved to Calgary in 1903 where she began piano study. In 1909, she was awarded a two-year scholarship to the Royal Academy of Music in London and was the youngest student and the first Canadian ever to receive this award. After receiving the silver medal in piano and bronze medal in sight singing, she moved to New York in 1911 to study under famous composers. She returned to Calgary in 1914, established a studio, married, and over the next fifty years dedicated her life to teaching piano and mentoring music students. She founded the Associated Studios of Music in the 1940's and, in 1965, received an honorary doctorate of laws from the University of Alberta, followed by the Centennial Award from the Canadian Federation of Music Teachers' Association (CFMTA) in 1967. She died in Calgary on 7 March 1968. The Dr. Gladys McKelvie Egbert Junior High School in Calgary was named in her honour in 1976. Excerpt from "The Encyclopedia of Music in Canada," The Canadian Encyclopedia Historica, at *www.thecanadianencyclopedia.com/index.cfm?PgNm=TCE&Params=U1ARTU0001104*

3 This event occurred at the first Calgary Stampede in 1912, when Tom Three Persons won a world championship in bronc riding, and was the only Canadian to achieve a championship in any major event at the Stampede. Born in 1896, he became a hero and a successful rancher

at a time when Canadians did not expect Indians to succeed, inspiring generations of Blood Indians in the rodeo arena. He died of ranch injuries in 1949 and was the first contestant inducted in the Canadian Cowboy Hall of Fame, 11 July 1983. See Hugh A. Dempsey, *Tom Three Persons: Legend of an Indian Cowboy* (Saskatoon: Purich, 1997).

Chapter 8: Laurie Finds a Family

1. Sarah Carter, *Lost Harvests: Prairie Indian Reserve Farmers and Government Policy* (Montreal and Kingston: McGill-Queen's University Press, 1990).
2. Norman Luxton (1876–1962) published Banff's *Crag and Canyon* newspaper (1902 to 1951), organized Banff's Indian Days from 1909 to 1950, and ran several businesses, including the Luxton Museum. He was named Chief White Shield by the Stoney.
3. The book that Mrs. Gorman is likely making reference to is Alexander Morris, *The Treaties of Canada With the Indians of Manitoba and the North-West Territories: Including the Negotiations on Which They Were Based, and Other Information Relating Thereto* (Toronto: Willing & Williamson, 1880).
4. Morris C. Schumiatcher, "The Buckskin Curtain: Citizenship and the Canadian Indian," *The Beaver* (Autumn, 1959): 12–15.
5. The potlatch was an elaborate gift ceremony celebrated by Aboriginal people on the northwest coast of North America. In 1884, the potlatch and all ceremonies similar were banned along the coast. These measures were not repealed until the 1960's with reforms made to the Indian Act. Olive Dickason, *Canada's First Nations: A History of Founding Peoples from Earliest Times*. 3rd ed. (Toronto: McClelland and Stewart (1992), 2002), pp. 182, 261, 288, 301–5.

Chapter 9: A History Teacher Studies History around the Campfire

1. Born in Mylor, England, in 1811, Reverend Robert Rundle, after only two months of theological training, was offered a missionary post for the Hudson's Bay Company's Saskatchewan District. In 1840, he left England for North America, and by October of that year found himself at Fort Edmonton. For the next eight years, Rundle spent the majority of his time travelling throughout the province, carrying his Methodist message to the people at various places. His travels took him as far north as Lesser Slave Lake and Fort Assiniboine, as far south as Big Hill Springs and as far east as Fort Pitt and Fort Carlton. He was fluent in English, French and Cree. Rundle befriended many Metis, Cree and Assiniboine, and he seemed to have developed cordial relations with most Hudson's Bay Company officials. When the Company began pressuring him to establish mission schools, he did not immediately comply; he never actually completed his task. He returned to England after a bad arm injury and died there in 1887. Excerpt from his biography at *www.edukits.ca/aboriginal/origin/grade11/biographies/rundle.htm*
2. G.A., Arthur Family Fonds, M 8188, Bull Plume's Winter Count.
3. Rene M. Caisse was a modest Canadian nurse who developed a natural herb formula in 1920 that she named Essiac (her maiden name in reverse) and never agreed to reveal the secret of its ingredients. She opened up a permanent cancer clinic in Bracebridge, Ontario, from 1934 to 1942, later continuing her nursing work from home. She died on Boxing Day 1978 at 91 years of age after having sold her herb recipe to the Resperin Corporation. Essiac is still in 2006 a non-governmentally approved cancer treatment formula. See James W. Demers, *Bridge of Hope: The Life of Rene M. Caisse, R. N., Canada's Cancer Nurse and the History of Essiac* (Bracebridge, ON: Bracebridge Publishing, 2004) or the Essiac website at *www.essiacinfo.org/caisse.html*

Chapter 10: A History Teacher Studies History in Books

1. *www.willrogers.org* for the Will Rogers's quote. Gorman was well aware of the many theories of migration, including those in the first pages of Olive Dickason's *Canada's First Nations*.
2. Ruth Gorman was not alone in her beliefs. In recent years, Edward W. Said, *Culture and Imperialism* (New York: Alfred Knopf, 1993), would have echoed these arguments.
3. Brian E. Titley, *A Narrow Vision: Duncan Campbell Scott and the Administration of Indian Affairs in Canada* (Vancouver: University of British Columbia Press, 1986) is the source used by Gorman for most of her reflections on Scott.

4   Pickersgill was born at Wyecombe, Ontario, 23 June 1905, and grew up in Manitoba.
5   See, for example, Jack W. Pickersgill, *The Road Back: By a Liberal in Opposition* (Toronto: University of Toronto Press, 1986), and Jack W. Pickersgill and D.F. Forster, eds., *The MacKenzie King Record*, 4 vols. (Toronto: University of Toronto Press, c.1960 – c.1970).
6   Ruth Gorman seems to have adopted many of her views on MacKenzie King from the work of C. P. Stacey, who edited the MacKenzie King diaries. See Charles P. Stacey, *A Very Double Life: The Private World of Mackenzie King* (Toronto: Macmillan, 1976).
7   Scrip was a piece of paper issued to a person of mixed blood ancestry in Manitoba, and later in the North West Territories, allowing them to claim a homestead. Scrip, which could be in dollars or in land, could also be sold to a willing buyer and speculators often acquired significant amounts. If an individual accepted scrip, it has been argued that his "Aboriginal" title was extinguished. Between 1885 and 1921, if Manitoba scrip is included, there were 24,326 claims, amounting to 2,609,772 acres in land scrip and $3,633,217 in money scrip. The best account is Joe Sawchuk, Patricia Sawchuk, and Theresa Ferguson, *Métis Land Rights in Alberta: A Political History* (Edmonton: Métis Association of Alberta, 1981).

Chapter 11: A Red Métis Meets a White Métis

1   See Peter Kulchyski, "Considerable Unrest: F.O. Loft and the League of Indians." *Native Studies Review* 4, nos. 1–2 (1988): 95–117.
2   There is much non-academic information available today from various native sources detailing the life of Oghema Niagara, a.k.a. Chief Thunderwater, including a family website run by his descendants. See, for instance, *www.snowwowl.com/swolfpastnotables2.html* and *http://chiefthunderwater.com/* In Ontario, Dr. P. Whitney Lackenbauer at St. Jerome's University is currently researching the life of Chief Thunderwater and his movement.
3   See Kulchyski, "Considerable Unrest," and also Titley, *A Narrow Vision*, pp. 101–9.
4   Ibid.
5   Ibid., p. 102.
6   See the book written by Morris, *The Treaties of Canada With the Indians of Manitoba and the North-West Territories.*
7   John Peter Turner, *The North-West Mounted Police*, 2 vols. (Ottawa: King's Printer, 1948).

Chapter 12: The Department and Enfranchisement

1   Diamond Jenness (1886–1969) is recognized as Canada's pre-eminent pioneer anthropologist. He documented Aboriginal life in Canada's North, the Inuit of the western Arctic, and First Nations communities across Canada.
2   It is difficult to know exactly the 'sit-in' that Mrs. Gorman is referring to here, but one possible example occurred at the University of Victoria, in 1996, where four Aboriginal students held a twenty-day hunger strike to protest the funding levels of post-secondary Aboriginal students. See *The Carillon* 38, no. 19 (29 February 1996).
3   Lucien Mason Hanks and Jane Richardson Hanks, *Tribe Under Trust: A Study of the Blackfoot Reserve of Alberta* (Toronto: University of Toronto Press, 1950).

Chapter 13: The Harsh Reality of Enfranchisement

1   *New Trail* 44, no. 3 (Winter, 1989): 5–6.

Chapter 14: Laurie and the Indians Find Me

1   John B. Tootoosis was born on the Poundmaker reserve on 18 July 1899. His grandfather was Yellow Mud Blanket, Poundmaker's brother. Tootoosis' history as a political leader goes back to 1920 when he was appointed chief of the band. His authority was denied by the Department of Indian Affairs because he was not yet 21. During the 1930's, he worked for the League of Indians of Western Canada and was elected secretary and organizer for the Prairie Region. He continued to organize Saskatchewan Indians in spite of attempts by government to restrict his movements, and ban him from reserves. He was also threatened with excommunication from the Catholic Church. He served as both president and executive member for the Union

of Saskatchewan Indians and, in 1959, was elected as the first president of the Federation of Saskatchewan Indians. In 1970, he was appointed to the newly formed Senate of the Federation and for the next nineteen years served his people as an active elder statesman. Excerpt from *The Saskatchewan Indian* (January/February, 1989): 1.
2. John Alexander Weir was the Faculty's first full-time teacher. Weir was born in North Dakota. His family moved to Regina then Saskatoon. He completed his BA and LLB at the University of Saskatchewan, where he was awarded the Governor-General's Gold Medal. He was chosen for a 1914 Rhodes Scholarship and, after three years of service in the R.A.F. as a Flying Officer, he earned a Bachelor of Arts with first-class honours from Oxford. Weir was hired as a lecturer in 1921 and became Dean of Law in 1926. He continued in that capacity until his untimely death in 1942. Excerpt from www.law.ualberta.ca/faculty/history/establishmenthistory.htm
3. Dr. Malcolm M. MacIntyre was a Mount Allison graduate who had obtained his LLB and later his doctorate at Harvard. He was noted as being a great teacher of torts and a sound pragmatist after his celebrated teacher Roscoe Pound. Like Dean Weir, his contributions to legal journals helped establish the scholarly tradition in legal writing in Canada. In 1934, he founded the *Alberta Law Quarterly*, a predecessor of the *Alberta Law Review*. Dr. MacIntyre served as Dean of Law from 1942 until 1945, when he returned to practice in New Brunswick. Several years later he joined the newly established Faculty of Law at the University of British Columbia. Excerpt from www.law.ualberta.ca/faculty/history/establishmenthistory.htm
4. Rex. v. Wesley, 26 Alta. L.R. 433 [1932] 2 WWR 337, 58 CCC 269, [1932] 4 DLR 774 (C.A.).
5. It should be noted that in his judgment Justice Buchanan, Chief Justice of the District Court, ruled the protests to remove 122 members of the Hobbema band invalid for procedural reasons. Whether the technical decision was because of the judge's humanity can only be speculated. For a full discussion, see Sanders, "The Queen's Promises."

Chapter 15: The Buckskin Curtain

1. Morris C. Schumiatcher, "The Buckskin Curtain: Citizenship and the Canadian Indian," *The Beaver* (Autumn, 1959): 12–15.
2. Sir John A. MacDonald held numerous cabinet positions simultaneously during his long political career as a Liberal-Conservative MP and was Superintendent General of Indian Affairs from 1878 to 1887 only.

Chapter 16: Department of Indian Affairs and the IAA

1. John Laurie spent a brief time teaching at Balmoral before transferring to Crescent Heights High School.
2. Adolf Hitler was a fan of Karl May novels about Indians and cowboys and he even instructed the German Army to distribute his books to soldiers on the Eastern front.

Chapter 18: I Take the Case

1. Chief John Snow is a Nakoda Elder, traditional storyteller, poet and published author. He was Chief of the Nakoda Nation of Stoney Indians at Morley, Alberta, from 1968 through 1990.
2. William Morrow, Q.C., later Justice Morrow of the Alberta Court of Appeal; Robert H. Barron Q.C.; John C. Gorman, Q.C., who later became Judge of the Provincial Court of Alberta; and William Major, Q.C. In 2003, all were deceased, except for Robert Barron, who had recently retired.

Chapter 19: The First Hobbema Hearing 1951

1. Appendix I provides a timeline for the events surrounding the hearings.
2. See Jean Goodwill and Norma Sluman, *John Tootoosis: Biography of a Cree Leader* (Kempville, ON: Golden Dog Press, 1982).
3. G.A., John Laurie Fonds, M656/14, Hobbema Case Literature, 1956–57 and written by Ruth Gorman.

Chapter 20: After the Hobbema Hearing / I Go Public

1. By reopening the hearings, Commissioner Grant effectively 'lost' the case for the Gorman camp, forcing Gorman to appeal the decision.
2. James Henry Gray, *Talk to My Lawyer: Great Stories of Southern Alberta's Bar and Bench* (Edmonton: Hurtig, 1987), p. 173.
3. If those indirectly associated with the 102 protested Indians were counted, the number of members who arguably could have been evicted would have been three or four times higher.
4. Douglas Harkness had a successful career in both the military and politics. In 1939, Harkness served in Britain, Sicily, Italy, France and Northwest Europe with the Canadian Army. In 1945, while still overseas, Lieutenant Colonel Harkness announced that he was running for Parliament in Calgary East. He would win this election, along with nine others, serving his constituents for twenty-seven years. Harkness served as Minister of Agriculture and Minister of National Defence in Conservative federal cabinets.
5. "The Bar Sinister," *Time Magazine*, Canadian edition (28 January 1957): 10.

Chapter 21: The Appeal

1. Sanders, "The Queen's Promises," p. 126, suggests that this may have been so.

Chapter 22: Senatorship

1. Gray, *Talk to My Lawyer*, p. 173.
2. The first female chief of police was Elizabeth (Liz) Scout.

Chapter 24: Laurie's Funeral

1. Pauline Johnson, "Calgary of the Plains," *The Calgary Daily Herald* (19 April 1913).

Chapter 25: Laurie's Magnificent Record of Change

1. He was published by a number of Western Canadian publishers, most notably *The Western Producer*, and *The Canadian Cattleman*. Many of his works are held at the Glenbow Museum, John Laurie Fonds, File M656/18, M656/23-25.

Chapter 26: The Brief / I Go North

1. Albert Lightning, sometimes spelled Lightening, was born Cree in 1900 on the Ermineskin Reserve in Alberta and spent much of his life reaching out to first peoples around the world, sharing cultural information with them. He was apparently fluent in Blackfoot, Cree, Stoney, and English. As a respected spiritual leader, he helped re-introduce the sweat lodge to the Miigmag and Maliseet people. He was also involved in the planning of the first ecumenical conference at Crow Agency in southeastern Montana, held in 1969. He passed away on 19 April 1991. Excerpt from Dianne Meili, "Albert Lightning, Cree, Ermineskin Reserve," in *Those Who Know: Profiles of Alberta's Native Elders* (Edmonton: NeWest Press, 1991), pp. 79–87.

Chapter 27: I Go to Parliament

1. The George Medal, created by the King of England in September 1940, was awarded only for acts of great bravery outside the realm of direct combat with enemy forces, but often resulting from enemy fire, bombing or torpedoing. Harkness won his medal during the naval invasion of Sicily in 1943, Canada's first major involvement of the Second World War in a European battlefield. To this day, only seventy-eight Canadians have ever received the George Medal. Interview with Stéphane Guevremont, military historian, University of Calgary, 4 February 2006.

Chapter 28: The Vote

1. Gorman was the publisher of the magazine from 1965 to 1970 and editor from 1965 to 1975.
2. John Wilton Littlechild, called to the bar in 1972, was appointed Queen's Counsel in 1976. Not only was he the first Alberta Treaty Indian to graduate from law school, he was the first Treaty Indian elected to Parliament in 1988.

3 John Melling was the first Executive Director of the Indian-Eskimo Association of Canada.
4 For example, see the actions taken by students in Victoria: *The Carillon* 38, no. 19 (29 February 1996).

Epilogue

1 Chief John Samson passed away on 12 May 2000.
2 In reality, the time that John Laurie knew Ruth Gorman was more likely fourteen years (1944 to 1959). This difference in dates can be blamed on Ruth's admittedly imperfect memory with respect to the time frame of twenty years.

INDEX

Aberdeen and Temair, Ishbel Gordon, Marchioness of, *xxv*, 138
Aberhart, William, *xviii, xxiv*, 20
Aboriginal art, 49, 61, 96, 98–99
Aboriginal dances, 61
Aboriginal funerals, 49
   burial rituals, 59
Aboriginal healing or medicine, 58, 60
Aboriginal humour, 129
Aboriginal peoples
   economic successes (Alberta reserves), 245
   economic successes (1880s and 1890s), *xxxii*
   labelled "savages," 45–46, 52
   last Canadians to get the vote, 255–56
   one of Canada's assets, 251
   portrayal in history books, 63–64
Aboriginal religious or spiritual ceremonies, 54
Aboriginal veterans, 26, 76
Aboriginal women
   admission to Indian Association of Alberta, 142
   denied treaty money, 79
   status of, *xxxiii, xxxviii*
Accounting for Genocide (Neu), *xxii*
Alberta Human Rights Commission, 87
Alberta: A New History (Palmer), *xv*
Albertan (newspaper), *xlix*, 28, 176
Albertans
   importance in getting vote for Indians, 239
Alberta's Dower Act, *xxiv*, 109
alcohol. *See* liquor
allotment, 69
"angry young men," 25–26, 54
assimilation, *xl*, 69, 253
average Canadian. *See* Canadian public; public opinion
Axworthy, Lloyd, 86

B

Banff School of Fine Art, 98–99
Barron, Robert (Bob) H., 154, 179
Battle, Robert Felix, 156
   made "Chief Mountain Chinook Wind," 157
Beaver, 119
Bedford, Judy, *ix, xii*

Beebe, Howard, *xxxi–xxxii*, 229, 248
Big Swan, *xxxii*
Bill 14. *See* Indian Act
Bill 268. *See* Indian Act
Black Horses, *xxxii*
Bobtail, Chief, 169
Bond, Marjorie, 16, 196
Borein, Edward, 28
brief to Parliamentary Committee (on compulsory enfranchisement), *xxix–xxxiv*, 220–23, 227–37
   Laurie's plan for, 221
British North America Act, 50
"brokers," *xl*
Brownlee scandal, 19
Brumlik, J.P., 179
Brusch, Dr., 60
Buchan, John, *Memory Hold-the-Door*, 196
Buchanan, Nelles, 180–81
buckskin curtain, 48, 119–21, 126, 213
Buffalo Bill's "Wild West Show," 28
Burns, Pat, 29
Burnsstick, Peter, *xxxii*

C

Caisse, Rene, 60
Calgary
   love of horses, 36
   oil city, *xiv*
   support during Hobbema Case, 256
   tolerant place for women, 110
   women's clubs, 110, 138 (*See also* names of individual clubs)
Calgary Herald, *xxvi, xxxii, xlviii*, 28, 88–89, 182, 239
   on brief to parliamentary committee, 229, 236
   Gorman as heroine, *xlix*
   on Hobbema Case, 171–73, 176, 227
Calgary Indian Friendship Centre, *xxiv, xlv, xlvi*
Calgary Local Council of Women, *xii, xlviii*, 171, 173, 175, 215
   assistance with Hobbema Case documents, 162
   political strength, 138–39
   power base for Gorman, *xvi, xxiv–xxv*
Calgary Rehabilitation Society for the Handicapped, *xxiv*
Calgary Stampede, 29, 34
   Native participation, 35–36, 58
Calgary's Women Liberal Club, 175
Calhoun, Alexander, 21, 47, 52, 64

269

Calihoo, John, *xl*, 128
Calvert, G. R., 203
Cameron Commission on Education, 139
Canada's First Nations (Dickason), *xiv*
Canadian Author's Association, 139
Canadian Cattlemen, 215, 239
Canadian Pacific Railway (CPR), 83, 110
    burden on native people of Canada, 71
    Hobbema documents, 162
    rail track issue, *xxiii, xxv, xlviii*, 110, 138
Canadian public, 124, 168, 170–71, 243
    failure to understand enfranchisement, 91
    ignorance of conditions on reserves, 90, 220
    on Meech Lake, 242
Cardinal, Harold, *xv, xxi*, 86, 247, 249
    red paper, 253
    Unjust Society, xxxix
Carter, Sarah, *Lost Harvests,* 42
Cavanaugh, Catherine, *xxiii, xliii*
Charles Camsell Indian Hospital, 217
Charter of Human Rights, 87, 94
children's allowance for Aboriginal peoples, 217
Chrétien, Jean
    'White Paper' (1969), 86, 249, 253
Citymakers (Foran), *xxxiv*
Colborne, Fred, 203
communism, 225
compulsory enfranchisement, *xiv, xxix*, 91–92, 95, 213, 219, 228–29
    Ellen Fairclough's announcement, 235
Confederation (1867), 64–65, 68
Constabaris, James, 109
Constitution (1992), *xiii, xxv, xliii*, 70, 248
Conway, Jill Ker, *In Her Own Words, xli*
Cooperative Commonwealth Federation (CCF), *xiv*, 21, 218
Cross, A.E., 29
Crowchild, Daisy, *xlv*, 59, 142, 208
Crowchild, David, *xxxi*, 35, 59, 128, 188, 199–200
Crowchild, Gordon, *xviii*
Crowchild, Regina, 248

D

"Darcy Tailfeathers Memorial Award," 101
Deane, Basil, 28, 171–72, 176, 182–83, 227
Dempsey, Hugh, *xxi, xxxii, xlv–xlvi*, 128, 188
    as "broker," *xl*
    on enfranchisement, 102
    Gentle Persuader, The, xxxv, xliv
    minimizes Gorman's role, *xliv*

Dempsey, Hugh (*continued*)
    view of Laurie, *xxxv–xxxvii, xxxix*
Department of Indian Affairs, *xxvii*, 60, 78, 87, 148, 251. *See also* enfranchisement
    Aboriginal veterans and, 76
    avoiding real aid by promoting culture, 244, 249–50
    bureaucratic control, 64–65, 95, 122
    Colonel Jones, 231–35
    as concealed dictatorship, 123
    control of access to reserves, 119, 121
    divide and conquer, 73, 137
    fostered anti-Indian attitude among public, 124
    Gorman's view of, *xxii, xxviii*
    grant system, 245, 247, 253–54
    during Hobbema Case, 158, 163, 168
    ignorance of Aboriginal peoples, 90
    Laurie's suspicion of, *xx, xxxvi*, 124, 226, 233
    mismanagement of moneys, 88, 251
    monetary motive behind expulsions, 154, 176
    patronage, 89
    persecution of persons who helped Indians, 137
    relation to eastern and Liberal parliament, 218, 226
    secrecy, 85
    self-sufficiency policy, *xiii*
    stifling initiatives, *xxxii*, 68
    taking back the land, *xiii, xxxii*, 68, 148 (*See also* reserves)
    "Trust Funds," *xxxii–xxxiv, xxxix*, 53, 77, 88–89, 95, 115, 127, 137, 145, 251
    White Paper (1969), 86, 249, 253
Deschamps, Joe, 158
Dickason, Olive, *Canada's First Nations*, *xiv*
Dickson, Betsy, 12
Diefenbaker, John, *xxxvi*, 203, 240
    Hobbema Case, 168, 175, 187, 214
    petition to Queen and, *xxxviii*
    removal of compulsory enfranchisement, 235
    voluntary legal work, *l*
Diefenbaker government, *xv, xxxvii*, 218, 227
    sympathetic to reform for Aboriginal people, 226
    vote for Canada's Aboriginal peoples, 239, 255
Dobbin, Murray, *One-and-a-Half Men, The*, *xl*
Dominion Elections Act, *xxxiii*

Douglas, Tommy, 175
Dover, Mary, *ix*
dower rights, *xxiv*, 109
Downe, Anne R., 140–41, 216
   aid to Indian Association of Alberta, 139
   aid to John Laurie, 139
Drees, Laurie Meijer, *xxxviii, xxxix–xl*
   Indian Association of Alberta, The, xxxvii

E

Edmonton Bulletin, 19
education, 42, 50–51, 87, 123
   access to, *xiii*
   community-based, *xxxiv, xlix*
   residential schools, 50–51, 75, 98, 139
Edwards, Manley, 55
Egbert, Gladys Alma, 34
enfranchisement, *xiv–xv, xxix, xxxiii, xxxviii*, 55, 69, 85, 119–20, 127. *See also* brief to Parliamentary Committee; Hobbema Case; vote
   compulsory, *xiv, xxi, xxix*, 69, 75, 91–92, 95, 213, 219, 228–29, 235
   definition, *x*
   encouraged by Indian Act amendments 1919, *xxxii*
   end of mandatory enfranchisement, 102, 235
   evictions through, 85, 90
   expulsion petitions, 152, 158
   failure to understand, 91
   Gerald Tailfeathers' experience with, 96, 100–102
   isolating Natives on reserves, 121
   serious threat to Aboriginal peoples, 90–92, 102, 121
   treatment in historical studies, *xv*
   voluntary, 69, 91, 95, 100
   from working off reserves, 121
Ermineskin tribe, 245
Ewing Commission, *xiv*
expropriation, 69

F

Fairclough, Ellen Louks, li, 231, 233–34
   announced removal of compulsory enfranchisement, 235
   visit to Sarcee reserve, 232
Family Home and Welfare Association, 138–39
"farm marriages," 79, 81
Female Persuasion (Thorp), *xli*
First World War, 23–24

First World War (*continued*)
   Aboriginal veterans, 26, 76
Foran, Max, *Citymakers, xxxiv*
Four Bears, 57
Fraser, Blair, 28
Fraser, Thelma M., 158
Frazer, Phil, 87
"Friends of the Indian Society," *xxix*, 140
friendship centres, *xlv, xlvi*, 243

G

Gale, Annie, *xxvi*
Geary, Affa Northcote, 76
Gentle Persuader, The (Dempsey), *xxxv*
   minimizes Gorman's role, *xliv*
Gershaw, Frederick William, 236
Gladstone, Fred, *xxx*
Gladstone, James, *xi, xvii–xviii, xxxvi, xxxviii, xlvi*, 102, 128, 230, 233
   on liquor on reserves, *xxix, xxxi, xxxvi*, 188–90
   Métis background, *xl*
   rift with Gorman, *xliv–xlv*
   saw Laurie as harsh Calvinist, 188
   senatorship, *xxxvi*, 187
Gladstone-Dempsey, Pauline, *xlv*
glass beads, 249
Gleichen reserve, *xiii*
Glenbow Museum, 15, 57, 133, 158, 195
Globe and Mail, 91
"A Good Samaritan: John Laurie" (Smith), *xxxiv*
Gorman, George, 32
Gorman, John, 154, 179, 191
Gorman, Linda, *xii, xvii*
Gorman, Ruth, *ix, xxi*
   ability to mobilize public opinion, *xvi*
   belief in justice and human rights, *xxiii, xlii, xlvii, xlviii*
   birth and early life, *xxiii*, 34
   brief to Parliamentary Committee (on compulsory enfranchisement), *xxix, xxx, xxxi, xxxii, xxxiii, xxxiv*, 220–23, 227–37
   as "broker," *xl*
   Calgary Local Council of Women, *xxiv, xxv, xxvi*, 109, 138
   CPR rail track issue, *xxiii, xxv, xlviii*, 110, 138
   differences of opinion with Laurie, *xi, xx, xxvix, xxviii*
   feminist activism, *x, xiii, xxiii, xxiv, xxvi*, 105, 109–10

Index   271

Gorman, Ruth (*continued*)
  funeral, *xxii, li*
  giving credit to Laurie, *xiv, xliii*, 173
  Hobbema Case, *xxxviii*, 154–70
  home and family responsibilities, *xli*, 118, 131
  Indian Friendship Centre, *xxiv, xlv, xlvi*
  on liquor on reserves, *xxviii, xxxi*
  made an Indian Princess (Mountain White Eagle Girl), *xviii, xxiv, xlviii*, 8, 112, 141
  met John Laurie, 110, 112
  modesty, *xiv, xliii*, 173
  as Mount Royal matron, *xxvi, xlii*
  My Golden West, ix, xii, xxi, xxiii, xxv–xxvii, xxvi, xxvii, xlii–xliv, xliii, xliv, 140, 242, 249
  newspaper coverage, *xlviii, xlix* (See also *Calgary Herald*)
  petition to Queen, *xxxviii*
  as populist, *xxv, xxviii, xlii*
  publicity campaign (Hobbema Case), *xxv*, 171–78
  Queen Mother of all Cree (Morning Star), *xlvi, xlix*, 182–83
  reforms for women, *xxiv*, 105, 109–10
  refusal to enter formal public life, *xxiv*
  relationship with Harold Cardinal, 249
  relationship with Indian Association of Alberta, *xvi, xxxi, xxxvii, xliv, l*, 114, 116–17, 127, 133, 247–49
  on repatriation of constitution, *xxiii, xxv, xlii*
  rift with Gladstone and Dempsey, *xliv, xlv*
  on role of women, *xxv*
  on self-government, *xxviii*
  on Senate, 238
  senatorship issue, *xxxvi, xxxvii*, 187–88
  on status of Aboriginal people, *xxiii*
  on status of Aboriginal women, *xxxiii*
  on status of Western Canadians, *xxiii*
  as steward of Laurie's incomplete legacy, *xxix*
  "strong-minded woman," *xli, xlii*
  suspicion of Department of Indian Affairs, *xxii, xxviii*
  tolerance and fairness, *xlvii, xlviii*
  on treaty obligations, *xxvii, xxxii*, 252–53
  trip to northern reserves, 221–23
  "troublemaker," 181
  at University of Alberta Law School, *xxvi*, 109

Gorman, Ruth (*continued*)
  as very much her father's daughter, *xliii*
  on vote, *xxviii, xxx, xxxix*, 116
  Western Canada Concept Party, *xxv, xxvi*
Graham, Fred, 27
Graham, W. H., 77
Grant (Commissioner in Hobbema hearing), 157, 159, 165, 167
grant system
  promoting intertribal rivalry, 245, 247, 249, 253–54
Gray, James Henry, 187
  "Queen Mother Morningstar," *xlix*
grudge fights, 152–53
  expulsion petitions, 158

H

halfbreeds. *See* Métis
Hanks, Jane Richardson, *xxxii*, 88
Hanks, Lucien Mason, *Tribe Under Trust, xxxii*, 88
Hanson, Bertha, 138
Harington, Florence, 173
Harkness, Douglas, *xviii, xxxvii*, 143, 146, 167–68, 175, 187, 203, 226, 239
  removal of compulsory enfranchisement, 235
Harper, Elijah, 242
Harris, Walter Edward, 145–46, 175, 182
Harvie, Eric, *xxxiv*, 15, 57, 162, 195–96, 203
Haynes, Reverend, 60
Heilbrun, Carolyn, *Writing a Woman's Life, xl*
Henderson, Don, 101, 193
Hiawatha, 79
Hobbema Case, *x, xxx, xxxvi, l*, 67, 85. *See also* brief to Parliamentary Committee
  appeal, 179–81
  Commission hearing (1951), 155–64
  Court of Appeal, 168, 179
  expulsion attempts, 151–52
  financial stakes (oil money), 186
  importance to Diefenbaker's success, 227
  Laurie's fear of involvement, *xxxviii, xlvi, xlviii, xlix*
  as precedent, 185
  publicity campaign, 170–78, 186
  Sanders on, *xl, l*
  winning of, 117
Hobbema reserve, *xiii, xiv*
  grudge fights, 152–53
Horner, Hugh, *xxxii*

Hudson's Bay Company, 79, 81, 83
Hunter, Eddie, *xviii*, 50–51, 188, 193
   violin, 40
Hunter, Enos, *xix*, *xxxvii–xxxix*, 8, 43, 49
   storyteller, 41
Hunter family, 206
hypocrisy, 66, 68

I

I Have Lived Here Since the World Began (Ray), *xv*
In Her Own Words (Conway), *xli*
Indian Act, 48, 69, 87, 90.
   See also enfranchisement
   amendment (1919), *xxxii*
   amendment (1961), *x, xiv–xv, xxix, xxxix, xlviii*
   Bill 14, 77, 90–91, 119–20, 149
   Bill 268 (revision 1951), l, 143–49
   Gorman's explanation to IAA, 113–14
   Section 112 (compulsory enfranchisement), 69, 102, 229
   ward system, 68, 106, 108, 118–19
   "White Paper" (1969), 86, 249, 253
Indian Affairs. *See* Department of Indian Affairs
Indian Association of Alberta, The (Drees), *xxxvii*
Indian Association of Alberta (IAA), *xiii, xv, xix, xxi, xxviii–xxix*, 88, 93, 126–27, 140, 151
   admission of Aboriginal women, 142
   brief on residential schools, 139
   built by "brokers," *xl*
   concern that Gorman was a woman, *xvi, xlix*
   democracy, 126, 130, 218, 254
   fear of reprisals, 136
   formation, *xiv, xl*
   Gorman's first meeting with, 114
   John Laurie and, *xix*, 126, 128, 130, 132–33, 137
   male only, 141
   meetings, 128–32, 136
   pow wows, 131
   retained both Gorman and Laurie for expertise, *xxxix*
   on vote, *xx, xxx, xxxi*
   woman president, 248
Indian Friendship Centre (Calgary), *xxiv*
Indian regalia. *See* traditional dress
IOU slips, 196

J

Jacques, Murray, 200
Jameson, Sheilagh, *xxxiv*
Jenness, Diamond, 86
Jiroux, Joe, *xxxi*
John Laurie Boulevard, 211
Johnson, Grace, *xlv, xlvi*
Johnson, Pauline, 86
Johnsons (scrip documents), 167
Johnston, Harry J. Crosby, 191
Joint Committee of the Senate and the House of Commons on Indian affairs
   brief to, *xxix–xxxiv*, 220–22, 227–37
Jones, Colonel (of Indian Affairs), 230, 232–35, 245
   resignation, 156

K

Kelly, Peter, 225
Kennedy, Fred, 28
King, William Lyon Mackenzie, 66, 69, 91–92
   hypocrisy, 67–68

L

Lane, George, 29
language, 45, 48, 58–59, 65, 126
   barriers, 42, 53, 72, 119, 121, 128, 132, 158, 213
   importance of, 57
   Stoney dictionary, 57, 207
Latour, Father, 60, 163, 165, 184
Laurie, John, 48, 70–71, 75, 110, 167
   adoption by Hunter family, *xviii*, 43–44
   ambassador for Indian people, 27, 68
   Anglican lay minister, 54
   "angry young man," 25, 66
   arrival in Calgary, 28
   birth, *xviii*, 11
   "broker," *xl*
   burial and grave, 35, 204–5, 208, 211
   Calgary Stampede, 34–35
   changed history of Canada, 215
   childhood, *xxxiv*, 12–13, 15
   children's allowance for Aboriginal people, 217
   claim of Aboriginal ancestry, *xvii, xix, xxxiv–xxxv*
   contacts and supporters, 27–28, 134, 138, 172, 182
   contribution to Indian race, 213
   Cooperative Commonwealth Federation (CCF), 21

Laurie, John (*continued*)
  credit for securing vote and ending enfranchisement, *xiv, xvi,* 212, 239, 241, 256
  death, *x,* 102, 191–94
  "deathbed" autobiography (Grey Owl childhood), *xvi, xxxiv,* 15–17, 194, 196–97
  dictionary of Stoney language, 57, 207
  enfranchisement and, *xxxviii,* 90, 92, 170, 219–20
  on expulsion petitions, 152–53
  First World War, 24
  funeral, *xxi, xxii,* 199–209
  heart attack (first), 164
  Hobbema Case, 155, 158, 174
  Hugh Dempsey's view of, *xxi, xxxv, xxxvii, xxxix*
  Indian Association of Alberta, *xix,* 126, 128, 130, 132–33, 137
  Indian family, *xviii,* 41, 43–48, 52, 206
  Indian healers and, 58
  Indian names, 206, 208
  Indian "sons," *xviii,* 96, 188
  John Laurie Boulevard, 211
  on liquor on reserves, *xx, xxviii, xxix, xxxi, xxxvi,* 189
  love of horses, 31–33, 35, 37, 46
  Métis history, 78
  Mount Laurie (*Iyamnathka*), *ix,* 8, 211
  newspaper coverage, *xlviii,* 173
  old age pension for Aboriginal people, 217
  personal papers, 195–96
  persuading with guilt or shame, 112, 116
  published articles, 215
  relationship with Gerald Tailfeathers, 99–102
  relationship with sister, *xvii,* 196
  respect for Senators, 236
  senatorship issue, *xxxvi,* 187–88
  study of Aboriginal stories and legends, 57–61
  summer on Stoney reserve, 39–55
  suspicion of Department of Indian Affairs, *xx, xxii, xxviii, xxxv, xxxvi,* 124, 226, 233
  as teacher, 30–32, 35, 63, 108, 110–11, 197, 214
  on treaties, *xx, xxviii*
  on vote for Aboriginal people, *xi, xx, xxviii, xxix, xxxv,* 54, 92–93, 218
League of Indians of Canada, *xix,* 76–77
Leatham, K. J., 167, 179
Leaven of Ladies (Norris), *xxiv, xliv, xlvii, xlviii*
legends, 47, 52, 57
Lethbridge Herald, 176
Liesemer, Gylman J. E., 191
Liesemer brothers, 21, 193, 203
Lightning, Albert, *xxxii,* 221
Lightning surname, 164, 167
liquor on reserves, 41, 218, 244
  Gladstone's support for, *xxxi,* 188–89
  Gorman on, *xxviii–xxix, xxxi,* 188–89
  Laurie's opposition to, *xx, xxviii, xxxi,* 188–89
Littlebear, Leroy, 87
Littlechild, John Wilton, 242
Loft, Frederick O., *xix,* 73, 75–78
Longfellow, Henry Wadsworth, 79
Lost Harvests (Carter), 42
Lougheed, James, 77
Luxton, Norman, 27, 43, 55, 239

M

Macdonald, John A., 65, 69, 71, 83, 122
Maclean, Archie, 29
MacLean, George (Walking Buffalo), *xxvii,* 53, 58–59, 120
MacLeod, Colonel, 159
Macleod, Mr. (United Church minister), 185
MacRae, Archibald Oswald, 31
Major, William (Bill), 154
The-Man-With-Tailfeathers-Around-His-Neck, 96
Manning, Ernest, 20, 203, 212
Many Wounds, Peter, *xxx*
Martin, Paul, 86
Massey, Vincent, 170
Matchatis, Nora, *xxxii*
Matheson, Shirley, 31
Mavericks (van Herk), *xv*
McClung, Nellie, *xxvi,* 138
McCrimmon, Malcolm, 157, 159
McDougall, George, 40, 51, 192, 239
McDougall, John, 192
McDougall Church, 39, 49, 191, 200, 204
McHugh, Clarence, *xxx*
McIntyre, Malcolm M., 109
medicine line, 119
medicine man, 58
Meech Lake agreement, 242
Meighen, Arthur, 74
Melling, John, 244
Memory Hold-the-Door (Buchan), 196
Métis, 78–79

Métis (*continued*)
    as "broker" people, *xl*
moccasin telegraph, 47, 75, 174
Moir, A. F. "Spud," 179–80, 185
Moon, Chief, *xxxii*
Morley, Alberta, *xxiii*, 87. *See also* Stoney reserve (Morley)
    cemetery, 35, 204
Morning Star, *xlvi, xlix*, 182–83
Morrow, William G. (Bill), l, 154, 179
Mount Laurie (*Iyamnathka*), *ix*, 8, 211–12
Mount Rundle, 59
Mountain White Eagle Girl (Gorman as Indian princess), *xviii, xxiv, xlviii*, 8, 112, 141
Mountie, xlviii
Mounties. *See* Royal Canadian Mounted Police
"Mrs. John Gorman Takes Indians' Brief to Ottawa," 229
Muir, Rodney, *xii*
My Golden West, ix, xii, xxi, xxiii, xxv–xxvii, xlii–xliv, 140, 242, 249

N

name loss, 96–97
Narrow Vision (Titley), *xii*
Neu, Dean, *Accounting for Genocide*, xxii
New Democrat Party (NDP), 175
"New Living Civilization Bill," 69
Niagara, Oghema, 74–75
non-violence, *xxvii*
Norris, Malcolm, *xix, xxxix, xl*, 73
Norris, Marjorie, *Leaven of Ladies, xxiv, xliv, xlvii, xlviii*
Norris, Ramsey, 21
North-West Company, 81

O

Ogilvie, Bob, 176
oil on reserves, *xiii, lxiv*, 147–48, 152, 154, 176, 186
old age pension for Aboriginal people, 217
Oliver, Frank, 69
One-and-a-Half Men, The (Dobbin), *xl*
Ottawa Citizen, 74, 236
Ottawa Journal, 91

P

Page, Patricia Kathleen, 34
Palmer, Howard, *Alberta, xv*
Palmer, Tamara, *xv*
Parker, Geoff, 35

Paul, Andrew, 225
Peacock, M.B., *xviii*, l, 55, 105, 108, 138
    connections with Aboriginal peoples, *xxiii*
    free legal advisor, 110
    Wesley case, *xxiii*
Pearson government (1963), *xv*
Persons Case, 137–38
Phillips, W.J., 99
Pickersgill, Jack, *xi, xxxii*, 67, 146–48, 170, 175, 177
Plainwoman, Percy (Two Gun), 98
Plume, Bull, 60
potlatch ceremony, 54
Prince's Island, *xxiii, xxv, xlviii*, 110, 138
Privy Council, 87, 137
propaganda, 63
public opinion, 168, 170–71, 243
    ignorance, 90–91

Q

"Queen Mother Morningstar" (Gray), *xlix*
"Queen's Promises" (Sanders), *xl, xlix*

R

Radio Europe, 176–77
Ragona, Paul, *xii*
Ray, Arthur, *I Have Lived Here Since the World Began, xv*
Red Crow, 206, 208
Reiss, Winold, 98
repatriation of constitution, *xxiii, xxv, xliii*, 70, 248
reserve system
    Canadian Pacific Railway (CPR) land and, 70–71
reserves, 88
    allotment, 69
    attempts to take back, *xiii*, 68–69, 152 (*See also* enfranchisement)
    changes and improvements, 241
    conditions prior to enfranchisement clause, 119–20
    direct sale of reserve land, 69
    like foreign countries, 45, 48
    like prison walls, 48, 83, 87
    oil, *xiii, lxiv*, 147–48, 152, 154, 176, 186
    press barred from, 121
    RCMP and, 121–22
    treaty promises, 251–52
residential schools, 50–51, 98, 139
Riel, Louis, *xl*, 81–82
Riel rebellion, 78–83, 121

Riley, Mrs. Harold, 138
Roosevelt, Eleanor, *xiv*, 94
Ross, George, 27, 55, 239
Rowan, Reta, 58, 140–41, 216
Rowan, William, 140
Royal Canadian Mounted Police, 79–80, 158
    access to reserves, 121–22
    attendance at IAA meetings, 136
    RCMP scouts, 153
Royal Proclamation of 1763, 65
Rundle, Reverend, 59
Ruttle's livery stable, 33–34

S

Saddle Lake reserve, *xiii*
Saddleback, Chief, 153, 167
Saint-Laurent, Louis, 147
Samson, John, 169, 173, 182–83, 188, 208, 230
    on education, *xxxiv*
    family name change, 97
    on liquor, *xxxi*
    Mother's Day cards for Gorman, *xlvi*
    president of IAA, 128
    trip to Ottawa, *xxxii*, 229, 248
    on vote, *xxx*
Samson Indian Band, 179. *See also* Hobbema reserve
    business successes, 245
Sanders, Douglas, *xxi*, 186
    analysis of the Hobbema Case, *xlix, l*
    "Queen's Promises," *xl, xlix*
Sarcee people
    business successes, 245
savages, 63, 122
scalping, 63–64
Schumiatcher, Morris, 48, 119, 175
Scott, Duncan Campbell, 67, 69, 74, 76–78, 86–87
    advocate of enfranchisement, 90–92
scrip, 69, 78, 158–62, 167, 180
Selkirk, Thomas Douglas, Fifth Earl of, 81
senatorship, issue of, *xxxvi, xxxvii*, 187–88
Shot on Both Sides, Chief, *xxx*
Sibbald, Mr., 51
Siksika people
    business successes, 245
Simeon, Leah, 61
Sitting Eagle, 206, 208
Small, Mary, 79
Smith, Donald, *x, xvii, xviii*, 16
    "A Good Samaritan: John Laurie," *xxxiv*
Smith, Gordon J., 77
Snell, Richard (Dick), 28, 171, 173–74, 182

Snow, John, 152
Social Credit, 20, 218
special status, 249
    need for, 250
St. Regis Hotel, 28
Staley, Reverend, 40, 51
Steer, A.C., 179
Steer, George H., 179
Steeves, Helen, 141
Steinhauer, Ralph, *xxxii*, 188, 223
Stonewall, Grace, 173
Stoney reserve (Morley), 37, 40–41, 45–46, 152, 207
    expulsion attempt, 151–52
    farming on, 42
    Laurie's final grave, 35, 204
storytelling, *xii*, 41, 46, 52, 57, 59, 61, 96. *See also* legends
strong-minded women, *xli, xlii, li*
Swanson, Cecil, 117, 206
Swanson, Frank, 236

T

Tailfeathers, Darcy
    first medical student at U of A, 102
Tailfeathers, Gerald, *xviii, xxxii*, 97, 188, 194, 207
    art (or painting), 96, 98–99
    Banff School of Fine Art, 99
    death, 102
    enfranchisement experience, 96, 100–102
    at Provincial Institute of Technology and Art, 99
    residential school, 98
    support from John Laurie, 99
Tailfeathers, Laurie Lee John, 207
Talk to My Lawyer: Great Stories of Southern Alberta's Bar and Bench, xlix
Taylor, Mrs., 216
Therrien, Richard, *xxii*
Thompson, David, 79
Thorp, Margaret, *Female Persuasion*, xli
Three Persons, Tom, 36
Thunder Chief, 96
Thunderwater, Chief (Oghema Niagara)
    establishment of council of tribes, 74–75
Time Magazine, 175–76, 186
Titley, Brian E., *Narrow Vision*, xii
Tootoosis, John B., *xl*, 106, 158
traditional dress, *xxi*, 43–44, 58, 182
treaties, 47, 72, 75, 83, 120, 148
    fear of abrogation or erosion, *xv, xxxvi*
    Laurie's belief in, *xx*

treaties (*continued*)
  obligations from, *xxvii, xxxii, xxxix*, 252–53
  promises, 251–52
  reserves established by, *xvi*
Treaties of Canada with Manitoba, the Northwest Territories and Kee-wa-ten, 48
Tribe Under Trust (Hanks), *xxxii*, 88
Trudeau, Pierre Elliott, 70, 121, 249
Trudeau constitution, *xiii, xxv, xlii*, 70, 248
"Trust Funds," *xxxii–xxxiv, xxxix*, 53, 77, 88–89, 95, 115, 127, 137, 145, 251
Turner, J. Peter, 79–80

U

United Farmers of Alberta (UFA), 19
University of Alberta Faculty of Medicine, 101
University of Alberta Law School, 109
Unjust Society (Cardinal), *xxxix*

V

Van Herk, Aritha, *Mavericks, xv*
Victoria, Queen, 169
  hypocrisy during reign of, 66, 68
violence, *xxii*
voluntary enfranchisement, 69, 91, 95, 100
vote, 90, 116, 144, 212, 219, 228–29. *See also* enfranchisement
  Aboriginal peoples' view of, *xi, xv, xxx–xxxi, xxxvi*
  Amendment to Indian Act (1961), *x*, 228–29
  end of despair and, 254
  as Euro-Canadian fight, *xv*
  freed tribes from dominance of Department of Indian Affairs, 240
  Gorman's views on, *xxviii*
  last Canadians to have, 54, 255–56
  Laurie on, *xi, xx, xxxv*, 218
  success of Hobbema Case and, 214
  turned to threat, 92, 94
  "We want bread, not votes," 93
  women, 94
"voyageurs," 81

W

Walking Buffalo, *xlvii*
War of 1812, 64
ward system, 106, 108, 118–19
Warne, Randi, *xliii*
Watson, Neil, *xii*

Weadick, Guy, 28
Weir, John Alexander, 109
Wesley case, *xxiii, xxiv*
Western Canada College, 31–32, 51
Western Canada Concept Party, *xxiii, xxv, xxvi*
Western Canadian thrust, 216
  Albertans, 117, 239
  Laurie's movement as, 5, 215
  pioneer tradition and, 110, 211
Western Canadian tradition of voluntary service, *l*
Western Canadian women, *xxiii*
Western narrative
  domination by men, *xli*
  women's role, *xliv*
White Cloud, *xvi*, 41, 52, 206, 208
'White Paper' (1969), 86, 249, 253
Whitney, Lawrence, *xlv*
Wild, James R., 157
Wilde, Mr., 158
Wildman, Dan, 37
Wilson, Woodrow, 25
winter counts, 58
  Bill Plume's, 60
  historical record of past, 59
woman's place, 118, 137–38
women's narratives, *xli*
Woodsworth, J.S., 20–21
Writing a Woman's Life (Heilbrun), *xl*

Y

Yamnuska. See Mount Laurie (*Iyamnathka*)